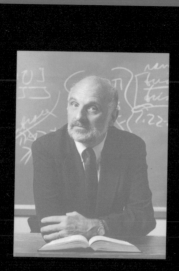

WALTER BRUEGGEMANN is the William Marcellus McPheeters Professor Emeritus of Old Testament at Columbia Theological Seminary in Decatur, Georgia. One of the most distinguished Old Testament scholars writing in English, he is a past president of the Society of Biblical Literature and a widely published authority on interpretive and hermeneutical matters. Brueggemann is an ordained pastor in the United Church of Christ.

SOLOMON

STUDIES ON PERSONALITIES OF THE OLD TESTAMENT

James L. Crenshaw, Series Editor

SOLOMON

ISRAEL'S IRONIC ICON
OF HUMAN ACHIEVEMENT

WALTER BRUEGGEMANN

University of South Carolina Press

© 2005 University of South Carolina

Published in Columbia, South Carolina, by the
University of South Carolina Press

Manufactured in the United States of America

09 08 07 06 05   5 4 3 2 1

Library of Congress Cataloging-in-Publication Data

Brueggemann, Walter.
    Solomon : Israel's ironic icon of human achievement / Walter Brueggemann.
        p. cm. — (Studies on personalities of the Old Testament)
    Includes bibliographical references and indexes.
    ISBN 1-57003-578-4 (cloth : alk. paper)
    1. Solomon, King of Israel. 2. Bible. O.T.—Criticism, interpretation, etc.
    I. Title. II. Series.
    BS580.S6B78 2005
    222'.53092—dc22

                                                    2005003205

For Gerald P. Jenkins, with abiding gratitude

CONTENTS

SERIES EDITOR'S PREFACE

Critical study of the Bible in its ancient Near Eastern setting has stimulated interest in the individuals who shaped the course of history and whom events singled out as tragic or heroic figures. Rolf Rendtorff's *Men of the Old Testament* (1968) focuses on the lives of important biblical figures as a means of illuminating history, particularly the sacred dimension that permeates Israel's convictions about its God. Fleming James's *Personalities of the Old Testament* (1939) addresses another issue, that of individuals who function as inspiration for their religious successors in the twentieth century. Studies restricted to a single individual—such as Moses, Abraham, Samson, Elijah, David, Saul, Ruth, Jonah, Job, and Jeremiah—enable scholars to deal with a host of questions psychological, literary, theological, sociological, and historical.

As a rule, these treatments of isolated figures have not reached the general public. Some were written by outsiders who lacked knowledge of biblical criticism (Freud on Moses, Jung on Job) and whose conclusions, however provocative, remain problematic. Others were targeted for the guild of professional biblical critics (David Gunn on David and Saul, Phyllis Trible on Ruth, Terence Fretheim and Jonathan Magonet on Jonah). None has succeeded in capturing the imagination of the reading public in the way fictional works like Archibald MacLeish's *J.B.* and Joseph Heller's *God Knows* have done.

It could be argued that the general public would derive little benefit from learning more about the personalities of the Bible. The conduct of those personalities, often less then exemplary, reveals flawed character, and their everyday concerns have nothing to do with our preoccupations from dawn to dusk. To be sure, some individuals transcend their own age, having entered the gallery of classical literary figures from time immemorial. But only these rare achievers justify specific treatments. Then why publish additional studies on biblical personalities?

The answer cannot be that we read about biblical figures to learn ancient history, even of the sacred kind, or to discover models for ethical action. But what remains? Perhaps the primary significance of biblical personages is the light they throw on the imaging of deity in biblical times. At the very least, the Bible constitutes human perceptions of deity's relationship with the world and its creatures. Close readings of biblical personalities therefore clarify ancient understandings of God. That is the important datum we seek—not because we endorse that specific view of deity, but because all such efforts to make sense of reality contribute something worthwhile to the endless quest for knowledge.

James L. Crenshaw
Duke Divinity School

PREFACE

A study of King Solomon as portrayed in Israel's tradition and memory opens up an investigation of immense complexity. It invites entry into some of the most demanding questions of Old Testament faith. By way of entry into those complexities and questions, I begin this study by noting the playful openness of the subtitle of the book.

There is no doubt that King Solomon is presented in memory and tradition in ancient Israel in relationship to *royal power*, that is, in relationship to the concentration of social, political, and economic leverage as it was established in David's Jerusalem. There is no doubt, moreover, that royal power was a dramatic *novum* in ancient Israel that entailed a deep break from older tribal patterns of social organization. The new power arrangements of the royal dynasty in ancient Jerusalem bespoke quite new patterns of social relationships that included social stratification, differentiation of social roles, and the accumulation of surplus value, all conditions earlier unknown in Israel.[1] Because these patterns of power represent something of a discontinuity with older patterns, it is not surprising that new emergent forms of social power were highly contested in ancient Israel. Some viewed the rise of monarchy under David and Solomon as a social emergent willed by YHWH, the God of Israel; others, in equally strong advocacy, viewed the monarchy as a betrayal of the older covenantal traditions of Israel. Consequently, great interpretive energy was utilized in the formation of the tradition in order to find an adequate accommodation between remembered tradition and newer social emergence. It is reasonable to say that "remembered Solomon" embodied all of the issues that swirled in ancient Israel around the reality of royal power. That reality is constituted by a concentration of socioeconomic political energy coupled together in intriguing ways with equally forceful theological-ideological interpretation. The interface of realpolitik and hermeneutical energy assured that royal power in ancient Israel remained under endless contestation. The figure of Solomon is inescapably a cipher for that endless contestation.

In what follows I will refer to Solomon as a model of royal power. The term "model" suggests that Solomon is, in the Old Testament, the paradigmatic presentation of royal power with all of the assets and liabilities that inevitably come with the newer emergent social relationships. The term "model," however, also deliberately begs important questions. In what follows it will be clear that the historicity of

Solomon as reported in the Old Testament is, in the present mood of scholarship, at best complex and laden with problems. Thus "model" allows for the possibility that the Solomon given us in the Old Testament text is a constructive paradigm that emerges out of Israel's longtime contested interpretive process, a contested paradigm that may or may not stand close to what "happened" in Israel's history. There is no doubt that the central presentation of Solomon in 1 Kings 3–11—and no less so the several derivative presentations considered in what follows—is an outcome of a complicated editorial and traditioning process laden with thick ideological traffic, even though that ideology carried by the text is itself not all of one piece.

Acknowledging that Solomon as model is a complex interpretive construct, the matter is made even more "thick" by the awareness that the hermeneutical construct of Solomon contains highly ironic dimensions, so that the text itself may bear more and other witness than a surface reading would indicate. It is not necessary for us to articulate a refined theory of irony in order to signal ironic dimensions of the biblical presentation of Solomon, most especially in the primary narrative of 1 Kings 3–11. The function of irony in rhetorical articulation is to distinguish between a "state of innocence" and the reality of experience; to shine light on the gap between appearance and reality; and to articulate elements of incongruity, complexity, and paradox that lie below the surface of what seems to be a single, tranquil, harmonious utopia.

All of these ways of defining the function of irony indicate that irony is a literary strategy for exposing contradictions where more usual perception does not notice those contradictions. This matter of irony is of great importance in reading the Bible alertly. On the one hand a pious reading of the Bible may tend to accept surface presentation in a way that refuses to acknowledge the complexity of lived reality. On the other hand, conventional positivistic historical criticism tends not to allow for imaginative playfulness that goes beyond a simple historical reading in a one-dimensional development. While irony is operative in many places, I shall explore the articulation of Solomon by examining the presence of irony in the narrative. The "surface" of Solomon is as a great, faithful, noble king. The thickness of the literature tells otherwise, however, even if the story of Solomon is taken not in terms of reportage but as a constructed model of royal power.[2]

The imaginative, artistic power of an ironic rendering of Solomon is crucial for reading the text. The ironic dimension of the literature is not only artistic and aesthetic but also directly serves the theological purpose of subverting absolute claims that were assigned in the tradition to Solomon. On the surface, Solomon is as fully absolute as any ruler in Israel could ever be, or as any ruler could be imagined or construed by Israel. The narrative presentation of Solomon, however, is given in literature that has a distinct, deliberate theological edge, that is, an awareness that the power of YHWH—variously enacted by direct or hidden means—serves to deabsolutize every human claimant to power and to render such claimants penultimate.

Thus the interface of *theological intentionality* and *ironic articulation* is pivotal for these narratives. This theological function of irony is noted by Wayne Booth, the master of the ironic:

> Irony is in things as they are, not merely in my view of them, and lacking the older vocabulary for dealing with our finitude, we do what we can. Of course, I know better than to expect anyone to accept any theological implications in what I am saying. I really do not want to claim that I have discovered a new proof of the existence of God, the ironological proof. All I would claim is that a serious look at how we use language ironically, and how we talk about irony, will lead us to recognize a striking parallel between traditional God-language and modern irony-language. The strongest religious traditions have always celebrated the Being who by his very existence dramatizes our finitude, our insignificance.[3]

The same matter is noted by Gail R. O'Day: "Despite its apparent attempts to conceal meaning, *irony is a mode of revelatory language.* It reveals by asking the reader to make judgments and decisions about the relative value of stated and intended meanings, drawing the reader into its vision of truth, so that when the reader finally understands, he or she becomes a member of the community that shares that vision, constituted by those who have also followed the author's lead."[4]

Thus the terms of the following investigation suggest that our subject, Solomon, is an intentional construct of Israel's theological imagination. That theological construct is a way of reflecting critically upon the meaning of human power in the face of the elusive presence of God. Such a perspective on the text of course begins with an awareness of the complexity of the text before us, and an equal awareness of the abiding significance of the questions posed by this textual tradition concerning human freedom and human responsibility in a world where God's will and governance are taken seriously.

ACKNOWLEDGMENTS

I am glad to express my appreciation to those most directly supportive of my completion of this study. I have benefited from the abiding generosity of Columbia Theological Seminary and from a season of generative hospitality in Clare Hall, University of Cambridge. I am grateful to Tia Foley, who brought the work to completion with her uncommon gifts of patience, technical competence, and good judgment. Tim Simpson labored, as he always does, to make my work better. Davis Hankins helped immeasurably with endnotes, and Richard Blake pursued arcane matters for me, especially with regard to chapter 13. I am grateful to Barry Blose at the University of South Carolina Press for initiating the book in the press's impressive series, to James L. Crenshaw, the series editor, and to Scott Evan Burgess, who diligently attended to the transformation of the manuscript into a book. This collaboration with James Crenshaw is the culmination of a long friendship around shared scholarly interests.

Dr. Gerald P. Jenkins, in his pastoral ministry, continues to exhibit a "listening heart," the kind of heart Solomon was promised but did not receive (1 Kings 3:9).

SOLOMON

CHAPTER I

BEGINNING POINTS

HISTORY AND CANONICITY

An attempt to write a "Life of Solomon" immediately runs into the problem that any historian characteristically faces, namely, that of finding reliable sources. Beyond the challenge of identifying sources, moreover, is the challenge of determining what actually happened: the question of historicity of the sources. For the historian studying the ancient world, the issue is exceedingly difficult because the sources are most often obscure and elusive. Beyond that, of course, one must bring to the sources a high degree of suspicion: the sources we have were most often not intended as reportage but were designed as vehicles for propaganda and ideology in the unending contestation to control and shape the past for the sake of the present and the future. (We may imagine that modern history, with its penchant for objectivity, more readily screens out such tendentiousness, except that we have ample evidence that deep passions related to gender, ethnicity, and imperial self-congratulatory culture continue to permeate historical study.)[1] Thus when we evaluate the sources concerning Solomon, we are not facing completely new issues; the problem of tendentiousness in sources is an ancient as well as a modern problem. A review of the recent history of the interpretation of the sources concerning Solomon readily indicates the way in which hermeneutical inclinations may affect the interpretation.

CHANGES IN RECENT OLD TESTAMENT STUDY

We may begin an exploration of the problem of sources by considering the drastic change of perspective in critical Old Testament study that has occurred within the last fifty years, and we will do so with reference to 1 Kings 3–11, the text commonly judged to be the most important and most reliable source concerning Solomon.

Old Testament study, especially in the United States, was dominated through the twentieth century by the scholarship of William Foxwell Albright and his most remarkable cadre of students, who in turn dominated U.S. Old Testament study in this period.[2] Albright, on the faculty at Johns Hopkins University, almost single-handedly developed the disciplines and methods of archeology so that a historical presentation of the Old Testament in its ancient Near Eastern environment was made possible on self-conscious critical grounds. That presentation of the biblical past was generated by an intense correlation between biblical historical evidence and the analysis of archeological data that was generated by immense creative activity as early as the 1930s and on through the middle of the century.[3] Albright was able to show remarkable confirmation of biblical historical presentation by archeological data that was nicely correlated with the biblical evidence.

Whereas Albright, in his immense erudition, paid primary attention to method and made arguments ad hoc about particular pieces of archeological evidence and particular biblical texts, it remained for his students, who were completely committed to his methods and perspectives, to present a more sustained, coherent presentation of the history of ancient Israel.

The most important, and still enormously valuable, synthesis of this primary scholarly achievement of the twentieth century is *A History of Israel* by John Bright, a book that has recently gone into its fourth edition.[4] In general, Bright has had confidence in the overall presentation of history that the Bible offers. At the same time, however, many readers have noticed that each successive edition of Bright's book makes less confident claims for the historical reliability of the biblical material. Thus we are able to see that Bright's own judgments follow a general line of scholarly development away from an easy credulousness about the biblical text rooted in profound confidence in Albright's methods, to a waning of such confidence as the twentieth century moved toward its close.[5]

Bright's presentation of the Solomonic material in the fourth edition provides a synthesis of material that has become common in Old Testament study.[6] On the whole, Bright's offer on Solomon follows the biblical line concerning the rise of Solomon's regime, the economic prosperity of his rule, the "flowering of culture," and the "theology problem" of the monarchy. Two matters covered by Bright will be important for our subsequent discussion. First, while Bright presents "history," he is convinced that the "history of Israel" cannot be accomplished without reference to the God who governs that history:

> For Bright, it all came down to one simple point: There is no authentic understanding of God without Israel's history, and there is no true understanding of Israel's history without God. Bright's "lively sense of history" provides the framework for a theology that enters into, rather than floats above, the fray of human existence. Bright urged his own students never to forget that "lively sense of history," for it embodies the life of discipleship amid the tension between grace and obligation, over and against the temptation of complacency. For a new generation of students and professional interpreters, Bright demonstrates that not only does history matter, but also theology.[7]

Thus Bright's history is a mix of facticity and theological attentiveness, a mix that is characteristic of Albright's approach and that dominated Old Testament interpretation at mid-century. While such an appeal to faith in the presentation of history is currently thought to be ignoble and compromising in some contemporary quarters, it is also important to notice that Bright's theological attentiveness provides the critical edge to his interpretive work. On Solomon's reported achievement of integrating the state into the central cult in Jerusalem, Bright concludes:

> The integration of state and cult, and the undergirding of the state with divine sanctions, had consequences by no means altogether healthy. The temptation was inevitable to hallow the state in the name of God and to suppose that the aims of the state and the aims of religion must necessarily coincide. In many minds the cult was accorded the wholly pagan function of guaranteeing the security of the state, of maintaining that harmonious balance between the earthly order and the divine which would protect the state from ill fortune both internal and external. In the autumn festival the covenant with David inevitably tended to crowd the Sinaitic covenant and its stipulations into the background, thereby setting up a tension between the two. In popular thought the promises to David and the presence of Yahweh in his Temple guaranteed the continuance of the state.[8]

Of less importance, we may notice Bright's characteristic judgment of the narrative report of 1 Kings 10:1–10 concerning the visit of the Queen of Sheba to Solomon in Jerusalem. This narrative anecdote strikes one as fanciful, but Bright takes it with seriousness as historical reportage:

> Solomon was also interested in overland trade with the south. The visit of the Queen of Sheba (I Kings 10:1–10, 13), an incident by no means to be dismissed as legendary, is to be understood in this light. The Sabeans, originally nomadic, had by this time settled and established a kingdom the center of which was in what is today eastern Yemen. Their strategic position astride the caravan routes from Hadhramaut northward toward Palestine and Mesopotamia enabled them to dominate the trade in spice and incense for which southwestern Arabia was famous. Exploiting the development of camel transport, they were beginning a commercial expansion which in ensuing centuries resulted in a trading hegemony over much of Arabia. It is possible that, taking advantage of the failure of the Egyptian trade monopoly in Ethiopia and Somaliland, they had also extended their interests there. The Queen of Sheba's visit is, therefore, intelligible. Solomon not only controlled the northern terminus of the trade routes; his maritime ventures had brought him into direct competition with the incipient caravan trade, stimulating the Sabean queen to act in its interests. She therefore visited Solomon, bringing samples of her wares:

gold, jewels, and spices. Since Solomon received her royally, she presumably gained the agreements she sought.[9]

From that opening concerning "trading hegemony over much of Arabia," Bright goes on to consider "the copper industry" and "trade in horses and chariots," matters noted in the biblical text and supported by the archeological data read in the world of Albrightian scholarship. The outcome of Bright's reading, long dominant in the United States, is that the narrative of 1 Kings 3–11 is, on the whole, a reliable rendition of tenth-century Solomon.

The general perspective of Bright is paralleled by the survey of James B. Pritchard in his "The Age of Solomon."[10] Pritchard, like Bright, is aware of the "folkloristic" character of the biblical text and of the tendency to "hyperbole."[11] Moreover, he notes the contrast between the biblical presentation of Solomon and the evidence of archeology:

> The general impression gleaned from a survey of the archaeological remains that have come from the 10th century—and they are considerable—is that cities were built on a small scale, that buildings were simple and modestly constructed from materials locally available, and that the standard of living was far from luxurious when compared to that prevailing in other parts of the ancient Near Eastern world. Solomon is mentioned in no Egyptian, or Mesopotamian, or Phoenician document. Only from the Bible do we learn that he lived. In contrast to this picture of life in the 10th century is that derived from I Kings 3–11, a life that might be termed a "Golden Age." Mentioned are huge amounts of gold, ivory carvings, bronze in abundance, woods imported from distant lands, chariots and horses, and international trade with distant and exotic lands. Everywhere the accent is upon opulence and extravagance measured in large but round figures. While in some respects the picture of grandeur is specific and dimensions of buildings are given, there is a noticeable lack of specific information about the principal characters. When accounts of the maritime adventures are given there is little specific data about the lands to which ships sailed except the names of two places, Ophir and Tarshish. In fact, references to geography outside Israel and Syria are either vague or nonexistent. Such is the broad, glittering picture of the age given in the biblical account. The divergences that exist between these two impressions of the Age of Solomon may be lessened, if not entirely reconciled, by one of two explanations. The first is that the sampling which archaeology has provided is not representative. . . . Another explanation for the discrepancy is that our only literary source for the Age of Solomon is late and to some extent legendary. It was composed—using a more ancient document as source to be sure—for a specific purpose, which was not that of the antiquarian or the historian.[12]

Thus Pritchard is aware of "historical problems" of the biblical narrative and adds due caution. At the same time, however, he securely locates Solomon in a credible tenth-century international environment. By a reference to the citation of a literary source in 1 Kings 11:41, moreover, Pritchard notes that the biblical text is "one stage removed" from the primary record:

> This relatively small segment of the Bible is particularly rich in anecdotes and details about people and places. But the author is careful to state in I Kings 11:41 that his is an account dependent upon a more primary and more detailed work, "The Book of the Acts of Solomon," a source which, alas, has not survived. Thus it is intimated that this preserved history that we possess is one stage removed from the primary record. The account in Kings is a compiled history, not a primary source, and the reader is referred, as it were, in the footnotes to a lost document for more detailed information and additional facts which the author of our document did not include.[13]

Pritchard does not, however, express a judgment on the reliability of the lost work cited in 1 Kings 11:41.

In this book I follow the dominant interpretation of Solomon in the United States under the aegis of Professor Albright. We may pause, however, to take note of the particularly acrimonious debate at mid–twentieth century between the U.S. Albrightians, represented by John Bright, and "the Germans," particularly Martin Noth.[14] The disagreement between these two lines of interpretation turned on the historical reliability of the biblical text, with particular reference to the traditions of Israel that recall the early founding events of the Pentateuch. Judgments about the historical reliability of the biblical text were, in the dispute, grounded on a judgment about the several genres of the text and what historical freight is carried by various literary genres. This dispute, characterizing much scholarship at mid–twentieth century, is of interest to us precisely because in a consideration of the Solomonic period the dispute is, for the most part, stilled. The biblical text concerning the Solomonic period, so much later than the "early traditions," was regarded even by Martin Noth as historically credible. Noth, the father of the Deuteronomic hypothesis, knows well of course that 1 Kings 3–11 in its present form is a late document, perhaps as late as the exile of the sixth century.[15] He is aware, not unlike Bright, that the text contains "legend."[16] He argues, however, that

> in the age of David and Solomon the historical chronicle took its place beside the popular legends and replaced them. The great historical events of this period, in which the Israelites had an active share, and such important historical figures as above all David himself, who had emerged from Israel, provided

sufficient incentive for recording the events of the time. Added to these incentives, however—and this is the novel and surprising thing—there was the ability to perceive the fundamental elements and underlying relationships within the events and to express them objectively and at the same time with literary skill. The result is by no means simply a register of historical events. Such reports were made, it is true—and they were also an innovation at the time—in the form of official royal annals which were no doubt kept by the "scribe" who was a leading royal official (cf. 2 Sam. viii, 17b; xx, 25a). The list of David's conflicts with neighbouring peoples in 2 Sam. viii, 1–14, was probably based on an extract from the royal annals; and under Solomon, who had two chief "scribes" (I Kings iv, 3a), the royal annals were probably kept with still greater thoroughness and provided the material for the "Book of the Acts of Solomon" (I Kings xi, 41). These historical works were, however, more than mere enumerations of individual events. Based though they were on solid firsthand knowledge, they were intended to expound the fundamental development and setting of a deliberately chosen segment of history.[17]

In this judgment, Noth follows Gerhard von Rad, who, in his essay of 1944, proposed that in Solomon's time a new model of literature emerged that focused on human initiative and human responsibility.[18] The outcome of such a hypothesis of "Solomonic–post-Solomonic humanism" was an Enlightenment that made possible actual "history writing" as a narrative about human initiative. Finally, it is remarkable that Noth, for all the charges of skepticism made against him, shares with Bright the conviction that Israel's history is infused with the reality of God, so that a theological dimension to the text is an appropriate one for this particular history.[19] Noth is cautious, perhaps more cautious than Bright, in making such a theological-historical connection, and he certainly believes that the direct theological claim is muted in Solomonic literature. This leads him to considerable confidence in the historical reliability of the text, but he will not deny the theological dimension.

As a consequence, Noth's presentation of Solomon is remarkably parallel to that of Bright. It is evident that the acrimonious disagreement between them focused on the earlier traditions; by the time of Solomon, however, both thought that the modern historian was on more reliable ground on the biblical text. Both appeal to archeological data and to the geopolitical reality of the ancient world. In the end both find the text of 1 Kings 3–11, for all of its complexity, on the whole reliable.

The fullest synthesis of the Albrightian portrayal of Solomon, a picture appealing to archeology but one that was primally informed by the biblical text of 1 Kings 3–11, is offered by G. Ernest Wright. In his book *Biblical Archaeology,* Wright correlated biblical attestation and archeological data, which he found on the whole to confirm the claims of the biblical narrative.[20] Wright summarizes the archeological data for the ancient cities of Hazor, Lachish, and Gezer (1 Kgs 9:15–19) and finds the archeology confirming the report of new fortifications: "Megiddo is thus a remarkable illustration of the energy of the illustrious king. The excavators have computed that the stables so far recovered at this one site alone would have housed some four hundred and fifty horses. In addition, the ruins of stables from the same period have been discovered at Ta'anach, near Megiddo, at Eglon on the Judean border; perhaps also at Gezer, though this is not certain; and there are many more important cities, of course, which have not been excavated."[21]

Wright comments on Solomon's commercial activity to the south (see 1 Kgs 9:26; 10:22) and relates the textual report to the trade out of Ezion-geber into the Red Sea. In addition to the function of Ezion-geber as a port, evidence is found of "a great smelting refinery" that contributed mightily to Solomon's economic prosperity. On the basis of buildings found in Beth Shemesh and Lachish, Wright finds a connection to the system of taxation outlined in 1 Kings 4:7–19. The most extensive part of Wright's exposition—commensurate with the length of the textual material in chapters 5–8—concerns the temple in Jerusalem that Solomon constructed. It is a common assumption of scholarship that the design and architecture of the temple followed the common three-room arrangement of temples from the period, for which the temple in Tell Tainat and more recently in Arad are commonly cited parallels. The temple of Solomon, moreover, was built by Phoenician artisans and— we may imagine—was open to religious practices and interpretations that were not rigorously Yahwistic, covenantal, or Mosaic. Wright is at pains to comment in detail upon the construction and furnishings of the temple in order to show their locus and meaning in a tenth-century environment on the basis of what is known from elsewhere. The conclusion of Wright's exposition is of course to insist that the temple of Solomon makes perfectly good sense in the common cultural environment and practice of the tenth century.

It is of particular importance for Wright that the temple in Jerusalem reflected and served a cosmic theology of creation that belonged to the perspective of the priests.[22] While Wright is preoccupied with the linkages to a tenth-century cultural and historical environment, it is worth noting that the interpretation he must, perforce, offer is deeply at odds with the definition of covenantal theology in Israel, and at odds with polemical dismissal of the mythological, the cultic, and the polytheistic that Wright himself has elsewhere insisted are alien to authentic Israel. In this particular exposition Wright does not pursue that abrasive interface between what became Solomonic theology and the old Mosaic tradition, but the matter is evident if one reads across the corpus of Wright's passionate interpretive writing.[23]

There are four major elements of the normative tradition of Solomon in 1 Kings 3–11—fortification, commerce, tax administration, and the temple. In each case Wright details the way in which these textual references correlate to the cultural environment that can be reconstructed from archeological remains. These elements have become standard in U.S. scholarship in attesting to the historical credibility of the normative tradition. In his book, Wright concludes his discussion of Solomon with a section entitled "The Theological Meaning of the Temple."[24] He is aware that the temple serves a theological claim that is in tension with the Sinai tradition. In his discussion of Solomon's temple, Wright largely confines his reflection to observations about its religious meaning and intentionality, and stays short of the theological claim that would be normative in such an environment: "The Sinai covenant had established a relationship between people and Deity which was prior to kingship and to the Temple, and sacramental rite was never allowed to gain precedence over covenant loyalty and vocational obedience. Indeed, whenever signs of such a reversal appeared, there were those who were ready to speak for the old order and to denounce king, priesthood and Temple."[25]

Wright is, of course, a critically informed biblical theologian. While he is here concerned with the symbolic significance and function of the temple in its historical setting, he does not include a theological statement concerning the temple. Perhaps he is restrained because he is here acting only as a historian. More likely, he senses that the implied religious claims of the temple tradition are inimical to what he affirms of biblical theology.[26]

Finally, in our survey of scholarship primarily informed by archeology, we may mention two books related to the work of J. Maxwell Miller and John H. Hayes. In the first, *Israelite and Judean History* (1977), Hayes and Miller are the editors, and the essay on Solomon is written by J. Alberto Soggin.[27] Soggin early on acknowledges that the narrative of 1 Kings 3–11 is not history in any critical sense:

> When we look at the biblical sources for the study of this period, we soon realize, however, that they are not "history" in our sense of the word. We are dealing, in effect, with that particular form of Israelite history which may be called "prophetic history" or "theocratic history" or with some other, semantically similar, definition. This type of history can hardly be considered as "A record or account, usually written in chronological order, of past events, especially those concerning a particular nation, people, field of knowledge or activity, etc." (Funk and Wagnall, *Standard College Dictionary*). Such is neither the content of this material nor its aim. Still, there can be hardly any doubt that the age of David and Solomon gave a major impulse to Israelite historiography,

inasmuch as it brought into being political, economic, and sociological factors which are usually the presuppositions for any kind of historiography.[28]

Soggin offers a summary of archeological materials related to Solomon, featuring matters that by now we have come to expect: fortifications at Megiddo, Gezer, and Hazor; temple parallels, especially at Arad; and commercial and smelting activity in the South.[29] When he comes to review the data in relation to the biblical narrative, Soggin comments on international and national affairs.[30] Of particular interest is his discussion of the development of royal ideology and the related subject of Solomon and the Jerusalem temple.[31] Soggin's concluding judgment on the temple coheres with the more cautious verdict of Wright: "The temple was dedicated to Yahweh, the God of Israel, but it was a Canaanite temple, where all the inhabitants of the region could have felt at home. Behind its official functions, the reality could hardly be concealed that the temple served the national cult more than it did the Lord of Israel."[32]

Even though Soggin is not in any way a part of the Albrightian tradition, his essay indicates the way in which that interpretive tradition became generally normative for scholars. While Soggin notes consensus judgments on archeological data, for the most part he follows the outline and substance of 1 Kings 3–11 and accepts that material as reliable. The other point is that Soggin is clear that the city-temple establishment was the generating force of a state cult that featured royal ideology deeply related to common royal ideology of the ancient Near East.[33] Scholars have continued to adjudicate the extent to which generic royal ideology in ancient Israel had a distinctive Israelite flavor, and the extent to which the distinctly Israelite was compromised in an embrace of the generic aspects of a broader cultural tradition.[34]

A decade after Soggin's essay, Miller and Hayes offered their own reading of the history of ancient Israel and Judah.[35] One can see reflected in their careful words a change in scholarly perspective away from the credulous naiveté of mid-century. The chapter on Solomon begins in this way:

> Solomon's reign was "the golden age" of Israelite and Judean history—or at least that is what one would conclude from a casual reading of the Bible. The compilers of Genesis–II Kings depicted Solomon as an exceedingly wise, exceptionally wealthy, and extremely powerful ruler whose empire stretched from the Euphrates River to the Egyptian frontier. The Chronicler pressed these claims even further, neutralizing all negative aspects of Solomon's reign and elaborating on his role as Temple builder and cofounder with David of the Jerusalem cult. The superscriptions to the books of Proverbs, Ecclesiastes, and Song of Songs appear to credit him for their wisdom. Not surprisingly, Solomon's reign came to be regarded as the epitome of splendor, opulence, and

wise government (see Luke 12:27). A more careful examination of the biblical texts, however, probing beneath the sweeping claims and generalizations, reveals certain ironies about Solomon.[36]

This opening statement acknowledges the claims of the Bible itself. But Miller and Hayes promptly offer a qualifying disclaimer, "or at least that is what one would conclude from a casual reading of the Bible." The quoted statement, moreover, ends with an acknowledgement of "certain ironies."

It is clear in this chapter that "Solomon's reign is the earliest point where a fairly good case can be made for a correlation between a specific item in biblical history and the archaeological record."[37] But then Miller and Hayes draw the careful preliminary conclusion: "When all of this is taken into account, a much more subdued and, in our opinion, realistic portrait of Solomon begins to emerge. Before attempting any observations about this more realistic Solomon, let us examine the biblical materials pertaining to his reign."[38]

After a quick view of 1 Kings 1–11, again a guarded verdict is offered: "This Genesis–II Kings presentation of Solomon is characterized throughout by editorial exaggeration. A cautious historian might be inclined to ignore it altogether if there were any other more convincing sources of information available. Unfortunately there are none. If we are to catch any glimpse of the 'historical' Solomon, it will have to come primarily from the materials included in I Kings 1–11 and so thoroughly editorialized in these eleven chapters. As a first step in that direction, it is necessary to distinguish and evaluate some of the different kinds of material involved."[39]

Miller and Hayes wisely begin by giving attention to the different kinds of materials that are offered in the biblical narrative. This question of literary genre is an old one and was at the center of the conflict between Bright and Noth, between the Albrightians and the Germans. The Albrightian zeal for the historical too readily ignored such literary distinctions and too easily expected some genres of literature to carry "historical reliability" that was not congruent with the genre. With respect to 1 Kings 1–11, Miller and Hayes not only recognize the ill fit between "sweeping claims" and "bits of information" but shrewdly conclude that the makers of the biblical tradition were themselves aware of the same conflict:

> The conflict noted at the beginning of this chapter between the sweeping claims about Solomon's wisdom, wealth, and power, on the one hand, and bits of information that seem to undercut these claims, on the other, was noticeable also to the compilers of Genesis–II Kings. They dealt with this conflict by distinguishing between the first and main part of Solomon's reign, during which they depict him as the faithful ruler who achieved "the golden age" (I Kings 3–10), and his last years during which they depict him as one led

astray by foreign women. Accordingly, the negative items reported for Solomon's reign—such as Jeroboam's opposition to the forced-labor policies and his escape to Egypt—are all placed in the last years. We have encountered the same pattern in connection with David—David under the blessing followed by David under the curse—and will see it later in the biblical presentations of other Judean kings. Needless to say, this is an artificial arrangement of the material.[40]

The strategy of those who formed the tradition was to edit the materials guided by a theological pattern of "Solomon under blessing" and "Solomon under curse," a pattern that R. A. Carlson had already seen in the David narrative.[41] It is clear, of course, that such a patterning of the "history" of Solomon is not neutral reportage but is instead an interpretive grid imposed upon whatever was available of reportage.

The remainder of the discussion by Miller and Hayes concerning Solomon is a review of historical issues that are by this time familiar to us, including both the development of economic interests and the development of royal ideology that was a *novum* in Israel. The discussion of Miller and Hayes is clearly more alert to the interpretive dimensions than was the older, more innocent historical positivism. Nonetheless, we are able to see that scholars, from the very beginning days of the archeological synthesis of the Albrightians into the latter part of the twentieth century, have inclined to take the biblical text as the reliable story line for historicity. That story line, moreover, is given us in 1 Kings 3–11, so that the other texts we shall consider—including Chronicles, sapiential and lyrical materials, and the Psalms—have been characteristically subsumed under the Kings narrative presentation whenever historical questions have been raised.

IS REAL HISTORY AT ODDS WITH SALVATION HISTORY?

A rendition of the biography of Solomon written at the outset of the twenty-first century cannot appeal to the credulous notions of the historical reliability of the biblical narrative that prevailed in the mid–twentieth century. The reason such an innocent reliance on the Bible is no longer possible is that in the last several decades, such a notion of historical reliability of the Bible has been severely subverted with a widespread suspicion that to some large extent concerns all of scripture. The simplistic notion of "God in history" that dominated mid-century interpretation under the so-called biblical theology movement has been under critique for a long time, most notably in a famous article by Langdon Gilkey.[42] In that article Gilkey suggested that the programmatic theme "God acts in history" to which G. Ernest Wright was committed is a kind of interpretive slogan without any clear substantive claim.[43] In the same context in which Gilkey wrote, it was increasingly clear that Gerhard von Rad, the towering figure in such an interpretive project, also could not factor out the relationship of *God* in *history,* and in the end could not find a way to relate "real history" to "salvation history":

> Thus there is a clear tension between the account actually given in the narrative and the intention of the narrator, whose aim was, with the help of this material, to describe the conquest of the land by all Israel, and who, in so doing, asked too much of it. In the end this conception was most succinctly given in the narrator's words that under Joshua Israel took possession of the whole land "at one time" ([*Hebrew*] Josh. x.42). This was the rounding off of the construction of that magnificent picture made by later Israel of Jahweh's final saving act. Beyond it no further unification was really any longer possible. But our final comment on it should not be that it is obviously an "unhistorical" picture, because what is in question here is a picture fashioned throughout by faith. Unlike any ordinary historical document, it does not have its center in itself; it is intended to tell the beholder about Jahweh, that is, how Jahweh led his people and got himself glory. In Jahweh's eyes Israel is always a unity: his control of history was no improvisation made up of disconnected events: in the saving history he always deals with all Israel. This picture makes a formidable claim, and actually in the subsequent period it proved to have incalculable power to stamp affairs. How this came about is quite interesting. Israel made a picture of Jahweh's control of history on his people's behalf whose magnificence far surpasses anything that older and more realistic accounts offered. Faith had so mastered the material that the history could be seen from within, from the angle of faith. What supports and shapes this late picture of Israel's taking possession of the land is a mighty zeal for and glorification of the acts of Jahweh.[44]

Of von Rad's work, Walther Eichrodt—the primary alternative to von Rad in Old Testament theology studies—offered this harsh verdict:

> On this view the OT narrators, invoking the licence of religious poetry, have dissolved the true history of Israel; the "acts of God in history" which they unwearyingly repeat (the call of the Patriarchs, the deliverance from Egypt, the granting of the land of Canaan etc.) are pictures of her history drawn by Israel in flat contradiction of the facts with the specific purpose of extolling and glorifying the God of Israel and his saving work. The formative intention from which this poetry springs is thus not aesthetic, but the urge of faith to understand, an urge which convinces itself of the special relationship of God to his people by drawing a "salvation-history." The spurious factuality of this

salvation-history ought not to be confused with historical truth; it rests on a quite different plane, and possesses a claim to validity only for the man who is prepared to "ask the same sort of questions and accept the same sort of answers." Anyone who agrees with this conception will have to divorce OT theology completely from the historicocritical view of Israel's history, and confine it to the presentation of Yahweh's relation to Israel and to the world as this is variously set forth by the different writers in accordance with their homiletic purpose, the "kerygmatic intention" (p. 112). In the circumstances "reportage," that is to say, the most precise description possible of these repeated attempts to base the meaning of Israel's existential situation on Yahweh's acts in history, commends itself as the best way of arriving at a realistic conception of that daring enterprise of faith on which Israel embarked again and again in order to be able to cling, in each new historical predicament, to her witness to Yahweh and to the salvation-blessings guaranteed by him.[45]

The challenge to that dominant hermeneutical assumption of God's action in history, however, is more powerfully reinforced by two other developments in critical scholarship. First, beginning in the 1970s, the Albrightian correlation between "biblical history" and archeological data began to unravel. The first critical review of that widely accepted interface, which had come to dominate scholarship in the twentieth century, concerned the ancestral traditions of Genesis 12–36. After a consideration of that "earliest memory," the same criticism in turn moved to the Moses traditions, and then to the traditions of David and Solomon. Over these several decades, some scholars have doubted the historical claims of the Bible for anything older than Hezekiah in the eighth century, and some have made the marker for what is reliable even later into the sixth or fifth century. In any case, there is currently a powerful inclination to date everything in the Old Testament as late as possible; for purposes of "historicity," that inclination means that texts are far removed from the "events" they report, and are inescapably suspect in terms of reliable history.[46] Thus the beginnings in this new development in scholarship concerned texts that did not in particular address the Solomonic question. The mood of skepticism that has come to permeate scholarship, however, applies to all of the traditions of ancient Israel including that of Solomon.

Two publications, offered almost simultaneously, initiated the process of historical skepticism that has now gained important momentum in Old Testament studies. In 1974 Thomas L. Thompson published *The Historicity of the Patriarchal Narratives: The Quest for the Historical Abraham.*[47] In his initial publication, Thompson subjected to rigorous scrutiny the primary archeological data upon which the Albrightian synthesis depended; he concluded that the correlations of the data to biblical reportage were on the whole not convincing and, consequently, that these data did not support the historicity of the Abraham narrative. Since the time of Thompson's publication, reliance upon archeological correlations to the biblical narrative has been treated with increasing skepticism by scholars. In the following year, 1975, John Van Seters published *Abraham in History and Tradition.*[48] In subsequent publications, Van Seters has continued to reflect on the questions he first addressed in 1975.[49] Van Seters brings to his work a particular theory of historiography that is informed by his study of Herodotus and Greek historiography. The outcome of his work is the conclusion that the "historical forces" in the Old Testament are quite late and cannot be thought close to reported events, and they therefore are not reliable as sources.

From these two primary works of Thompson and Van Seters has flowed a spate of other books, the sum of which is to argue that the biblical claim to historicity must be regarded with acute skepticism. Most important in advancing the argument of Thompson and Van Seters is a trio of scholars who are variously labeled "minimalists," "revisionists," and, in a more polemical way, "nihilists." This trio is constituted by Keith Whitelam, Niels Lemche, and Philip Davies. Philip Davies has drawn the most skeptical conclusions concerning the historical reliability of the biblical narrative. In his book *In Search of "Ancient Israel,"* Davies has come to the conclusion that the "actual" history of ancient Israel is related almost not at all to the presentation of the Old Testament, the Old Testament account being a constructed memory to serve other, later ideological purposes.[50] Perhaps the clearest judgment in this interpretive trajectory is offered by Niels Peter Lemche in his book *The Israelites in History and Tradition.*[51] (It is worth noting that the same word pair, history and tradition, was the subject of Van Seters's first book, the argument being that the biblical account is "tradition" and not "history.") In his conclusion, Lemche writes of the entire modern project of the "history of Israel"—from Wellhausen to Albertz—as being an "indolent" work of "rationalistic paraphrase" of the biblical narrative, without any critical perspective upon that narrative.[52] In his final section, Lemche critiques Wellhausen and von Rad, but he clearly intends to indict the entire scholarly enterprise: "They forgot to read the texts as evidence of themselves, of the intentions of their authors. Modern scholars created an image of ancient Israel in this way. It was little more than a repetition of the image of Israel as found in the Old Testament, however, transferred into the historical world of which it had no part, being the creation of the imagination of the biblical authors."[53]

Insofar as the Old Testament narrative is "the creation of the imagination," it plays no useful role as a source for the "history of Israel," and historians must look elsewhere in the data for the sources to be used in such history. It is to be noticed that this development in scholarship has focused primarily upon the ancestral traditions of Genesis, the Mosaic narrative, and the "tribal period" of Joshua, Judges, and Samuel.

This push toward skepticism has not gone unanswered. Concerning the ancestral material of Genesis, attention may be paid to the conservative valuing of the text as "reliable source" in *Essays on the Patriarchal Narratives,* edited by A. R. Millard and D. J. Wiseman (1983).[54] With more critical finesse, Baruch Halpern has soberly argued for the historical intentionality and seriousness of the biblical writers. It is worth noting that Halpern himself is a third-generation Albrightian and knows the data in great detail and with acute discernment.[55]

Following the emergence of scholarly skepticism concerning archaeological data as a means of substantiating historical claims for the biblical narrative, the second major source of skepticism has been the more recent awareness among scholars that the biblical text is shot through with ideology. The term "ideology" can of course have a variety of meanings, ranging all the way from Karl Marx's mention of "distorted truth" to Clifford Geertz's claim that ideology is the baseline of meaning for any society.[56] In current Old Testament studies the word ideology is widely used but without great precision. The usages of both Marx and Geertz are operative. For the most part, when the term is used in Old Testament studies, the usage tilts in the direction of the meaning of Marx. That is, ideology is understood as a meaning imposed on memory, tradition, or text as a strong advocacy for a certain version of reality. Thus a vested interest is imposed on an available truth or reality, eventually skewing what might have happened or what is remembered in the interest of a contemporary political, economic, or even theological agenda.[57]

The force of "ideology critique" in current Old Testament studies needs to be understood in the wake of the hegemony of historical criticism that was for several centuries a practice of positivism. That is, historical criticism was conducted with the assumption that it was a neutral, objective, scientific enterprise that took the text as it was and read it without imposing anything alien upon the text. Such an assumption, of course, is difficult to maintain when it is clear that such interpretive work was not at all disinterested.[58] Rather, the project of historical criticism is itself a form of advocacy in the service of a certain rationality that issues in control of the text. (A clear example is the whole matter of source analysis that has dominated Old Testament historical critical study, whereby scholars with a certain rationality broke apart the tensions and incongruities in texts that violated that rationality. Indeed, as biblical readers outside the "First World" of Euro-American Enlightenment have gotten voice enough to interpret the Bible, it becomes clear that our conventional Western ways of reading the biblical text are not at all neutral but are undertaken by and in the service of certain sociopolitical and theological interests.)[59]

Those engaged in the enterprise of ideology critique insist that every reading of the Bible is to some extent an interested advocacy. Such critique, however, concerns not only reading the Bible; it is now widely recognized, in addition, that the biblical texts themselves are vehicles for advocacy whereby certain interests have been imposed upon the tradition of ancient Israel. In addition to the biases of race, gender, and ethnicity that operate in the Bible, we may identify four important aspects of ideology that are regularly noted in current scholarship.

1. The "Deuteronomist" is now thought to be the most generative and influential framer of texts in the Old Testament. The Deuteronomist—a person or a movement—imposed a particular theological vision upon the historical memory of Israel.[60] The imposition of a particular vision is ideological in that these authors had certain views about Torah and kingship, about God's judgment and mercy, and about the destiny of Jerusalem that were made normative, even though other views of the matter are hinted at in the text and can be quite readily imagined. The power of the Deuteronomic vision, as it has dominated subsequent interpretation, is taken by many scholars to be the clearest example of ideology in the Old Testament.

2. It is widely argued in skeptical circles that the notion of "exile" is an ideological construct designed by a small group of displaced urban elites who were able to establish themselves as the "superior" Jews who became the carriers of "true Judaism."[61] One can see the effect of that claim of the "exiles" transposed into political power—in cooperation with Persian authorities—in the "reforms" of Ezra and Nehemiah. The verdict that exile is an ideological claim is based on the premise that the claim is completely disproportionate to the historical reality concerning these deportees and those who remained in the land in the sixth century.[62] Jeremiah 24 is a clear and unmistakable example of the textual advocacy concerning this group in Babylon that claims entitlement to the future of Jerusalem.

3. The process by which *tradition* became *canon* is an obscure one. A high theological view of the matter of canon is that the community of faith was led by the gift of discernment to settle as normative canon their pieces of literature that carried the core truth of the faith.[63] Such a high theological notion is of course in tension with what must have been the practical and, surely, disputatious human route to canon. In any case, those who engage in critique of ideology are able to view "canon" as the outcome of a powerful, interested advocacy, whereby certain interpretive forces in the community were able to establish canon as a means of control of the levers of power in society. By this means they were able to "read out" of the community interpretive trajectories and variations that were unacceptable to their particular advocacy that was powerful enough to establish canon in the first place. The result of such a perception is that even canon, the settled claim of scripture, is—not unlike the perspective of the Deuteronomists and not unlike the interpretive claims of the exilic community—shot through with vested interest.

4. To these disputes concerning the interrelationship of "interpretive imposition" and "historical reliability," we may add one other dimension concerning current scholarly discussion. The sequence of interpretive maneuvers by the Deuteron-omists, by the exilic elite, and eventually by the canon makers of Judaism mobi-lized the tradition in order to claim a singular distinctiveness of Israel as the people of God. This interpretive achievement, moreover, appeals to the covenan-tal traditions of Moses, the land promised to the ancestors in Genesis, and the conquest traditions in the book of Joshua. Scholars, notably Keith Whitelam, have taken this interpretive achievement (made over the generations) to be an ideological act that not only served the claims of Israel but also, as a counter-point, silenced the legitimate history of the Palestinians.[64] Thus it is readily seen, on this reading, that such ancient interpretive imposition serves contemporary ideology needs, in this case, the assertiveness of the state of Israel.[65]

Discussions concerning the waning of confidence in archaeological data and the awareness of ideology in text making and text reading have created a powerful skep-ticism about the biblical claims for history. The present book is of course not about the ancestral, Mosaic, or tribal traditions wherein most of the scholarly dispute has been located. The purpose for laying out the dispute has been to characterize the present interpretive scene as one of skepticism and one of attentiveness to the gen-erative power of ideology in text making and text reading. In tracing the movement of contemporary scholarship, one is struck by how the current perspective of schol-arship has moved from an earlier Albrightian *credulity* to the current skepticism. The thought may be entertained that there is nothing in principle to commend skepti-cism rather than credulity, though as a critical scholar I would not go so far.[66] Rather, I want only to note the present mood of scholarly skepticism as the milieu of our study of Solomon. If we are skeptical of the historical claims made for Solomon in the primary narrative of 1 Kings 3–11, then we are prepared to recognize the ideological force of a narrative articulated through an irony that functions in order to subvert the dominant claims of the literature itself. Thus our present study in-escapably must be conducted within a context of scholarship dominated by a certain skepticism. While the causes of scholarly skepticism are deep and complex, it is nonetheless the case that simplistic confidence in historical critical methods can no longer be a beginning point for our work.

ASSESSING THE HISTORICITY OF THE SOLOMON TRADITION

In tracing the development of scholarship from credulity to skepticism, we may now—at last—consider the present state of studies concerning the Solomon narra-tive. Two studies, representing very different perspectives, are helpful in assessing the historicity of the Solomon tradition.

Israel Finkelstein and Neil Asher Silberman's *The Bible Unearthed: Archaeology's New Vision of Ancient Israel and the Origin of Its Sacred Texts* takes a quite skeptical perspective in general and is fully sympathetic to the insights and claims of the revisionists, identified above.[67] Finkelstein and Silberman begin their critical analysis of the evidence for the Solomonic period with a bold question: "Did David and Solomon exist?"[68] On the basis of the now famous Tell Dan inscription concerning the "House of David," they judge there is enough ground to conclude that David and Solomon existed, although they notice that the revisionists who deny their existence have "some points" in their favor. Most importantly, they observe that archaeologists cannot find "significant evidence for a 10th century occupation" of Jerusalem, and they judge that at the most Jerusalem would have been "a typical hill country village."[69] "In fact, it is highly unlikely that this sparsely inhabited region of Judah and the small village of Jerusalem could have become the center of a great empire stretching from the Red Sea in the south to Syria in the north. Could even the most charismatic king have marshaled the men and arms needed to achieve and hold such vast territorial conquests? There is absolutely no archaeological indication of the wealth, manpower, and level of organization that would be required to support large armies —even for brief periods—in the field."[70]

Major attention is given to the stables and the gates that are credited to Solomon, an important feature of the older synthetic reconstruction of the period. Attention is given to the archaeological finds of Megiddo, Hazor, and Gezer, with particular reference to the work of Yigael Yadin. In the end, however, Finkelstein and Silberman conclude, on the basis of ceramic evidence plus carbon-14 dating of samples of wood, that the evidence to which archaeologists have appealed is to be dated "long after the time of David."[71]

> Essentially, archaeology misdated both "Davidic" and "Solomonic" remains by a full century. The finds dated to the time just before David in the late eleventh century belonged in the mid–10th century and those dated to the time of Solomon belonged in the early ninth century B.C.E. The new dates place the appearance of monumental structures, fortifications, and other signs of full statehood precisely at the time of their first appearance in the rest of the Levant. They rectify the disparity in dates between the *bit hilani* palace structures in Megiddo and their parallels in Syria. And they allow us finally to understand why Jerusalem and Judah are so poor in finds in the 10th century. The reason is that Judah was still a remote and undeveloped region at that time. There is hardly a reason to doubt the historicity of David and Solomon. Yet there are plenty of reasons to question the extent and splendor of their realm.[72]

Finkelstein and Silberman conclude that David and Solomon presided at best over exceedingly modest chiefdoms. The development of the hyperbolic tradition of dynasty and empire was accomplished, they propose, in the seventh century B.C.E. by the Deuteronomic historian who appealed to the royal ideology that had subsequently been developed in Jerusalem. The ideological development from a modest historical base is enacted in and through the rule of Josiah, the darling of the Deuteronomists (see 2 Kgs 22–23), who is, in fact, the great unifier of the traditions of North and South.[73]

> It was Josiah's ambition to expand to the north and take over the territories in the highlands that once belonged to the northern kingdom. Thus the Bible supports that ambition by explaining that the northern kingdom was established in the territories of the mythical united monarchy, which was ruled from Jerusalem; that it was a sister Israelite state; that its people were Israelites who should have worshiped in Jerusalem; that the Israelites still living in these territories must turn their eyes to Jerusalem; and that Josiah, the heir to the Davidic throne and to YHWH's eternal promise to David, is the only legitimate heir to the territories of vanquished Israel. On the other hand, the authors of the Bible needed to delegitimize the northern cult—especially the Bethel shrine—and to show that the distinctive religious traditions of the northern kingdom were all evil, that they should be wiped out and replaced by centralized worship at the Temple of Jerusalem. . . . Under Josiah, however, the time comes for Judah to rise to greatness.[74]

Thus Finkelstein and Silberman go far in the direction of the skeptics, though not so far as to deny the existence of Solomon. It is of particular interest that in their assessment of the traditions of Solomon no mention of the temple is made, a fact noteworthy because of the cruciality of the temple in the older Albrightian argument.

A somewhat different assessment of the data is offered by William G. Dever's *What Did the Biblical Writers Know, and When Did They Know It?*[75] Dever is an heir to the archaeological synthesis of G. Ernest Wright and is the foremost authority on what remains of "biblical archaeology," a term from which Dever vigorously distances himself. Dever clears the ground for his investigation of the historical question of Solomon by reducing the pertinent biblical material to the historical books of Samuel and Kings. He of course recognizes that in the main these books are part of the "epic history" of the Deuteronomists about which he makes a conventional scholarly judgment:

> In short, the Deuteronomistic history as a composite literary work is largely "propaganda," designed to give theological legitimacy to a party of nationalist

ultra-orthodox reformers, what has been called (along with the prophetic reform movements of the time) a "Yahweh alone" party. . . . The work as a whole comprises the *entire* "epic history" of Israel mentioned above, that is, it contains not only whatever basic document the Deuteronomists produced, but also presumably a radically edited and reworked version of earlier literary works, most of them lost to us. The Deuteronomists claim to be a story not only of late "Mosaic" reforms, but of Israel's entire history; it is "theocratic history" on a grand scale.[76]

Given that premise, Dever proceeds to seek out "historical nuggets" in the midst of the ideological reconstruction offered by the "historical" text.[77] Proceeding in a very careful fashion by way of answering the revisionists and their offer of "more non-histories," Dever lines out the texts of evidence upon which he will rely.[78] It seems clear that Dever's approach is much more disciplined in terms of method than the work of the revisionists.

With this theoretical basis clearly articulated, Dever enumerates a series of "convergences" between the biblical texts concerning "early Israel" and archaeological data from the Iron I period.[79] He then takes up several pertinent data. Concerning the gates at Gezer, Megiddo, and Hazor, he says: "If the biblical Solomon had not constructed the Gezer gate and city walls, then we would have to invent a similar king by another name."[80] Dever stresses the evidence that would link the biblical text to the archaeological evidence of the invasion of the Egyptian Shishak (see 1 Kgs 14:25–28).[81]

Dever offers a detailed analysis of the possible correlation between tax districts in 1 Kings 4 and proposed sites that were likely administrative centers, with particular reference to Tirzeh and Beth Shemesh. The discussion is concluded with an extended consideration of the temple in Jerusalem.[82] A study of the design and architecture, the furnishings, and decorations and iconography show detailed correlation with temples known from the Iron I period. Dever's conclusion, not far removed from the earlier judgment of G. Ernest Wright, is that the temple of Solomon is best understood precisely in the tenth century:

> The fact is that we now have direct Bronze and Iron Age parallels for *every single feature* of the "Solomonic temple" as described in the Hebrew Bible; and the best parallels come from, and only from, the Canaanite-Phoenician world of the 15th–19th centuries. . . . The point is simple: the *only* life-setting for "Solomon's temple," whether there was a biblical Solomon or not, is to be found in the Iron Age, and in the 10th–8th centuries at *latest*. Perhaps the question is simply this. Which strains the reader's credulity more: the supposedly "fanciful"

descriptions of the temple in the Hebrew Bible; or the revisionists' scenario of its "total invention" by writers living centuries later?[83]

On the basis of an important theoretical issue, Dever challenges the revisionist judgment that Jerusalem could not have been a center for power as claimed in the biblical text.[84] Whereas the revisionists judged that there were not enough people, Dever makes the argument that the small number of people is no argument against Jerusalem as such a center of power because "it is not urbanization that 'causes' states to form, but the other way around."[85]

On all these counts, Dever's claim that the root of the tradition of Solomon is in "history" is indeed credible. He recognizes the overstatement of the Deuteronomic version of the tradition, but believes that the evidence suggests a claim of historicity for the tenth-century city. When we compare the work of Dever—rooted in Albrightian traditions but attentive to methodological issues in a fresh and disciplined way—and Finkelstein and Silberman, who are skeptical and inclined toward revisionist judgment, we may arrive at a more or less common judgment, though my own predilection, not unlike that of Dever, is against extreme skepticism. If we take Dever and Finkelstein and Silberman as representative of the spectrum of the field, we see a general agreement of genuine historical rootage in the text, greatly enhanced by hyperbolic extravagance, an overstatement perhaps generated by normal royal ambition or perhaps more intentionally an ideological imposition in the service of later political claims. Either way, the "historical Solomon" is a modest figure presiding over a modest state in what was likely a modest economy.

TURNING FROM THE HISTORICAL SOLOMON
TO THE CANONICAL SOLOMON

I have taken this long to situate the following study of the Solomonic tradition in current scholarship because biography characteristically concerns a historical character. We have arrived in our argument on the judgment that Solomon was a modest historical character from the tenth century who presided over a modest court, a modest economy, and a temple apparatus in Jerusalem. (An even more skeptical conclusion is drawn in some quarters, but such a conclusion seems to me an unnecessary speculation.) Thus one might imagine our work to be preoccupied with that modest historical personage.

It is the case, however, that that modest historical personage is not the subject of our study. Rather, our study concerns the Solomon of the Bible, so that we may say we are considering "canonical Solomon," the one given us in the canonical literature of the Hebrew Bible. Thus the following discussion is limited to and informed by the canonical shape of the portrayal of Solomon, a portrayal that is no doubt some distance from "history." The canonical achievement of presenting Solomon, that is, the imposition of a normative, interpretive shape upon whatever was available historically, evokes the following comments.

"Canonical Solomon" is the true Solomon of faith, the one blessed and approved by God, whose work was to transform what had been a modest tribal community into a powerful urban culture. It does not matter if the impetus for this portrayal is rooted in the ambitions of Josiah, as Finkelstein and Silberman suggest. The reader of the Bible takes what is offered. There is no doubt that this triumphant, glorious Solomon has been important for much subsequent interpretive reflection, not least with the production of the Masons in the contemporary world.[86]

Canonical Solomon is surely a product of interpretive imposition, that is, of ideology. The emergence of canonical Solomon is not happenstance but instead is an intentional result of careful advocacy. If it is the case that Josiah is the model king intended by the Deuteronomists, then Solomon is the countermodel, the one who violates Torah even as Josiah is the perfect Torah keeper. Thus, as Finkelstein and Silberman conclude:

> In order to revive the golden age, this new David needs first to undo the sins of Solomon and Jeroboam. The path to greatness must pass through the cleansing of Israel, mainly the destruction of the shrine of Bethel. This will lead to the reunification of all Israel—people and territory—under the Temple of YHWH and the throne of David in Jerusalem. The important thing to remember, then, is that the biblical narrative does not see the partition of the united monarchy of David and Solomon as a final act, but as a temporary misfortune. There can still be a happy ending. If the people resolve to change their ways and live again as a holy people apart from foreign idols and seductions, YHWH will overcome all their enemies and give them eternal rest and satisfaction within their promised land.[87]

The recognition that canon is a carrier of ideology is an important one for our purposes. As canon is the imposition of a normative view on tradition, so ideology is an advocacy imposed on tradition. In the case of Solomon, canonical normativeness and ideological advocacy converge in the offer of a Solomon who is triumphant in every regard.

The canonical Solomon is triumphant—except that the construction of Solomon is, in the very text of 1 Kings 3–11, subverted from triumph by the ironic exposé of his would-be success. The narrative ends in indictment and demise (11:1–13). That subverted ending serves canonically to advocate Torah. The same advocacy, understood ideologically, is the work of "a party of nationalistic ultra-orthodox reformers" of the "Yahweh alone" party.[88] Thus, for canonical reasons of Torah and for ideological reasons of reform, the narrative, in the end, would never let Solomon finish with triumph. His would be the wrong kind of triumph, the kind countered by Josiah (2 Kings 23:25). For that reason, attention to the ironic is crucial in seeing the subtlety of the canonical and the ideological when allowed an ironic dimension.

Even if canonical ideological Solomon is to some extent deconstructed in 1 Kings 3–11, nonetheless he remains for many generations to come a generative symbol of power. It is for that reason that beyond 1 Kings 3–11—in the Chronicler, in song and singing and poetry—Solomon is still a treasured symbol for Israel when Israel is completely in touch with worldly reality. The continuing generativity of Solomon would not be possible were he merely "historical." Whatever of "historical" he is, Solomon is a force of creativity who continues to feed the lyrical imagination of Israel. Always implied in that developing tradition concerning Solomon is something of a misgiving, a misgiving that appears only as a trace here and there but enough to keep Israel's most imaginative overstatement tenaciously in the matrix of the Deuteronomists. Thus the Deuteronomists "made" Solomon; once made, however, Solomon could not be confined to or controlled even by the force of the Deuteronomists. Solomon takes on a durable life that endlessly pushes the edges of Israel's faith. We will trace the way in which historical Solomon became the Solomon of imaginative tradition and thereby opened Israel toward Torah and beyond Torah.

CHAPTER 2

THE LARGER NARRATIVE IN WHICH "SOLOMON" IS EMBEDDED

TRACING THE TRADITION OF ISRAEL IN THE PRIMARY NARRATIVE

T he key narrative concerning Solomon, found in 1 Kings 3–11, of course does not stand alone but is embedded in a larger narrative. The primary narrative of the Old Testament canon is the most extended narrative memory of ancient Israel, the literary corpus that stretches from Genesis 1 through 2 Kings 25. (This extended narrative excludes the book of Ruth, which is situated differently in the canon of the Hebrew Bible.) The narrative traces the tradition of Israel from *Creation* to the *deportation* of Israel from the land of promise (along with a concluding, suggestive note concerning King Jehoiachin in 2 Kings 25:27–30). This arrangement of the literature suggests that for these traditionist shapers of the narrative, the goal of all human history is to situate Israel in exile, the perspective from which the completed tradition proceeds. Thus the primary narrative dares to imagine that the largest vista of the creation of the world has as its reference point the demise of Jerusalem, which in Israelite imagination is indeed the epicenter of all reality.

The notion of a "primary history" has been argued with force by David Noel Freedman:

These nine books (really scrolls) comprise just about 150,000 words, or half of the entire Hebrew Bible. This rearrangement (and it is hardly more than a relabeling, since the nine books—Genesis to Deuteronomy and Joshua to Kings—remain in exactly the same order as before) reveals the true nature of the initial main and central content of the Bible. I have termed this nine-book collection the Primary History, chiefly because I have never found a name for it in the literature. I have also called it the First Bible because that is what it is. It is central and basic, the core and foundation of the rest of the books, which are related to it, dependent on it, and do not make much sense without it.[1]

Freedman goes further to propose that the books of this literary corpus are arranged in relationship to the sequence of the Ten Commandments. This judgment seems excessively speculative and has not been followed by scholars generally. More recently, David Harman Akenson has explicated the primary history that he terms the "Great Invention."[2] By this he means that the literature from Genesis through

Kings is a daring, imaginative construct, hence the word "invention." Akenson hypo-
thesizes that one "young man" created this literature as a response to the "woe" of
the exiles:

> Before his hair had turned gray or his eyes dimmed, the young man had col-
> lected, with the help of his allies, young and old, the traditions and manu-
> scripts of his people and turned them into nine scrolls, which became the first
> nine books of the Hebrew Bible (the Christian "Old Testament" has things
> out of sequence at this point); Ruth belongs later: Genesis, Exodus, Leviti-
> cus, Numbers, Deuteronomy, Joshua, Judges, Samuel (broken in early medi-
> eval times into two separate volumes) and Kings (also broken into two in the
> early medieval era). These nine books are a unity. They take the story of the
> covenant—the interaction of Yahweh and the Chosen People—from the cre-
> ation of the earth down to the 560s B.C.E., when after thirty years as a prisoner
> in the equivalent of a gilded cage in Babylon, Jehoiachin, former King of
> Judah, was set free. The Books of Kings ends with marvellous ambiguity.
> Jehoiachin, released, is set upon a throne by his Babylonian host, and it is a
> higher throne than that of the other conquered kings who are with him. And
> he was given a daily allowance of food for the rest of his life (II Kings
> 25:28–30). That is an end to an historical chronicle written by someone who
> had hope, but who had no idea of what the next chapter of the Chosen Peo-
> ple's history would contain.[3]

Here, the word "invention" is used for the product of the great and nimble
mind that produced the first nine books of the Hebrew Bible. Inventors do not
create, for creation is to make something where there was nothing. Inventors
use what is to hand, and then they add something of their own genius,
whether it is new ways of recombining old elements, or tiny little improve-
ments in existing parts so that what otherwise would not work does; or they
take out their tools and make a part of new design and suddenly everything
works. And the really good ones do so with marvellous efficiency and little
flash. One thinks with admiration of the medieval inventor who first whittled
from a piece of oak the eccentric cam, and attached it to the rim of a wagon
wheel, thereby permitting the translation of rotary motion of linear force; on
that elegant simplicity hangs all modern mechanical transportation.

Between the very good inventors and the few really great ones, there is a
line: the truly great ones instinctively and fully collaborate with their users.
There is nothing more useless than a physical invention that is ahead of its

time or a cultural invention that is ahead of its audience. (The sadly risible nineteenth-century Frenchman who invented a perfectly workable facsimile machine comes to mind.) If ever there was a case of successful collaboration between inventor and audience, it is the first nine books of the Hebrew Bible. Not only were they embraced by their exilic audience, they were carried, eventually, back to the city of Jerusalem where they became the reference point for the establishment of a spiritual world. One cannot read these nine books of history without entering into their world, arguing with them, interrogating them for hidden meanings. Genesis through Kings: a truly great invention.[4]

For our purposes, it is of special interest that Akenson reckons Solomon's temple to be particularly remarkable in this literary invention:

> This fact is what the young religious genius understood, and to understand that man's genius, we must break through the subsequent belief (one that has been normative for at least the last 1,500 years) that the Chosen People had no idols. They did, but they did not denominate them as such. While denouncing the iconic idols of their neighbours, the Chosen People produced an aniconic idol whose dimensions exceeded those of almost any religious artifact in ancient history: the Temple of Solomon. Just as Yahweh could be limned only in the covenant, so the covenant could be touched only in the Temple. There, in the Holy of Holies, in the tabernacle in which the earliest Israelites had travelled with their god in the Ark of the Covenant, Yahweh was physically present (see Exodus 29:42, 33:9). There one killed all manner of beasts, their blood being a direct offering to him. By an easy act of association, one did not merely worship in the Temple. One worshipped the Temple. This form of aniconic idol is not as unusual as one might think. What is unusual is the direct denial of its function. But, as we shall see, such denial of reality was one of the ways in which the ancient Hebrews and their heirs transcendent, by-passed reality.[5]

We have the knowledge that the Temple eventually was rebuilt, the idol repaired, the sacrifices reinstituted, the covenant again physically honoured, and thereby reaffirmed. However, the young man had no such foreknowledge. He was proceeding, with the same kind of faith that is ascribed to Moses, to lead the people spiritually, yet, unlike Moses, to some destination that he knew not. In collecting the central traditions of the Chosen People, in editing them so that they fit together rather better than they otherwise would, in writing down ancient oral tales and fitting them into his text, and in adding touches of his own, the young man was inventing a great religion. This is not the same as creating one; inventions are made by the imaginative recombination of pieces that are lying around a culture's workshop, with the addition of the occasional newly-machined part. This was invention, not creation.[6]

The hypothesis of the primary history, as voiced by Freedman and Akenson, echoes two observations that are pertinent for our study. First, it is noteworthy that in Akenson's rendering, the temple is front and center in the long concern of this historical memory in Israel. Consequently, we are entitled to see that the Solomonic narrative of 1 Kings 1–11—with the great temple dedication of 1 Kings 8 at its center—is the pivot point of the entire primary history. It is of course the case that 1 Kings 9:1–9, immediately after the dedication of the temple in 1 Kings 8, offers a decisive warning against land loss:

> If you turn aside from following me, you or your children, and do not keep my commandments and my statutes that I have set before you, but go and serve other gods and worship them, then I will cut Israel off from the land that I have given them; and the house that I have consecrated for my name I will cast out of my sight; and Israel will become a proverb and a taunt among all peoples. This house will become a heap of ruins; everyone passing by it will be astonished, and will hiss; and they will say, "Why has the Lord done such a thing to this land and to this house?" Then they will say, "Because they have forsaken the Lord their God, who brought their ancestors out of the land of Egypt, and embraced other gods, worshiping them and serving them; therefore the Lord has brought this disaster upon them." (1 Kgs 9:6–9)

That land loss, governed through three verbs—cut off, cast out, become a heap of ruins—is the beginning of the demise that is the theme of 1 and 2 Kings and that culminates in the deportation described in 2 Kings 24–25. Thus the entire primary history takes Solomon as a key marker in its recital.

Second, it is worth observing that the primary history begins in Genesis 1:1–2, 11–12, 22, 24, 28, vv. 4–6, with an accent on "earth" ('eres):

> In the beginning when God created the heavens and *the earth, the earth* was a formless void and darkness covered the face of the deep, while a wind from God swept over the face of the waters. . . . Then God said, "Let *the earth* put forth vegetation: plants yielding seed, and fruit trees of every kind on earth that bear fruit with the seed in it." And it was so. *The earth* brought forth vegetation: plants yielding seed of every kind, and trees of every kind bearing fruit with the seed in it. And God saw that it was good. . . . God blessed them, saying, "Be fruitful and multiply and fill the waters in the seas, and let birds multiply on the earth.". . . And God said, "Let *the earth* bring forth living creatures

of every kind: cattle and creeping things and wild animals of the earth of every kind." And it was so. God made the wild animals of the earth of every kind, and the cattle of every kind, and everything that creeps upon *the ground* of every kind. And God saw that it was good. . . . God blessed them, and God said to them, "Be fruitful and multiply, and fill *the earth* and subdue it; and have dominion over the fish of the sea and over the birds of the air and over every living thing that moves upon the earth. . . . In the day that the Lord God made *the earth* and the heavens, when no plant of the field was yet in *the earth* and no herb of the field had yet sprung up—for the Lord God had not caused it to rain upon *the earth,* and there was no one to till the ground; but a stream would rise from *the earth,* and water the whole face of *the ground.* (See also 1 Kgs 1:17, 26, 30; 2:13)

The primary history is preoccupied with the "earth" as a life-giving system ordered by the Creator. At the end of the primary history, in 2 Kings, the narrative is preoccupied with "the land":

He carried away all Jerusalem, all the officials, all the warriors, ten thousand captives, all the artisans and the smiths; no one remained, except the poorest people of *the land.* (2 Kgs 24:1)

But the captain of the guard left some of the poorest people of *the land* to be vinedressers and tillers of the soil. . . . He appointed Gedaliah son of Ahikam son of Shaphan as governor over the people who remained in the land of Judah, whom King Nebuchadnezzar of Babylon had left. (2 Kgs 25:12, 22)

This account of the emptying of the land is signified positively by the removal of "temple vessels" away from the land (2 Kgs 25:13–17).[7] Negatively, the emptying of the land is signified by the remainder in the land of "the poorest" (24:14; 25:12). Such a statement indicates the radical depletion of a life-sustaining infrastructure.

Now it is to be recognized that the same term functions differently in the two clusters of texts. At the outset *'eres* pertains to the whole earth as creation; in the conclusion *'eres* pertains only to the environs of Jerusalem. Nonetheless, the same term suggests a coherence to the stretch of the narrative: at the outset the land is *full of blessing;* at the end it is *emptied of real life.* Thus the whole of the primary narrative is about the fullness and the emptiness of *'eres,* a story Israel takes as its own.

It is plausible, moreover, that the mentions of Solomon in 2 Kings 24:13 and 25:16 are intended to draw the reader to the centrality of the Solomon narrative and the temple, and perhaps to suggest that the anticipated curses of 1 Kings 9:6–9 are now fully operative as Israel, disobedient to Torah, comes to a current crisis that has been, from the beginning, an anticipated sentence for disobedience. Such a possible connection gives force to the curses of Genesis 3:14–19 and the way in which they become, through extended editorial work, a leitmotif of the entire primary history.[8] The outcome of this reading of the material from Genesis through Kings is to locate the Solomonic narrative at the center of Israel's formative, imaginative interpretation of its past.

THE PRIMARY NARRATIVE IN CURRENT CRITICISM

While a notion of the primary narrative with a sweep from creation (Gen 1:1) to exile (2 Kgs 25:30) makes good canonical sense and offers rich interpretive possibility, the critical matters beneath such a canonical judgment are inescapably more complex. Through the nineteenth and twentieth centuries, critical interpretation has hypothesized that these traditional materials are constituted by diversity of sources brought together by a complicated editorial process.[9] At the beginning of the twenty-first century, that hypothesis is in some disarray and does not command a consensus as in previous generations of scholarship. Nevertheless, the literary complexity of what may have turned out to be the primary narrative is undeniable. Scholars now are not wont to work out that apparent editorial complexity in much detail. At a minimum, nonetheless, the following may be said to be a near consensus in current criticism.

The prevailing judgment is that the scrolls constituting the primal narrative arrived in something like final form in the sixth-century exile, due to the articulation of two quite distinct interpretive trajectories, both of which exercised immense authority in the exilic community, and both of which are reckoned to be authoritative and crucial for the final canonical form of the tradition. First, current critical opinion would support the judgment that the materials in Genesis through Numbers are canonically shaped by the Priestly traditionalists, who utilized old sources, but the materials reached final form in the exile. Their purpose is to advocate and urge Israel as a holy people, preoccupied with proper rules and practices of worship and purity. This Priestly material, a powerful shaping advocacy in the development of the canon, focuses upon the commandments that will guide and maintain a community of holiness. It shows the way in which the cultic practices of holiness (e.g., Sabbath and circumcision) pervade even the narrative memory of Israel, and record and celebrate the "generations" of the faithful, thus articulating a continuity of the holy community through time, even time that is historically filled with disruption and discontinuity. This continuity is articulated through a series of genealogies (*toledoth*) that shape the literary corpus. For the most part, this interpretive trajectory does not bear upon the Solomon traditions, except insofar as the temple of Solomon shares the horizon of the cultic traditions of the Pentateuch and appears connected with traditions of Tabernacle. As we will see, such a connection, while present, is of little import for the burden, program, and intention of the Solomon tradition.

The second interpretive trajectory that is constitutive for the primal history is the Deuteronomic theology articulated in the book of Deuteronomy that then functions as the interpretive grid for the historical reportage of Joshua, Judges, Samuel, and Kings.[10] Clearly this interpretive trajectory more directly concerns us because the Solomonic material of 1 Kings 3–11 is presented in this corpus. It is clear that the Deuteronomic corpus of Deuteronomy—Joshua, Judges, Samuel, and Kings—is in every way distinct from the Priestly textual traditions of Genesis through Numbers. Thus the primal history is constituted by the interface of these two interpretive trajectories. It is clearly the second that concerns us as we take up the study of Solomon.

The book of Deuteronomy constitutes a major, if not the predominant, theological articulation of Old Testament faith. Plain and simple, it introduces into Israelite faith and thought the idea and practice of covenant, the conviction that YHWH, the God of Sinai, and Israel are bound in a relationship of mutual fidelity that entails obligations of each party to the other and makes assurances of each party to the other.[11] This venturesome articulation of faith insists that biblical faith is at bottom a dialogic, interactive relationship whereby each party impinges upon the other. While the full-blown articulation of Deuteronomy surely has antecedents and claims to be rooted in traditions that go back to the hidden, ancient days of Sinai, it is generally thought that Deuteronomy constitutes an important *novum* in Israel's theological enterprise.

The covenantal theology of the book of Deuteronomy was already fully delineated in 1938 by Gerhard von Rad, who identified the following elements of a covenantal structure:

Historical presentation of the events at Sinai, and paraenetic material connected with this event (Deut 1–11);
The reading of the law (Deut 12:1–26:18);
The sealing of the covenant (Deut 26:16–19);
Blessings and curses (Deut 27ff.)[12]

Von Rad, in a variety of subsequent studies, moreover, noticed the interpretive dynamic of the tradition of Deuteronomy, paying particular attention to the reiterated word "today," a signal that the interpretive tradition was kept endlessly contemporary.

There is, however, one feature constantly recurring throughout *Deuteronomy*, which shows very clearly how intimately its provisions were formerly bound up with the cultus. We refer to the persistent repetition of the word "today," which is the common denominator of deuteronomic homiletic as a whole: e.g. "Today I command you . . ." (*Deut.* xv.15); "Today you are to pass over Jordan"

(*Deut.* ix.1); "Today you have declared concerning Yahweh that he shall be your God" (*Deut.* xxvi.17); "Today you have become Yahweh's people" (*Deut.* xxvii.9); "Today I have set before you life and prosperity, death and misfortune" (*Deut.* xxx.15); "Today I call heaven and earth to witness against you" (*Deut.* xxx.19).

It cannot be maintained that this is merely an effective stylistic device which the deuteronomist has chosen to make more vivid what he has to say. On the contrary, it is a quite fundamental feature of *Deuteronomy,* reminding us that this is a vivid reconstruction of the events of the redemption story such as only the cultus can furnish. No literary composition, however skilful, could ever bring the events to life in this way. Or let us read from this point of view a passage such as *Deut.* v.2–4: "Yahweh our God made a covenant with us in Horeb. Not with our fathers did Yahweh make this covenant, but with us here, who are all of us still alive today. Yahweh has spoken to you face to face out of the fire upon the mountain."

Here the immediacy of the event is still more evident. The divine revelation on Sinai is not something in the past, a matter of history so far as the present generation to whom it is addressed is concerned. It is a present reality, determining the way of life of the very same people who receive it. In a literary presentation of the matter it would be meaningless so to discount the passage of time; such a procedure could carry no conviction with a post-Mosaic generation. But within the framework of the cultus, where past, present, and future acts of God coalesce in the one tremendous actuality of the faith, such a treatment is altogether possible and indeed essential.[13]

Thus the covenant tradition of Deuteronomy continues to exercise enormous influence on the ongoing interpretive practice of Israel.

What von Rad expressed so imaginatively in the text received further impetus in 1955 when George Mendenhall published his influential study *Law and Covenant in Israel and the Ancient Near East.*[14] Mendenhall argued for the great antiquity of the covenantal tradition, finding its source in the old treaties among the Hittites in the fourteenth century. Aside from the claim of antiquity and the identity of the covenantal genre as a political one, Mendenhall's great contribution was to make clear the dynamic and practical contemporaneity of the religious practice of ancient Israel. He understood that the covenant, with stipulations and oath at its center and reinforced by sanctions (blessing and curse), fully characterized the life and faith of the community.

Mendenhall's appeal to Hittite parallels caused an enormous stir in scholarly circles. The next generation of scholars, however, found the citation of Hittite parallels to be less convincing than had been thought at mid-century. In place of the Hittite parallels, attention is currently given to Assyrian treaties in the eighth and seventh centuries.[15] Many of the gains of the work of Mendenhall remain—the accent of contemporaneity and the political dynamism of the genre. Only now the preferred linkage is to Assyrian parallels in the eighth and seventh centuries, the time that scholars take to be the period of the Deuteronomic school that initiated a quite new theological model into Israel. Consequently, the book of Deuteronomy is reckoned to be an articulation of the eighth and seventh centuries that fixed Israel's faith in a canonical pattern of *command and sanction*. The tradition is thoroughly centered on YHWH, the God of Sinai, who at Sinai issued the ten commands (Exod 20:1–17).

The book of Deuteronomy, however, is quite explicit in its acknowledgement that it is not a Sinai document. It is a post-Sinai tradition that has the commands of Sinai as its premise (see Deut 5:6–22). The teaching of Deuteronomy itself, however, is situated in the territory "beyond the Jordan in the land of Moab" (1:5). What became "the book of Deuteronomy" receives its name from the word *deuteros* that occurs in the Greek translation of Deuteronomy 17:18. Whereas we conventionally render the term "copy," it is as well to take the term as "second version," so that Deuteronomy constitutes a second version of commands after the first proclamation at Sinai. The second version serves the dynamism of the commandments by keeping remembered commandments contemporary through interpretation, expansion, and innovation.

The first large unit of Deuteronomy—Deuteronomy 1–11, or more precisely, Deuteronomy 5–11—makes an urgent appeal for obedience. It recognizes that the inculcation of the young into this obedience of covenant is an urgent, life-or-death matter. The second, central portion of the book, chapters 12–25, constitutes the commands of Deuteronomy. It is argued that this extended, complex series of commandments that pertain to every sphere of life is in fact an ordered exposition of the Ten Commandments.[16] Whether that is the case or not, it is clear that the sequence of commands offered here intends to bring every sphere of Israel's life—cultic and economic—under the rule and will of YHWH. The rhetoric of this corpus offers a Yahwistic ethic as an alternative to the seductive options of the "Canaanites" in the land. Israel's existence and future are said to be constituted and assured by obedience to this alternative, covenantal ordering of communal life. Thus according to the dynamics of Deuteronomy 5:1–5 (see also 31:9–13), Israel is expected and required to reaffirm its loyalty to covenant with YHWH on a regular and public basis. Indeed, without such public reenactment, the covenant expires and Israel ceases to be Israel.

This urgency is reinforced in the blessings and curses of Deuteronomy 28, with a more modest recital of curses in Deuteronomy 27:15–26. While chapter 28 begins with a series of blessings related to obedience (28:1–14), the great body of the chapter concerns curses for disobedience (28:15–68). There is no doubt that this inventory of curses draws from a common stock of curses in ancient Near Eastern culture.[17] In context, however, the curses constitute a severe threat and warning to Israel, indicating that everything for the life, survival, well-being, and future of Israel finally depends upon compliance to Torah commands, which in this instance means specifically the commands of Deuteronomy 12–25.

Thus the tradition of Deuteronomy is simplistic in championing obedience to Torah as the clue to life. This advocacy, in quite direct fashion, allows no slippage, makes no exceptions, and understands that life is reduced to the single yes or no of compliance:

> See, I have set before you today life and prosperity, death and adversity. If you obey the commandments of the Lord your God that I am commanding you today, by loving the Lord your God, walking in his ways, and observing his commandments, decrees, and ordinances, then you shall live and become numerous, and the Lord your God will bless you in the land that you are entering to possess. But if your heart turns away and you do not hear, but are led astray to bow down to other gods and serve them, I declare to you today that you shall perish; you shall not live long in the land that you are crossing the Jordan to enter and possess. I call heaven and earth to witness against you today that I have set before you life and death, blessings and curses. Choose life so that you and your descendants may live, loving the Lord your God, obeying him, and holding fast to him; for that means life to you and length of days, so that you may live in the land that the Lord swore to give to your ancestors, to Abraham, to Isaac, and to Jacob. (Deut 30:15–20)

The power and passion of this teaching is to be understood in terms of the urgency of the seductions that are felt concerning both religious and political-economic options in the land of promise, options characterized summarily as "Canaanite." Thus the Canaanite system—religious and political-economic—will lead to land loss and to death:

> When the Lord your God has brought you into the land that he swore to your ancestors, to Abraham, to Isaac, and to Jacob, to give you—a land with fine, large cities that you did not build, houses filled with all sorts of goods that you did not fill, hewn cisterns that you did not hew, vineyards and olive groves that you did not plant—and when you have eaten your fill, take care that you do not forget the Lord, who brought you out of the land of Egypt, out of the house of slavery. The Lord your God you shall fear; him you shall serve, and by his name alone you shall swear. Do not follow other gods, any of the gods of the peoples who are all around you, because the Lord your God, who is

present with you, is a jealous God. The anger of the Lord your God would be kindled against you and he would destroy you from the face of the earth. (Deut 6:10–15)

If you do forget the Lord your God and follow other gods to serve and worship them, I solemnly warn you today that you shall surely perish. Like the nations that the Lord is destroying before you, so shall you perish, because you would not obey the voice of the Lord your God. (Deut 8:19–20)

If you will only heed his every commandment that I am commanding you today—loving the Lord your God, and serving him with all your heart and with all your soul—then he will give the rain for your land in its season, the early rain and the later rain, and you will gather in your grain, your wine, and your oil; and he will give grass in your fields for your livestock, and you will eat your fill. Take care, or you will be seduced into turning away, serving other gods and worshiping them, for then the anger of the Lord will be kindled against you and he will shut up the heavens, so that there will be no rain and the land will yield no fruit; then you will perish quickly off the good land that the Lord is giving you. (Deut 11:13–17)

While this theology is no doubt rooted in older tradition and purports to be faithfully reminiscent of Moses, there can be no doubt that it is a remarkably fresh and demanding interpretive innovation, conducted by a radical group that came later to be designated as the YHWH Alone party.[18] It is plausible that the actual religious practices of Israel at the time were much more tolerant and latitudinarian than this interpretive tradition acknowledges. This advocacy, in contrast to conventional practice, envisioned an Israelite community deeply committed to the most stringent demands and requirements of Yahwistic covenantalism.

It is clear that this theological trajectory, when juxtaposed to that of the Priestly tradition, offers an alternative theological vision. Together with the Priestly tradition, it constitutes the canonical voice of the primary history. Whereas the Priestly interests focused upon purity and the maintenance of a "holy people," the Deuteronomic tradition focuses upon the specific claims of Deuteronomic Torah, which is more fully focused upon social-political-economic interests. Thus the book of Deuteronomy, which stands fifth in the canon, produces a quite distinct interpretive accent that will be important for the literature that follows.

DEVELOPMENT OF THE DEUTERONOMIC HISTORY

The book of Deuteronomy, with its taut theology of covenant obligation and covenant guarantees, was close to its final form in the seventh century. It represented a nervy theological initiative by a group of radical advocates who offered an alternative vision of faith championed by the Jerusalem establishment of dynasty and temple. This advocacy insisted that for all the claims of power and promises asserted by Jerusalem ideology, the inescapable condition of Israel's well-being—temple Israel and royal Israel included—was obedience to the Torah requirements given in this tradition.

On the basis of that firm conviction formulated in the scroll found in 2 Kings 22, some from the same "Deuteronomic" circles proceeded to offer an alternative version of Israelite history. Following publication of Martin Noth's bold hypothesis, biblical scholars now generally hold that the entire historical narrative of Joshua, Judges, Samuel, and Kings in their present form was shaped according to the claims and perspectives of the theology of the book of Deuteronomy, thus the "Deuteronomic history."[19] Noth's proposal, even though perhaps overly simple, continues to shape interpretive conversations, and there is a large contemporary critical literature based on his ideas.[20] Noth's hypothesis is that the entire corpus of the history was written at one time, by one hand, from one perspective, as a critical reflection on Israel's destiny in the sixth-century exile. Noth, moreover, proposed that the entire history was offered about 550 B.C.E., thus soon after the final paragraph of 2 Kings 25:27–30, as a report of events in 562 B.C.E. There is no doubt that this historian appealed to a rich variety of antecedent sources including both folklore and archaeological records from the archives of Jerusalem. What interests us, however, is the impact of a theological vision imposed on antecedent materials in order to "explain" how Israel ended in exile, perhaps to offer a promise beyond exile, perhaps to offer a program of restitution for the generation soon to depart from exile.[21]

The term "Deuteronomic"—always linked to the theological vision of the book of Deuteronomy—is used somewhat loosely in critical conversation to refer to a variety of interpretive matters. Most closely, the term refers to certain terms and phrases that are most readily recognized as having rootage in the rhetoric of the book of Deuteronomy. When the term "Deuteronomic" is used expansively, as it often is, the interpretive outcomes include the following.

The Book of Joshua

In the book of Joshua, the Deuteronomic history takes what may have been included as "conquest traditions" and frames them into a unified report concerning a systemic seizure of the land, all led by Joshua as an act of obedience to YHWH.

Joshua 1 declares Joshua to be the proper successor to Moses who will enact the ancient promise of the land. The mandate to Joshua includes a characteristic formula of military encouragement, only the formula is transposed into a concern for Torah obedience:

Only be strong and very courageous, being careful to act in accordance
with all the law that my servant Moses commanded you; do not turn
from it to the right hand or to the left, so that you may be successful
wherever you go. This book of the law shall not depart out of your
mouth; you shall meditate on it day and night, so that you may be careful to act in accordance with all that is written in it. For then you shall
make your way prosperous, and then you shall be successful. I hereby
command you: Be strong and courageous; do not be frightened or dis-
mayed, for the Lord your God is with you wherever you go. (Josh 1:7–9)

The community in turn responds to Joshua with a pledge of obedience: "They
answered Joshua: 'All that you have commanded us we will do, and wherever you
send us we will go. Just as we obeyed Moses in all things, so we will obey you. Only
may the Lord your God be with you, as he was with Moses. Whoever rebels against
your orders and disobeys your words, whatever you command, shall be put to death.
Only be strong and courageous'" (Josh 1:16–18).

Thus the "history" begins with the assertion that *Torah obedience* is the clue to and
condition for life in the land.

Joshua 8:30–35 reports on the enactment of covenant that entails a deposit of
a "copy of the Torah" (8:32) together with covenantal sanctions from "the book
of the Torah," that is, from Deuteronomy:

And there, in the presence of the Israelites, Joshua wrote on the stones
a copy of the law of Moses, which he had written. All Israel, alien as
well as citizen, with their elders and officers and their judges, stood on
opposite sides of the ark in front of the levitical priests who carried the
ark of the covenant of the Lord, half of them in front of Mount Gerizim
and half of them in front of Mount Ebal, as Moses the servant of the Lord
had commanded at the first, that they should bless the people of Israel.
And afterward he read all the words of the law, blessings and curses,
according to all that is written in the book of the law. (Josh 8:32–34)

Joshua 11:16–20 reports on the enactment of *herem* in compliance with the
requirement of Deuteronomy 20:16–18, an act of inordinate violence. The term
is used to refer to wholesale destruction that is understood as a "burnt offering"
in abundance to YHWH. The term bespeaks social violence rooted in faith.

Joshua 23, the narrative conclusion to the taking of the land, consists of a
speech of Deuteronomic theology placed in the mouth of Joshua. The accent is
upon rigorous Torah obedience as the Deuteronomic condition for well-being:

> Therefore be very steadfast to observe and do all that is written in the
> book of the law of Moses, turning aside from it neither to the right nor
> to the left (Josh 23:6).

The warning is that the distinctiveness of Israel—maintained through Torah obedience—should protect Israel from being mixed with non-Israelite culture: "so that
you may not be mixed with these nations left here among you, or make mention of
the names of their gods, or swear by them, or serve them, or bow yourselves down
to them" (Josh 23:7). This concern for distinctiveness maintained through obedience to the commands of the book of Deuteronomy concerned the seduction of
Canaanite religion and Canaanite patterns of social relationships. When this text is
read a second time, in the sixth-century exile, then clearly the threat is not Canaanite culture and religion but instead is the culture to which Israelites have been
deported from Jerusalem. The consequence of such steadfast obedience is protection
and well-being: "For the Lord has driven out before you great and strong nations;
and as for you, no one has been able to withstand you to this day. One of you puts
to flight a thousand, since it is the Lord your God who fights for you, as he promised you" (23:9–10).

That assurance is more than balanced by the negative threat connected to disobedience to Torah:

> For if you turn back, and join the survivors of these nations left here among
> you, and intermarry with them, so that you marry their women and they
> yours, know assuredly that the Lord your God will not continue to drive out
> these nations before you; but they shall be a snare and a trap for you, a scourge
> on your sides, and thorns in your eyes, until you perish from this good land
> that the Lord your God has given you. (Josh 23:12–13)

> If you transgress the covenant of the Lord your God, which he enjoined on
> you, and go and serve other gods and bow down to them, then the anger of
> the Lord will be kindled against you, and you shall perish quickly from the
> good land that he has given to you. (Josh 23:16)

Thus already in the Joshua tradition concerning the receiving of land, the Deuteronomist is building the case for the ultimate loss of the land in the sixth century. The
Deuteronomic shaping of the book of Joshua exhibits the way in which the text
requires a double reading, first in the alleged context of the text itself, and second in
the exile that is the context of Deuteronomic interpretation. The sense of the book
of Joshua is to accent the Torah as the condition of land occupation and retention, a
tradition rooted in the book of Deuteronomy where the negative sanctions of curse
bespeak deportation.

The Book of Judges

The central part of the book of Judges consists of "hero stories" (Judg 3:6–16:31). These narratives have now been organized by the Deuteronomist into a more or less coherent account of life in the land of promise before the rise of the monarchy. (Judges 17–21, normally excluded from the Deuteronomic materials, reflects the crisis of social power prior to the rise of the monarchy.)

The primary feature of the editorial process of constructing a coherent narrative—along with the arrangement and juxtaposition of materials—is the imposition of a theological formula in four parts. That formula is clearly exhibited in the brief narrative concerning Othniel in Judges 3:7–11. First, there is the disregard of the first commandment and the worship of other gods (see Deut 5:6–7): "The Israelites did what was evil in the sight of the Lord, forgetting the Lord their God, and worshiping the Baals and the Asherahs" (Judg 3:7). Second, there follows the consequent punishment of disobedient Israel by subjecting Israel to the control and abuse of foreign peoples: "Therefore the anger of the Lord was kindled against Israel, and he sold them into the hand of King Cushan-rishathaim of Aram-naharaim" (3:8a).

The third piece of the formula is a return to dependence upon YHWH: "But when the Israelites cried out to the Lord, the Lord raised up a deliverer for the Israelites" (Judg 3:9a). And fourth, YHWH intervenes to deliver this repentant people by raising up a deliverer, a feature of the formula that prepares the way for the narrative of rescue through an already extant hero tale: "The Lord raised up a deliverer for the Israelites, who delivered them, Othniel son of Kenaz, Caleb's younger brother" (Judg 3:9c).

This most characteristic Deuteronomic formula is constructed by a combination of two older formulae that voice Israel's most elemental faith.[22] First, the initial two elements of the formula—*sin* and *punishment*—reflect the oldest conviction of Deuteronomy and likely attest to a "deeds-consequences" notion whereby certain deeds produce anticipated consequences. Second, the other two elements of the formula—*cry* and *save*—characterize the faith of the Psalter, expressed especially in lament and thanksgiving as, for example, in Psalm 107:4–32. The four elements together articulate the full drama of alienation and restoration to covenant.

The account of the book of Judges clearly pertains to the initial period of Israel in the land as the Deuteronomists present the history of Israel. This account may also be read, however, in the context of sixth-century exile. When read in this latter way, the crisis of Israel in the sixth century is given a certain theological illumination. Elements one and two (sin and punishment) articulate the way in which Israel came into exile: Israel disobeyed and so was "sold into the hand" of the enemy, in this case Babylon. Thus the plight of exile is articulated in the "deeds-consequences" scheme of Deuteronomy. The third element, "cry out," represents a return to dependence upon YHWH, and the fourth element anticipates a rescuing deliverer; in the actual historical circumstance of exile, that deliverer was Cyrus the Persian (see 2 Chron 36:22–23; Isa 44:28; 45:1). This latter identification of the rescuer sent by YHWH is beyond the horizon of the Deuteronomist, but is later attested in the tradition of Israel. Thus the Deuteronomist, in the book of Judges, analyzes the entry into exile and anticipates a return from exile that will be triggered by a cry of repentance.

We are able to see, then, that the book of Judges permits—and requires—a double reading. It is to be read, according to the imaginative memory of Israel, as a time of intense interaction with non-Israelite populations in a context where Yahwistic faith was both resource and vexation. The material is then to be read, in canonical context, as a Yahwistic formulation of the crisis of exile. In canonical formation exile is said to be a consequence of infidelity to YHWH.

The Book of Samuel

According to the initial hypothesis of Martin Noth, the beginning of the book of Samuel—until the appearance of Saul—was a continuation of the book of Judges.[23] If we begin our consideration of the book of Samuel with the appearance of Saul, we are plunged into a dispute about kingship.[24] It is conventional to take the texts of 1 Samuel 8, 10:17–27, and 12—the so-called antimonarchal source—as sounding the sentiments of the Deuteronomist. In these several speeches on the lips of Samuel, the text sounds advocacy for Torah obedience and anticipates that the monarch to come will depart from Torah and cease to practice the neighborliness required by Torah. Specifically, the warnings against the usurpatious character of monarchy in 1 Samuel 8:11–17 are thought by many scholars to be a critical reflection precisely upon the exploitative policies and practices of Solomon. In any case, it is clear that monarchy constitutes a peculiar and important issue for the Deuteronomist, an issue to which we will return.

In the text that includes 2 Samuel 9–20 and 1 Kings 1–2, dubbed since Rost as the Succession Narrative, the literature traces the inexorable movement of David's throne toward the empowerment of Solomon.[25] Indeed, a good case can be made that this entire literature is designed to substantiate Solomon as the proper successor to David. Most interesting for our study is the fact that this so-called Succession Narrative bears none of the marks of the Deuteronomist. It is as though in the final form of the text the traditionists were prepared to let the complex, sordid course of the monarchy speak for itself, without any explanation or heavy-handed theological indictment. We will return to the explicit references to Solomon in the Succession Narrative.

The Books of Kings

In the books of Kings, the Deuteronomist draws more closely to the agenda of the destruction of Jerusalem, a theme that has been in purview since the beginning of the corpus. In common critical judgment 1 Kings 1–2, bringing Solomon to the throne, concludes the Succession Narrative begun in 2 Samuel 9–20. As noted, 1 Kings 3–11 constitutes the primary narrative of Solomon to which we will return. The remainder of the books of Kings are constituted by reportage and verdict upon the series of kings in Israel and Judah, a series interrupted by the Elijah-Elisha narratives in the middle of the books of Kings.

The formulaic account of the several kings has as its centerpiece a theological verdict upon each king concerning fidelity to the Jerusalem temple—the criterion upon which every northern king perforce defaults—and fidelity to Torah obedience.[26] The sequence of kings in such a perspective is indeed a dismal one, with only Hezekiah and Josiah winning unreserved commendation:

> He [Hezekiah] trusted in the Lord the God of Israel; so that there was no one like him among all the kings of Judah after him, or among those who were before him. For he held fast to the Lord; he did not depart from following him but kept the commandments that the Lord commanded Moses. The Lord was with him; wherever he went, he prospered. He rebelled against the king of Assyria and would not serve him. (2 Kgs 18:5–7)

> Before him [Josiah] there was no king like him, who turned to the Lord with all his heart, with all his soul, and with all his might, according to all the law of Moses; nor did any like him arise after him. (2 Kgs 23:25)

Indeed, in the case of Hezekiah that positive verdict would seem to be subverted by the narrative report that follows in 2 Kings 18:13–15.

In calculating the larger intentionality of the Deuteronomic historian, special attention should be given to Josiah, the quintessential Torah-keeping king and no doubt the primary model king for the Deuteronomist. Josiah responded properly and appropriately to the finding of the scroll, a document most scholars take to be some form of the book of Deuteronomy (2 Kgs 22:10–13). It is a matter of dispute whether this reported incident in 2 Kings 22–23 has historical grounding. Even if it does not, the narrative articulates a clear Deuteronomic advocacy, namely, that kings must respond obediently to Torah as Josiah himself does. Thus the Josiah report constitutes the spectacular example of a Deuteronomic notion of how Jerusalem might have conducted itself.

After the positive verdict concerning Josiah, however, the Deuteronomic history follows immediately with a judgment that the sins of Manasseh, his grandfather, override Josiah's Torah righteousness; consequently, even Josiah's Torah obedience could not save Jerusalem from the fate wrought by Manasseh: "Still the Lord did not turn from the fierceness of his great wrath, by which his anger was kindled against Judah, because of all the provocations with which Manasseh had provoked him. The Lord said, 'I will remove Judah also out of my sight, as I have removed Israel; and I will reject this city that I have chosen, Jerusalem, and the house of which I said, My name shall be there'" (2 Kgs 23:26–27).

In the final chapters of 2 Kings 24–25, the narrative report moves quickly to portray the savage demise of Jerusalem and the loss of the land. Thus the story of kingship is steadily, if not uniformly, downhill to demise and deportation.

A TALE OF LAND LOSS

The hypothesis of the Deuteronomic corpus suggests that these several pieces, seemingly with great theological intentionality, coherently tell the tale of land loss in a community that failed to practice Torah in a way that would, according to Deuteronomy, have assured land retention and well-being.

We may notice two literary elements that suggest a coherence of the whole. First, it is credible to suggest, along with Marvin Chaney, that Joshua is understood by the Deuteronomists to be the counterpoint to King Josiah.[27] Consequently, if we take Joshua, Judges, Samuel, and Kings to be a coherent corpus, the whole is framed and bracketed by the Torah of Joshua (Josh 1:7–8 and 23:6, 16) and the Torah of Josiah (2 Kgs 22:13, 25). The whole is one advocacy of Torah as the clue to Israel's life in the land. Second, the Deuteronomic corpus appears to be organized around a series of extended speeches wherein this voice of powerful theological advocacy makes its clear statement.[28] Among the most prominent of these speeches are the following:

Joshua 23

The speech in Joshua 23 asserts Torah obedience as the condition of retention of the land just given: "Therefore be very steadfast to observe and do all that is written in the book of the law of Moses, turning aside from it neither to the right nor to the left, so that you may not be mixed with these nations left here among you, or make mention of the names of their gods, or swear by them, or serve them, or bow yourselves down to them, but hold fast to the Lord your God, as you have done to this day" (Josh 23:6–8).

1 Samuel 12

In 1 Samuel 12, Samuel warns Israel against disregard of the commandments. Most remarkably, the rhetoric of this speech three times reduces royal claims by the assertion that the king is reckoned alongside all other Israelites subject to the Torah and with no special claim or entitlement: "If you will fear the Lord and serve him and heed his voice and not rebel against the commandment of the Lord, and if both you and the king who reigns over you will follow the Lord your God, it will be well; but if you will not heed the voice of the Lord, but rebel against the commandment of the Lord, then the hand of the Lord will be against you and your king. . . . But if you still do wickedly, you shall be swept away, both you and your king" (1 Sam 12:14–15, 25).

All, including the king, are subject to the Torah; this means that all claims of royal legitimacy and priority are erased before the commanding authority of Torah.

2 Samuel 7

This curious pivotal chapter, as McCarthy has shown, occupies a decisive place in the Deuteronomic narrative even though much of verses 1–16 are not themselves marked by Deuteronomic characteristics. This oracle in the mouth of the nation gives legitimacy to David and his longstanding dynasty that came to dominate the books of Kings. It is clear that from the perspective of the rigorous Torah require- ments, YHWH's unconditional promise to David is a radical innovation, one that requires the Deuteronomic historian to move beyond the simple calculus of Deu- teronomy: "I will be a father to him, and he shall be a son to me. When he commits iniquity, I will punish him with a rod such as mortals use, with blows inflicted by human beings. But I will not take my steadfast love from him, as I took it from Saul, whom I put away from before you. Your house and your kingdom shall be made sure forever before me; your throne shall be established forever" (2 Sam 7:14– 16).

It is clear, moreover, that the text as it now stands envisions Solomon as the car- rier of the unconditional, long-term promise of YHWH to David: "When your days are fulfilled and you lie down with your ancestors, I will raise up your offspring after you, who shall come forth from your body, and I will establish his kingdom" (2 Sam 7:12). Thus the chapter enunciates a decisive turn in the perspective of the history, a move that no doubt was signaled, in the final form of the text, in the hints of 1 Samuel 2:10, 13:13–14, 15:28, 24:20, 25:28, 26:25, and 28:17.

1 Kings 8

The speech found in 1 Kings 8 portrays the building and dedication of the temple by Solomon as a pivot point for the entire narrative. Indeed, the temple in Jerusalem became the marker by which all subsequent kings are measured and most are found wanting.

2 Kings 17:5–41

This speech is an extended statement by the Deuteronomists on the failure of the northern kingdom and on the failure of any part of YHWH's people that does not adhere to Torah. Special attention should be given to the several statements in the larger articulation. In the midst of the indictment of the North, 2 Kings 17:13 asserts that the prophets sent by YHWH constantly issued warnings and appeals for repentance: "Yet the Lord warned Israel and Judah by every prophet and every seer, saying, 'Turn from your evil ways and keep my commandments and my statutes, in accordance with all the law that I commanded your ancestors and that I sent to you by my servants the prophets.'"

The prophetic appeal was to no avail; thus the northern kingdom, by disregard of such prophetic summons, perished, as the Deuteronomic historian had understood that it would, leaving only Judah: "Therefore the Lord was very angry with Israel and removed them out of his sight; none was left but the tribe of Judah alone" (2 Kgs 17:18).

In turn Judah resisted the commandments and so was cast out into exile, as had been the North (see 2 Kgs 17:23). These verses altogether articulate a full scribal theology of history. The rigor of Deuteronomy is apparent, except that the option of repentance is voiced. With that option rejected, however, we are back at the simple, direct calculus of Deuteronomy: obedience leads to blessing; disobedience leads to curse. This promise is found as early as the Torah entrusted to Joshua: "They answered Joshua: 'All that you have commanded us we will do, and wherever you send us we will go. Just as we obeyed Moses in all things, so we will obey you. Only may the Lord your God be with you, as he was with Moses! Whoever rebels against your orders and disobeys your words, whatever you command, shall be put to death. Only be strong and courageous'" (Josh 1:16–18).

This teaching culminates in 2 Kings 24–25. Recalcitrant Israel stands under judgment. Consequently, the gift of the land is revoked and the promise is nullified in Deuteronomic perspective. Israel ends in landlessness, now outside the territory and on the terms of another (see 2 Kgs 25:27–30).

THE INTERFACE OF DIVINE JUDGMENT AND DIVINE FIDELITY

In the earlier mention of 2 Samuel 7 and the dynastic promise to David, we noted that the oracular promise concerning the dynasty is a radical *novum* in Israel. It is the merit of Gerhard von Rad to have articulated the odd interface of *Torah* and *dynasty* as the defining theological datum for the Deuteronomic historian; von Rad takes the royal oracle of 2 Samuel 7 as an articulation of divine forbearance that provides something of a foil for the rigor of the demand of Deuteronomy for obedience: "With the history of the kingdom of Judah the position is different. That history, too, appears in the first instance as a story of human disobedience, with the cloud of God's judgement gathering ever thicker. How in this case is the divine forbearance, the much more extended span of divine patience, to be explained? This leads us to mention an element in the Deuteronomist's theology of history which we have so far left out of consideration."[29]

There then follows in von Rad's discussion a series of textual citations, each of which features an adversative "but" concerning royal futures that counters the more general statement of divine judgment (see 1 Kgs 11:32, 36; 15:4; 2 Kgs 8:19). Von Rad regards these texts as the juxtaposition of Torah rigor with a royal promise that is "wholly undeuteronomic": "It is interesting to see how in the Deuteronomist this prophetic tradition is fused with the Deuteronomic theology of the cult-place and the name; that is, how two traditional elements of completely different provenance are here united into a whole (cp. especially I Kings II.36)."[30] The outcome is "the special theological *schema* within and around which the Deuteronomist built his work, and therefore have a special significance for the ends he had in view. They exhibit a traditional element which is wholly undeuteronomic, namely, a cycle of definite Messianic conceptions."[31]

This "Messianic conception," moreover, leads to a profound deterrence of divine judgment: "It is the Nathan promise which runs through the history of Judah like a katéchon and wards off the long merited judgement from the kingdom 'for the sake of David.'"[32]

Thus the Deuteronomic presentation of Israel's royal history—with themes already inchoate in the early portion of the "history"—plays with and plays upon the interface of judgment for Torah disobedience and promise of divine fidelity: "For him both of these, the torah of Moses and the dynasty of David, were concrete historical powers: like the dynasty, the revelation of Jahweh's will to Moses was also something clearly discernible; it had in fact already been handed over in trust to the kings in the form of a sacred book. Thus the Deuteronomist sees the main problem of the history of Israel as lying in the question of the correct correlation of Moses and David."[33]

The large plot line of the books of Kings is that eventually Torah judgment will win, in the form of destruction and deportation. Except . . . perhaps a big except. Second Kings 25:27–30 adds a final note of durability for the dynasty that is enigmatic and may offer royal hope beyond judgment. That, however, is well beyond our concern with Solomon.

Our purpose in this chapter is to consider the larger literary context in which Solomon is presented. We may take the large social corpus of the primary history that stretches from Genesis through 2 Kings as our proper context. More immediately, we consider that the Deuteronomic corpus stands beside the Priestly tradition and that our proper focus is the literature from Deuteronomy to 2 Kings. Either way, it is clear that Solomon is located in a very large plot, and he is subject to canonical editorial work, interpretation that transforms him from whatever he may have been in ancient Israelite history into the primary carrier of theological affirmation and theological problematic.

CHAPTER 3

THE BELOVED SON AMID
ROUGH-AND-TUMBLE POWER

At the center of the Deuteronomic history—and at the center of the primal narrative—stands the Solomon narrative of 1 Kings 3–11. Solomon of course did not appear de novo in the memory and imagination of Israel. From the outset, he is a son of David. Both his claim to legitimacy and his compromised destiny are surely rooted in David, who also claimed legitimacy and who also, before his son, compromised his own destiny. For that reason, before we take up the Deuteronomic presentation of Solomon in 1 Kings 3–11, we may consider the appearance of Solomon in the so-called Succession Narrative, a text not especially marked by Deuteronomic interpretation. In this antecedent narrative that may indeed be an apologia for Solomon, Solomon appears as a passive recipient of the throne who received royal power according to divine will, with vigorous contestation but without active engagement on his part. The following elements in the antecedent narrative are important for our consideration of Solomon in the primary narrative of 1 Kings 3–11.

TWIN THEMES: BLESSING AND CURSE

In his rereading of the David narratives, R. A. Carlson has proposed that the narrative of 2 Samuel be understood as a twofold presentation of "David under Blessing" and "David under Curse."[1] The material that Carlson subsumes under "blessing" is 2 Samuel 2–7. It will be noted that this includes material in 2 Samuel 2:1–5:5, conventionally regarded as the conclusion of the narrative of "The Rise of David," along with chapters 6 and 7, that help to legitimate "institutional David." It is worth noting that David Gunn, against common critical opinion, has proposed that chapters 2–4 be taken as an introduction to the Succession Narrative that conventionally begins in chapter 9.[2] In any case, Carlson is correct that in chapters 2–7 David goes from strength to strength and from success to success.

Conversely, 2 Samuel 9–24 is taken by Carlson as an account of "David under Curse."[3] This material includes the main body of what is, since Rost, commonly taken as the Succession Narrative (2 Sam 9–20), plus chapters of material usually regarded as appendix in chapters 21–24.[4] In this material the power, wisdom, and prestige of David begin to unravel.

Thus Carlson proposes a reading of the final form of the text that is unimpeded by older critical distinctions. The twofold narrative, taken as Carlson takes it, is important on its own terms because it suggests, in both parts, that the fortunes of David were not just of his own choosing; rather, he is acted upon in decisive ways. There is no doubt, moreover, that the turn from blessing to curse is situated in the narrative of 2 Samuel 11. This chapter of course is accompanied by the theological response of 2 Samuel 12, the account of David's "original sin," whereby in hubris the king imagines that he is not accountable to Torah (see the indictment of 2 Sam 12:9). Nathan's curse upon the house of David is searing and succinct: "Now therefore the sword shall never depart from your house, for you have despised me, and have taken the wife of Uriah the Hittite to be your wife" (12:10).

It is credible to conclude that this future-shaping verdict of Nathan is designed as a counterpoint to the climax of Nathan's oracle of royal legitimization: "But I will not take my steadfast love from him, as I took it from Saul, whom I put away from before you" (2 Sam 7:15).

In this latter verse, the term "sur" occurs three times: "take from," "took," and "put away." The same term is decisive in 2 Samuel 12:10, where it is rendered "depart." Thus David, in the two speeches by Nathan, is the carrier of two forces that will not depart: YHWH's steadfast love (ḥesed), and the sword (ḥereb). David and his dynasty are carriers of both, both generated through prophetic oracle. The outcome is the assertion of the claim that the life of David's family is deeply marked by an irresolvable, inescapable ambiguity. (We may note that by the twofold use of the verb "sur," the wordplay gives voice to the large thematic tension in the Deuteronomic history noted by von Rad concerning Torah obedience and divine promise. The promise is one of abiding ḥesed. The curse for Torah disobedience is ḥereb. The narrative that follows stays well within this ambiguity and refuses to resolve it in either direction.

Given our interest in Solomon, this twofold characterization under ḥesed and ḥereb, under blessing and curse, is of interest because this is the legacy into which Solomon entered. Carlson's paradigm for reading 2 Samuel concerning blessing and curse prepares us to read the Solomon narrative of 1 Kings 3–11, for here as well we see the same themes. It is credible to see the Solomon narrative arranged as "Solomon under blessing" in 1 Kings 3–8 and "Solomon under curse" in 1 Kings 9–11. Taken as reportage, this would suggest that Solomon learned and received a great deal from his father, David. Taken as Deuteronomic interpretation, however, we may suggest that these twin themes emerged as a decisive perspective and pattern through which every life is inescapably read. The emergence of this pattern on the one hand is a theological one, witnessing the sovereign claim of God:

I form light and create darkness,
I make weal and create woe;
I the Lord do all these things. (Isa 45:7)

Taken as critical response to context, however, the twin themes together suggest that the shaping of the narrative of Solomon, not unlike the shaping of the narrative of David, is under the impetus of exile with its embodiment of curse and its daring anticipation of blessing yet to come. In this regard, as in much else, Solomon is his father's son.

SOLOMON AS SYMBOLIC CIPHER

The culmination of "David under blessing" in Carlson's reckoning is with the divine oracle in the mouth of Nathan in 2 Samuel 7:1–16. This text, we have already noted, introduces divine commitment to the house of David and is thus pivotal for the structure and shape of the Deuteronomic history. For our immediate purposes, we focus on 2 Samuel 7:12–15: "When your days are fulfilled and you lie down with your ancestors, I will raise up your offspring after you, who shall come forth from your body, and I will establish his kingdom. He shall build a house for my name, and I will establish the throne of his kingdom forever. I will be a father to him, and he shall be a son to me. When he commits iniquity, I will punish him with a rod such as mortals use, with blows inflicted by human beings. But I will not take my steadfast love from him, as I took it from Saul, whom I put away from before you."

These verses may in the long run refer to the long succession of Davidic kings. In the first instance, though, they refer directly to Solomon, the son whose kingdom will be established. Three things are important here. First, Solomon is given an unconditional promise of divine favor, a claim of entitlement, and an assurance of an established kingdom. Solomon's future in power is, by divine oath, fully guaranteed. Second, though the motif is subordinated, this fully legitimated, guaranteed coming king will be "God's son"; in that role nonetheless Solomon is subject to punishment for disobedience. In the articulation of these verses, the punishment for disobedience is penultimate while divine assurance is ultimate; but the dimension of punishment is emphatically voiced. Third, Solomon's great work will be temple building. As many scholars have noted, this notice in 2 Samuel 7:13 is a most curious statement, given the divine refusal of a temple in verses 5–7. Indeed, the statement is so curious that some scholars believe the verse to be an interpolation into the text. In any case, the final form of the text manages to connect the divine commitment of this text to the royal temple of 1 Kings 8, so that Solomon's great work is the fulfillment of his primary mandate from YHWH.

This oracle is of fundamental importance, for it intrudes the divine promise of unconditional fidelity into the Deuteronomic horizon. For our purposes the oracle is important because it provides the initial anticipation of Solomon as a bearer of immense theological freight. It is clear, in this articulation of royal ideology, that we are not dealing with the modest historical figure we discovered in chapter 1. Rather, we are dealing with a symbolic cipher who enters Israel's narrative as the embodiment of Israel's deepest promises and best hopes.

THE SUCCESSION NARRATIVE'S CULMINATION IN SOLOMON

In the Succession Narrative of 2 Samuel 9–20, the account found in 1 Kings 1–2— or what Carlson terms "David under curse"—is the account of David's family after David has come to royal power. Rost proposed naming the passage the Succession Narrative because the narrative is dominated by and points to the question on the lips of Nathan: "Has this thing been brought about by my lord the king and you have not let your servants know who should sit on the throne of my lord the king after him?" (1 Kgs 1:27). While scholars are now less clear about this focus to the narrative, Rost surely saw correctly that the narrative in turn disposed of would-be candidates for the succession to the throne among the sons of David, in turn, Amnon (2 Sam 13–14, especially 13:30–33), Absalom (15–19, especially 18:9–18), and finally Adonijah (1 Kgs 1–2, especially 2:13–25). The narrative moves to its culmination with Solomon, the son of David. As the narrative moves episode by episode through the sons of David, there is no doubt that the critical encounter of David with Bathsheba and Uriah (2 Sam 11)—the encounter that evokes Nathan's harsh condemnation in 12:10—dominates the entire narrative and places the future of David's house in jeopardy. Indeed, though the Deuteronomist seems to have no direct impact on the Succession Narrative, it is clear in 1 Kings 15:4–5 that the Deuteronomist had reckoned this narrative encounter to be decisive for all that follows: "Nevertheless for David's sake the Lord his God gave him a lamp in Jerusalem, setting up his son after him, and establishing Jerusalem; because David did what was right in the sight of the Lord, and did not turn aside from anything that he commanded him all the days of his life, except in the matter of Uriah the Hittite."

From the perspective of the Deuteronomist, the issue in the narrative of 2 Samuel 11 is that David violated Torah (as is made explicit in 2 Sam 12:9). Or, as the narrative prefers to say, "The thing that David had done displeased YHWH" (11:27). This verdict is remarkable because the narrator, as von Rad has seen, is reticent to include YHWH explicitly as an actor in the narrative.[5] The verdict, moreover, stands in sharp contrast to the easy, dismissive message of David to Joab concerning the death of Uriah:

> David said to the messenger, "Thus you shall say to Joab, 'Do not let this matter trouble you, for the sword devours now one and now another; press your attack on the city and overthrow it.' And encourage him." (2 Sam 11:25)

Unfortunately, the NRSV renderings of "do not let this matter trouble you" in 2 Samuel 11:25 and "displease the Lord" in 2 Samuel 11:27 together constitute a weak and misleading translation. In fact, the two statements, one of easy judgment and one of harsh warning, are exactly symmetrical: "Do not let this matter be *evil in your eyes*" (11:25) and "was *evil in the eyes of YHWH*" (11:27).

The issue is the *autonomy* that David practiced and *accountability to YHWH* that the narrative advocates in an uncompromising way.

For our purposes, the important matter is the narrative that follows after the confrontation with Nathan in 2 Samuel 12:1–15. The subsequent narrative is in two parts. First, in 2 Samuel 12:15–23, the child born to this illicit relationship that required a violent cover-up dies. Indeed, Nathan at the end of his speech had anticipated that death as a consequence of David's "scornful" action (2 Sam 12:14). And then immediately and second, to the same troubled relationship, now made legitimate by narrative (see 11:27), is born a second son, Solomon. Verses 24–25 announce the birth that follows immediately upon the preceding episode of death.

In 2 Samuel (2 Samuel 12:24–25), Bathsheba is now made "his wife," having been made so in 11:27. The verbs "he came to her" (*bo'*) and "he lay with her" (*skv*) are the same verbs as in 11:4, only there the first verb is feminine and the woman is the subject. The second verb in both cases has David as the subject, so that the narrative report of the two couplings is closely parallel. Perhaps the narrator wishes to call attention to the replication of the initial action, this time legitimate . . . but only so by a hair, a legitimacy that Nathan (and the Deuteronomist) would scarcely sanction.

The next statement is a marvel of succinctness. It consists of three members, the central one of which is "YHWH loved him" (2 Sam 12:25). This is an astonishing assertion in context, a beloved child out of such sordidness. The statement, moreover, is not given through Nathan, for mention of Nathan follows; nor is there any other identification of the mode of disclosure. The statement is a simple, raw, theological datum that provides a clue to the entire Succession Narrative and tells where the narrative is headed. Von Rad comments:

As a theological comment on the history it is if anything even more completely detached from its context than the previous one. It lays a positive emphasis quite unexpectedly on one of the characters in the drama. The statement is sufficiently paradoxical in itself, since the reader is told nothing about the child except that he exists. Who would have foreseen a magnificent future for the child of such a union? Quite evidently the author has something more important to do than write an essay on this newborn infant. Yet here is a note of the quite irrational love of God for this child, and at the end of the long story when Solomon is left in command of the field after untold complications, the reader will recall this sentence and understand that it is not human merit and virtue which have made the throne secure, but a paradoxical act of election on the part of God.[6]

The term "love" that von Rad takes as an irrational initial commitment is illuminated by the fact that the term also functions for formal covenant commitments. Such a nuance binds the baby to the purposes of YHWH.[7]

Around this pivotal assertion, the child receives two names. The first, given by David, is "Solomon." The name is not here commented upon. Nonetheless the name clearly pertains both to the capital of Jeru*salem,* where "David remained" (2 Samuel 11:1) and over which, as "David's city," Solomon is destined to preside, and to the era of well-being that Solomon would establish and over which he would preside. We may note three subsequent uses of the term *"shalom,"* peace, concerning Solomon.

First, at the end of the Succession Narrative, in the midst of the killing that serves the throne, *shalom* is assured to the Davidic house: "So shall their blood come back on the head of Joab and on the head of his descendants forever; but to David, and to his descendants, and to his house, and to his throne, there shall be *peace* from the Lord forevermore" (1 Kgs 2:33).

In the primary narrative of Solomon (1 Kgs 3–11), moreover, the term occurs twice in ways that concern us. In 1 Kings 5:12 (Heb v. 26), Solomon has peace with Hiram, clearly a political-economic settlement. More important, in 1 Kings 4:24 (Heb 5:4), in the wake of Solomon's huge tax-collecting engine and an inventory of royal opulence, we learn: "For he had dominion over all the region west of the Euphrates from Tiphsah to Gaza, over all the kings west of the Euphrates; and he had *peace* on all sides."

The peace of Solomon, as we shall see, is a near-global economic order with a concentration of power in Jerusalem to provide great comfort for the privileged company around Solomon. If we consider the uses of the term in 1 Kings 2:33 and 4:24, we are permitted to note that the naming of the baby perhaps includes a soft note of irony, for this coming king named "peace" will establish a peaceableness for some at the expense of others. Thus David's act in naming is itself perhaps to be understood as a statement of immense royal ambition wherein the father anticipates the son as rich, powerful, and effective beyond his own achievements. *Shalom* in context is not to be read gently or romantically but as the imposition of an order of power that has a monopoly on violence, trade, and symbols of legitimacy. There is much current talk, as I write this, about a Pax Americana that replicates the ancient Pax Romana. Solomon and his pax is an antecedent to all such impositions that provide benefits for some (see 1 Kgs 10:8), but that also produce long-term, seething disgruntlement, as in 1 Kings 12:1–19.

In the birth announcement, Solomon receives a second name, this one from the Lord via Nathan. He is called Yedidiah, "beloved of YHWH." Not much is made of this name in the tradition, except that this name, along with the phrase "YHWH loved him," delineates Solomon's special, privileged connection to YHWH that begets legitimacy and surely destines him for success and well-being.

Nothing is said in the tradition about the interplay of these two names, one from his ambitious father and the other from the Lord. Perhaps it is legitimate to suggest a juxtaposition wherein the name Solomon bespeaks his worldly prominence to come and Yedediah affirms his theological identity. In quite derivative Christian tradition, these same accents are taken up theologically to assert Jesus as "truly man, truly God." These terms do not require us to overread concerning David's favored son. Together, however, they do suggest "the two bodies of the king," with the mythological and the vulnerably historical.[8] It is curious that the narrator ends this terse birth comment and resumes the plot concerning David and Joab, holding in abeyance for an extended period the next moment in Solomon's rise to power and his embrace of his peculiar destiny.

SOLOMON'S DESTINY, IN THE MIDST OF AMBIGUITY AND DECEIT

The narrator in the Succession Narrative has now tipped his hand. It is Solomon! It is Solomon twice named, by father David and by YHWH, "peace" and "beloved." It is Solomon, beloved of YHWH but also Solomon born out of this vexed palace family at the tail end of violence, cover-up, disobedience, and judgment. It is Solomon, carrier of Israel's best promises and embodiment of Israel's deepest embarrassments. So it is written, front and center in Israel's hymnal, "after he had gone into Bathsheba" (Ps 51:2):

> For I know my transgressions,
> and my sin is ever before me.
> Against you, you alone, have I sinned,
> and done what is evil in your sight,
> so that you are justified in your sentence
> and blameless when you pass judgment. (Ps 51:3–4)

In wondrously restrained language, the narrator has placed this king-to-be in a context of profound ambiguity, a condition he will not easily shake off.

Having put the matter so artistically, the destiny of Solomon is put on hold by the narrator, who now resumes the story of David. The entire account of Uriah and Bathsheba (2 Sam 11:1–27), the denunciation of the king by Nathan (12:1–15a), the death of the first-born to this now exposed couple (12:15b-23), and the birth of the beloved (12:24–25), is bracketed by David's war against the Ammonites (11:1;

12:26–31). That war in turn was triggered by the affront committed by the king of Ammon against David's troops (10:1–5). The narrator now closes that bracket in 12:26–31, at the end of which the persistently successful David can return to Jerusalem and resume the important story of his family (12:31; 13:1ff.). The narrator thus details the family soap opera of son Amnon, who is killed by Absalom, and son Absalom, who is killed as a rebel by Joab. Through all of this narrative, Solomon is "nowhere," perhaps a "u-topian" figure waiting for the family to exhaust itself in intrigue and violence. It is clear in this extended narrative that the sword anticipated by Nathan (12:10) is alive and active in this community, in this city of *shalom* (!), and in this family. The time passes without notice by the narrator—or by us—until we reached a climactic moment: "King David was old and advanced in years . . . he could not get warm (1 Kgs 1:1)." Old people have poor circulation and David may have been among them. If, however, the verdict of 1 Kings 1:1 is linked to the presence of Abishag, the young virgin in verses 2–4a and the verdict of verse 4b, "the king did not know her," then it is clear that the issue is that David could not maintain his virility. And if no virility, then it is time to find the next king!

This sorry status of David, the narrator carefully reports, reminds us that the entire David narrative monitors the close interface of power and sexuality.[9] It is clear that David's failed virility evokes the climactic episode in the Succession Narrative in 1 Kings 1–2. First Kings 1 is an account of immense intrigue offered in careful literary crafting, intrigue evoked according to the evident enfeeblement of the aged king.

In 1 Kings 1:5–8 the narrator establishes the sides in the life-or-death struggle to come concerning the future of the crown. It is noteworthy that in these verses, Solomon is not even mentioned. He is only the unnamed alternative to Adonijah, who in verses 9–10 postures as king. The narrator adds a "but" in verse 10 to signal what is to come. Thus verse 10b follows the same adversity conjunction as in verse 8, the two statements indicating organized opposition to Adonijah's royal ambition.

In 1 Kings 1:11–27, that organized opposition is led by Bathsheba and Nathan, who have appeared before in tandem. In 2 Samuel 12:1–15a, Nathan's speech follows upon the indictment of verse 9: "You have taken his [Uriah's] wife to be your wife."

And in 12:24–25, Nathan announces God's name for the son of Bathsheba who is to become king. Now, in 1 Kings 1:11–27, Nathan takes the initiative and instructs Bathsheba, who seems eager to cooperate.

The plot is hatched in 1 Kings 1:11–15, in which Nathan dissembles (1:11; see v. 18). In fact, Adonijah has not been made king, according to the narrative (see 1:9). Quite clearly Nathan's instruction to Bathsheba is urgent because the stakes are very high. If Adonijah "wins," the lives of Solomon and Bathsheba are at risk . . . to say nothing of the life of Nathan. Nathan scripts Bathsheba and anticipates his own intervention in the scene around the old king.

The plot is executed to perfection. Bathsheba opens the ploy with David (1 Kgs 1:15–21). She also dissembles, for nowhere has David "sworn" the throne to Solomon (1:17). Nor, as indicated, has Adonijah become king. The only true report is Solomon's exclusion from the party (1:19; see v. 10). As Nathan has spoken of the great risk (1:12), so now Bathsheba anticipates that she and her son would be "offenders" to Adonijah (1:22).

The second part of the plot exhibits Nathan's plan to interrupt Bathsheba's speech (1 Kgs 1:22–27). Again the false claim is made that Adonijah has become king (1:25). Indeed a formula of acclamation is reported that in our narrative has in fact not occurred. Again the only correct part of the report is the exclusion of Adonijah's opposition (1:26; see vv. 10, 19).

The scheme enacted by Nathan and Bathsheba works to perfection; the old king is duped, evoking the assertion of a promise to Solomon that had not heretofore been made (1 Kgs 1:28–31). The old king lines out the actions of anointing and king making. The conspirators act promptly upon the king's now explicit authorization, anointing Solomon and evoking an acclamation of his kingship (1:38–40). In all of this, the narrator is restrained if not reticent. The reader, however, is aware of the high irony whereby the old king takes an action he had not previously imagined or intended. The sense that Solomon's throne is secured through manipulation and intrigue depends upon the premise that David had nowhere earlier promised the throne to Solomon, a claim expressed in turn in the plot by Nathan (1:13), and by Bathsheba (1:17). Nathan's own address to the old king is more circumspect, as he does not make an appeal to such an oath, even though he had instructed Bathsheba to make a claim upon an imagined royal oath. It is of course imaginable that such a promise was made and that it is simply not reported in the text. We are, however, dealing with a textually constructed plot and, in the end, a textually constructed Solomon. On that ground, the alleged oath of David is clearly a fiction, a fiction that gives ground for an ironic reading of the whole.

David Jobling has explored with great alertness the role of women in the narrative of 1 Samuel.[10] He observes the way in which women have been co-opted to serve the career of David. In our narrative, we may take Bathsheba as an initiative taker in her own right who is determined to create the future for her son. Whatever we are to make of her intention, Bathsheba's role is crucial even if not extensive. She may be taken, for what follows in the Solomon narrative, as a harbinger of the way in which women function as signals in the narrative and are in the end used by the narrator to problematize Solomon's reign.

By 1 Kings 2, Solomon is situated on the throne (1 Kgs 1:46). His first act of *shalom* is his treatment of Adonijah, his brother and rival (1:41–53). In this life-or-death struggle for power, one might have expected Solomon to execute Adonijah promptly. Apparently Adonijah expects the same (1:49–50). Solomon, however, does not immediately kill his brother. Instead, he grants his brother a quite conditional reprieve: "if . . . if." The first positive "if" requires the full allegiance of Adonijah to Solomon. The second, negative "if" leaves an ominous threat hanging in the air over the brother who has lost the game. Solomon is not generous toward Adonijah, only prudent. At the outset, Adonijah seizes the opportunity granted by his triumphant brother and signs on with Solomon (1:53). The second "if" threat is unresolved and remains to haunt the narrative.

By chapter 2, Solomon is fully in charge at the death of his father, David (1 Kgs 2:10–12). Chapter 2, however, reports on the finishing of unfinished royal business by the son at the behest of the father. David, for a moment, is not the feeble man of chapter 1 but is instead the voice of practical, calculating royal wisdom. David's speech in 1 Kings 2:1–9 includes two accent points together that voice the kind of profound tension that the narrative characteristically offers concerning the royal family.

On the one hand, in 2:5–9 David urges his son and heir Solomon, beloved of the Lord, to be as ruthless as his dangerous circumstance requires. David has a vivid memory of three particular characters from his past who must be dealt with. The sequence of events is in a negative-positive-negative pattern; in this conversation, the negative prevails in the most violent way concerning the counsel the father gives to the son.

Joab has been David's primal agent in every circumstance in the Succession Narrative, on which see 2 Samuel 11:14–21 and 19:1–8. David, however, has other memories. Even in his devotion to David, Joab has twice carefully protected his own number two role with David. David had reassigned military leadership at the expense of Joab, and twice Joab had eliminated his challenger. He eliminated Abner, then head of the northern Saul movement (2 Sam 3:27); later Joab eliminated Amasa, who was his competitor as head of the military after the elimination of Abner (2 Sam 20:9–10). Joab's affront to David, in both cases, is that Joab had perpetuated blood feuds in a regime that was bent upon becoming more "rational" in its rejection of such destructive tribalism.

David's counsel to Solomon is terse and indirect: "Act therefore according to your wisdom, but do not let his gray head go down to Sheol in peace" (1 Kgs 2:6). The two terms of note are *wisdom* and *peace*. It is the first mark of wisdom, in royal perspective, to do what must be done to secure and retain power. The term "peace" here is contradicted in its obvious meaning in order to authorize state violence. Thus Solomon does what must be done to assure his own *shalom*.

Barzillai was a worthy landowner, now old, who had sided with David in the civil war with Absalom and was part of his coalition of landowners (2 Sam 17:27–28;

19:31–40). David's counsel to Solomon concerning the old man and his family is to do *ḥesed* toward them. This counsel is not an act of generosity but a careful maintenance of alliances upon which the throne depends. Even Solomon could not rule in a vacuum but depended upon support from big-time economic players who could be allies or who could readily become adversaries.

Shimei, "a man of the family of the house of Saul," had cursed David in public and condemned him as a "murderer" and "scoundrel" (2 Sam 16:5–7). Upon David's return to Jerusalem after the civil war, David had resisted the urge of Abishai, brother of Joab, to kill Shimei as an enemy of the king. In a remarkable act, David spared Shimei: "You shall not die" (2 Sam 19:23). The narrative gives no reason for David's act of mercy to the family of Saul. More likely, it appears that David is coalition building and needs to evoke no additional enmity at this point in his career that had become so fragile.

David's memory, however, is longer than his oath concerning Shimei (1 Kgs 2:8–9). David recalls his oath to spare Shimei, and quotes himself here more than the narrator had reported in 2 Samuel 19. That oath, however, only pertains to David and not to his son. And so in rhetoric not unlike the previous rhetoric concerning Joab in verses 5–6, David counsels Solomon to be "wise" in the interest of the crown.

In all three cases, David settles old scores in a way that will aid Solomon's securing of power. On the other hand, David becomes a mouthpiece for the Torah theology of the Deuteronomists. The charge David issues to Solomon in 1 Kings 2:1–4 is not unlike that issued to Joshua at the outset of the Deuteronomic history in Joshua 1:7–8:

> I am about to go the way of all the earth. Be strong, be courageous, and keep the charge of the Lord your God, walking in his ways and keeping his statutes, his commandments, his ordinances, and his testimonies, as it is written in the law of Moses, so that you may prosper in all that you do and wherever you turn. (1 Kgs 2:2–3)

> Only be strong and very courageous, being careful to act in accordance with all the law that my servant Moses commanded you; do not turn from it to the right hand or to the left, so that you may be successful wherever you go. (Josh 1:7–8)

In both cases, obedience leads to prosperity in a direct and simple way. The statement of David in verse 4 is somewhat different, reiterating the divine promise to David but nonetheless casting it within a conditional, Deuteronomic "if."

David's appeal to the old tradition of commandment refers explicitly to the written Torah of Moses, a phrase characteristic of Deuteronomic rhetoric that no doubt pertains to the commandments of Deuteronomy. A very similar formula is offered in Deuteronomy 17:18 that concerns king and Torah. Thus David counsels his "greater son, Solomon" that obedience to the commands of Deuteronomy is the precondition of prosperity and longevity on the throne. Indeed, it is Torah obedience that assures a successor in the dynasty.

The "if" of verse 4 is a signature term of Deuteronomic theology that seems rooted in the old "if" of Moses in Exodus 19:6. This cadence of conditionality swarms over the tradition of Deuteronomy, before and after the commandments of chapters 12–25:

If you heed these ordinances, by diligently observing them, the Lord your God will maintain with you the covenant loyalty that he swore to your ancestors. (Deut 7:12)

If you do forget the Lord your God and follow other gods to serve and worship them, I solemnly warn you today that you shall surely perish. (Deut 8:19)

If you will only heed his every commandment that I am commanding you today—loving the Lord your God, and serving him with all your heart and with all your soul—then he will give the rain for your land in its season . . . and you will gather in your grain, your wine, and your oil. (Deut 11:13–14)

If you will diligently observe this entire commandment that I am commanding you, loving the Lord your God, walking in all his ways, and holding fast to him, then the Lord will drive out all these nations before you. (Deut 11:22–23)

If you will only obey the Lord your God, by diligently observing all his commandments that I am commanding you today, the Lord your God will set you high above all the nations of the earth. (Deut 28:1)

But *if* you will not obey the Lord your God by diligently observing all his commandments and decrees, which I am commanding you today, then all these curses shall come upon you and overtake you. (Deut 28:15)

If you obey the commandments of the Lord your God that I am commanding you today, by loving the Lord your God, walking in his ways, and observing his commandments, decrees, and ordinances, then you shall live and become numerous, and the Lord your God will bless you in the land that you are entering to possess. (Deut 30:16)[11]

But *if* your heart turns away and you do not hear, but are led astray to bow down to other gods and serve them, I declare to you today that you shall perish; you shall not live long in the land that you are crossing the Jordan to enter and possess. (Deut 30:17–18)

Everything depends upon obedience. Clearly such a conditionality is a serious contradiction of the unconditional promise that we have seen in the dynastic oracle of 2 Samuel 7:1–16. The Deuteronomic tradition, it is clear, is bold and skillful in inserting the "if" of Torah obedience into the midst of unconditional royal promise. This is made unmistakably clear by a comparison of two versions of the dynastic promise, both of which are derived from the oracle of 2 Samuel 7. In Psalm 89:29–37, on the one hand, there is a conditional "if," but that "if" is clearly penultimate. The bottom line is the unconditional, steadfast love of YHWH toward David's line:

> I will establish his line forever,
>   and his throne as long as the
>   heavens endure.
> *If* his children forsake my law
>   and do not walk according to
>   my ordinances,
> *if* they violate my statutes
>   and do not keep my
>   commandments,
> then I will punish their
>   transgression with the rod
>   and their iniquity with
>   scourges;
> *but* I will not remove from him
>   my steadfast love,
>   or be false to my faithfulness.
> I will not violate my covenant,
>   or alter the word that went
>   forth from my lips.
> Once and for all I have sworn by
>   my holiness;
>   I will not lie to David.
> His line shall continue forever,
>   and his throne endure before
>   me like the sun.

> It shall be established forever
>> like the moon,
>> an enduring witness in the
>> skies. (Ps 89:29–37)

By contrast, the same dynastic oracle is rephrased in Psalm 132 so that the "if" of conditionality becomes the bottom line without the addition of any ultimately unconditional assurance:

> The Lord swore to David a sure oath
>> from which he will not turn back:
> "One of the sons of your body
>> I will set on your throne.
> *If* your sons keep my covenant
>> and my decrees that I shall teach them,
> their sons also, forevermore,
>> shall sit on your throne." (Ps 132:11–12)

While the psalmic elements appear to be rhetorically parallel in the two psalms, in fact they make claims quite antithetical to each other. Thus 1 Kings 2:1–4 is remarkable because the "if" of Deuteronomy in David's own mouth is here the bottom line of fatherly counsel to royal son. In this attestation, Solomon's future depends upon Torah obedience.

From this remarkable assertion on the part of David, we may note two important connections. First, the traditioning process had placed this Deuteronomic oracle in tight juxtaposition to the harsh advice of David to Solomon in 1 Kings 2:5–9. In this latter text, David speaks an unmitigated harshness, a harshness framed in a long memory of vengeance that has forgotten nothing. Some notion of retaliation might justify these death sentences on Joab and Shimei in terms of the law of retaliation. But no effort is made to offer such a justification. The counsel to execute enemies of the dynasty stands in bald contrast to the Torah injunction without any attempt to connect them or accommodate one to the other. It appears that such an interface is quite intentional, for it articulates in powerful fashion the profound contradiction of *ḥesed* and *ḥereb* that pervades the royal story that is antecedent to Solomon's own reign.

A second textual connection of larger scope is to entertain the notion that 1 Kings 2:1–4 at the outset of the books of Kings is intentionally placed as a counterpoint to the concluding paragraph of 2 Kings 25:27–30. In that deeply enigmatic conclusion to the royal recital, it is clear that Jehoiachin has no son to sit on the throne. (He may have had sons, but none who will sit on the throne after him.) According to the

Deuteronomic presentation, the royal line ends here and has run out of steam, power, and legitimacy. No comment is made in 2 Kings 25:27–30 concerning why this ending has come, though much is implied in Deuteronomic horizon. It is clear that the dynasty ends in this paragraph because of a failure of Torah obedience.

Father David had said precisely to son Solomon in 1 Kings 2:4: "Then the Lord will establish his word that he spoke concerning me: 'If your heirs take heed to their way, to walk before me in faithfulness with all their heart and with all their soul, there shall not fail you a successor on the throne of Israel.'" If this connection between the two texts at the beginning (1 Kgs 2:2–4) and end (2 Kgs 25:27–30) of the Kings corpus is sustainable, it means that the books of Kings are framed by two texts that bracket monarchy with Torah. Such a bracketing does not immediately touch upon Solomon, to whom 1 Kings 2:4 is addressed. Except that in the Deuteronomic tradition Solomon is the one endowed for "hearing" (shema‘) and the one who flagrantly violates Torah and so sets in motion the process of royal rejection and dynastic failure: "Then the Lord was angry with Solomon, because his heart had turned away from the Lord, the God of Israel, who had appeared to him twice, and had commanded him concerning this matter, that he should not follow other gods; but he did not observe what the Lord commanded" (1 Kgs 11:9–10).

With the death of David, Solomon is securely situated on the throne in Jerusalem (1 Kgs 2:10–12). According to conventional hypotheses, the Succession Narrative concludes in 1 Kings 2:13–46 with "mop-up action" whereby Solomon will fully secure his throne. While this violent mop-up action does not correlate precisely with David's specific counsel to him in 1 Kings 2:5–9, Solomon's ruthless consolidation of power is unmistakably in the spirit of David's "wisdom."

Whereas David had urged on Solomon two executions (Joab in 1 Kgs 2:5–6 and Shimei in 2:8–9), in fact Solomon's settling of scores pertains to four persons. Solomon does indeed move ruthlessly against Joab and Shimei as David had urged: Joab is struck down by Benaiah, Solomon's new hatchet man (2:28–35; see 1:10). That death is presented as a necessity for the resolve of old bloodguilt from the deaths of Abner and Amasa implemented "without cause." Shimei is dispatched as well by Benaiah (2 Kgs 2:36–46). It is reported that Solomon had given Shimei a deferred sentence of death and placed him on probation (2:36–37). Shimei, however, violated that probation in what was, according to the narrator, an innocent journey outside royal surveillance. Innocent or not, the violation was enough to bring death as father David had urged.

Beyond David's immediate counsel concerning Joab and Shimei, Solomon still had to deal with his brother, Adonijah, his rival for the throne. In 1 Kings 1, Adonijah had been given a reprieve by Solomon, even though one might have expected his immediate execution in the high-stakes struggle for power between the brothers.

Solomon had set the condition for Adonijah's survival and issued a stock royal warn-ing that Adonijah, having no option, readily accepted: "So Solomon responded, 'If he proves to be a worthy man, not one of his hairs shall fall to the ground; but if wickedness is found in him, he shall die.' Then King Solomon sent to have him brought down from the altar. He came to do obeisance to King Solomon; and Solo-mon said to him, 'Go home'" (1 Kgs 1:52–53).

The follow-up narrative concerning Adonijah is curious. Adonijah asks for Abi-shag to be his wife (1 Kgs 2:17). This is the "young virgin" who could not "warm" David (1:1–4) who by now was surely in Solomon's entourage as a concubine. The narrator has already told us that possession of concubines is a dramatic, public sym-bol of loss or seizure of royal power (see 2 Sam 12:11–13; 16:20–23). Given aware-ness of that symbolism, the request of Adonijah for the "young virgin" is an act of astonishing daring or astonishing foolhardiness. The request, moreover, is mediated through Bathsheba, who is Solomon's mother but also Solomon's strong advocate. Thus we may wonder about Adonijah's request and Bathsheba's message, whether the queen mother manufactured such a death wish on the part of her son's nemesis. The narrator gives no signal to indicate such a possibility, and the thought only occurs because the act is so odd. Whatever may have been the inclination of Adoni-jah or the intrigue of Bathsheba, the reaction of the king is prompt and unsurpris-ing: "Then King Solomon swore by the Lord, 'So may God do to me, and more also, for Adonijah has devised this scheme at the risk of his life! Now therefore as the Lord lives, who has established me and placed me on the throne of my father David, and who has made me a house as he promised, today Adonijah shall be put to death'" (1 Kgs 2:23–24).

One other opponent of Solomon remains to be dispatched. *Abiathar*, royal priest to David, had been aligned with Adonijah against Solomon from the outset (1 Kgs 1:7), and so still represents within the royal entourage a dissenter. David's advice to Solomon had not reached as far as Abiathar, but Solomon is evidently capable of extrapolation from such parental wisdom.

As Solomon disposes of his adversaries, he comes to Abiathar, who "deserves death" for his support of Adonijah. Solomon, however, spares Abiathar, ostensibly an act of regard for Abiathar's Priestly loyalty to David, perhaps because of Solomon's practical reluctance to kill a priest. Either way, Solomon has resolved not to kill Abi-athar "on this day," a phrase suggesting that the threat of the sword will hang over Abiathar to perpetuity. The pivotal importance of Abiathar for the larger tradition should, in passing, be noticed. It is most likely Abiathar who is in purview in the earlier threat against the Priestly house of Eli: "Then in distress you will look with greedy eye on all the prosperity that shall be bestowed upon Israel; and no one in your family shall ever live to old age. The only one of you whom I shall not cut off from my altar shall be spared to weep out his eyes and grieve his heart; all the members of your household shall die by the sword. The fate of your two sons, Hophni and Phinehas, shall be the sign to you—both of them shall die on the same day" (1 Sam 2:32–34).

It is, moreover, plausible that Jeremiah, many years later, is of the Priestly house of Abiathar, for that prophet is "of the priests who were in Anathoth in the land of Benjamin" (Jer 1:1), the very village to which Abiathar is banished. If this latter connection between Abiathar and Jeremiah is sustained, then the sparing of Abiathar by Solomon has immense implications—Solomon has left alive the most abrasive voices of critique of the monarchy, an abrasion that comes to full voice in the tradition of Jeremiah (see 22:11–30, for example).

In three of these four cases, the narrator is at pains to portray Solomon as patient and generous, and willing to give his adversary "time for amendment of life." Concerning Adonijah: "So Solomon responded, 'If he proves to be a worthy man, not one of his hairs shall fall to the ground'" (1 Kgs 1:52a); concerning Abiathar: "The king said to the priest Abiathar, 'Go to Anathoth, to your estate; for you deserve death'" (2:26a); and concerning Shimei: "Then the king sent and summoned Shimei, and said to him, 'Build yourself a house in Jerusalem, and live there, and do not go out from there to any place whatever. For on the day you go out, and cross the Wadi Kidron, know for certain that you shall die; your blood shall be on your own head.' And Shimei said to the king, 'The sentence is fair; as my lord the king has said, so will your servant do.' So Shimei lived in Jerusalem many days" (2:36–38).

In stark contrast, there is no mitigation of the deathly punishment of Joab, who is abruptly and without pause executed (1 Kgs 2:29). The treatment of Joab, who had "grasped the horns of the altar" (2:28), and the treatment of Adonijah, who "went to grasp the horns of the altar (1:50), is very different, though at the end both are executed as enemies of the new king.

The mitigation of a death sentence in the cases of Abiathar, Adonijah, and Shimei is worth noting, perhaps to establish that Solomon proceeded by a rule of law, or perhaps to show his generosity. In any case, the mitigation is in each case coupled with an ominous and durable threat. Concerning Adonijah: "But if wickedness is found in him, he shall die" (1 Kgs 1:52b); concerning Abiathar: "But I will not at this time put you to death, because you carried the ark of the Lord God before my father David, and because you shared in all the hardships my father endured" (2:26a); and concerning Shimei: "For on the day you go out, and cross the Wadi Kidron, know for certain that you shall die; your blood shall be on your own head" (2:37). In the end, it all comes to death, except for the case of Abiathar.

Three observations conclude our discussion of this narrative antecedent to the primary narrative of Solomon.

First, the juxtaposition of the Deuteronomic charge of 1 Kings 2:1–4 and the ruthless advice of David (1 Kgs 2:5–9, implemented in 2:13–46) creates an awesome, nearly unbearable tension in the final form of the text. Solomon's actions in chapter 2 are appropriately triggered by David's advice; Solomon is an eagerly responsive son. It is astonishing that no reference is made in the long chapter 2 back to the charge of 1 Kings 2:1–4. It is as though the theological charge concerning Torah obedience lingers in the air without acknowledgement or receptivity. The stunning disregard of Torah is itself an enormous commentary on what follows in the Solomon narrative. The charge of David to his son to keep Torah lingers powerfully, held in abeyance for subsequent utilization.

Second, while the disregard of the charge of Torah is spectacular, we may notice a second disregard that is quite small but surely noteworthy. In his advice to Solomon, David sandwiched between his warning about Joab (1 Kgs 2:5–6) and Shimei (2:8–9), a brief mention of Barzillai, the Gileadite: "Deal loyally, however, with the sons of Barzillai the Gileadite, and let them be among those who eat at your table; for with such loyalty they met me when I fled from your brother Absalom" (2:7). As noted above, Barzillai had been among the powerful landowners who rallied to support David in generous ways in his acute time of need (2 Sam 17:27–29; 19:31–41). No doubt in early days David's throne depended upon the support of such powerful allies. In acknowledgement of that indispensable gesture of kindness by Barzillai in a crucial time of crisis, David tersely urged his son to "deal loyally," that is, to show faithfulness commensurate with Barzillai's own fidelity toward David. This urging of quid pro quo is not a great act of generosity, but only repayment in kind to Barzillai for his venturesome generosity that sustained David.

In the paybacks of Solomon in 1 Kings 2:13–46, there is nothing concerning Solomon's action that matches David's urging concerning Barzillai, as there is in the cases of Joab and Shimei. The omission is stunning. Solomon pays back his *adversaries* ruthlessly; he has, however, no payback for *allies*. He exhibits no capacity for loyalty (*hesed*). The default concerning Barzillai may be understood as a personal deficit; Solomon simply is not into generosity. Or the default may reflect the development of policy that no longer operates on faithful connections but only on the basis of raw, utilitarian power. If Solomon is on his way to a "power state," then he need expend no energy on a friendship that sustains power relationships, a position that perhaps anticipates the decision of his son Rehoboam concerning tax policy: "So Jeroboam and all the people came to Rehoboam the third day, as the king had said, 'Come to me again the third day.' The king answered the people harshly. He disregarded the advice that the older men had given him and spoke to them according to the advice of the young men, 'My father made your yoke heavy, but I will add to your yoke; my father disciplined you with whips, but I will discipline you with scorpions'" (1 Kgs 12:13–14).

The disregard of David's charge concerning Barzillai is even more elemental than the disregard of the Deuteronomic charge of 1 Kings 2:1–4. The Deuteronomic charge is an interpretive imposition upon the narrative of David and his son. The charge concerning Barzillai, however, is intrinsic to the narrative itself and to the cast of characters upon which the narrative and the throne depends. Disregard of the Deuteronomic charge bespeaks a waywardness from the Torah championed by the Deuteronomists. The disregard of the charge concerning Barzillai is surely a cynical, callous disregard of the political realities that make the processes of state formation viable in long-term ways.

A third observation pertains to the conclusion of the so-called Succession Narrative as it voices Solomon's settlement in power. The narrative account that is antecedent to the rule of Solomon curiously has two endings. First, in 1 Kings 2:12, the formula of Solomon's settlement on the throne appropriately follows the report of the death of David, for David's death is clearly a prerequisite for Solomon's formal ascent to power: "So Solomon sat on the throne of his father David; and his kingdom was firmly established." But then, at the end of chapter 2 (where Rost ended his Succession Narrative), we are given a second formula that concludes the entire narrative: "So the kingdom was established in the hand of Solomon" (1 Kgs 2:46c). Perhaps too much should not be made of this double formula, for each is clear in its own place, the first following the death of David and the second ending the entire narrative.

We may nonetheless notice two variations in the twofold formula. First, in 1 Kings 2:12, the adverb *"me'od"* is rendered "firmly": "His kingdom was firmly established." This adverb is missing in the second formula of verse 46, suggesting perhaps that the series of executions in chapter 2 made Solomon's grip on power less firm. Second, the final formula asserts that the kingdom was established "by the hand" (*beyad*) of Solomon, that is, by his power. The preposition *b* is open for translation; and NRSV renders *beyad* as "in his hand." In light of the narrative account of 1 Kings 2:13–46, I prefer "by the hand," which suggests that Solomon's aggressive, ruthless acts of power are what secured the throne. This is in contrast to the formula of 1 Kings 2:12, which suggests that the kingdom came to him by inheritance. It may be that the two formulae are synonymous. It is possible, however, to conclude that the two formulae bespeak, yet again, the deep and remarkable ambiguity in Solomon's rise to power, power received and power seized.

In any case, we arrive at the primary narrative of Solomon in 1 Kings 3–11 concerning the one born to rule. As we shall see, that rule is shot through with ambivalence. It may be that worldly power is always and everywhere marked in such a way, a primal theme in the interpretive work of Reinhold Niebuhr.[12] In any case, it is surely so in this narrative, for the king rules—it is claimed—at the behest of YHWH.

It is, however, this same YHWH who eventually destabilizes the absolutism of power for which Solomon so much yearned. This strange visitation of holiness in the midst of power assures that the narrative to come will be characteristically interesting and surprising.

CHAPTER 4

HOW A MODEST SOLOMON BECAME A LARGE NARRATIVE SOLOMON: 1 KINGS 3–11

We have set the stage for the primary Solomon narrative in 1 Kings 3–11 by exploring three aspects of the larger narrative. First, we have considered the claim of historicity made for the Solomon era and concluded at best that the historicity of Solomon reflects a modest pre-state chiefdom. Second, we have considered that the force of theological interpretation in the account of this modest chieftain is situated in Israel's larger narrative that runs from creation in Genesis 1 to exile in 2 Kings 25. Specifically we have considered the interpretive energy and power of the Deuteronomists, who assure that power in Israel is always in proximity to the elemental reality of Torah commandments. Third, we have traced the way in which narratives antecedent to this primary narrative situate Solomon in a family and community deeply marked by ambiguity, an ambiguity that bespeaks the abiding assurance of *ḥesed* (steadfast loyalty) and the equal accent that bespeaks the abiding threat of *ḥerev* (sword). Solomon is a child of such ambiguity and will, in what is to come, fully enact that profound ambiguity.

In this chapter, as we take up 1 Kings 3–11, we will be concerned with two tasks. First, we will study the shape and substance of these chapters in 1 Kings as an integrated, intentional whole; second, we will consider the source of interpretive energy that resulted in the remarkable transposition of Solomon from a modest chieftain to a majestic figure of international proportion.

THE TRANSFORMATION OF SOLOMON INTO "SOLOMON"

The narrative of Solomon (1 Kgs 3–11) is a complex gathering of materials that draws upon a variety of sources articulated in a great variety of literary genres. While the outcome is not a neat linear articulation of the kind produced in the modern West, it is likely that all of this diversity of literature has been ordered into a coherent and intentional whole. Thus the outcome of the traditioning process is a canonical, normative Solomon, perhaps rooted in historical reality, but now the consequence of bold, interpretive imagination.

The materials gathered into this corpus include *folklore material,* the kinds of legendary narratives of success and wonderment that may attach to any folk hero.

Without doubt Solomon attracted such materials, which in the final form of the text contributed to what must have been the popular image of the great king. There are traditional *royal narratives,* more or less courtly conventions necessary to the royal presentation. These materials would include particularly the dream narrative of chapter 3, for the claim to the throne must eventually be rooted in divine authorization and legitimacy, even if the ascent to the throne was in reality accomplished by a violent palace coup. There are materials that either arise from *royal and temple archives* or are imitations of such archives. Such materials include the details of temple construction and the meticulous inventory of royal wealth that sounds like a budget report (for example, 1 Kgs 6:14–36; 10:14–22). There are *liturgical materials* perhaps reminiscent of actual liturgical performance, though these materials now serve a secondary literary function and are not now to be taken as materials for liturgical significance (see 8:1–13). Finally, it is clear that *explicitly theological materials* are included, most spectacularly the verdict rendered against Solomon in the concluding section of 1 Kings 11:1–13. At the very end, moreover, 1 Kings 11:41–43 adds the stereotypical paragraph of closure that is conventional through the royal recital of the books of Kings. All of these materials—folklore materials, royal narratives, royal and temple archives, liturgical materials, and theological interpretation—stand together in an uneasy combination, the sum of which results in "canonical Solomon." It will be clear in what follows that the way in which these materials have been ordered and juxtaposed is neither a random, ad hoc accumulation nor an easy, seamless narrative. Rather, the sequence of texts provides for breaks, gaps, and jolts that are characteristic of Hebrew narrative, disruptive interfaces that invite or even require discerning and imaginative interpretation.[1] The following review illustrates the way in which the materials in 1 Kings 3–11 are situated for interpretive effect.

Solomon the Temple Builder

There is no doubt that the material concerning the construction and dedication of the temple (1 Kgs 5:1–8:66) stands at the center of the narrative of Solomon. There is no doubt, moreover, that the final form of the text intends to feature the erection of the temple as Solomon's major achievement, an achievement that stands pivotally central in the primary history of Israel, midway between creation (Gen 1–2) and exile (2 Kgs 24–25).

The material on the temple is a quite complicated collage. The account of temple building begins in 1 Kings 5 with the resolve of Solomon to build the temple that he understands as a mandate from YHWH (1 Kgs 5:5 with reference to 2 Sam 7:13), the securing of resources for the temple from his Phoenician (Sidonian) ally Hiram (1 Kgs 5:6–12), and the mobilization of a coerced workforce to engage in the actual construction of the temple (5:13–18). As we shall see, each of these elements—the allusion to 2 Samuel 7:13 as divine authorization, the alliance with Hiram and the utilization of cedar, and the mobilization of "forced labor"—all are tag words for major points of interpretation. Attention to these notations precludes our reading the material on the surface, as the text itself provides signals for access to deeper interpretive probes.

First Kings 6 details the construction of the temple, notably the specifications, the expensive materials, and the fine craftsmanship that were involved. According to this evidence, no expense or effort was spared in the construction. Particular notice may be taken of the term "finish" (*klh*) in verses 44 and 38, a term elsewhere important in Israel's articulation of major achievements in the life of faith (see Gen 2:1; Exod 39:32, 40:33; Josh 19:51).[2] Attention will be given to verses 11–13 because these verses are an intrusion into the narrative. Not only are the verses curiously an oracle of divine utterance in the midst of a long descriptive text, but the substance of the divine utterance is a characteristic Deuteronomic "if," a conditionality that parallels the Davidic charge of 1 Kings 2:1–4. The appearance of these two verses indicates that the narrative account, even here, is not preoccupied with mere descriptive reportage but is characteristically committed to interpretation.

First Kings 7:15–50, continues the report on the splendid detail of temple construction with an appreciation of both the cost and the artistic achievement of the whole. It is of interest that Solomon recruited "Hiram from Tyre" as the master craftsman, thus a foreigner, to complete the temple (1 Kgs 7:13–14). It is probably the case that this Hiram, a craftsman, is to be distinguished from Hiram the king of Sidon already noted in 5:7–12. In 1 Kings 7:14 and 50 the verb "finish" (*klh*) again is utilized, echoing the use of chapter 6.

It is of particular interest that the temple report of 1 Kings 6:1–7:51 is interrupted in 7:1–12 in order to report on the remainder of Solomon's immense building project whereby he "finished" a series of important public buildings in Jerusalem (1 Kgs 7:1). The appearance of this list of buildings in the midst of the temple reports suggests that from a royal perspective, the temple is a part of the grandeur of an elaborate reconstruction of the central city, all of which is designed to create a proper public sense of the monarchy.

The temple report culminates in 1 Kings 8:1–66 with an elaborate reminiscence of the great festival of dedication over which Solomon presided. As in the previous chapters concerning the temple, chapter 8 is enormously complex. The report of the actual liturgical procession, whereby the ancient symbol of divine presence, the ark of the covenant, comes into the new temple, extends only through verse 13. This liturgical report is followed by a series of utterances that serve as a rich and variegated interpretive field concerning the temple: Solomon addresses the congregation and articulates divine authorization of the temple and, incidentally, divine approbation of Solomon's rule (1 Kgs 8:14–21); he articulates a prayer that binds YHWH to YHWH's promises to sustain the dynasty (8:22–26); and an additional speech, ostensibly in the mouth of Solomon, redefines the temple away from the claims of the preceding verses in order to characterize the temple not as a place of divine presence but as a place of Israel's access to divine attentiveness (8:27–30). Then follows a series of prayers making provision for forgiveness of those who sin, culminating in verses 46–53, with special provision for those "carried away captive to the land of the enemy" (8:31–53). The dedication ends with a blessing for the community (8:54–61), an elaborate offering of sacrifices (8:62–64), and a dismissal of the community (8:65–66).

This complex material makes clear that the temple, in this Solomonic rendition, is no single thing. Rather, the temple is a visible, accessible matrix of interpretation in which many interpretive voices in Israel had their say. It is evident, moreover, that the cacophony of interpretations offered here is not limited to the voice, time, or context of Solomon but in fact stretches long into Israel's future well beyond Solomon. Thus the temple functions in this rendering as an opportunity for ongoing reinterpretation of the recurring crisis of divine presence in the life of Israel.[3]

Solomon the Exploiter

There is no doubt that in the imagination of Israel, Solomon is primally the temple builder. But of course he was not only a temple builder, for the construction of the temple required an extensive economic infrastructure to support a sustained building project. Thus gathered in the narrative before and after the temple materials of 1 Kings 5:1–8:66 are reports on Solomon's economic successes, materials that are a combination of seemingly sober reportage together with more imaginative folkloristic materials.

First Kings 4:1–28 articulates Solomon's economic success, which appears to be rooted in his administrative finesse. We are given a roster of his high officials, seemingly a well-developed bureaucracy (1 Kgs 4:1–6). This is followed by a careful description of his tax-collecting apparatus, which must have been greatly effective in providing royal revenue (4:7–19). The report describes the means whereby revenues were maintained. Finally the report cannot resist a comment on the immense opulence of the Solomonic apparatus, whereby the entire royal entourage established in Jerusalem lived exceedingly well (4:20–28).

This is a picture of peace and prosperity that purports to offer a stunningly high standard of living for the royal entourage. Two notices are included that reflect the underbelly of such extravagance. First, in 1 Kings 4:21, it is suggested that Solomon's great wealth has resulted from the economic network over which he presides, so that the wealth and ease experienced by the urban elite in Jerusalem were in fact from tribute (*minhah*); thus Solomon was on the receiving end of a coercive, usurpatious international economic system. This notion of a tributary system of income, moreover, is reinforced in verse 24 with the specification of "dominion" (*rdh*) and "peace" (*shalom*): "For he had dominion over all the region west of the Euphrates from Tiphsah to Gaza, over all the kings west of the Euphrates; and he had peace on all sides" (1 Kgs 4:24). That is, the peace (*shalom*) of Solomon is an imposed one coercively financed by vassal states, thus a Pax Solomon, the sort that great imperial powers characteristically impose on other states. Second, the mention of "horses, chariots, horsemen, officers" suggests the military muscle that imposes and maintains the international flow of revenue to the well-lived capital city (4:26–27). The outcome of the entire report of verses 1–28, including the euphoric note of verses 20–21, suggests a well-ordered, well-financed state that stood on the receiving end of a coercive economic system that enjoyed the produce of an exploitative international system. The reality is perhaps not unlike the lyrical anticipation of the coming economic well-being of Jerusalem after the exile, the city to which will flow the produce of the nations (note particularly the flow of gold, frankincense, and myrrh in the birth legend of Jesus after the fashion of Isaiah 60:6):

> Then you shall see and be radiant;
> your heart shall thrill and rejoice,
> because the abundance of the
> sea shall be brought to you,
> the wealth of the nations shall come to you.
> A multitude of camels shall cover you,
> the young camels of Midian and Ephah;
> all those from Sheba shall come.
> they shall bring gold and frankincense,
> and shall proclaim the praise of the Lord.
> All the flocks of Kedar shall be gathered to you,
> the rams of Nebaioth shall minister to you;
> they shall be acceptable on my altar,
> and I will glorify my glorious house. (Isa 60:5–7; see Matt 2:11)

The economic success of Solomon, rooted in administrative finesse (and, now we see, in military muscle) so well characterized in 1 Kings 4, is matched by the celebration of Solomon's economic prowess in 1 Kings 9:10–10:29, situated on the other side of the temple report. In this report on the economy, several contributors to Solomon's dominant position in the international context are named: building construction in addition to that of the temple, as well as a face-down with his ally, Hiram (1 Kgs 9:10–14); forced labor, the mobilization of conscripted men to accomplish the ambitious building projects in the earlier chapters (9:15–24); a commercial fleet, giving Solomon access to the economic opportunities and resources to the south (9:26–28); alliances with Hiram in naval commerce (10:11–12); huge gold resources (10:14–25) ; and arms dealing (10:26–29).

In 1 Kings 9:25 there is an odd, terse mention of Solomon's Priestly function as he presided over the great state festivals in the temple. (On the three festivals see Deuteronomy 16:16–17.) Two matters of note: First, nothing is made in the text of this Priestly action of Solomon. While the verse may be designed to exhibit Solomon's public role as liturgy leader, nothing should be deduced from the notice about his piety. Since this performance is listed in a long inventory of royal achievements, we may surmise that his acts of piety are simply "business." Second, this note again reports that Solomon "completed" the temple, though this time with an alternative verb, *slm*. The offer of sacrifices is simply attestation to Solomon's spectacular work as temple builder.

In addition to these paragraphs that are offered as sober, factual reports, three other items indicate Solomon's large international affluence. Most important is the narrative of his encounter with the Queen of Sheba (1 Kgs 10:1–10, 13). This was a trade summit meeting between two big-time commercial giants. The queen herself is no slouch, for she comes "with a very great retinue" to impress Solomon (10:2). It turns out, not surprisingly, that she did not impress Solomon; rather, she is the one impressed, for Solomon's affluence and administrative apparatus literally "take her breath away" (10:5). It is likely that this narrative includes folkloristic hyperbole that served to enhance Solomon's popular image, a king widely celebrated in Israel, one easily capable of "topping" the celebrated queen to the south.

Further evidence of Solomon's international significance is found in 1 Kings 9:24, a brief notation that calls attention to his wife, daughter of Pharaoh. Her mention here and in several other passages in the Solomon narrative signifies the way in which Solomon is involved in a political-economic-military network with the great power figures of his time. He stands allied with and at the center of international power. (The mention of this wife may also hint at the ways in which Solomon replicates the old pharaonic policies, which had reduced Israel to slavery.)

A third mention of Solomon's international stature occurs in the lyrical summary of 1 Kings 10:23–25, an unreserved affirmation of Solomon's success that is also voiced in 4:20 and 10:8, all statements of the same sort in which the voice of the narrator (or in one case, the voice of the queen) reaches the limit of explanatory discourse and breaks out in emotive affirmation. The economic achievements of Solomon are nearly beyond words:

Judah and Israel were as numerous as the sand by the sea; they ate and drank and were happy. (1 Kgs 4:20)

Happy are these your servants, who continually attend you and hear your wisdom! (1 Kgs 10:8)

Thus King Solomon excelled all the kings of the earth in riches and in wisdom. The whole earth sought the presence of Solomon to hear his wisdom, which God had put into his mind. Every one of them brought a present, objects of silver and gold, garments, weaponry, spices, horses, and mule, so much year by year. (1 Kgs 10:23–25)

The material concerning the temple in 1 Kings 5:1–8:66 is bracketed by the affirmation of economic success in 1 Kings 4:1–18 and 9:10–10:29.

Solomon the Wise Ruler

A third prominent, though less developed, motif is Solomon's reputation for wisdom. While the term "wisdom" may be used in a variety of ways in the Old Testament, with reference to Solomon the term refers to the capacity to govern wisely, shrewdly, and effectively in order to enhance the realm over which he presides. That reputation of Solomon as a wise king essentially rests on two very different texts. First and most prominently, the narrative report of 1 Kings 3:16–28 evidences Solomon's cleverness in sorting out the tangle of competing claims for which there is no clear evidence. There is no doubt that this narrative is a popular tale that attached itself to Solomon and established Solomon as a wise, pragmatic king capable of acting for *shalom*. This pragmatic accent is indicated in the final verse of the narrative whereby "wisdom" is connected to "justice": "All Israel heard of the judgment that the king had rendered; and they stood in awe of the king, because they perceived that the wisdom of God was in him, to execute justice" (1 Kgs 3:28). This same pragmatic wisdom, moreover, is recognized by those outside Israel, both the Queen of Sheba and "the whole earth":

So she said to the king, "The report was true that I heard in my own land of your accomplishments and of your wisdom, but I did not believe the reports until I came and my own eyes had seen it. Not even half had been told me; your wisdom and prosperity far surpass the report that I had heard." (1 Kgs 10:6–7)

The whole earth sought the presence of Solomon to hear his wisdom, which God had put into his mind. (1 Kgs 10:24)

Without reference to Israel's particular traditions of faith, those outside Israel were able to recognize and affirm Solomon's acumen in matters of administration and economics. Indeed, Solomon's wisdom acts as a magnet for international wealth. The king knows how to make it work for the benefit of Israel's regime.

The other text that has been centrally committed to Solomon's reputation as a wise king is 1 Kings 4:29–34. Here "wisdom" concerns not pragmatic governance but rather the capacity to categorize and organize worldly knowledge. Solomon is here portrayed as a patron of the arts, one who supports the gathering, organizing, and maintaining of the cultural legacy of his regime. In that context, it is important to notice the international scope of this wisdom: "He was wiser than anyone else, wiser than Ethan the Ezrahite, and Heman, Calcol, and Darda, children of Mahol; his fame spread throughout all the surrounding nations" (1 Kgs 4:31). Solomon's operation in international scope caught the attention of "all peoples," as did his economic success (4:34). On counts of both governance and economics, Solomon has placed little Israel, only recently emerged from rustic hill country existence, on the map of the weighty ones of the world. On both counts Solomon is the one who has transposed Israel and made it a community to be noticed in the largest international scope.

Solomon's success as an economic manager and his reputation as a purveyor of wisdom accent his worldly effectiveness. His legacy as a temple builder, moreover, is to be understood not simply as an enterprise of royal piety, though it may have been that (see the comment above on 1 Kgs 9:25). Temple building in that ancient world (as in the contemporary world) is the supreme act of the management of public symbols, which constitutes an indispensable element of maintaining social authority through divine legitimacy. One need not be exclusively cynical to judge that Solomon's temple building may be understood, in some major part, as a worldly act of dynastic promotion.

The Solomon narrative, however, is not merely a report on worldly success, though it is that. On two counts it is more than that. First, it was impossible in that ancient world to imagine a genuinely worldly or secular royal regime, for all legitimate power was understood to be a gift of divine purpose. Thus the dynasty of David and Solomon was permeated with theological claim. And second, the text of 1 Kings 3–11 does not purport to be descriptive reportage. Indeed, the note of 1 Kings 11:41 cites an antecedent document, "The Book of the Acts of Solomon," to which the reader is referred for extended reportage. Though that cited document is unknown to us, the citation indicates the intention of the present textual tradition. Rather than reportage and description, the present text intends to be theological interpretive commentary that rereads the career of Solomon with reference to the faith claims of ancient Israel and, in the end, with reference to the theological passions of the theological tradition. Though these traditionists did not explicitly write to "create scripture," it is obvious why this theological interpretation that rereads according to theological conviction readily became scripture in the community of early Judaism.

Thus moving beyond celebrations of worldly success, the Solomon narrative seeks to root Solomon's governance in the will and purpose of YHWH, the God of Israel. We have seen in the antecedent report of 1 Kings 1 that Solomon received the throne through a carefully managed pattern of intrigue that culminated in a palace coup. In the Solomon narrative, however, the rule of Solomon is grounded not in a political coup but in a divine approbation mediated through a dream narrative (1 Kgs 3:5–15). The genre of dream report is not an uncommon mode for divine communication in that ancient world. It is a strategy of biblical narrative (found in the culture of the Near East more generally) whereby the divine world may contact and impinge upon the human world. Whatever we may make of the authenticity of this dream report, we pay primary attention to its function in the Solomon narrative.

In that narrative, Solomon is located at Gibeon, a great high place for the conduct of great public rituals that will exhibit the king as both authorized and pious. The opening assertion of YHWH in 1 Kings 3:5 is abrupt: "Ask what I should give you." The dream offer indicates not only YHWH's willingness to be generous to Solomon; it also makes clear that Solomon is on the receiving end of the transaction. Solomon's response to the divine command constitutes the primary content of the dream encounter (1 Kgs 3:6–9). The response of Solomon to the divine command consists of three parts that are not unlike the prayer of David in 2 Samuel 7:18–29. The response begins with praise of YHWH for previous *hesed* to David that culminates in the gift of a son to David, Solomon himself (3:6). The accent is on YHWH's *hesed* to the dynasty. The second element, introduced by "and now," is a statement of modesty on the part of the new king before the task of governance, and appropriate humility and deference to the God who will give him these gifts (3:7–8).

The specific request of Solomon, a request invited by YHWH, occurs in 1 Kings 3:9 and exhibits the central feature of "good kingship" in that ancient world. The petition is for an "understanding mind," a listening heart to discern good and evil, wisdom and foolishness, life and death. The term *spt* (govern) occurs twice in this verse, indicating that a primary responsibility of kingship is a judicial one, to rule wisely in matters of justice where the evidence is not clear.[4] It is worth noting that this responsibility, here recognized by Solomon as a primary one, is remote from economic success and temple building, though perhaps not so removed from the royal capacity for wisdom.[5]

The divine response to the royal petition fully appreciates Solomon's selflessness in his petition (1 Kings 3:10–13). The divine response enumerates three matters a more self-aggrandizing king might have requested: long life, riches, and victory over enemies, all things that would make a regime secure and prosperous. The contrast between what Solomon asked and what he might have asked but did not is spectacular. The contrast sets the bar very high for "good kingship" and nicely reflects distinctions in the command of Deuteronomy concerning kingship (Deut 17:14–20). Solomon thus receives divine appreciation and approval. YHWH now makes two responses to this new, selfless king: first, Solomon will receive that for which he asked, a heart wise and discerning. The phrasing is somewhat different from the petition of 1 Kings 3:9, but the substance is the same. Solomon will be without peer in his capacity for wise judgment. But second, Solomon will receive from YHWH that for which he did not ask: riches and splendor ("honor"). On both counts, concerning what he asked and what he did not ask, Solomon's endowment will be unmatched in the world around him. The formula of incomparability in the two cases is however different. In the first case of the "wise and discerning mind," there is no parallel ever, before or after. In the second case of "riches and honor," there is no parallel in his lifetime. We may notice, in the latter case, the nice irony that he is *given* what he did not *ask*. Had he asked, however, he would have been under judgment for his greediness. The interface of verse 11 and verse 13 is a subtle anticipation of the later riddle of gaining and losing one's life (see Mark 4:34–37).

This dream narrative of 1 Kings 3:5–13 establishes the theological legitimacy for the reign of Solomon and for the narrative that is to follow concerning Solomon. But it does more than that. It also provides the criteria for judgment of the reign of Solomon, for in fact his reign, as narrated for us, is dominated most especially by the pursuit of "riches," a facet of which includes domination of enemies and their economies. Thus we are able to see that this narrative of legitimacy is buoyant, affirmative, and without reservation. It immediately slides over into theological verdict that in the hands of the Deuteronomist takes the form of divine judgment. That is, the trust of royal power so readily given by God to Solomon is immediately placed in a framework of accountability to YHWH. This move from *legitimacy* to *verdict* is signaled in 1 Kings 3:14, a verse that appears to continue the divine response of 3:11–13. In fact, though, 3:14 takes a sharp rhetorical turn by introducing a Deuteronomic "if" into the divine speech that is quite unanticipated in verses 11–13. The gift of "riches and honor" so grandly guaranteed by YHWH in verse 13 is now made conditional upon obedience to the commands of Deuteronomy, so conditional as to be quite retractable on the part of YHWH.

Whereas the dream narrative of 1 Kings 3:5–13 serves legitimacy, that dream narrative is matched by a second dream narrative in 1 Kings 9:1–9 that sounds the cadences of the Deuteronomists. This second dream narrative issues a severe warn-ing to the king, who has just "finished" the temple (1 Kgs 9:1), a warning that amounts in context to a harsh judgment. The second dream narrative, also placed at Gibeon, issues a symmetrical utterance that revolves around a characteristically Deutero-nomic "if." After an introductory assurance that YHWH will be attentive to the Jerusalem temple—by name, by eyes, and by heart—for all time to come (9:3), the oracle is in two parts. First, verses 4–5 line out a theory of *obedience and prosperity* that is faithful to Deuteronomic assumptions:

Positive condition: "*if* you walk before me . . ." (1 Kgs 9:4)

Good consequence: "*then* I will establish . . ." (1 Kgs 9:5)

This latter promise alludes back to the royal oracle of 2 Samuel 7:

Negative condition: "*if* you turn aside . . ." (1 Kgs 9:6)

Bad consequence: "*then* I will cast off . . ." (1 Kgs 9:7–9)

These verses altogether constitute an exposition of the "if" of 1 Kings 3:14 (see also 1 Kgs 6:11–13) that stands in profound tension with the free assurance of 3:11–13. It is moreover noteworthy that the negative "then" of verses 7–9 is much more exten-sive and perhaps much more passionate than the positive "then" of verse 5. The imbalance between the two is an indication that the textual tradition already has in purview the unambiguous verdict of 11:1–13 and the awareness of the coming loss of the land (in effect the loss of the northern territory). In our text, the term is "cut off" (*krt*) (9:7). In 11:11, the term is "tear" (*qr'*), with an infinitive absolute for emphasis. The unmistakable point in the two uses, however, is the same. By this time in the narrative the regime of Solomon stands under a negative theological verdict. The text tradition no longer has much interest in the celebration of Solomon as tem-ple builder, wise man, or economic genius. Now the energy of the narrative is all focused on the Torah, and the news for Solomon is not good.

The verdict for which the "if" of 1 Kings 3:14 and 6:12 prepares us and which is more frontally anticipated in 9:6–9 comes to full articulation in 1 Kings 11:1–13 with a subsequent narrative implementation in 11:14–40. The negation of Solomon in 11:1–13 is marked by characteristic Deuteronomic rhetoric and turns on the com-mand of Deuteronomy 7:3 that is cited in 1 Kings 11:2:

Do not intermarry with them, giving your daughters to their sons or taking their daughters for your sons. (Deut 7:3)

You shall not enter into marriage with them, neither shall they with you; for they will surely incline your heart to follow their gods; [but] Solomon clung to these in love. (1 Kgs 11:2)

The failure of Solomon is constituted by marriage to "many foreign women," marriages that were no doubt expressions of Solomon's network of political and economic alliances. The "many foreign women," with their home-based religious commitments, caused Solomon to depart from exclusive loyalty to YHWH, or at least that is the judgment of the narrative: "For when Solomon was old, his wives turned away his heart after other gods; and his heart was not true to the Lord his God, as was the heart of his father David" (1 Kgs 11:4). The *indictment* of 1 Kings 11:1–8 is followed in characteristic prophetic rhetoric with the *sentence* of 11:11 concerning land loss: "Therefore the Lord said to Solomon, 'Since this has been your mind and you have not kept my covenant and my statutes that I have commanded you, I will surely tear the kingdom from you and give it to your servant.'" Thus the speech of verdict is shaped, as in familiar prophetic pattern, as a speech of judgment constituted by indictment and sentence.[6] We observe, now only in passing, that 11:12–13, introduced by "yet" ('ak), adds the characteristic proviso of Davidic exception that here, as elsewhere, mitigates the Deuteronomic judgment based on Torah. The Davidic proviso is, as we have seen, grounded in theological conviction; but it also reflects the "facts on the ground," namely, that the family of David persisted in power in Jerusalem and in Judah for a very long time to come.

We are now prepared to map out the complexities of the whole of the narrative. Remarkable interfaces expressed as disjunctive Hebrew rhetoric evidence the double-minded judgment about Solomon that permeates the entire tradition.[7]

Introduction: 3:1–2
   Premise of legitimacy and piety: "Solomon loved the Lord" (3:3)
      Dream narrative of legitimacy (3:4–15)
         The Deuteronomic "if" (3:14)
      Narrative of wisdom and justice (3:16–28)
         Solomon as economic genius (4:1–28)
            The royal bureaucracy (4:1–6)
            The royal tax-collecting apparatus (4:7–19)
            Royal success and contentment (4:20–21)
            Royal extravagance (4:22–28)
         Solomon as patron of wisdom (4:29–34)
         Solomon as temple builder (5:1–8:66)
            The Deuteronomic "if" (6:11–13)
            The larger royal building project (7:1–12)
   Second dream narrative (9:1–9)
      Solomon as economic genius (9:10–10:29)
         Solomon and Sheba (10:1–10, 13)
         Solomon and wisdom (10:6–7, 23)

Verdict: "Solomon loved many foreign women" (11:1)
 The indictment (11:1–10)
 The sentence (11:11)
 The Davidic proviso (11:12–13)
 Narrative implementation (11:14–40)
Conclusion (11:41–43)

The narrative is too complex for easy summary. We may, however, notice several elements that are decisive for the shape of the whole. The conclusion in 1 Kings 11:41–43 is characteristic Deuteronomic formulation. The narrative lacks such a stereotypical introduction, suggesting that the beginning of the reign of Solomon is problematic for the Deuteronomist. There is no doubt that the formulae of 1 Kings 3:3 and 11:1 are deliberately twinned, so that the narrative is framed with a beginning in good covenantal obedience and a deterioration into radical disobedience. This sense of deterioration is evident in 11:4: "For when Solomon was old, his wives turned away his heart after other gods; and his heart was not true to the Lord his God, as was the heart of his father David." It is likely that such a theory of deterioration that groups positive materials early and negative materials later is an editorial contrivance designed to keep Solomon reputable and innocent until he completes the building of the temple. As we will see, the introductory note of 1 Kings 3:1–2 suggests a problematic dimension to the Solomonic regime that is present from the very beginning of the narrative.

At the center of the narrative stands the great section on temple building, a textual section designed to dominate the whole of the narrative, with other materials intentionally grouped around this central section. We are treated to a verdict on Solomon at beginning and end; at the center is the temple report grouped around the temple report, with the bracket of verdicts, are the narratives of Solomon's wisdom and success in 3:16–4:34 and 9:10–10:29. The dream narratives of 3:5–14 and 9:1–9 provide clues about the shape of the whole; the first dream narrative is affirmative and the second dream narrative is a warning. Thus the whole is arranged around good king (3:1–4:34) . . . temple builder (5:1–8:66) . . . bad king (9:1–11:40) (11:41–43).

The whole is an enormous literary, interpretive achievement, pieced together from a variety of sources, each of which carries into the whole the suasion of its own perspective. It is evident that the completed narrative amounts to a great deal more than the sum of the parts, and a great deal other than the sum of the parts. The tradition begins with remembered Solomon, at best a modest chieftain. Tradition then transformed that modest, remembered Solomon into an artifact of critical, faithful imagination that presented Solomon as the most celebrated figure in Jerusalem, a figure so noted and celebrated that he became an engine for enduring interpretive tradition as different as the political myths of Ethiopia and the bourgeoisie myth of the Masonic lodge in Western Europe and the United States. The remarkable achievement of the tradition is the transformation of remembered Solomon into imagined Solomon, an act grounded in an inaccessible memory of some kind, carried to the future with enormous daring, freedom, and imagination.

THE COUPLING OF POLITICS AND THEOLOGY

Here we reflect on the source of the remarkable, interpretive energy that made possible the transposition of Solomon. The community of Israel did not live in a cultural vacuum, and the monarchy of David and Solomon did not emerge in a context free of ideology. Rather, the state formed by David emerged in a sociopolitical environment of the ancient Near East with longstanding practices of kingship and well-developed theories of kingship. The minor states around Israel, much like Israel, had monarchies. The ideological force of kingship, however, was fostered in the great imperial states of Mesopotamia and Egypt, from which we have important residues of theoretical-liturgical-ideological material.

There was a common theory of divine kingship that pertained to all states, but with important distinctions in the different cultural contexts of the Near East.[8] Scholars commonly believe that the great states regularly conducted temple rituals in order to assert and reenact the primacy and sovereignty of the high God of that culture, who would provide stability, security, and prosperity for the realm. Such primacy and sovereignty were understood to have mythic-ontological reality, but that mythic-ontological reality received concrete, existential force by the regular liturgic reenactment of God as divine king who is primal and sovereign. The evidence we have of such liturgies is in the form of the great myths of creation, which were in fact the scripts for regularly recurring liturgies. The status of the divine king, moreover, was understood as the indispensable antidote to the forces of chaos that threatened social stability and well-being, forces of chaos that might take natural form in the shape of floods or droughts, or historical form in the shape of military enemies. Either way, it was the capacity of the God king to fend off such threats. Social and cosmic ordering assured by the divine king required regular liturgical renewal and reenactment whereby the ontological reality was liturgically mediated. In each such liturgical mediation the will of the divine king for order and stability was reestablished, thus countering the threat of chaos through the next liturgical season.

The drama of *order over chaos* was enacted, in these ancient great states, in the central temple that was presided over by the human king, who presumably played a major role in such dramas.[9] Thus the concrete, political dimension of divine rule was consigned to the human king, who thereby received both divine legitimacy through

liturgy and concrete responsibility for the maintenance of order, security, and prosperity in the realm. The liturgies of divine kingship had an important political component that was regularly utilized for the political legitimacy of the status quo,
a legitimacy that easily lent itself to propaganda and/or ideology. This deep liturgic
heritage was certainly on the horizon of ancient Israel as the dynasty of David
emerged.

The common liturgical-rhetorical strategy whereby the *God king* ordered chaos
and the *human king* maintained social order articulated an intimate relationship
between the two. In Egypt that formulation was taken with ontological seriousness
so that the king was indeed God's son and so divine. In Mesopotamia, by contrast,
the formula was a political one that characteristically did not carry any ontological
connotation. In either usage, the formula was a powerful device to assure divine
legitimacy for a human institution, thus easily linking theological legitimacy and
political concreteness.

It is plausible to think that the same notion of YHWH the high God as king over
Israel and over creation prevailed in ancient Israel. Martin Buber long ago considered the way in which the Sinai covenant was a "kingly covenant," and the way in
which the Old Testament witnesses to the liturgic notion of the enthronement and
kingship of YHWH:

> The unconditional claim of the divine Kingship is recognized at the point
> when the people proclaims JHWH Himself as King, Him alone and directly
> (Exodus 15:18), and JHWH Himself enters upon the kingly reign (19:6). He
> is not content to be "God" in the religious sense. He does not want to surren-
> der to a man that which is not "God's," the rule over the entire actuality of
> worldly life: this very rule He lays claim to and enters upon it; for there is
> nothing which is not God's. He will apportion to the one, forever and ever cho-
> sen by Him, his tasks, but naked power without a situationally related task He
> does not wish to bestow. He makes known His will first of all as constitution—
> not constitution of cult and custom only, also of economy and society—He
> will proclaim it again and again to the changing generations, certainly but sim-
> ply as reply to a question, institutionally through priestly mouth, above all,
> however, in the freedom of His surging spirit, through every one whom His
> spirit seizes. *The separation of religion and politics which stretches through history
> is here overcome in real paradox.*

Is this—which takes its place beside the oriental conception of the divine
kingship—only a doctrine, or is its core an experience? Is it historicizing
theology or is it history that a confederation of half-nomadic Semitic tribes at

some time, undoubtedly more than three thousand years ago, on their wanderings from Egypt to Canaan, instead, perhaps, as other Semitic peoples did in such an hour of unification and high-spirited onward advance, of elevating its human leader as *melekh* (although under divine authority with the same title), proclaimed its God, JHWH, as *melekh*? That, accordingly, this confederation of tribes which called itself Israel, dared as a people, first and once-for-all in the history of peoples, to deal seriously with exclusive divine rulership? As people—to be sure, in the unceasing dialectic of the divine conflict between subjects and rebels, between Gideons and Abimelechs, yet, even so, acting as people: proclaiming, obeying, following?[10]

In addition to Exodus 15:18 and 19:6, Deuteronomy 33:5 also is an ancient text attesting to the divine kingship of YHWH:

> There arose a king in Jeshurun,
> when the leaders of the people assembled—
> the united tribes of Israel.

More recently, Frank Cross has made the case, concerning Exodus 15:1–18, which culminates in the enthronement formula of verse 18, that the tradition reflected in the song is very old and appeals to common creation myths: "Mythic elements were present at the beginning of Israel's history when Yahwism emerged from its mythopoeic environment. The cultus of the league was strongly shaped by historical patterns; however, it is best expressed in the Epic tradition of Israel as shown by A. Alt and his students. The myths of creation and kingship became recrudescent with the introduction of kingship and its ideology, especially in the Solomonic era with the institution of the dynastic temple."[11]

Thus Israel, especially in the Solomonic tradition, embraced much of the mythic-liturgic-ideological world of divine kingship.

It is likely the case, however, that in the earliest traditions of ancient Israel it was sufficient that YHWH was divine king; in that ancient liturgical practice of Israel reflected in old texts, there was no human king, and Israel indeed resisted human kingship as an act of mistrust in YHWH's kingship. That high view of *YHWH as king* is reflected in the poetry of Second Isaiah, who in the sixth century seized upon the older ideology of divine kingship in order to provide ground for hope among the deported Jews. Buber observed:

> The covenant at Sinai signifies, according to its positive content, that the wandering tribes accept JHWH "for ever and ever" as their King. According to its negative content it signifies that no man is to be called king of the sons of

Israel. "You shall be for Me a kingly domain," "there was then in Jᵉshurun a King"; this is exclusive proclamation also with respect to a secular lordship: JHWH does not want, like the other kingly gods, to be sovereign and guarantor of a human monarch. He wants Himself to be the Leader and the Prince. The man to whom He addresses His will in order that he carry it out is not only to have his power in this connection alone; he can also exert no power beyond his limited task. Above all, since he rules not as a person acting in his own right, but as "emissary," he cannot transmit power. . . . There is in pre-kingly Israel no externality of ruler-ship; *for there is no political sphere except the theo-political,* and all sons of Israel are directly related (*kohanim* in the original sense) to JHWH, Who chooses and rejects, gives an order and withdraws it.[12]

The primary case that supports Buber's judgment is the narrative of Gideon. After his great victory that was understood as a gift of YHWH, Gideon is recruited to be king; but he refuses on theological grounds. "Then the Israelites said to Gideon, 'Rule over us, you and your son and your grandson also; for you have delivered us out of the hand of Midian.' Gideon said to them, 'I will not rule over you, and my son will not rule over you; the Lord will rule over you'" (Judg 8:22–23). This self-understanding of Israel given in the tradition represents a profoundly held theopolitical position in ancient Israel: YHWH is king and there is no king in Israel save YHWH. This view is belatedly reflected in the curious text of Ezekiel 34:23–24 where a new David is anticipated. He is treated as a "prince" (*ns'*) and not more than a prince, because YHWH is the only king.

There was in Israel, however, an alternative theopolitical view that a human king was an articulation of YHWH's divine rule and not an antithesis to it. This view more nearly replicated the common view of the ancient Near East and offered a powerful challenge to the covenantal ideology voiced by Gideon. After acrimonious dispute over human kingship that entailed both theological passion and political-economic-military interests (on which see 1 Sam 7–15), the view prevailed in Israel that a human king was willed by YHWH and gave concrete force to YHWH's rule in the world. Thus was founded the dynasty of David, informed and legitimated by that common royal ideology. Thus Solomon is both the product and the beneficiary of that newly emergent notion in Israel.

It is an old hypothesis in Old Testament scholarship, first proposed by Sigmund Mowinckel, that in monarchal Israel there was a great enthronement festival whereby YHWH was annually enthroned yet again as king in Jerusalem and as king over all creation (see Pss 47, 93, 96, 97, 98, 99).[13] In that festival, according to the hypothesis, the Davidic king occupied a central dramatic role and thereby received liturgical legitimacy as the effective regent for YHWH on earth. That hypothesis, which can never be more than a hypothesis, has recently been reaffirmed by J. J. M. Roberts, who draws an important conclusion:

> In my view, this festival developed as an important part of the preexisting autumn agricultural festival early in the period of the united monarchy to celebrate Yahweh's rise to imperial rank. I think it was influenced by general Near Eastern modes of thought, but that it was adopted in response to Israel's particular political development in a period of imperial power, not just as an aping of insignificant Israel's more powerful neighbors. I think it included a ritual reenactment of Yahweh's accession to the throne symbolized by a procession of the ark into the sanctuary, and the placing of the ark under Yahweh's cherub throne in the inner sanctum of the temple. Finally, after all the linguistic and syntactical debate, I would argue that the ritual meaning of the Hebrew expressions *mlk yhwh* and *yhwh mlk* is still best captured by Mowinckel's translation, "Yahweh has become king!"[14]

If we allow for some such public imagination and celebration of YHWH's kingship in which the human king played a crucial role, then we are able to understand the immense interpretive energy whereby the tradition eventuated in "royal Solomon." We have seen that in 2 Samuel 7:14, in the founding oracle of the Davidic dynasty, it is asserted of Solomon, the anticipated heir: "I will be a father to him, and he shall be a son to me. When he commits iniquity, I will punish him with a rod such as mortals use, with blows inflicted by human beings." That language of father and son, so crucial in binding divine king to human king, moreover is echoed in 1 Kings 8:19–21, where David's son is charged with temple building. That is, Solomon is charged with the creation of a proper liturgical venue for the practice of the state liturgy of enthronement.

It is clear that the Psalter reflects this same developed liturgic practice and mythic ideology. Scholars have identified certain psalms as "royal psalms" that celebrate the cruciality of the human king for the community as YHWH's regent and son:

> I will tell of the decree of the Lord:
> He said to me, "You are my son;
> today I have begotten you." (Ps 2:7)

See also Psalm 110 as an authorization of the peculiar role of the king as an intimate of YHWH. Beyond that, it is credible to think that Psalm 8 celebrates the "royal man" who is "little less than God" and who is to exercise "dominion" as is the Davidic king who has responsibility for the maintenance of creation:

> Yet you have made them a little
> lower than God,

and crowned them with glory
and honor.
You have given them dominion
over the works of your
hands;
you have put all things under
their feet,
all sheep and oxen,
and also the beasts of the field,
the birds of the air, and the fish
of the sea,
whatever passes along the
paths of the seas. (Ps 8:5–8)

It is clear in the psalm that such human dominion is subordinate to the divine sovereignty:

O Lord, our Sovereign,
how majestic is your name in
all the earth!" (Ps 8:9)

Thus we see that the transposition of remembered Solomon into imagined Solomon was an immense achievement in ancient Israel, accomplished through great interpretive imagination, and that that interpretive imagination embraced the ideology of kingship available in Near Eastern culture and dominant in the great states around Israel. To be sure, that liturgical practice and ideology was adapted to Israel's own sense of itself. Even with such adaptation, however, it is clear that this way of self-understanding was a profound *novum* in Israel, requiring a considerable departure from the covenantal conviction that held only YHWH to be king. The move toward more common cultural models and away from a lean sense of covenantal Israel at Sinai was in part a pragmatic move for the sake of order and security.

We should not, however, miss the point that such a broad interpretive maneuver was, at the same time, a move toward common theology rooted in the great states.[15] As Israel became more ambitious to participate in and compete with the great states, it was compelled to accommodate itself to such patterns of power and legitimacy. That accommodation was an act of immense imagination that remained endlessly in dispute in the ongoing tradition of Israel. As with every such act of imagination, there were important gains and losses in the maneuver that continued to be assessed through the traditioning process. Solomon was an imaginative interpretive product; he became, moreover, the point man for such an assessment—a disputatious assessment that is deeply evident in the narrative construal of 1 Kings 3–11.

A CRITIQUE OF SOLOMON: MOVING FROM COVENANT TO ROYALTY

The transposition of remembered Solomon into imagined Solomon made appeal to and practice of an innovative ideology in Israel. Our reading of 1 Kings 3–11, moreover, requires us to be attentive to the innovative interpretive perspective now in play and the way in which it was variously welcomed and resisted in Israel.

What follows in this text is a discussion of a broad field of competing interpretive convictions. It is commonplace that the formula of 1 Kings 3:3—"Solomon loved the Lord"—functions as an entry point into the narrative that is nicely matched to the formula of 11:1. If we begin with 1 Kings 3:3, however, that leaves 3:1–2 as an odd preliminary comment, and therefore I consider the significance of these two verses for our reading of Solomon.

We may of course take the verses simply as reportage, a communication of two facts: Solomon's marriage to Pharaoh's daughter, and the practice of sacrifice at "high places." It is entirely possible to take these verses as innocent reportage. If, however, we recognize that the Solomon narrative is a matrix for contested interpretation, then it is plausible, even probable, that these verses are not mere reportage but are in fact polemic. In what follows then, I consider these two verses as a plunge into interpretive disputation, the kind that gathers everywhere around the imagined Solomon.

If we begin with the happy affirmation that "Solomon loved the Lord," and know from the outset that this formula is twinned to 1 Kings 11:1, then the notice in 3:1 already calls attention to the seduction of "many foreign women," for Pharaoh's daughter is the lead character among "many foreign women." Thus to begin the narrative in this way may signal from the outset that the narrative is deeply critical of this king and proceeds in an ironic tone. There is no doubt that the marriages to "many foreign women" were political arrangements that helped solidify Solomon's global economic network. It is significant that reference to Pharaoh's daughter as the wife of Solomon occurs five times in the Solomon text, distributed before the temple account (1 Kgs 3:1), within the temple account (7:8), and after the temple account (9:16, 24; 11:1). (Notice, moreover, that in 1 Kings 11:19–20 the same practice of marriage alliance pertains to Pharaoh's daughter with reference to "Hadad the Edomite.")

This recurring mention of Pharaoh's daughter we may take as an intentional interpretive sign on two counts. First, Egyptian royal ideology, as Frankfort has shown, holds the highest view of kingship so that in that environment the human king is divine.[16] This ideological claim of divinity could of course move governance in an absolutizing direction, absolutism expressed perforce as exploitation. The narrative clearly wants to attach Solomon to that high ideology. Second, in Israelite memory, "Pharaoh" inescapably bespeaks oppression and exploitation, the undoing of the miracle of the exodus. Thus we may imagine that Solomon's political-economic policies were committed to exploitation that was expressed in theoretical absolutism and in the practice of self-aggrandizement. In this reading the initial mention of Pharaoh's daughter—the very first verse of the narrative—signals to the reader that from the very outset this final form of the narrative is positioned in a critical stance toward Solomon.

The second claim of these initial verses, popular sacrifice in high places, may also be taken as reportage on the status of religious practices prior to the completion of the temple, a completion mentioned in verse 1. In general, however, the critical stance of the tradition is not preoccupied with such a "history of religions" perspective. It is unmistakably clear that the final form of the narrative of the books of Kings takes a quite negative view of "high places," condemning kings who foster them and commending kings who purge them (see 1 Kgs 12:31–32; 13:2, 32, 33; 14:23; 15:14; 22:43; 2 Kgs 12:3; 14:4; 15:4, 35; 16:4; 18:4, 22; 21:3; 23:5, 8, 9.)[17] Moreover, the climactic verdict of the Deuteronomist in 2 Kings 17:9, 11, 29, 32 indicates a harsh negation of such heterodox shrines. In light of such recurring usage, we notice that "high place" in 1 Kings 11:7, linked to "many foreign women," constitutes a vigorous feature of Torah disobedience. Given such a relentless and sustained condemnation of high places, it is not likely that the note in 1 Kings 3:2 on high places is innocent reportage. More likely it is a polemic at the outset that corresponds to and looks toward the final indictment of Solomon in chapter 11.

Thus both items—Pharaoh's daughter and high places—are likely signs of a major critique of Solomon. The force of this initial critique is further enhanced when the two items are taken together. The mention of high places in 1 Kings 3:2 and 11:7 bespeaks heterodox worship that this critical perspective condemns. The ground of such high places, moreover, is in alliances through "many foreign women" (1 Kgs 11:1–5), among them Pharaoh's daughter (3:1). Taken altogether then, 1 Kings 3:1–2 begins the narrative with a subtle critique of Solomon, who has moved drastically away from covenantal Israel toward common royal theory that is characteristically untroubled about "many foreign women" or "high places." Thus 3:1–2 constitutes a powerful signal that the embrace of common ancient Near Eastern ideology of the kingship, an embrace specified by Solomon, is under heavy critique. The juxtaposition of these verses alongside 3:3–13 is a characteristic parataxis in Hebrew rhetoric that refuses to adjudicate the tension. The tension between an excessive accommodation to culture in royal practice and a responsive covenantal perspective is acute from the outset. As we read the narrative that follows, we are thus prepared for a contested interpretation of Solomon, child of the Torah, product of royal ideology, and arena for dispute whereby Israel conducts its traditioning process.

CHAPTER 5

"SOLOMON" AS TEMPLE BUILDER

I n the narrative of 1 Kings 3–11, there is no doubt that the central and most celebrated achievement of the imagined Solomon is the building of the temple. The
account of the temple in 1 Kings 5:1–8:66 occupies the dominant position in
the entire narrative, an accomplishment authorized in the dynastic oracle of 2
Samuel 7:13 (see the reiteration of 1 Kgs 5:5 and 8:19). The building of the temple
by Solomon may be understood first in terms of the common theory of temple in the
ancient Near East, an enterprise in large states that Solomon sought to replicate, and
second in the particular circumstance of Solomon in the consolidation of his imperial regime.

THE TEMPLE'S FUNCTION AS A SYMBOL OF ORDER AND POWER

The temple in common ancient Near Eastern understanding functions as a core symbol of an integrated society; it provides assurances of reliable *cosmic order*, and con-
solidates and legitimates concrete *political power*. Thus Solomon's achievement is to
be understood as a powerful but not disinterested act of symbolization.

In its most comprehensive symbolization, the temple replicates and embodies
cosmic order. Its stability and reliability amid threats of chaos are clearly expressed
in Psalm 46, which familiarly celebrates the durability of the temple:

> Therefore we will not fear,
> though the earth should change,
> though the mountains shake in the heart of the sea;
> though its waters roar and foam,
> though the mountains tremble with its tumult.
> There is a river whose streams make glad the city of God,
> the holy habitation of the Most High.
> God is in the midst of the city, it shall not be moved;
> God will help it when the morning dawns.
> The nations are in an uproar, the kingdoms totter;
> he utters his voice, the earth melts. (Ps 46:2–6)

The temple is characteristically on a high mountain, signifying preeminence and
durability.[1] Thus Solomon provided a fixed reference point in Israelite imagination
whereby Israel in its vulnerability could be reassured. The cosmic significance of the

temple, so well articulated by John Lundquist, is, however, not simply an offer of reassurance.[2] It also serves a much more utilitarian, political purpose, a point not fully appreciated by Lundquist.

Carol Meyers has underscored the political achievement of the temple for Solomon.[3] She makes clear that the kingdom of Solomon was an exceedingly diverse and complex one that required intentional symbolic integration:

> The formation of the monarchy must be understood in terms considerably more complex than the assertion that the rise to power of Saul and David was a response to the pressures exerted upon the Israelite tribes by the Philistine hegemony. . . . The kingdom ruled by David and then Solomon was hardly a "gigantic homogeneous bloc" but rather was a remarkably varied structure, composed of at least five discrete levels of political interrelationships. The political organization achieved by roughly the midpoint of David's forty-year reign was that of a true empire, which can be conceived schematically as consisting of five concentric circles, each of which represents both a different stage in the formation of the empire and a different category of domination by the central government in Jerusalem.[4]

The temple functioned as an important instrument of consolidation and political power, for it could appeal to a broad population in its articulation of cosmic symbolization: "Solomon's architectural program can be seen as the logical and essential continuation of the national unification and imperial expansion achieved by David."[5] Such symbolization could appeal to the non-Israelite elements of the regime, whereas the ark of the covenant, now housed in the temple, could in parallel fashion appeal to the traditional Israelites. By constructing the temple, Solomon joined the ranks of kings in the ancient Near East who exhibited their piety and devotion to the high God, creator of heaven and earth, and who did so in a way that served the pragmatic ends of the Jerusalem establishment.

Temple Architecture and Furnishings

A good deal of attention has been given to the architecture of the temple as it is variously traced through 1 Kings 5–8 and more or less parallel presentations in the books of Chronicles and Ezekiel, plus the tabernacle traditions of Exodus 25–40. It is clear in all of these renditions that the temple of Solomon reflects the characteristic patterns of temple architecture and furnishings of the Near East generally. G. Ernest Wright long ago traced the architectural parallels elsewhere in the Near East and lined out the cosmic symbolic significance of the architecture.[6] Of all of the elements of scholarship concerning Solomon, this understanding of the temple has remained a constant as a way of connecting Solomon to an Iron Age cultural context.

In more recent scholarship, William Dever has made a strong case for the parallels to cultural context, insisting that *"every single detail* of the temple can now be correlated by archaeological examples from the Late Bronze and Iron Ages."[7] It is rather remarkable that in their minimalist discussion of Solomon, Finkelstein and Silberman do not take up the temple in any detail.[8] One must not think too much of an argument from silence; it may be, however, that the data concerning the temple ill serves a minimalist perspective, because that data would seem to support a genuine cultural link. The data that are commonly cited in order to appreciate the temple as a theological-cultural achievement include the use of foreign materials and forced labor, an architectural design familiar throughout the ancient Near East, and the presence of fine craftsmanship and opulent decoration.

The use of cedars from Lebanon as the predominant material for the temple suggests both a planned opulence signified by such exotic lumber and a readiness to utilize materials that are from non-Yahwistic sources outside Israel (1 Kgs 5:1–12). The lead artisan, Hiram, moreover, is from Tyre, surely a non-Israelite (7:13–14).

The labor force for the construction of the temple is "forced labor out of all Israel," suggesting that the temple construction was an elitist royal project and not a populist enterprise (1 Kgs 5:13–18). With reference to both materials and manpower, it is clear that Solomon is proceeding in ways that are quite alien to the requirements of covenantal Israel, which would have looked askance at such foreign materials and would have resisted any coercive labor policy.

The design of the temple is in three chambers: the vestibule (*ulam;* 1 Kgs 6:3), the holy place (*hekel;* 6:17), and the most holy place ("holy of holies," *debir;* 6:16). The basic sketch of the temple in 1 Kings 6:1–22 exhibits a plan known elsewhere in the ancient Near East; it is consequently probable that the temple replicated a common Phoenician model, for which archaeology has produced a parallel at the Syrian site of Tell Tainat.[9] This three-chamber design represented an important departure from the older Israelite sanctuary that was characteristically undifferentiated and without any hint of distinct chambers. The architectural design (also reflected in the characterization of Ezekiel 41) is significant because it suggests the view that Solomon moved as much as possible away from simple covenantal Israelite modes of public life in the direction of common cultural patterns that were more complex and eventually hierarchical. In temple design Solomon certainly went outside any narrow Israelite notion into broader cultural perspective. Beyond that, however, the three-chamber room reflects a theory and practice of gradations of holiness whereby almost anyone could enter the "vestibule," only certain qualified people could enter the "nave," and only the priest—the most holy person—could enter into the "holy of holies." This practice of gradations of holiness reflects not only notions of differentiated piety or liturgical purity but also a class structure with different levels of social worth and social value. Thus the architecture reflects and reinforces political-sociological judgments that were introduced into a society of differentiated roles, a practice of differentiation unknown in covenantal Israel. Meyers comments:

> The rapid emergence of Israel as an imperial power in the lifetime of David marked a radical change not only in political orientation but also in socioeconomic structure. The leadership of Saul and of David in his early years set Israel on a course marked by the increasingly centralized organization of local communities and a growing body of individuals whose statuses in the community were hierarchically ranked. These two principles of social organization can be identified with a chiefdom stage in the evolution of a complex state. . . . Not only can monumental architecture be identified as a diagnostic feature of the shift to nonegalitarian societies but it also can be perceived as signifying institutional and societal transitions involved in state formation.[10]

Thus while the temple in Jerusalem may have been a device for the integration of a complex society, it was an integration that was differentiated and variegated with self-conscious rankings, a practice alien to the covenant community that apparently antedated the monarchy. I have suggested elsewhere that the three-chambered distinctions are not unlike the three chambers on jet airplanes with a tourist cabin, a first-class cabin, and a cockpit.[11] The various chambers of an airplane reflect distinctions of social class and social power. The unqualified worshiper could no more enter the holy place than could a "cheap fare" enter the first-class cabin, at least not until the "curtain is rent" (see Matt 27:51).

It is important to notice the accent upon the fine craftsmanship in the finishing of the temple (1 Kgs 6:18–20, 23, 29, 32–36; 7:17–20, 24–26, 36, 41) and the opulent decoration in gold (6:21–22, 28, 30, 32, 35; 7:48–50). On counts of both artistry and opulence, the temple is richly extravagant, with no effort or resource being spared. The significance of such extensive finery is no doubt twofold, as such temple construction characteristically is. On the one hand, the whole is surely designed to glorify God, to enhance YHWH as sovereign in the face of competitor gods, and to articulate "the beauty of holiness." On the other hand and at the same time, there is little doubt that such extravagance—in text if not in fact—is a piece of propaganda designed to enhance the dynasty, to promote its theological legitimacy, and to exhibit its hugely successful economy. But then, the success of the economy can characteristically be claimed as evidence that the blessing of an effective God abides with his people and particularly with this king.

Thus Solomon as temple builder has built a characteristic ancient Near Eastern sanctuary of a generic kind. We may suspect, moreover, that the theological intentionality of the temple is also more or less generic without any of the awkward particularity of the old covenantal tradition that might have hindered the theopoliti-cal integration of the complex realm over which Solomon presided as regent for YHWH. The account of construction in 1 Kings 5–7 (excluding the Deuteronomic accent of 1 Kgs 6:11–13 and excluding the rest of Solomon's building program in 7:1–12) is a generic achievement without affront to anyone and without any hint of a demanding theological commitment. As Meyers writes,

> The extent of the ideological impact of the written or even the spoken word would have been necessarily limited in the ancient world. Consequently, other forms of propaganda, notably those employing visual symbols, were extremely important. Both verbal and visual modes of communication stressed that dynastic power derived its legitimacy from its close connection with divine sovereignty. With the religious sphere existing as an integral and critical aspect of political authority, divine sanction of a regime provided the ultimate and incontrovertible justification for its coercive power. A religious text could con-vey that sanction to a privileged, literate audience; a religious symbol or edi-fice could provide that message to a wider public.[12]

THEOLOGICAL REFLECTIONS ON THE TEMPLE

The building and finishing of the temple in 1 Kings 5–7 is more or less generic and accommodating. When we reach chapter 8, however, the text moves in a quite dif-ferent direction. Unlike the materials in chapters 5–7 that could pass for reportage, chapter 8 is one of the great chapters of biblical faith that offers a complex, critical theological reflection on the temple, a probe into the demandingly complex problem of divine presence.[13] This text purports to be a rendering of the one day of temple dedication, with Solomon as the definitive actor in the drama of temple imagina-tion. As we shall see, however, this long chapter is more like a sustained, variegated meditation that stretches over time; it includes material from several sources that reflect quite different interpretive perspectives. The temple is an interpretive refer-ence point not unlike Solomon himself, a magnet for contested and contesting inter-pretive claims.

First Kings 8 begins with a purported account of the key element in dedicating the temple, namely, the transport of the ark of the covenant into the newly com-pleted temple (8:1–13). This liturgically accomplished interplay of *ark* and *temple* is an extraordinary achievement in the management of defining religious symbols. On the one hand, as we have seen, the temple itself is a generic sanctuary of Phoenician style that was essential to the large claims of dynastic legitimacy assured through localized divine presence. The temple gives articulation to the claim that the Davidic king is at the center of cosmic order. The narrative account of the construction and decoration in 1 Kings 5–7 has made this clear. On the other hand, the ark of the covenant is the core religious symbol of old tribal memory that signifies the presence of YHWH, the God of Sinai, in the midst of Israel:

The Ark of the Covenant surely served as a prime symbol of Yahweh's presence among the tribes and of divine support for the king who had possession of it. Scholars widely recognize that the coming of the Ark to Jerusalem signified the granting of Yahweh's favor for the new era, the bestowal of divine blessings upon and through the regime that was inaugurating the shift from tribal organization to statehood, and God's approval of the new status of Jerusalem as the center of a far-reaching polity. Bringing the Ark to the new capital helped immeasurably in transferring the ancient religionational traditions of pre-monarchic Israel to the new dynastic order and hence in securing the support of the tribal components of the national kingdom. If the Ark itself signified God's legitimating presence, the procession and the festivities connected with it constituted a media event that reached "all the people, the whole multitude of Israel, both men and women" (2 Sam 6:19). . . . The presence of the Ark in Jerusalem was apparently a powerful and effective instrument for securing both monarchic and dynastic legitimacy in the eyes of the people who were heirs to Israel's ancient order. . . . It was the major symbol in the religious sphere for sanctioning the reordering of Israelite national life.[14]

The old tribal conviction is evidenced with reference in 1 Kings 8 to the "ancestral houses" (*'aboth;* 8:1) and "elders" (8:3). The new generic, imperial horizon is connected to the scene of "the city of David, which is Zion," a phrase that indicates that the city as locus of the new temple is the personal, private property of the dynasty and is not beholden to old tribal traditions. Thus the interplay of symbols old and new, covenantal and cosmic, makes the temple a draw for the several populations that constitute the new complex kingdom of Solomon. The ark, moreover, is carried into the inner sanctuary (*debir*), into the holy of holies, indicating that the ark, formerly a quite egalitarian symbol, has now been subsumed in the three-chamber temple structure bespeaking social stratification and hierarchy (8:6). Thus it can be suggested that the Solomonic liturgy hijacked the old symbols in the service of the new royal ideology.

The extravagant procession that included representatives of the new populations culminates in 1 Kings 8:10–13 with two climactic affirmations. First, in verses 10–11, Priestly language is employed to articulate the real, palpable presence of YHWH in the temple, in the "most holy place": "And when the priests came out of the holy place, a cloud filled the house of the Lord, so that the priests could not stand to minister because of the cloud; for the glory of the Lord filled the house of the Lord"

(1 Kgs 8:10–11). The language of a cloud-filled house, and "the glory of God filled the house," is parallel to the tabernacle language of Exodus 40:34; this rhetoric is the most characteristic way in which a Priestly discourse asserts "Real Presence" in the holy place. The liturgy has effectively located YHWH in the temple as patron to the dynasty and as guarantor of the city. Thus, for example, the reason Psalm 46 can be so certain of the well-being of the city is because of divine presence: "The Lord of hosts is with us; / the God of Jacob is our refuge" (Ps 46:7; see also 46:11). "Real Presence" is a huge theological claim but also an enormous political resource that, in the language of Meyers, readily functions as propaganda.

Second, that affirmation in 1 Kings 8:10–11 is reinforced by the remarkable anthem of verses 12–13 in which Solomon—or the temple choirs—sings of YHWH's abiding presence in the temple. These verses articulate the highest view of divine presence in the temple given anywhere in the Old Testament, and represent the highest Priestly claim made for the temple. Verse 12 quotes (alleges) that YHWH had promised to dwell in "thick darkness." That term bespeaks the numinous, hidden, powerful presence of God who is accessible but ominous:

The English term "thick darkness" represents an approximate way of rendering a difficult Hebrew word, 'araphel, which designates total and ominous obscurity, a portent of danger but also a harbinger of life. It appears in one of the narratives of the Sinai-Horeb theophany. One of the narrators spoke of lightning and of the thick cloud which attended the descent of Yahweh upon the top of the mount. He also mentioned the 'araphel "where Elohim was" and which Moses dared to approach (Exod. 20:21). The term admirably fitted the ambiguity of the Hebraic theology of presence, for the meaning which it carried, gloom, also conveyed the symbol of the hiddenness of God at the exact moment of his proximity.[15]

Thus the term refers to God situated upon the ark in the "most holy place," a presence that can be counted on without intimacy. Whereas YHWH is quoted in 1 Kings 8:12, in verse 13 Solomon speaks. Now Solomon is the initiative taker who "makes a house" for YHWH (a verb expressed intensely with an infinitive absolute). Solomon takes this initiative even though in the oracle of 2 Samuel 7 it is only YHWH who must make a house for David. The capacity of Solomon to take such initiative toward YHWH indicates the powerful force of royal ideology. Three other items in this statement of Solomon merit attention: First, the term "exalted" (zbl) refers to the mountain location of the temple and hints at the mythical claim of "cosmic mountain" that the temple embodies, thus a tilt toward generic temple ideology. Second, the verb "dwell" (ysv) is immensely important because it literally means to "sit" in a permanent way as a king "sits" on the throne. The verb is rarely used for the divine presence and bespeaks permanence. The verb is quite in contrast to the verb in verse 12 also rendered "dwell" but translating *skn,* a term meaning to take up temporary residence while maintaining mobility and freedom. Thus YHWH's utterance in verse 12 asserts freedom, whereas Solomon's expression in verse 13 serves to deny that very freedom. The two lines together with the two verbs articulate the tension Israel knows about "presence"; in this usage, however, Solomon's flattened verb is the last one and thereby seems to prevail. The temple "sit" has overcome the ark "sojourn" in the interest of the dynasty:

> According to the second colon of the first poetic verse of the dedication formula (vs. 12), the promise of Yahweh to sojourn in the ʿaraphel is not to be construed as a commitment to dwell forever in a holy place. On the contrary, the use of the nomadic term *shaken,* originally meaning "to alight for the night," "to encamp for a time," "to sojourn," reiterates the traditional stance of Yahwism on the transience of divine manifestations. Moreover, the verb *yashabh,* "to dwell" (literally, "to sit down,") which is used in the second verse of the poem (vs. 13*b*), is precisely that which Nathan's oracle to David emphatically placed in the negative when it stated that Yahweh walks about but does not sit down (2 Sam. 7:6). It appears that Solomon purposely attempted to link the two phrases by the adverb "therefore" in order to promote a shift of meaning toward the synonymity of the two verbs. The relation of cause and effect between Yahweh's promise and the erection of the new edifice inevitably tended to identify the ʿaraphel of intermittent presence with the total obscurity of the innermost room in the temple that was being consecrated. Through contextual juxtaposition, the power of innuendo was capable of transforming the notion of a nomadic transitoriness of presence into that of a cultic permanence of proximity. Yahweh dwelt in his temple. His inaccessibility to human eyes was preserved, but the worshippers' secure feeling of his residence on the rock of Zion could not fail to be a welcome one. In the course of the following centuries, the verb "to sojourn" became synonymous with the verb "to dwell" and acquired the meaning of abiding presence. The temple of Jerusalem was henceforth the residence of Yahweh on earth.[16]

It is evident, then, that the careful language of 1 Kings 8:10–13 shows the way in which royal-temple theology claimed YHWH as permanent resident and therefore patron of the Jerusalem establishment.

Before moving on, we should pay special attention to 1 Kings 8:9, for it strikes a remarkable deconstructive note in the midst of the royal pageant of presence. While verses 1–13 in general take a high view of divine presence in the temple via the ark, verse 9 dissents and serves to deny such presence. All that is there in the ark, it is claimed, are the tablets of the Torah given at Sinai, that is, the Ten Commandments. This dissent is a protest against a high theology of presence and voices a "low church" insistence that all that Israel is granted of presence is the articulated will of the sovereign God who will be obeyed. True *presence* is known through *obedience*, a claim that lies behind the prophetic articulation of Jeremiah 22:16, where it is asserted that "knowledge of God" is given in and through obedience:

> He judged the cause of the poor
> and needy;
> then it was well.
> Is not this to know me?
> says the Lord. (Jer 22:16)[17]

The juxtaposition of 1 Kings 8:9 together with verses 10–13 wondrously signals the profound and unresolved issue concerning the presence of YHWH in the midst of Israel. In this context, a high view of divine presence seems to prevail. Israel, however, could never assert such a high view without at the same time indicating some unease with it. Obviously, dynastic propaganda could not countenance such a voice of dissent; even in this canonical text, however, the Jerusalem establishment is not able to eliminate the voice of dissent that is so characteristic of Israel's faith.

The high claim for presence in 1 Kings 8:12–13 and the dissent in verse 9 together indicate that Israel struggled with and disputed about a sense of YHWH's presence in the temple. The remainder of chapter 8 evidences the ongoing continuation of that struggle.

First Kings 8:14–26 provides an articulation of the high claims of legitimacy for the dynasty, claims that are closely linked to the temple. These verses make clear how liturgical utterance can be put to the service of institutional legitimacy. Verses 14–21, with reference back to 2 Samuel 7:13, indicate Solomon's designation as the proper temple builder. Verses 22–26 move from temple-building authorization to the establishment of the monarchy. The two themes of temple and dynasty are characteristically linked as the twin gifts of YHWH in Jerusalem, a twinning made clear in the Davidic psalm 78:

> He rejected the tent of Joseph,
> he did not choose the tribe of Ephraim;
> but *he chose the tribe of Judah,*
> *Mount Zion,* which he loves.
> He built his sanctuary like the high heavens,
> like the earth, which he has founded forever.
> *He chose his servant David,*

and took him from the sheepfolds;
from tending the nursing ewes he brought him
to be the shepherd of his people Jacob,
of Israel, his inheritance. (Ps 78:67–71)

The text of 1 Kings 8:23–24 makes clear the way in which the *dynastic covenant* is presented as a subset of the *Sinai covenant* with Israel. This unit of text culminates with the claim of verse 26 that the dynastic promise to David has come to fulfillment in Solomon.

Three notices in these verses tell against high Jerusalem ideology. First, the temple is to be a house "for my name." This formula, rooted in the tradition of Deuteronomy, is a dissent from any claim of palpable presence (see Deut 12:11). This formulation understands that YHWH is fully present *in heaven,* and only YHWH's name is fully present in the temple (see Deut 26:15; 1 Kgs 8:29–30). This distinction between YHWH and YHWH's name makes a claim for presence in the temple but qualifies that claim in order to maintain the freedom of the God who dwells in heaven. Second, the reference to the ark of the covenant in verse 21 permits the temple to be understood primarily as shelter for the ark. The ark, moreover, is the primal symbol of old covenantal notions of YHWH's sojourning presence in which YHWH did not "dwell" anywhere permanently (see Num 10:35–36). Third, the "if" of verse 25, a characteristically Deuteronomic "if," submits the claim of dynasty to Torah and so prevents any absolutist royal claim. On all counts the broad claim of verses 12–13 for temple presence and the implied dynastic claim are subtly subverted by the Torah tradition.

That subversion of the claims of Solomon is further advanced in 1 Kings 8:27–30. Verse 27 states negatively that God's large, free sovereignty cannot be confined in the ideologies of temple or throne, and verses 28–30 then offer a sense of presence congruent with that free sovereignty of YHWH. YHWH's *name* is in the temple; YHWH's *eyes* are upon the temple; YHWH's *ears* are attentive to the temple, for God hears what is addressed toward the temple. The temple is not a place of presence but a place of divine attentiveness from YHWH who "dwells" in heaven. This shrewd formulation makes a momentous affirmation on behalf of the temple of Solomon, but surely less of an affirmation than his entourage might have claimed. The conclusion of this unit of text is "hear and forgive" (8:30). The articulation of the theme of forgiveness opens the text to an entirely new direction. It is most plausible that forgiveness emerges in the Old Testament as a primary theological theme in the sixth-century exile, for it is in meditation upon the guilt that produced the exile that Israel begins to ponder the conditions necessary for forgiveness, and the free gift of forgiveness from YHWH (see Jer 31:34; 33:8).[18]

There follows in 1 Kings 8:31–53 an extensive, wondrous expression of exilic theology focusing upon forgiveness. In these verses, the text enumerates a conventional
series of troubles (curses) that can come upon Israel when Israel violates covenant:
defeat and war (8:33), drought (8:35), famine, plague, blight, mildew, and locust
(8:37), reception of foreigners (8:31), risk in war (8:44), and exile ("captivity")
(8:46–53). This list is not quite symmetrical in all its parts, because verses 33 and
44 both consider "the enemy," because verses 41–43 about the foreigner are somewhat odd in this list, and because verses 46–53 on exile are disproportionately long.
Nevertheless, the pattern of each case is roughly the same, namely, the reality and
recognition of sin that has caused the trouble, the option of repentance ("turn")
along with prayer toward the temple, and the petition for forgiveness that is to
be offered by YHWH because YHWH attends to prayers that are prayed toward the
temple.

Scholars commonly judge these verses as representing a struggle with the guilt of
exile and with a theology of repentance whereby Israel's return to Torah could permit a return to the land.[19] These prayers proceed on the assumption that genuine
repentance would evoke and permit YHWH's generous forgiveness, but that divine
forgiveness has as its precondition repentance that is verbalized in prayer. The entire
transaction of repentance and forgiveness, moreover, is toward, in, and through the
temple. Thus the temple, even in ruins and even for those who understand themselves as distant from Jerusalem, continues to be the pivotal instrument for life with
YHWH.[20] This same theology of repentance, here linked to the temple of Solomon,
is also voiced in two exilic texts that now frame the older corpus of the book of
Deuteronomy:[21]

From there you will seek the Lord your God, and you will find him if you
search after him with all your heart and soul. In your distress, when all these
things have happened to you in time to come, you will *return* to the Lord your
God and heed him. Because the Lord your God is a merciful God, he will neither abandon you nor destroy you; he will not forget the covenant with your
ancestors that he swore to them. (Deut 4:29–31)

When all these things have happened to you, the blessings and the curses that
I have set before you, if you call them to mind among all the nations where
the Lord your God has driven you, and *return* to the Lord your God, and you
and your children obey him with all your heart and with all your soul, just as
I am commanding you today, then the Lord your God will restore your fortunes and have compassion on you, gathering you again from all the peoples
among whom the Lord your God has scattered you. . . . For the Lord will again

take delight in prospering you, just as he delighted in prospering your ancestors, when you obey the Lord your God by observing his commandments and
decrees that are written in this book of the law, because you *turn* to the Lord
your God with all your heart and with all your soul. (Deut 30:1–3, 9–10)

For purposes of understanding the temple built by Solomon, this unit of text makes
clear that the temple functioned, long after Solomon and long after the context and
horizon of Solomon's ideological interpreters, as a magnet for Israel's faith and for
Israel's most serious symbolization of that faith. The theological-liturgic function of
the temple, for the exiles of the sixth century, is very different from its purported
function in the tenth century. In the purported tenth century, the temple fulfilled the
function of legitimacy of high dynastic claims for what was said to be a successful
urban establishment. By contrast, in the exile what is needed is a visible, identifiable
matrix for forgiveness and reconciliation and the opportunity to return to the home-
land. In the traditioning process, it is clear that the temple is remarkably supple as
an instrument to satisfy the needs of the community. Quite clearly, the temple built
by Solomon is not held within the confines of his intended purposes but is used in
rich and imaginative ways for new needs of faith in newly emerging circumstances.
The conclusion of verse 53, for all the cosmic significance of the temple that we have
noted, celebrates the distinctiveness of Israel that is rooted in old Exodus traditions:
"For you have *separated* them from among all the peoples of the earth, to be your
heritage, just as you promised through Moses, your servant, when you brought our
ancestors out of Egypt, O Lord God" (1 Kgs 8:53). There is a touch of irony in the
claim of this verse; the imagined Solomon clearly intended the temple to serve cosmic symbolism and moved determinedly away from the particularities of Israel's
covenantal traditions. Such a development in the tradition back toward the particular in this verse attests that the temple, as a matrix of faithful imagination, would not
be held enthralled to "original intent."

In 1 Kings 8:56–61, Solomon issues a second blessing of the Lord, matched to
the blessing of the Lord in verses 15–21. In this latter case, however, the rhetoric is
thoroughly Deuteronomic, a fact indicating the way in which the temple has been
resituated, in the traditioning process, to serve the Deuteronomic shaping of the
royal narrative. The celebration of "rest" together with the "good promises" in verse
56 is reminiscent of the Deuteronomic formula of Joshua 21:43–45, on which see
also Deuteronomy 25:19. Indeed, through 1 Kings 8:56 it may be said, in royal
claim, that Solomon is indeed the giver of *shalom* on every side. Verse 57 makes an
appeal to Torah obedience that is clearly in the cadences of Deuteronomy, and verse
60 culminates with an allusion to the first commandment concerning "no other
god," a commandment that is of course linked to Moses and exodus, as in 1 Kings

8:56; see verses 21 and 53. The paragraph of the royal blessing concludes in verse 56 with yet one more appeal for Torah obedience.

It is clear from this long chapter 8 concerning the significance of the temple that Israel's traditioning process concerning Solomon is complex and disputatious. For our purposes, the wonder is that the temple of Solomon that can be the arena of vibrant pluriform traditioning, some of which, even in temple precincts, can tell profoundly against Solomon's royal ideology. As elsewhere, Solomon here is a liturgic construct to give voice to the complexities of the tradition. In this text, moreover, the temple itself is a literary construct that exhibits the complexity of the tradition, each part of which is seriously offered and each part of which merits serious interpretive tension.

The final form of the text concerning the temple is cast in the rhetoric and convictions of the Deuteronomists, in order to serve the community in its exilic or postexilic circumstance. In the midst of that traditioning process, however, it is equally clear that the Deuteronomic editors worked with extant temple materials that reflected the temple tradition common in the Near East. Frank Cross has shown the way in which the theology of Zion accomplished a compromise of common Canaanite traditions that he links to the high God "El" and the older Israelite tradition of covenant:

> In fact Israel's temple incorporated compromises between the older traditions of the league tent-shrine and the dynastic temple of Canaanite kingship. The portable Ark with its cherubim became the "centerpiece" usurping the place of the divine image of Canaanite temples. According to one tradition, the Tent of Meeting was taken up and placed in the Temple. The language of tent and temple continues to be mixed in psalms of the First Temple. The conditionality of temple and dynasty—*bêt* Yahweh and *bêt* David—persisted, albeit intermittently, until the end, thanks to the prophetic and traditional insistence that kingship was forfeited when the ancient covenant was violated, and that the temple in which Israel trusted could be destroyed as was the shrine at Shiloh.[22]

The Zion tradition that lies behind the temple and forms the royal theology of the Jerusalem dynasty has been fully explicated by Ben Ollenburger.[23] While I believe that the temple tradition and the royal tradition were more closely intertwined than Ollenburger does, we may consider his analysis of the latter: "As the dwelling-place of Yahweh, creator of the cosmic order and defender of Israel, Zion functions preeminently as a symbol of security. This component of Zion symbolism has been traditionally viewed as the predominant aspect of the Zion tradition, leading scholars to speak of the inviolability of Zion/Jerusalem. For our present purposes it is sufficient to note that the security symbolized by Zion is rooted first of all in *Yahweh's presence*."[24]

In the temple YHWH is presented as creator and defender, as patron of the city and of those who dwell therein. This claim is best known in Psalm 46, a song that confidently trusts that YHWH in the "city" will prevail against every threat of chaos:

> God is our refuge and strength,
> a very present help in trouble.
> Therefore we will not fear,
> though the earth should change,
> though the mountains shake in
> the heart of the sea;
> though its waters roar and foam,
> though the mountains tremble with its tumult.
> There is a river whose streams
> make glad the city of God,
> the holy habitation of the Most High.
> God is in the midst of the city;
> it shall not be moved;
> God will help it when the morning dawns.
> The nations are in an uproar, the kingdoms totter;
> he utters his voice, the earth melts. (Ps 46:1–6)

This temple, as the seat of the Creator God, is the theater in which the ongoing drama of struggle between God's order and the threat of chaos is enacted.[25] This has produced the scholarly hypothesis of an annual temple ritual whereby God the creator again, each year, defeats chaos and assures order, fertility, peace, and prosperity for the coming year. This hypothesis—proposed by Mowinckel, reviewed by Ollenburger, and confirmed recently by Roberts—is based on the enthronement psalms (Pss 47, 49, 96–99) that dramatically claim YHWH as king before whom the chaotic waters and the competing gods all flee in terror:[26]

> God has gone up with a shout,
> the Lord with the sound of a trumpet.
> Sing praises to God, sing praises;
> sing praises to our King, sing praises.
> For God is the king of all the earth;
> sing praises with a psalm. (Ps 47:5–7)

> Say among the nations, "The Lord is king!
> The world is firmly established;

it shall never be moved.
He will judge the peoples with equity." (Ps 96:10–13)

The Lord is King! Let the earth rejoice;
let the many coastlands be glad! (Ps 97:1)

Let the sea roar, and all that fills it;
the world and those who live in it.
Let the floods clap their hands;
let the hills sing together for joy
at the presence of the Lord, for
he is coming to judge the earth.
He will judge the world with righteousness,
and the peoples with equity. (Ps 98:7–9)

The Lord is king; let the peoples tremble!
He sits enthroned upon the
cherubim; let the earth quake!
The Lord is great in Zion;
he is exalted over all the peoples.
Let them praise your great and awesome name.
Holy is he!
Mighty King, lover of justice,
you have established equity;
you have executed justice
and righteousness in Jacob.
Extol the Lord our God;
worship at his footstool.
Holy is he! (Ps 99:1–5)

On the basis of this theological affirmation, liturgically mediated in songs sung in the temple, the temple of Solomon serves as a public assurance against chaos, an assurance that transcends the threats of history and nature and takes on ontological proportion. Thus the temple belongs, in Zion theology, to the structure of creation willed by the Creator. Consequently, the Jerusalem temple is a place of safety and well-being not subject to the vagaries of lived history.

In this theology, the key issue is *order versus chaos,* with attention to the great cosmic reality of the threat of chaos that was signaled immediately in Genesis 1:1–2. In this theology, YHWH is the creator who guarantees order and who fends off chaos. This is a remarkable theological articulation, when we remember that in 1 Kings 8:31–53 the program is one of guilt and forgiveness. Thus if we recast these accents in the phrasing of conventional Christian theology, the temple is oriented to issues of *creation*, whereas the Deuteronomic extrapolation moves the accent to *redemption*. In the final form of the text, the accent on redemption prevails, but it has not ever completely overrun the matter of *creation versus chaos*, a theme that recurs, for example, in the exilic texts of 2 Isaiah (see Isa 43:16–21; 45:18–19), and eventually in the narrative of Jesus (Mark 4:35–41).

Finally, attention may be called to the remarkable study by Fredrik Lindström of individual psalms of lament. Lindström makes a powerful case in three regards: first, the psalms of lament are spoken by those who are helpless before the power of death or chaos; second, the reason for that condition of powerlessness, it is asserted, is that YHWH has been negligent; and third, the work of such prayers, consequently, is to summon YHWH back into action on behalf of the speaker, for when YHWH takes an initiative, the powers of death and chaos will flee for they cannot withstand the reality of YHWH. Such negating powers as death and chaos only occupy the vacuum left by YHWH's absence. Most remarkably, Lindström notices that these psalms regularly are uttered with reference to the temple, for the temple is the context in which the God of order and well-being faces and overcomes the powers of death. Thus Lindström comments on Psalms 61 and 63 concerning the cruciality of the temple:

The temple is, in the capacity as the meeting place between heaven and earth, "the gateway to heaven" (Gen 28:17), a microcosmos. Here, the divine presence which fills the whole earth (Isa 6:3) is manifested. When the individual in YHWH's house seeks protection under the Divine wings (Ps 61:5b), it is with the knowledge that these wings, that is, the roof/ceiling of the temple, have a cosmological meaning in that they symbolize the protective heavenly firmament. . . . Ps 63 is an individual complaint psalm, i.e., composed in order to be used in an acute situation of danger. Its theological profile is comprised of the temple theological experience that YHWH is the power who helps the threatened individual with his protection and care. These experiences of the petitioner of the central aspects of the character and activity of the present YHWH are manifested by the temple on Zion. This symbol of the presence of God provides the individual with categories by which he can interpret the blessings and woes of life. Suffering is interpreted by this understanding of life as the withdrawal of YHWH's saving presence so that the hostile sphere is able to get the petitioner in its grasp (vv 2, 10f., 12c). The origin of the life-threatening situation even in Ps 63 remains obscure. By the meeting with YHWH's presence in the worship service, affliction is overcome (vv 3–5). Here, the sufferer is assured of being once again admitted into the life of fellowship with YHWH which he has previously experienced (vv 7–9) and which means protection from the attacks of the evil realm.[27]

This latter point concerning the temple as the venue for such personal prayer is especially important, for it attests that the great liturgic claims made for the Creator God in the temple have been transposed even into the practice of personal piety. What Zion theology and Solomon set out to do in terms of state legitimacy has also become a resource for personal faith. This development from *public liturgy* to *personal piety* indicates the way in which the temple of Solomon is a huge and dominating engine for Israel's faith and imagination. Indeed, this observation about the cruciality of the temple for personal piety suggests that, for all of the movement of Deuteronomic critique and redescription of Zion theology, Zion theology persists as a power resource in Israel into later Judaism. Indeed it is later asserted in Christian tradition:

> Our ancestors worshiped on this mountain, but you say that the place where people must worship is in Jerusalem. Jesus said to her, "Woman, believe me, the hour is coming when you will worship the Father neither on this mountain nor in Jerusalem. You worship what you do not know; we worship what we know, for salvation is from the Jews. But the hour is coming, and is now here, when the true worshipers will worship the Father in Sprit and truth, for the Father seeks such as these to worship him. God is spirit, and those who worship him must worship in spirit and truth." (John 4:20–24)

Such a twist on worship away from the temple and into "spirit and truth," however, does not in the meantime tell against the powerful resource that the temple continued to be in the ongoing tradition of Israel. It is then no wonder that Solomon is celebrated in this primary narrative of 1 Kings 3–11 principally as temple builder.

CHAPTER 6

"SOLOMON" AS WISE KING

Solomon, in the primary narrative, enjoyed a reputation as a wise king, and this aspect of his reputation became defining in the subsequent traditions. Indeed, his reputation as wise king was, in the end, more important than even his accomplishment as a temple builder. As far as the tradition is concerned, his reputation for wisdom is based on only a few texts. At the outset, Solomon is celebrated because of his request from God to be given a listening heart that is able to discern (1 Kgs 3:9), a request granted by God: "I now do according to your word. Indeed I give you a wise and discerning mind; no one like you has been before you and no one like you shall arise after you" (3:12). The key issue of wisdom for the king is to rule effectively, particularly in judicial matters, when the facts lack clarity and require imagination.[1]

The narrative of 1 Kings 3:16–28 is designed to give evidence that the king has indeed been given the wisdom he requested: "All Israel heard of the judgment that the king had rendered; and they stood in awe of the king, because they perceived that the wisdom of God was in him, to execute justice" (1 Kgs 3:28). And again, in 1 Kings 4:29, Solomon, with very great wisdom, discernment, and breadth of understanding, is championed as a great source of wisdom, wisdom so spectacular as to impress people and kings of all the nations: "People came from all the nations to hear the wisdom of Solomon; they came from all the kings of the earth who had heard of his wisdom" (4:34). Whereas the narrative of 3:16–28 impressed all Israel, Solomon's generativity in 4:29–34 in a parallel way reached beyond all Israel to all nations. (On the latter, see also 5:7, 5:12; 10:23–24.)

Again, Solomon is shown to be a wise king, illustrating the claim of 1 Kings 4:34, as he exhibits his wisdom in a breathtaking way to the Queen of Sheba in her state visit (1 Kgs 10:3–8).

Finally, we see in the concluding Deuteronomic summary of the life of Solomon that wisdom is reiterated as the hallmark of his reign (1 Kgs 11:41). In a later discussion, we will inquire whether this final verdict is in some puckish way ironic, for clearly the outcome of his reign is one of destructive foolishness. Thus all parts of the primary narrative of 1 Kings 3–11 attend to this feature of Solomon's public performance. The evidence is not extensive, but it may be taken as an epitome of how the tradition constructed and remembered Solomon.

WISDOM, THE ACCUMULATED TRADITION OF DISCERNMENT

As presented in the Old Testament and as understood by critical scholarship, wisdom is an elusive yet many-splendored phenomenon. We may, as a beginning point, characterize wisdom as *sustained critical reflection on lived experience in order to discern the hidden shape of reality that lives in, with, and under the specificities of daily life.*[2] Such a characterization proceeds on the assumption that in the very concreteness of life there is a buoyant, intractable givenness that must be honored and respected because it cannot be circumvented or outflanked. Such a characterization that asserts such givenness, moreover, stands as a warning against and critique of any surface utilitarianism, any facile technical reason, and any assumption that life in the world is infinitely supple and subject to human ingenuity. The wisdom tradition, that is, the accumulation of observations about the hidden shape of reality, understands the discernment of such shaping and compliance with such shaping to be "the path of life"; conversely, resistance to that shaping or contradiction of it is inescapably harmful and is "the way of death." Thus wisdom, the voice of the accumulated tradition of discernment, invites and warns:

> And now, my children, listen to me:
> happy are those who keep my ways.
> Hear instruction and be wise,
> and do not neglect it.
> Happy is the one who listens to me,
> watching daily at my gates,
> waiting beside my doors.
> For whoever finds me finds life
> and obtains favor from the Lord;
> but those who miss me injure themselves;
> all who hate me love death. (Prov 8:32–36)

Wisdom is not only the route to well-being. In the ancient world—in Israel as well as in its larger cultural environment—all matters are referred to God or gods, so that wisdom intrinsically has a theological reference point.[3] That is, the buoyant, intractable givenness of lived reality is the will of God, so that the pragmatic categories of wise and foolish—conformity to that buoyant, intractable givenness or resistance to it—are for the most part readily transposed into theological-ethical categories of righteous and wicked. Or as Walther Zimmerli has observed, "Wisdom thinks resolutely within the framework of the theology of creation."[4] Wisdom is sustained, critical reflection about the interconnections of various parts of creation that are willed and upheld in their patterned existence by the intent of the Creator.

Sometimes such reference of lived reality to the Creator is explicit; more often and everywhere, the connection is assumed and implied. Thus "wisdom" is an ongoing work bringing life into concrete conformity to the "really real" that is not subject to human pressure, whether that pressure takes the form of wealth, of power, or of learning. Wisdom is the ongoing awareness, applied to every sphere of life, that life comes to us and is given to us on terms other than our own. Those who yield to the way in which the Creator gives creation to us may receive life in all of its joyous abundance.

It is readily recognized, and surely assumed by scholars, that wisdom, since the beginnings of human community and human consciousness, has discerned theological reality that is intrinsic to the processes of life. The enterprise of wisdom requires neither formal learning nor any explicitly critical categories in order to reflect on the hidden, inscrutable dimensions of lived life.[5] And surely human community has always had a dimension of wonder that was rooted in daily experience but sought understanding of daily experience beyond that given in surface observation. Thus scholarship has judged that one important facet of wisdom is that given in the family, clan, or tribe, wherein the adult community nurtures and inculcates its young into the received tradition of how life works well.[6]

Such "tribal wisdom" is characteristically given in terse and pithy sayings that summarize vast amounts of observation and that in artistic articulation bespeak a dimension of hiddenness that is beyond immediate control. Thus, popularly: A bird in the hand is worth two in the bush. . . . Still water runs deep. . . . Where there's smoke there's fire. . . . He who laughs last laughs best. Such artistic articulation depends upon metaphor and characteristically voices a larger generalization that is readily understood with reference to concrete reality. Thus wisdom arises from daily interaction that in an important way is common and shared across many cultures. That is, in every culture families are concerned about the safety of children, have anxiety about sexuality, worry about money, and want their children to know that life is not—to use a metaphor—"a piece of cake." Because the experiences that lie behind such observations are common, scholars have been able to notice the ways in which tribal wisdom, reflected in the book of Proverbs, has important parallels in other cultural communities, as, for example, in African tribal communities.[7] In each culture there is something of a particular reference, but "the things that make for peace" (Luke 19:42) do not vary and are everywhere the same. To be sure, Israelite wisdom was particularly attentive to Israel's peculiar life, history, and culture and surely was impacted by the Yahwistic claims of Israel's faith.[8] Nonetheless, the teaching given in Israel is a common one found elsewhere as well. Thus Erhard Gerstenberger could suggest that Proverbs 3:7 functions as a "motto" for clan wisdom: "Do not be wise in your own eyes; / fear the Lord, and turn away from evil" (Prov 3:7).[9]

Except for the citation of YHWH, the same motto could be offered everywhere, for it warns against autonomy, it refers to life beyond the child being instructed, and it testifies to the risks of what the community defines as evil. No doubt such teaching in Israel was old and deep long before Solomon and the rise of the monarchy.

DEVELOPMENT OF AN INTELLECTUAL TRADITION OF WISDOM

In addition to the wisdom of family, clan, and tribe, there is a second broadly based wisdom tradition that is more urbane, self-aware, and intellectually disciplined. This is the critical tradition that was based in urban communities, linked to the great centers of political power, often tied to the crown, and likely situated in schools that instructed well-connected young people. We have available an extensive corpus of such wisdom teaching that clearly was international in scope, the development and sponsorship of which no doubt represented an important cultural achievement.

It is fair to assume that the propagators of such elite practices of wisdom—not unlike modern, state-sponsored universities—had arrived at the awareness that "knowledge is power." For that reason, great urban centers of power already in the Late Bronze Period were committed to the collating of traditions of cultural learning and perhaps, in limited ways, to the production of new learning. Again, we may recognize that this collection and production of knowledge was international in scope and not tied to any particular community. Indeed, we may imagine that the practitioners of such cultural activity knew each other across national and ethnic boundaries, perhaps exchanged data and learned from each other.

As royal administration grew increasingly complex, a competent and skilled bureaucracy was needed to manage affairs of state.[10] Such officials, moreover, had not only to know the particular skills of their respective tasks but had to be competent in the ways of power as well. This latter awareness meant, among other things, a sustained awareness of the possibilities and limits of power. Because such concentrations of power aim at continuity, there was an immediate need to assure, in each subsequent generation, a rising class of the competent. Thus it is plausible that the court sponsored schools to educate the sons of the urban elite in power, and quite clearly, power in sapiential traditions is much more subtle and complex than the simple conviction that "might makes right."

A useful analogue on this theme of nurture to power is the book *The Wise Men* by Isaacson and Thomas.[11] The book traces the management of U.S. foreign policy over several generations, featuring six stars of the system who were skillfully and commonly "wise" in the ways of the world. The culmination of the book, perhaps not unlike the culmination of the wisdom of Solomon, ends in the debacle of war policies in Vietnam, policies that turned out to be exercises in foolishness, as though nothing wise had ever been learned.[12]

There is no doubt that the wisdom of family, clan, and tribe was transmitted orally, for such social groups are inevitably oral cultures. The great states, however, moved from oral to written discourse, a practice needed for administrative complexity and for institutional continuity.[13] The officials who managed the written processes —urban writing largely being a monopoly of the state—were the scribes. The scribes, skilled in writing, kept the records (scrolls) that gave established power a settled memory.[14] It is entirely likely that in the environment of the state, those we refer to as wise men were the scribes, the ones who perhaps generated wisdom insight but who certainly collected and organized the tradition of learning upon which the management of power depended. Thus it is plausible, but cannot be demonstrated, that the state provided the matrix in which an intellectual tradition could be fostered and practiced.[15] This tradition was surely aimed at the management of power, but at its best it understood that power is immensely complex and has intractable limits.

Such intellectual enterprises reiterated old learnings, consolidated them, and added to them. Thus it is likely that one of the features of such urban wisdom traditions was the gathering together of older wisdom teaching and communal lore. Perhaps this matter of collation is not unlike the current practices of charitable foundations—funding arrangements designed to benefit through tax advantage the well-connected urban elite—to fund projects of collection, consolidation, and organization of folklore of subcultures of the past, particularly with a contemporary accent on African American lore.[16]

Insofar as knowledge is power, the organization of all available knowledge in encyclopedic fashion is an epistemological function of political totalism. As the state seeks to have a monopoly on violence, so the state might also seek a monopoly on knowledge, on everything known about the true shape of reality. The wisdom teachers had a capacity for and interest in such comprehensiveness. Perhaps two current forms of such totalism include government intelligence communities that clearly proceed on the conviction that knowledge is power, and the funding of research by large corporations, often by the government, in the interest of developing military capacity. There is no doubt that such collation and production has an immediate pragmatic intent. The trick, often not executed, is to pursue such pragmatic intent while at the same time remembering that true wisdom consists not of sheer utilitarianism; true wisdom pauses before mysteries that are beyond human control.

A contemporary example of the juggling of the mysterious with a utilitarian agenda may be that of the academically and politically inclined children and grandchildren of Leo Strauss, the great Jewish intellectual at the University of Chicago, who have mobilized his intellectual tradition and teachings in the service of neoconservative ideology—except that Strauss's daughter has attested that Strauss himself had no interest in such neoconservatism per se.[17] The case of Strauss is a good example of how a wisdom teacher can be ill-used by his students in a way that betrays his enterprise of discernment.

Insofar as the state can sponsor an intellectual tradition of scribes and courtiers who organize all that is known, there is no need, surely, that such learning should be immediately and flatly practical. Thus it is clear that the sapiential tradition rooted in urban culture had enough freedom and leisure to develop in artistic and intellectual ways beyond the pragmatic. We are able to identify wisdom teaching in Proverbs 1–9, for example, that is sophisticated and to some extent speculative, without pressure to produce immediate behavioral instruction. The learned tradition of wisdom could move away from observed particularities to more general, almost lyrical affirmations, as, for example:

> The Lord by wisdom founded the earth;
> by understanding he established the heavens;
> by his knowledge the deeps broke open,
> and the clouds drop down the dew. (Prov 3:19–20)

Characteristically there is nothing that is particularly Israelite in such teaching and reflection, except for the naming of the deity that in every culture including Israel would have been specific. Those who value and preserve such teaching are clearly urbane in their thought, making them citizens of the larger world of mystery and responsibility that takes delight in playful human thought and that walks around the edges of the truth ordained in the fabric of the world.

It is clear on all counts that urbane wisdom is quite distinct from the old lore of clan wisdom, and surely reflects an environment of power, ease, security, and leisure. The critical reflection of urbane wisdom both arises from and contributes to the wonder of the urban achievement. For all of that, however, we may ask about the relationship of court and school wisdom situated among urban elites to the long-standing wisdom of clan and tribe. The connection between the two is not obvious.

There is no doubt that *tribal wisdom* on the one hand and the *wisdom of the school and court* on the other are very different. The school and court were preoccupied with the management of power and the capacity to "master" and to dominate amid the vagaries and intrigues of big-time politics. The wisdom of the tribe did not think so ambitiously about power and control, but more modestly about staying out of harm's way. The horizon of concern is no doubt very different; however, both trajectories were engaged in critical reflection. Both invited a kind of reflective distance so that practitioners of wisdom could stand back enough to observe what was happening and critique their own participation in it. Both enterprises focused on what is human and what is mysterious in the very midst of what is human. Both had the practical aim of giving some control over what is hidden in life. And both, in the end, referred that hiddenness beyond self to the God who hides God's self in the particulars of creation. Both traditions understood that wisdom consists of attending to that which is hidden; in the very act of knowing what is hidden, moreover, what matters most remains inaccessible. Thus:

> It is the glory of God to conceal things,
> but the glory of kings is to search things out.
> Like the heavens for heights, like the earth for depth,
> so the mind of kings is unsearchable. (Prov 25:2–3)

> But where shall wisdom be found?
> And where is the place of understanding?
> Mortals do not know the way to it,
> and it is not found in the land of the living. (Job 28:12–13)

The enterprise of wisdom does not reach a conclusion in either clan or court. It is an enterprise of critical reflection that is always under way, always processing the new data of lived life, and always referring what is known, long known, and newly known to the God of all wisdom. The aim is knowledge as power; but the decisive point of sapiential knowledge is to know that wisdom is incomplete and power is penultimate. The wisdom traditions always seek to complete the incomplete and to push the penultimate toward ultimacy; the discerning wisdom teachers know that that must be their goal and yet they cannot succeed. What a marvel that in every human community, and in every powerful court in the ancient world, there were those who made the sustained effort to know better. The God of wisdom is the God who occupies all that is experienced and observed and is governor and giver of life, who stands as limit and curb at the edges of human ambition and autonomy.[18] The wise know about God at the center and at the edge, and keep up the process of probing rigorously and vigorously, but at best not arrogantly.

THE RELATIONSHIP OF POWER TO WISDOM

All of this enterprise of *power via knowledge* was long established in the ancient Near East before Solomon. There were serious sages of local reputation known in many Israelite villages from the earliest days. And surely every family and clan devised aphorisms by which to inculcate their young into their vision and practice of the world. There was, moreover, a long collection of international reflection long before Solomon, pondering the burden and limit of power. Solomon is born to power and born to the chance for wisdom.[19] Our narrative exhibits the way he received his inheritance of power and pursued his chance for wisdom. The Solomon given us in the narrative needs a large stage for the enactment of power, he being no longer content with the hill country tribal community that adored his father, David. Indeed, it is plausible that the life-or-death contest of 1 Kings 1 aligning Solomon against the old order in Israel is a harbinger of the large vista of power and prestige that Solomon will pursue. The initial mention of Pharaoh's daughter in 1 Kings 3:1, moreover, indicates the horizon of the narrative and of Solomon for which the narrative will vouch. Solomon is said to participate in the international arena, and one marker of that international community is the practice of wisdom that transcended every ethnic or local context. Thus behind Solomon is the well-developed sapiential lore of Egypt and Mesopotamia, the world in which Solomon will eagerly participate.

One decisive feature of this intellectual inheritance that must have been to the liking of Solomon is that even in Israel this intellectual inheritance bore few of the marks of Israelite faith or tradition. Clearly if Solomon is to be among "the great ones of the earth," he cannot linger too long over the specificities of the old covenantal community of Israel. Thus an embrace of wisdom is in part an emancipation from local conditions, an act that is parallel to the resituating of the old tribal ark in the cosmically oriented symbolization of the temple. As a result, the wisdom tradition, even in Israel, lacked the old categories of promise and covenant and spoke not at all about God's miraculous interventions in the life of the world. Thus the urbane practice of wisdom here supersedes the primitiveness of old tradition. As a consequence Solomon would seem to be presented as a key figure in the transition of the community of Israel from the primitive to the urbane. The theme of Solomonic wisdom is announced in the dream narrative of 1 Kings 3:3–15, although the entry of Solomon into international scope is already signaled in verse 1 with reference to Pharaoh's daughter. In the dream narrative, a characteristic way of establishing legitimacy and divine approval, Solomon evidences his resolve to be a good king by his simple request in 1 Kings 3:9: "Give your servant therefore an understanding mind to govern your people, able to discern between good and evil; for who can govern this your great people?"

The petition is from "your servant," an address of submissive deference. The request of a "discerning mind" in Hebrew is "listening heart," in order to perform juridical functions properly and responsibly. In that ancient world as in many preindustrial societies, a key feature of leadership is to sort out disputes in the constituency.[20] Thus the focus is upon juridical function, and that in a society that perhaps lacked well-developed rules of evidence and procedure but relied on an authorized capacity to do "what is best for all parties." Short of rules of evidence and procedure, such juridical performance depended upon the intuition and imagination to go beneath the surface of disputatious claims in order to render healthy, community-enhancing decisions. The accent upon the judicial function of the king is indicated in the double use of the verb "judge" (spt) that requires a capacity for discernment of good and evil, that is, right and wrong or justice and injustice, word pairs that bespeak life-producing or death-dealing decisions.

The selfless petition of Solomon in 1 Kings 3:9 is granted in quite parallel language by YHWH in verses 11–12: "God said to him, 'Because you have asked this, and have not asked for yourself long life or riches, or for the life of your enemies, but have asked for yourself understanding to discern what is right, I now do according to your word. Indeed I give you a wise and discerning mind; no one like you has been before you and no one like you shall arise after you.'"

Interestingly, the word in 1 Kings 3:11 rendered "discern" is a translation of "shema'," to listen, thus to "hear justice." The verb thus is reiterated from the petition of verse 9, "listening heart." It is remarkable that the phrase is not "to speak justice" or "do justice," but instead to "hear justice," suggesting that justice is not in the verdict or in the imagination of the king but is intrinsic to the case itself, if only the king listens well enough to hear and receive the proper ruling. In verse 12 Solomon is granted the "heart" he requested in verse 9; the term in both cases is rendered "mind." Both uses understand the heart to be the decision-making organ of human rationality. The request is a heart to "hear." The gift from God is a heart "wise and discerning" (hkm wenabōn), thus a double usage that reinforces the term "discern" (bin) used in the request. The word pair "wise and discerning" is variously arranged in a number of texts concerning responsible public conduct:

> Wisdom is at home in the mind
> of one who has understanding
> but it is not known in the heart of fools. (Prov 14:33)

The word pair characterizes Joseph as an able and competent administrator for Pharaoh: "Now therefore let Pharaoh select a man who is discerning and wise, and set him over the land of Egypt. . . . So Pharaoh said to Joseph, 'Since God has shown you all this, there is no one so discerning and wise as you'" (Gen 41:33, 39). The same word pair, moreover, is used both to characterize the people Israel who attend to Torah and the judicial officers whom Moses will appoint:

> You must observe them diligently, for this will show your wisdom and discernment to the peoples, who, when they hear all these statutes, will say, "Surely this great nation is a wise and discerning people!" (Deut 4:6)

> Choose for each of your tribes individuals who are wise, discerning, and reputable to be your leaders. (Deut 1:13)

In the latter uses, the phrasing is eventually linked to adherence to Torah; in the Genesis narrative, however, the phrase refers to a much more pragmatic, generic capacity to govern. Thus it is plausible that the phrasing in the narrative of Solomon leaves open the play between generic capacity for governance and an Israelite attentiveness to Torah, exactly the kind of play that pervades the narrative of Solomon. The formula of incomparability concerning Solomon in 1 Kings 3:12 ("no one like you has been before you and no one like you shall arise after you") is an exercise in rhetoric that intends to establish Solomon as the most characteristic and celebrated model of wisdom that partakes both of Israel's traditional commitments and the generic wisdom of international culture. The formula of incomparability in verse 12 is not unlike that employed for Moses (Deut 34:10), for Josiah (2 Kgs 23–25), and, in a less developed way, for Joshua (Deut 11:25; Josh 1–5). We recognize Deuteronomic influence in this element of the dream narrative. We may notice, moreover, the way in which wisdom and Torah are linked in Deuteronomic rhetoric: "You must observe them diligently, for this will show your wisdom and discernment to the peoples, who, when they hear all these statutes, will say, 'Surely this great nation is a wise and discerning people!' For what other great nation has a god so near to it as the Lord our God is whenever we call to him? And what other great nation has statutes and ordinances as just as this entire law that I am setting before you today?" (Deut 4:6–8).

The Torah connection is less explicit in the Solomonic formulation but surely never far from the horizon of the narrative. Thus on all counts Solomon is equipped and authorized to be the quintessential ruler, endowed by YHWH with a capacity to hear and, consequently, to do what is best. The defining adjective twice used (*shema'*: understanding, 1 Kgs 3:9; wise and discerning, 3:11) makes clear that Solomon is not autonomous, nor left to his own devices, nor free to enact his own imagination, but is bound to the reality of lived life wherein YHWH's resolve for justice is concretely at work and evident to those who are able to discern. It is worth noting that in the divine response of 1 Kings 3:11, unlike the royal petition of verse 9, the term *"miōpaṭ"* is used. The goal of royal judicial activity is *miōpaṭ*, a term that refers to the initiation and maintenance of well-being by the community on behalf of all of its members, without excessive respect for power or wealth. The same word, twice used, becomes a tag word for Torah adjudication in the tradition of Deuteronomy: "You must not distort *justice;* you must not show partiality; and you must not accept bribes, for a bribe blinds the eyes of the wise and subverts the cause of those who are in the right. *Justice,* and only *justice,* you shall pursue, so that you may live and occupy the land that the Lord your God is giving you" (Deut 16:19–20).

The rhetoric of the dream narrative situates Solomon in the company of such traditions of wisdom that through just administration may produce a community of life-giving, life-sustaining environment for all.

The dream narrative of 1 Kings 3:3–15 is followed immediately by the narrative of 3:16–28, the only specific case reporting the concrete judicial activity of Solomon. There can be little doubt that this narrative, certainly rooted in folklore that models "case rulings," is placed as it is to attest in concrete ways that Solomon did indeed receive the promised gift from YHWH of a wise and discerning heart, and that the king is able to act on such a heart. It is clear that the outcome of this narrative is made possible by shrewdness that goes beyond the hard evidence that the case itself offers.

The case presented to the king in 1 Kings 3:16–22 is a dispute concerning an alleged switching of babies of two prostitutes. It is clear that the case presented to the king boils down to "she said . . . she said," and offers no evidentiary grounds for a decision. The king observed that one mother was saying, "This is my son that is alive, and your son is dead," while the other mother was saying, "Not so! Your son is dead, and my son is the living one" (1 Kgs 3:23). The response of Solomon to the problematic case exhibits enormous freedom and cleverness on the part of the king as the supreme judicial officer of the realm. Solomon introduces a high-risk ploy in order to educe more evidence, because the initial evidence is inadequate. Obviously the king's ploy in verse 24 is designed to break the inadequate dispute of "she said . . . she said" and to force the case into a more telling condition: "So the king said, 'Bring me a sword,' and they brought a sword before the king" (3:24). The ploy works. The two alleged mothers respond quite differently to the king and the case is resolved because the real mother—unlike the other woman—responds as one would expect "because compassion for her son burned with her" (3:26). The hard-nosed royal proposal was designed to evoke maternal compassion, although the reader might not have expected the nonmother to be so completely indifferent and void of passion for the child.[21]

The wisdom of Solomon is exhibited because the king had the imagination to probe beneath the facts of the case and to insist that motherly compassion be the ground of the verdict, a ground not suggested in the initial presentation of the case. The new feature that the king introduces into the case is the deep, passionate commitment that a mother has to a child (a son in this case) that wills the well-being of the son no matter what. If we understand wisdom as the deposit of insight accumulated over time from many observations, we may take it that mother love is an observed phenomenon (see Hos 1:6–7; 2:6, 25; Isa 49:15; Jer 31:20).[22] This passion (compassion) of the mother is of course attested in every society, and in the Old Testament in every kind of literature. While it is not distinctive to the wisdom sayings of the book of Proverbs, we may particularly notice Proverbs 17:12: "Better to meet a she-bear robbed of its cubs / than to confront a fool immersed in folly." The foolishness of the fool is said to be even more dangerous than the threat of a she-bear separated from her cubs. Used as a norm for the assessment of foolishness, the proverb recognizes the profound attachment of bear to cub, that is, mother to child.

The narrative of Solomon's judicial wisdom is indeed terse. It is clear, nonetheless, that the king has resources for this case in what must have been consensus teaching in the sapiential tradition about motherly attachment to child. It required no special royal wisdom to recognize that reality, for everyone no doubt recognized it. The wisdom of the king, rather, is that the king "stepped out of the box" and brought a new, imaginative insight to the case, after which resolution of the case was obvious; the nonmother exhibited no such attachment to the child and so her claim was dismissed by the king.[23] The practice of imagination in judicial ruling, so crucial and so readily evident in this case, is particularly appreciated by Martha Nussbaum in her study of judicial imagination.[24] Anthony Amsterdam and Jerome Bruner, moreover, have shown the way in which *judicial norm* and *innovative imagination* are both required for the sake of wise governance.[25] Solomon did indeed "discern" beyond the facts of the case, a capacity here taken to be a gift from YHWH. The conclusion of the case is a simple, obvious, uncontested verdict: "She is his mother" (1 Kgs 3:27).[26]

It is no surprise that the narrative concludes with a report on the public response of awe (fear; *yr'*) at the king's ruling. The case is narrated in order to verify the king's peculiar capacity for governance, a verification that is universally embraced in Israel. Public response, moreover, credits the wisdom of Solomon as a gift of God. This verdict twice uses the term "justice" (*miōpaṭ*), with the verb "judge" (*ōpṭ*) used one time. The first usage of *miōpaṭ* perhaps refers simply to royal procedure. The second use, however, as the last word in the narrative, goes much further to connect *divine wisdom* with *human justice,* that is, the enactment of fairness and equity in ways that enhance the community. In this case, there is no doubt that Solomon can be relied upon to serve the good of the realm, to utilize his peculiar gift from God for the sake of the entire realm. In this case, a prostitute received a cunning royal ruling that assured her right, which confirmed her role as mother. No wonder Israel is in awe.

In 1 Kings 4:29–34 (Heb 5:9–14), yet another text concerning royal wisdom, we are in a very different world, the world of international learning and prestige.[27] This unit of the text begins in 4:29 with a general affirmation not unlike that seen in 1 Kings 3:9, 3:12, and 3:28. Only here, the claim is much greater, consisting of three terms all of which we have heard before: *wisdom, discernment*—modified by the strong adverb "very great," and *listening heart,* a phrase echoing 3:9. Thus the text self-consciously appeals to the dream narrative and the divine gift of chapter 3. The three terms, moreover, are reinforced with the concluding formula "as vast as the sand on the seashore," that is, inestimable in scope. That much of this new narrative episode squares with chapter 3.

But then, in 1 Kings 4:30–31, the narrative report claims much more: On the one hand, the wisdom of Solomon is greater than that from "the east," the location of old inscrutable wisdom.[28] On the other hand, Solomon is wiser than Egyptian wisdom, a great deal of which is known in preserved texts. The references to "east" and "Egypt" intend to encompass the entire world of learning that was on the horizon of the narrative. Verse 31, moreover, moves from the general to the particular and identifies well-known wisdom teachers who had international reputations; thus the reputation of Solomon as a wise king was established in international scope that made him the most learned and most discerning of all public figures. In this report Solomon is not content any longer simply to dazzle Israel, as he was in 3:28; his royal ambition causes him to compete in the Olympic games of discernment, and even there he is a winner. It is clear that Solomon, in this presentation, has moved Israel and the Jerusalem court into big-time play. Perhaps the mention of the Pharaoh's daughter that was noted above is a harbinger of the scope of both Solomon's ambition and his achievement. In this telling there is little left of the old tribal alliance that constituted the covenantal community even of his father, David. Clearly Solomon now is operating in a very different, much more demanding intellectual and artistic arena.

The ground of Solomon's reputation is that the king is said to be enormously imaginative and energetic in the production of proverbs and songs, thus possessing not only insight (as in 1 Kgs 3:16–28) but also an artistic flair for aesthetic utterance. Since we are dealing with Solomon of an exaggerated reputation and not simply Solomon, we do not ponder the implausibility of a king who could formulate so many wise sayings. If, however, we wanted to understand this claim historically in the tenth century—which I do not suggest—one might imagine that the royal court was an arena for sapiential activity, with the king as patron while recognized teachers in the court collected and collated international lore and learning. Gerhard von Rad, two generations ago, proposed a "Solomonic Enlightenment" that he likened to the great eighteenth-century European Enlightenment of "man come of age" as the manager of his own destiny.[29] There is now a consensus that such a claimed tenth-century achievement is not historically credible.[30] If, however, we take Solomon as an imagined figure, then the narrative claim of this text shows Israel, albeit in a later time, imagining Solomon with such an intellectual achievement. In that construal, through its king Israel is able to compete with the great courts of the ancient Near East and need not rely upon or appeal only to the remembered revelation of Mount Sinai.

The subject of such proverbs and songs is what von Rad termed "natural science," whereby observations from "nature" are collected, collated, and organized to provide an encyclopedic grasp of all available knowledge:

We can see the same process in the sphere of "natural science." If we read, for example, concerning the bee, a particularly insignificant winged creature, that we have to thank her for one of the most wonderful things (Sir. II.3), then this is simply the stating of an astonishing fact and contains no moral appeal. Alongside such unpretentious sentences, one can at once place the magnificent animal descriptions in the divine speech in the book of Job, for the difference here is only in the more ambitious, artistic presentation. We select from the available material (ostrich, Job 39.13–18; horse, Job 39.19–22; crocodile, Job 40.25–41.26) the description of the hippopotamus.

> See the hippopotamus beside you.
> He eats grass like an ox.
> See his strength in his loins
> and his power in the muscles of his body.
> He lets his tail hang down like a cedar;
> the sinews of his thighs are firmly knit together.
> His bones are tubes of bronze,
> his loins are bars of iron.
> He is the first of the works of God,
> "made to have dominion over his fellows."
> For the mountains provide wood for him,
> and all the wild beasts play there.
> He hides under lotus bushes,
> in the covert of reed and marsh.
> The lotus bushes cover him with their shade,
> and the poplars by the stream surround him.
> Even when the stream rushes, he is not afraid,
> he remains calm even when Jordan flows into his mouth.
> "Who" could grasp at his eyes
> or pierce his nose in the snare? (Job 40.15–24)

As a result of its insertion into the divine speech, this passage has been placed in a definite theological light. If one removes it from this particular theological shadow, it at once becomes clear that in its original form it never gave expression to anything religious or to any moral interest. References to the animal as a model for specific human virtues—that universally acknowledged requirement of moral instruction—had a part to play in education in Israel, too, but above all in that of ancient Egypt ("Go to the ant, you sluggard. . . ," Prov. 6.6ff.). In ancient Babylon, too, there were detailed descriptions of animals and their parts. There, however, they belonged to sacral literature and

served the science of prognostication. How different the biblical animal descriptions are! In them the concern is only with the description of the phenomenon itself and with its peculiarity. In this attitude towards a part of man's
puzzling environment, in this concentration on the phenomenon itself without immediately referring it to man and his world, one can see a specific characteristic of ancient Israel's knowledge of the world, for Egyptian wisdom did
not know animal descriptions of this type with no moral aim.[31]

Von Rad also suggested that the speeches of God in the whirlwind of Job 38–41 evidence the same kind of comprehensive ordering of knowledge.[32]

The text in 1 Kings 4 goes on to specify that this new body of learning, grounded
in concrete observation, includes conclusions gathered about trees, animals, birds,
reptiles, and fish, that is, all creatures that inhabit God's creation. The detail of poetic
description of Behemoth (Job 40:15–24) and Leviathan (41:1–34) are perhaps
examples of such careful observation. Perhaps in our contemporary world we may
think of studies like those of Annie Dillard's *Pilgrim at Tinker Creek* or, more broadly,
the work of John Muir as examples of the world observed with some reference to
faith.[33] Such works are not quite "scientific" in a proper sense, but they are respectful of the modes of knowledge that are geared to disciplined, cumulative observation. Taken theologically, this enterprise of collected observation is a study of
creation and all of its creatures, perhaps with an implied acknowledgment of the
Creator that need not in every case be explicit.[34] Clearly, the enterprise credited to
Solomon moves beyond "historical miracles" that have so preoccupied Old Testament scholarship, and beyond the tricky concrete cases of judicial contestation such
as the one narrated in 1 Kings 3:16–28. The vast enterprise of comprehending all of
creation leads to a conclusion in 1 Kings 4:34 that Solomon's reputation was gladly
international: "People came from all the nations to hear the wisdom of Solomon;
they came from all the kings of the earth who had heard of his wisdom." It is worth
noting that the two narrative verdicts in 3:28 and 4:34 both concern the wisdom of
Solomon. The conclusion in 3:28, on the one hand, concerns "all Israel" and "justice." The conclusion in 4:34 concerns people of "all the nations" and "all the kings
of the earth" and the comprehension of all creation. The two verdicts together nicely
voice the ambiguity concerning Solomon that pervades the narrative, namely, the
extent to which Solomon remains rooted in Israel's concrete traditions and the ways
in which Solomon is by ambition, achievement, and reputation well beyond these
traditions, perhaps indifferent to them, perhaps alienated from them.

The pressure of interpretation pushes Solomon and his reputation for wisdom
always in the direction of the international. Thus in 1 Kings 5:7 and 5:12, Solomon's
wisdom is recognized by his ally Hiram. In 1 Kings 10:23–24, moreover, Solomon's

reputation for "wisdom and riches" is known in "the whole earth." In this usage, the notion of wisdom is not explicated. It is clear that these verses intend to relate to the dream narrative of chapter 3, for in 3:12–13 the king is granted not only the wisdom for which he had asked but "riches and honor" for which he did not ask. The international reputation of his wisdom in 10:24, moreover, recognizes his wisdom as a gift from God: "The whole earth sought the presence of Solomon to hear his wisdom, which God had put into his mind" (1 Kgs 10:24). Because wisdom is here linked to riches and because verse 25 is focused on riches, we are likely to take wisdom as an acknowledgement of Solomon's skill in statecraft and his competence in economics. Clearly this reputation is not grounded in judicial discernment (as in 3:16–28) nor in the collection of lore (4:29–34). Thus we may take wisdom in this international scope to consist of success, which in the characteristic phrasing of diplomatic language is linked to piety of a generic kind. The truth for all to see is that Solomon makes it work.

The test case for the international reputation of the king identified in 1 Kings 4:34 and 10:23–24 is the specific narrative encounter with the Queen of Sheba in 10:1–13. This narrative, like that of 3:16–28, is marked by folklore elements; it features a great economic summit between Solomon, like whom there is no other in the political world of that time, and the Queen of Sheba, apparently understood to be the counterpart of Solomon and his rival in the great and inscrutable economy to the south. The queen herself is a very great lady with a great retinue, loaded with precious goods, no doubt brought in order to exhibit her wealth and success and to put the Jerusalem king on notice that she is no second-rate player in this drama.

Despite her success and posturing, however, Solomon more than lived up to his reputation. Quite literally, the king took her breath (rûaḥ) away (1 Kgs 10:5). He took her breath away by "all the wisdom," by his house (that is, the royal foundation in Jerusalem, on which see 7:1–12), by his extravagant table (see 4:22–23 [Heb 5:2–3]), and by his many burnt offerings (10:4–5). It is clear that Solomon's wisdom, like Solomon's temple piety, is now a function of the state in which neither wisdom nor piety counts in itself for anything; they are simply components of a general reputation whereby this queen and any other competitor must be impressed. The very appreciation of wisdom in this list of impressive qualities has the effect of reducing the importance of wisdom per se, for now it is simply a mark of generic royal achievement. One can imagine at such a summit meeting not only the exchange of gifts but perhaps artistic and intellectual performances by star performers as well, for in fact staged summit meetings are rarely for the conduct of business but are instead a political apparatus for exhibition and mutual admiration. Such was this meeting.

The response to the queen's loss of breath is in two parts. First, the queen speaks (1 Kgs 10:6–9). In the speech that tradition places in her mouth, the queen from the

South concedes everything to Solomon and is presented as an awestruck subordinate sovereign, thus furthering Solomon's capacity to surpass all others. She connects Solomon's wisdom to his prosperity (ṭov), suggesting that his wisdom here is his capacity to manage the state economy well.

The remainder of the speech of commendation of the queen is a complex, perhaps ironic, statement in two parts. First, in 1 Kings 10:8, in a twofold statement, the queen recognizes that those around Solomon are happy, that is, fortunate. The political-economic system is working for them. The text, though, poses an interesting problem. In Hebrew, the twofold "happy" formula in verse 8 offers two synonymous statements—"happy are your men, happy are your servants"—in both cases referring to those who are close to Solomon in court and who participate in his achievements and benefits. Other versions followed by the NRSV, however, take the first "happy" formula to refer to wives, thus alluding to Solomon's network of seven hundred political marriages, including one to Pharaoh's daughter (see 1 Kgs 11:3). (In Hebrew the terms for "men" and for "wives" vary by only one letter; thus it is easy to see how there may be confusion on this point.) Either way, the double formula alludes to the close entourage of the king, thus a statement that lacks any larger social vision.

But then, such extravagant formulae are not unfamiliar in contemporary public life. With the recurring economic summits of the Group of Seven and the International Monetary Fund and the World Bank, we are regularly reminded that the horizon of such summit meetings is characteristically limited to those with economic access, accompanied by systemic disregard of those beyond the pale of such access. Thus it is not surprising that the queen limits her commendation to those who cluster around the royal apparatus and totally disregards any others. The statement of the queen is a credible one, albeit a quite parochial one. The term "blessed" ('ashrê) here need imply no intentional theological dimension but refers in the first instant to "good luck." And indeed, the prosperous most often tend not to notice the mechanisms that provide affluence, but innocently celebrate "good fortune."

Having read the queen's statement in 1 Kings 10:8, perhaps innocent or perhaps ironic, we are quickly jolted by a formally parallel statement in verse 9: "Blessed be the Lord your God, who has delighted in you and set you on the throne of Israel! Because the Lord loved Israel forever, he has made you king to execute justice and righteousness" (1 Kgs 10:9). This most remarkable statement makes a theological accent that is rare in the world of Solomonic discourse. The word "bless" is an acutely theological word that is characteristic in Israel's prayer and here constitutes an act of praise toward YHWH. The term "blessed be" (brk) is rhetorically in parallel to 'ashrê (happy), which can also be rendered as "blessed" as in Psalm 1:1. The term "brk," however, is frontally theological, whereas 'ashrê is much more utilitarian.

Thus the speech of the queen shifts, in moving to 1 Kings 10:9, from a pragmatic observation to a theological affirmation. The statement of the queen affirms that Solomon has the throne as a gift from YHWH. The statement of the queen, moreover, grounds the gift of royal governance in terms of YHWH's abiding commitment ("love") toward Israel; note well that YHWH's love is toward Israel and not toward Solomon as it was voiced in 2 Samuel 12:24, nor toward David nor toward David's family nor toward Zion or Jerusalem . . . but toward Israel (see by contrast Ps 78:68). Thus grounding for the doxological statement of the queen in 1 Kings 10:9 is in the traditions that are antecedent to the Davidic monarchy; we may imagine a rootage in the old covenantal memories of Moses in the Sinai. The purpose of Solomon's rule, as articulated by the queen, is justice and righteousness, a common word pair in Israel's faith but not elsewhere used of Solomon. That word pair, familiar in prophetic rhetoric (see Amos 5:7, 24; 6:12; Isa 5:7; Jer 22:3), bespeaks a covenantal ethic of distributive justice whereby the resources of the community are mobilized on behalf of all its members, most particularly the needy and the marginalized.

This is an astonishing utterance by a Gentile queen, of which we may make three observations. First, the speech of the queen is freighted with Israel's most distinctive covenantal cadences, with particular reference to YHWH, the God of Israel. It is remarkable that this splendid piece of Israelite rhetoric is placed on the lips of the Gentile queen, as though the foreign queen must instruct the Israelite king in his covenantal obligations. That the queen knows of this royal responsibility may suggest, as John Barton has noted, the awareness that some semblance of "natural law" is operative in the Old Testament; consequently, even outsiders to the revelation of Sinai know something of the requirements of the Creator God.[35] Second, taken in sum it is clear that this mandate of "justice and righteousness" is fundamentally alien to the reign of Solomon. To be sure, in 1 Kings 3:16–28 Solomon did rule in a way to "execute justice" (see 1 Kgs 3:28). That episode, however, is an exception to the larger presentation of Solomon. Third, it seems evident that this advocacy of justice and righteousness, introduced by *brk* and with explicit reference to YHWH, is in deep tension with verse 8 and its celebration of the royal apparatus, wives, and courtiers. Thus on all counts this utterance of the queen is remarkable and, in a subtle way, provides a judgment upon Solomon, whose regime delivered wealth and prestige, largely to the neglect of justice and righteousness. This verse, moreover, occurs in an episode that celebrates Solomon's achievements, and thus it is a daring rhetorical maneuver of narrative irony.

After the extended speech of the queen whereby the king is subtly recalled to his proper royal burden, the queen showers the Jerusalem king with extravagant gifts, thus acknowledging his primacy and apparently indicating her readiness to sign trade agreements: "Then she gave the king one hundred twenty talents of gold, a great quantity of spices, and precious stones; never again did spices come in such quantity as that which the queen of Sheba gave to King Solomon" (1 Kgs 10:10). This verse evokes from the narrators a parallel act of commercial extravagance from Solomon's northern neighbor, Hiram the Phoenician (10:11–12), after which the encounter with the queen ends with her departure (10:13). This particular episode, asserting Solomon's preeminence in the world of international commerce, has an echo in the notation of 10:23–25. As with the Queen of Sheba, Solomon is favorably compared to "all the kings of the earth," so that "the whole earth" is drawn to his wisdom. Thus the notation twice alludes to Solomon's wisdom. This notation, however, not unlike verses 10 and 11–12, tails off into wealth and opulence, suggesting that Solomon's attraction among the nations is his enormous economic success: "Every one of them brought a present, objects of silver and gold, garments, weaponry, spices, horses, and mules, so much year by year" (10:25). Solomon's wisdom here is his practical capacity in statecraft and his enormous success in economic matters. He understands how the world works. Now it may be that one can find here a theological component to the narrative, that is, that Solomon understood his interconnectedness to the world through the will and the purpose of the Creator, the true perception of wisdom. There is, however, little evidence of that dimension of wisdom in the purview of his international advisors or in the horizon of Solomon as given in the text. The chief claim of the wise Solomon is his economic prosperity. But from the perspective of worldly powers, who would have asked for more?

The wisdom of Solomon in the primary narrative of 1 Kings 3–11 is a complex matter, including at least the capacity for wise governance that may produce justice, an encyclopedic organization of available knowledge in the awareness that knowledge is power, and a programmatic capacity for political and economic success. The concluding verdict on Solomon in 11:41 alludes to his wisdom, without detailing the complex dimensions of that wisdom. It is enough for the editors to summarize his reputation.

Later on, in taking up the literature of Proverbs, Ecclesiastes, and Song of Solomon, we will have more to say concerning wisdom. Here we may notice that the imagined Solomon of these narratives puts on the table the large, tricky question of faith and reason. Without supporting any claim for a tenth-century Enlightenment (as was made by von Rad), the text suggests an imagined royal enterprise that shifts from a revelation-rooted faith to a pragmatic sapiential awareness drawn away from the revelation of Sinai and toward the large world of international learning. Such a move that in the narrative is both celebrated and critiqued is an enormous venture in the biblical tradition, for it draws royal power away from the specificity and radicality of covenantal ethics into a pragmatism guided by the pursuit of "success." It is too much to claim in that ancient world any "autonomous reason," as was known in the eighteenth-century Enlightenment.[36] No doubt the available epistemologies of that old context were religiously rooted. Nonetheless it is clear that the imagined Solomon moves a distance toward the norms, criteria, and techniques of his prestigious international neighbors and consequently away from the specificity of the God of Sinai. This deep shift, signified by the large category of "wisdom," is perhaps signaled at the very outset of this primary narrative concerning Solomon by the initial mention of Pharaoh's daughter (1 Kgs 3:1) and the acknowledgement of "high places" that bespeak heterodoxy (3:2). To be sure, 1 Kings 3:3 focuses the new king on YHWH; but the love of YHWH is placed in a context that is open to the world of international pragmatism in a way that "older Israel" could never countenance. Wisdom, as given in the imagination of Solomon, is immensely complex. We may judge as well that this imagination of the great king is never narrated innocently, but surely with an ironic sense of gain and loss. Most likely the Queen of Sheba did not object to serving as a mouthpiece for that remarkably shrewd presentation of royal ambiguity.

CHAPTER 7

"SOLOMON" AS ECONOMIC GENIUS

A t the outset, Solomon asked YHWH for "an understanding mind," that is, for wisdom (1 Kgs 3:9). YHWH, however, is endlessly generous to the family of David and so promises Solomon much more than he requests. YHWH promises Solomon, in addition to wisdom, "riches and honor" so that "no other king shall compare with you" (3:13). YHWH, moreover, is as good as the promise; Solomon did indeed receive riches and honor in abundance. Indeed the primary narrative of 1 Kings 3–11 is preoccupied with the wealth of Solomon that is beyond measure and the consequent "honor" that is inescapably a byproduct of such enormous wealth. In this chapter I consider the data of the text itself concerning the wealth of Solomon, then reflect on the social revolution that is signified in this narrative account of the wealthy king.

SOURCES OF THE WEALTH OF SOLOMON

The biblical text identifies five sources of the wealth of Solomon, three of which figure prominently. That is, YHWH's promise of riches and honor is secured for and by Solomon not by a supernatural, miraculous act but by shrewd, cunning, and powerful acts of state. There can be little doubt, in this imaginative account, that the primary source of the wealth of Solomon is his aggressiveness and effectiveness in international commerce, an enterprise apparently rooted in his alliance with Hiram the Phoenician that gives him access to the sea, and signified by the summit meeting with the Queen of Sheba that apparently secured trading opportunities for Solomon in the rich resources of the south (1 Kgs 5:1–7; 10:1–13). The narrative account would have us believe that Solomon, given the location of Israel and Jerusalem at the intersection of trade routes north and south, occupied the strategic position to be the broker and middleman for international trade between the Arabic countries to the south and the great kingdoms of the north. Two texts in particular evidence this peculiar and productive enterprise of Solomon.

In 1 Kings 9:26–28, in cooperation with his ally Hiram, Solomon exploited commercial traffic to the south out of the port of Ezion-geber and its access to the Gulf of Aqabah. Archeologists have proposed that near the port was a foundry that processed copper and iron, thus contributing to the wealth of Solomon.[1] The location of Ophir, the goal of commercial sailing, is uncertain, but the term signifies for the narrator an opportunity for enormous wealth. Our terse textual report does not indicate on what basis Solomon received from Ophir the huge stores of gold reported in 9:28; it is in any case clear that "gold" in this narrative signifies the almost unlimited financial success of Solomon.

The second account of international commerce is in 1 Kings 10:26–29, which presents Solomon as an international arms dealer, the middleman in arms traffic north and south.[2] It is not likely that the large number of chariots and horses maintained in verse 26 concerns Solomon's defense program, but rather refers to his commercial investment in "rolling stock." The king imported horses from the south "at a price" and relayed them to the northern states, no doubt at a different, higher price. The narrative report cannot restrain itself from ogling at the royal wealth that made silver "as common in Jerusalem as stones" (1 Kgs 10:27). It is to be noted, of course, that none of the products that generated wealth were produced by Solomon or in Israel. The king is a trader; he capitalizes on the produce of other states to his own benefit. Though no doubt on a modest scale if at all, the Solomonic achievement is an enterprise of a global economy that is characteristically of primary benefit to the single preeminent economy, as is the case in the contemporary global economy with the United States being the single preeminent beneficiary. In the imagination of this narrative, Solomon occupies a singularly preeminent position to his singular benefit. It may be that "a rising tide raises all boats," but we have no indication that this generation of economic wealth benefited others as it is said to have benefited Solomon.

The external gains of commerce have an internal match, namely, taxation, the second source of the wealth of Solomon. The report of 1 Kings 4:7–19 concerns twelve tax officers who preside over twelve tax districts. According to verse 7, the revenue expected from these districts was equal, each one to cover regime expenses for a month each year. The peculiar note in verse 19 suggests that Judah, Solomon's own tribe and territory, may not have been overly taxed. Two things strike one about this catalog. First, it is quite terse and businesslike, which means that tax collection had been routinized and was not subject to debate or negotiation. The flatness of the report likely indicates the hardnosed firmness of the regime in securing revenues from its subjects. Second, a number of tax officers are identified in terms of their fathers, suggesting that the Department of Internal Revenue was a network of powerful families, all of whom could get "to the trough" regularly in order to partake of the royal largess. Note especially that two of Solomon's sons-in-laws, Benabinadab and Ahimaaz, were among the twelve, as well as Baana, son of Hushai, the advisor who had duped Absalom on behalf of David (1 Kgs 4:11, 15, 16; see 2 Sam 17:5–14). Thus the tax apparatus of Solomon was apparently administered by those closest and most intimately linked to the king, for above all a "wise king" must pay his bills. The report indicates a no-nonsense collection policy with an in-house clique of most trustworthy agents of the king. As we shall see in 1 Kings 12:1–19, the policies of royal taxation were much more contested than the laconic report of chapter 4 may indicate.

A third source of revenue was simply cheap labor, whereby the powerful Jerusalem establishment could grow wealthy at the expense of those conscripted for government at low pay.[3] The two reports on forced labor yield different scenarios, perhaps indicating that the policy of forced labor was in dispute or at least that there was a difference of opinion on how best to report this ominous underside of royal prosperity (1 Kgs 5:13–18 [Heb 5:27–32]; 9:15–23). The practice of such conscripted labor is not elsewhere unknown in the Old Testament. Thus it is provided that conquered peoples can be reduced to such a status (Deut 20:11; Josh 16:10; 17:13; Judg 1:28, 30, 33, 35). Characteristically these reports are matter-of-fact and unblinking about the harshness of policy that is understood simply as a legitimate benefit of victory. Most ominous for our present consideration, the initial report of Israelites in Egyptian bondage described them as a forced labor unit engaged in building supply cities for Pharaoh: "Therefore they set taskmasters over them to oppress them with forced labor. They built supply cities, Pithom and Rameses, for Pharaoh" (Exod 1:11). The reports on the labor policies of Pharaoh and of Solomon are surely too closely paralleled to be mere coincidence. This same practice, moreover, is anticipated among the harsh expectations of 1 Samuel 8:11–17 concerning the prospect of an Israelite monarchy. It is anticipated that if you have seen one example of centralized, absolute power, you have seen them all: "He said, 'These will be the ways of the king who will reign over you: he will take your sons and appoint them to his chariots and to be his horsemen, and to run before his chariots; and he will appoint for himself commanders of thousands and commanders of fifties, and some to plow his ground and to reap his harvest, and to make his implements of war and the equipment of his chariots. He will take your daughters to be perfumers and cooks and bakers'" (1 Sam 8:11–13).

This severe warning, apparently based on much observation (perhaps ex post facto in Israel), reflects an understanding that opulence and extravagance at the peak of the economic pyramid in any society require exploitation at the bottom.[4] And that of course is what Solomon undertook. In 1 Kings 5:13–18, Solomon recruited a huge force of cheap labor from Israel in order to secure materials for building the temple. That is, the opulent temple is to be built on the backs of regimented peasants who had no voice in economic policy. The narrative specifies the order of work (a month on duty in Lebanon, two months at home), and the provision of supervisors to expedite the process. (See Exodus 5 on the harsh, demanding role of supervisors who act in order to meet production quotas in the Egyptian system.) The entire project was supervised by Adoniram, identified among the high officials of

Solomon as "in charge of forced labor" (1 Kgs 4:6). The report of 5:13–18 strikes one as shameless in its economic arrangement, assuring that royal command of peasant labor is a proper and unquestioned practice, legitimated according to royal ambition.

The second text concerning forced labor, in 1 Kings 9:15–23, would seem to suggest some uneasiness with the practice of forced labor, whether an uneasiness "on the ground" or only concerning the later report. The widespread practice of forced labor is again taken for granted. The projects completed according to this practice of cheap labor are extensive, pertaining to royal cities, royal gates, and royal storage cities. The term for "storage cities" in verse 18 is the same as the term in Exodus 1:11, surely no coincidence! That is, the report on Solomon is crafted so that the alert reader does not miss the allusion to the context of slavery in the Exodus narrative, here elusively portraying Solomon in the role of Pharaoh.

The important point in 1 Kings 9:15–23, however, is the crucial disclaimer in the deployment of forced labor that is not on the horizon of 5:13–18. In 9:20–21 the roster of forced labor is given, all of the "foreigners" subjected to the demanding rule of Solomon: "All the people who were left of the Amorites, the Hittites, the Perizzites, the Hivites, and the Jebusites, who were not of the people of Israel—their descendants who were still left in the land, whom the Israelites were unable to destroy completely—these Solomon conscripted for slave labor, and so they are to this day" (1 Kgs 9:20–21).

But then, in the crucial proviso of 1 Kings 9:22, it is asserted—against the claim of 5:13—that Solomon's own close-to-home subjects were exempted from such duty and served only as supervisors. There is of course no way to adjudicate this distinction between the texts. The dispute is presented not to reach a historical judgment but rather to highlight the interpretive ambiguity at work in the formation of the narrative. Thus the narrative makers are in dispute on the precise portrayal of Solomon, how harshly to portray him, and how alert he will be to the covenantal claims of his Israelite and Judean subjects. It seems evident that even given the proviso of 9:22, exploitation is in the air and oppressiveness swirls around the imagined Solomon. Indeed, the narrators know that it could not have been otherwise! The concentration of wealth required for royal opulence had to come from somewhere; the chosen source of easy revenue is exploited peasants, whether homegrown or foreign.

These three primary sources of wealth—*international commerce, taxation,* and *cheap labor*—make a pyramid of "wealth and honor" possible. (Alongside these three, a fourth source of wealth is the royal bureaucracy that serves to administer international commerce, taxation, and cheap labor.) Such a pyramid, imposed by the king, required muscle to establish and sustain, just as benign neocolonialism in the current global economy requires muscle for domination. Solomon had two enforcement arms, the bureaucracy and the military, each enabling the other. First, Solomon is imagined to have put his government on a more rational basis than that of his father, David, by establishing a bureaucracy that would supervise the complex apparatus of revenue production.[5] The list in 1 Kings 4:1–6 provides a sketch of a rational bureaucracy, a notable advance over the quasi-tribal arrangement of David in 2 Samuel 8:15–18. The Solomonic apparatus is thought by some interpreters to be an imitation of some aspects of Egyptian governance, a parallel that is intentional if the forced-labor policies of the regime are reminiscent of those given in the Exodus narrative. The presence of Pharaoh's daughter in the narrative, moreover, may indicate a ready influence that made such a foreign apparatus workable in Israel.

The list of officers set forth in 1 Kings 4:1–6 ends with the name of Adoniram, "in charge of forced labor," who is named in the arrangements of 5:14 and whose name will reappear in the account of the demise of Solomon's apparatus (see 12:18). The narrative report indicates immense hostility toward Adoniram and all that he represented, a hostility that suggests that the exclusionary proviso of 9:22 is not entirely persuasive: "When King Rehoboam sent Adoram, who was taskmaster over the forced labor, all Israel stoned him to death. King Rehoboam then hurriedly mounted his chariot to flee to Jerusalem" (1 Kgs 12:18). (Almost certainly the official named here is the same as in 4:1–6. There is a slight variation in citing the name.)

The second mode of enforcement of this triad of commerce, taxation, and cheap labor is of course *military*, enough to make stick the demands for revenue, both externally and internally. Of course every colonial and neocolonial power must make a sufficient show of military capacity along with a willingness to act decisively for the sake of revenue collection. (Thus it is said currently, in some quarters, that the U.S. invasion of Iraq was to make a show of power for the surrounding states in order that they might be more amenable to the will of the last standing superpower.) Not a great deal is made in the narrative of the standing army of Solomon, for he is primarily an arms dealer. But clearly Solomon had sufficient garrisons and fortifications to sustain his avaricious will, including the three great cities where gates and fortifications are evident:

This is the account of the forced labor that King Solomon conscripted to build the house of the Lord and his own house, the Millo and the wall of Jerusalem, Hazor, Megiddo, Gezer (Pharaoh king of Egypt had gone up and captured Gezer and burned it down, had killed the Canaanites who lived in the city, and had given it as dowry to his daughter, Solomon's wife; so Solomon rebuilt Gezer), Lower Beth-horon, Baalath, Tamar in the wilderness, within the land, as well as all of Solomon's storage cities, the cities for his chariots, the cities for his cavalry, and whatever Solomon desired to build, in Jerusalem, in Lebanon, and in all the land of his dominion. (1 Kgs 9:15–19)[6]

It is clear that Solomon had sufficient military power that he seldom needed to exercise it. But all parties knew that his military capacity was there, and so they complied with the king's revenue requirements. Thus the three modes of revenue collection, reinforced by bureaucratic forcefulness and military power, made this imagined regime into an operation of immense wealth, apparently the very wealth that had been promised at the outset of the narrative by YHWH. And as always, wealth breeds "honor." Solomon is a king of immense gravitas, so the narrative sees, based on a complex money machine. The narrative takes care to exhibit the opulence, enough ground from which to gloat over this regime so recently come of age in that ancient world. Solomon is rich, very rich and very famous.

THE COST OF WEALTH

This carefully constructed scenario of economic generativity, according to our imaginative report, worked uncommonly well. It placed Solomon at the center of a revenue-producing international economy that was matched at home by confiscatory revenue-producing arrangements. The narrative, a vehicle for Israel's imagination, cannot resist reporting in detail on the effectiveness of the economic arrangements of Solomon, whether the celebration of the genius of Solomon or the affirmation of the fidelity of the God who promised riches and honor to the king who did not request them.

A small note in 1 Kings 9:10–14 indicates the aggressive capacity of Solomon, even toward his primary ally, Hiram. It is noted that Hiram supplied cedar, cypress, and gold "as much as [Solomon] wanted." The narrative clearly indicates Solomon to be the senior party in the alliance. Solomon is a big-time trader, redeploying whole cities (villages?) as a part of royal policy. The report suggests that characteristically the Jerusalem king took the best for himself. This leaves his ally disgruntled (1 Kgs 9:13). Nonetheless the disgruntled Hiram sends gold to Solomon (9:14). Clearly Solomon need not be loved, perhaps not even respected, but only feared. Even as he takes advantage of his ally, the gold pours in.

As with the deployment of cities, so with the erection of great state buildings. The report on royal buildings in 1 Kings 7:1–12 suggests a vast royal complex (see also 1 Kgs 9:24). Perhaps the materials for the buildings are supplied from the sometimes willing ally Hiram. But the manpower for this extended project is surely forced labor, whether of the king's own people (5:13) or of his subjugated peoples (9:20–22). Indeed forced labor is intimately linked to state buildings in 9:15–22. We are not able to identify each of the buildings in the remarkable complex of 7:1–12. One may imagine, however, any major imperial city with its endless state buildings designed in part to serve state functions and in part merely to articulate grandeur and splendor, order and legitimacy. Thus in the imagination of Israel, Solomon sponsored such a project that is marked by cedar, an especially exotic commodity (7:2–3), and by "costly stones" (7:9–11). Nothing is spared in the exhibit of royal splendor.

The international dimension of this enormous wealth is dramatically indicated in the aftermath of the visit of the Queen of Sheba in 1 Kings 10:14–22, 23–25. Cross-reference is made in 10:17 and 10:21 to the "House of the Forest of Lebanon" (1 Kgs 7:2–5), so that royal income is directed to the building project. The report, however, is not about buildings but the accumulation of wealth per se. Indeed the rhetoric of this paragraph sounds like a rich man repeatedly letting his gold coins trickle through his fingers with deep self-satisfaction; the point of wealth here is not as a means for a program but as an end in itself. The report is honest that it is trade that produces wealth, the trade we have seen in 9:26–28 and 10:26–29. The accent is on the commodity itself: gold (10:14), gold (10:16), gold (10:17), ivory and gold (10:18), gold and silver (10:21), gold, silver, ivory, apes, and peacocks (10:22), and, in 10:25, "Every one of them brought a present, objects of silver and gold, garments, weaponry, spices, horses, and mules, so much year by year." The wealth is limitless. Solomon and his court engage in opulence beyond imagination: "Nothing like it was ever made in any kingdom" (10:20b).

And of course, the key use of much of the wealth wrought through trade and usurpatious labor policies is for the building of the temple that further enhances the remarkable reputation of Solomon. Clearly nothing is spared by way of expense in the erection of the temple; the narrative cannot resist reporting on every opulent, exotic detail of the temple that is designed as a suitable residence for God and as a worthy achievement of this greatest of all kings.

The entire temple report is saturated with the expensive; we may notice two elements in the report in particular. In 1 Kings 6:19–22, the inner sanctuary (holy of holies) is YHWH's most intimate abiding place, it is also the most opulent:

The inner sanctuary he prepared in the innermost part of the house, to set there the Ark of the Covenant of the Lord. The interior of the inner sanctuary was twenty cubits long, twenty cubits wide, and twenty cubits high; he over-laid it with pure gold. He also overlaid the altar with cedar. Solomon overlaid the inside of the house with pure gold, then he drew chains of gold across, in front of the inner sanctuary, and overlaid it with gold. Next he overlaid the whole house with gold, in order that the whole house might be perfect; even the whole altar that belonged to the inner sanctuary he overlaid with gold. (1 Kgs 6:19–22)

Everything is gold, pure gold. This is the edifice of a king who had more money than he could possibly spend; everything is lavish.

In parallel fashion, the concluding report on the temple construction in 1 Kings 7:48–50 is all about gold: "So Solomon made all the vessels that were in the house of the Lord: the golden altar, the golden table for the bread of the Presence, the lampstands of pure gold, five on the south side and five on the north, in front of the inner sanctuary; the flowers, the lamps, and the tongs, of gold; the cups, snuffers, basins, dishes for incense, and firepans, of pure gold; the sockets for the doors of the innermost part of the house, the most holy place, and for the doors of the nave of the temple, of gold" (see also 1 Kgs 7:51).

Clearly the urban elite who both sponsored and benefited from such an imaginative emphasis had no memory of the God who resisted a temple and went to and fro in tent and tabernacle (2 Sam 7:6). This God is now the benefactor of Solomon, who has contained God in such opulence that one might imagine a God wholly committed to urbane extravagance. Perhaps this God is now as protected from the cry of the poor as were the temple custodians who provided such a winsome mode of divine confinement.

The high economic privilege enjoyed by Solomon (and mirrored in the extravagance designed for the God of Solomon) is detailed in the inventory of opulence in 1 Kings 4:22–28 (Heb 5:2–8): "Solomon's provision for one day was thirty cors of choice flour, and sixty cors of meal, ten fat oxen, and twenty pasture-fed cattle, one hundred sheep, besides deer, gazelles, roebucks, and fatted fowl" (1 Kgs 4:22–23).

The "bread of Solomon" for one day is immense, most especially the voracious appetite for meat in the midst of a peasant economy where meat was a rare luxury. The narrative boasts but then must quickly explain how such opulence is possible. The explanation sweeps from description of Solomon's dominion, to the domestic economic benefits of an imposed peace abroad, to the effectiveness of the bureaucratic and military structure created and maintained by Solomon.

Solomon had "dominion," according to this vista of Greater Israel, from Egypt to the Tigris and Euphrates Rivers; all the wealth of this vast region flowed to Jerusalem both as appropriate commercial revenue and as "tribute" (see 1 Kgs 4:21). The latter term suggests that this is protection money characteristically gathered by the greater power from the lesser power (4:24). Solomon had *shalom* on every side, that is, an imposed political-military settlement that evoked respectful conformity among coerced subject peoples. The soft language of the text bespeaks a hard-nosed economic-military arrangement so that peace abroad permitted prosperity at home.

The consequence of an imposed peace abroad is a stable economy at home. As a result Solomon is presented as the one who fulfills the peasant dream of "vine and fig tree" (1 Kgs 4:25). Or as the prophetic poem has it:

But they shall all sit under their
own vines and under their own fig trees,
and no one shall make them afraid;
for the mouth of the Lord of hosts has spoken. (Mic 4:4)

"No one shall make them afraid," for all of the political threats have been curbed by the king who taxes and imposes forced labor even as he imposed tribute on foreign peoples.

The military muscle whereby the entire opulent arrangement is made possible is suggested in 1 Kings 4:26. Also necessary to maintenance of Solomon's economic privilege are "those officials" in 4:27, referring back to the revenue officers of verses 7–19, the ones who maintained the military equipment of verse 28.

The outcome of this complex economic-military arrangement is that Solomon's officials "let nothing be lacking" (1 Kgs 4:27). This is a most extraordinary claim. It suggests that Solomon's achievement was flawless, that he and his people were so completely safe, secure, and sated that nothing remained to be accomplished. The overheated, grandiose language in the verse perhaps anticipates the sweeping verdict of Francis Fukuyama, who, with the fall of the Soviet Union and the defeat of the ideology of socialism, announced "the end of history."[7] Fukuyama celebrated what he took to be the complete and irreversible victory of Western liberal democratic capitalism over any competitive system or theory. Apparently the achievement of Solomon is imagined in something like the same terms as "the end of history." All has been accomplished; it is indeed "finished," the complete presentation of "realized eschatology" with nothing left undone.[8] It does not get any better than this. This congratulatory verdict on the achievement of Solomon imagined the end of all social restlessness, it entertained no thought that the Pax Solomon imposed on other peoples was in any way coercive or resisted. All is well and all will be well. The *shalom* of Solomon is a coherent, completely integrated system of well-being.

This remarkable enumeration of the facets of royal opulence reaches its congratulatory summary in 1 Kings 4:20: "Judah and Israel were as numerous as the sand by the sea; they ate and drank and were happy." The verdict this report offers is that the people of Solomon's own community, Israel and Judah, prospered immensely.

The formula "as numerous as the sand by the sea" recalls the old ancestral promise to Abraham (Gen 22:17) and Jacob (32:12). It speaks to Solomon as the fulfillment of Israel's best, oldest hopes. The fact that Israel and Jerusalem have "multiplied," moreover, might also suggest that the fruitfulness and abundance of all creation has come to fulfillment here, especially since "multiplying" (as in 1 Kgs 4:20) and "dominion" (as in 4:24) together may echo the creation hope of Genesis 1:28 (see also Exod 1:7). Thus Solomon is the fruition of all of the best hopes of Israel and of creation. The "bread and [circuses]" that Solomon would offer in terms of the performance of the economy and the pageantry of the temple here allegedly won him wide public support, a public that now gladly becomes consumers of what Solomon can offer . . . that is, "eating, drinking, and rejoicing," or "eating, drinking, and making merry," seemingly without critical edge or awareness. Solomon has transformed his population from a community with engaged face-to-face interaction into a consumerist society. This verdict near the beginning of the Solomon narrative is a counterpoint to the expostulation of the Queen of Sheba near the end of the Solomon narrative that we have already considered: "Happy are your wives! Happy are these your servants, who continually attend you and hear your wisdom" (1 Kgs 10:8). Both articulations portray a populace deeply sated and that in an uncritical way affirms the royal achievement from which it benefited so deeply.

The verdict of 1 Kings 4:20, moreover, is given a basis in the next verse, namely, that such satiation is rooted in the international economy over which Solomon presided: "Solomon was sovereign over all the kingdoms from the Euphrates to the land of the Philistines, even to the border of Egypt; they brought tribute and served Solomon all the days of his life" (1 Kgs 4:21; Heb 5:1). It is all based on *tribute!* This economic achievement would seem to be the culmination of the dream of Israel that is reiterated in the old covenant tradition: "For the Lord your God is bringing you into a good land, a land with flowing streams, with springs and underground waters welling up in valleys and hills, a land of wheat and barley, of vines and fig trees and pomegranates, a land of olive trees and honey, a land where you may eat bread without scarcity, where you will lack nothing, a land whose stones are iron and from whose hills you may mine copper. You shall eat your fill and bless the Lord your God for the good land that he has given you" (Deut 8:7–10). Here, as in 1 Kings 4:27 (Heb 5:7), Israel lacked nothing. Moses had promised that Israel would lack nothing; now Solomon accomplishes it. Everyone is an uncurbed consumer, the capacity for which is detailed in 4:22–23 (Heb 5:2–3).

The verdict of 1 Kings 4:20 is all-inclusive. But because the parallel statement in 10:8 had limited the "happiness" to courtiers and wives, we are permitted to probe by asking: "All Israel?" "All Judah?" Well, yes. That is what the narrative says and wants us to believe, because the narrative asserts that Solomon is the embodiment of Israel's deepest hope for *shalom.*

But all? Well, we recall that the extravagance of royal provisions was matched by the assertion of tax-collecting procedures. We recall the immense, even grandiose, building projects that were made possible by forced labor. We may at least entertain a reservation about the comprehensiveness of "all" in 1 Kings 4:20. That reservation is reinforced in and informed by the narrative of 12:1–19, a text that lies outside the bounds of the Solomon narrative of chapters 3–11 but that reflects on the wake of the work of Solomon. The report is that the tightly controlled system of Solomon promptly came unglued at his death in a tax revolt. It is attested, in the mouth of Solomon's son Rehoboam, that "my father made your yoke heavy" (1 Kgs 12:14). That is, at his death, so the report goes, the taxpaying population had had enough of royal policy that took and took and took, that took by tax and by forced labor (see 1 Sam 8:11–18).

Now if we credit this critical report and spin it back to 1 Kings 4:20 and 10:8, we may judge that "Israel and Judah" in 4:20 and "courtiers and wives" in 10:8 did not include all in the consumer economy. Rather some, those who ate at the king's table (1 Kgs 4:22), "those who continually attend you" (10:8), benefited immensely. They did so, however, at the expense of the labor-delivering, tax-paying populace that had no access to the table of the king's extravagance and did not participate in "royal happiness." One may at least suggest that there is something ironic about 4:20 and 10:8, though the full disclosure of that irony awaits chapter 12. On the basis of these texts, we may opine that the economic miracle of Solomon, like many economic miracles of global proportion, offers less than meets the eye. Such a high level of consumerism, then or now, comes at an immense cost of cheap labor and accompanying social costs that some must pay. The ones who ate and drank and were happy did not notice. The ones at the royal table were perhaps narcoticized. Such a narcotic, of course, only works if the dosage is endlessly intensified. And such an endless intensification of economic extravagance is unsustainable. The verdicts of 4:20 and 10:8 at best would seem to be penultimate.

THE ROLE OF SOLOMON IN THE IMAGINATIVE
SELF-UNDERSTANDING OF ISRAEL

The economic reports of Solomon are a mixed lot of texts. The data of 1 Kings 9:26–28 and 10:26–29 have busied archaeologists, as though these texts are reliable reportage.[9] The summit meeting of 10:1–13 no doubt has folkloristic dimensions, and the report of 4:20–23 contains the extravagant congratulatory rhetoric of court language, whether or not it contains any ironic dimension.

In this area as much as any concerning Solomon, it is important to move beyond the innocence of the text to gather together clues that are offered us concerning this systemic achievement of Solomon. Even accepting that the report of Solomon is an act of immense imagination, it is clear that this imagination-generating figure of Solomon decisively transformed the imaginative self-understanding of Israel. Thus scholars more historically inclined would say that the monarchy decisively altered social relations in Israel.[10] And if not historically, then rhetorically and artistically, Israel's textual imagination entertains a changed set of social relationships. The setting of Solomon, historical or imagined, is in a tribal society with a segmented society of small social units. David had moved that small fluid economy toward larger coherence in his role as a chieftain.[11] The move to monarchy, however, featured a concentration of wealth and authority, a concentration that in the Solomonic narrative approximates totalism.[12] This concentration of wealth and power represented a sharp departure from the old segmented arrangements and clearly evoked resistance, evident not only in 1 Kings 12:1–19 but also in the hint of 2 Samuel 20:1. Thus the new course of imagination leads to deeply altered social relations and practices.

There is no doubt that the Solomonic experiment led to important social stratification. It is plausible that the imagined Solomon of our text was a product of the urban elites who counted on the cheap labor of village peasants to produce the wealth that made affluent urban society possible.[13] Such social stratification is likely signaled in the articulation of the Queen of Sheba in 1 Kings 10:8. Certainly that same stratification is assumed in the temple structure that endorsed and legitimated varying degrees of holiness among the "more acceptable" and the "less acceptable" in terms of ritual qualification.[14] Such stratification would suggest that not everyone in Israel and Judah "ate, drank, and rejoiced" (1 Kgs 4:20).

Social stratification of course produces differentiation of social function; some members of society perform more valuable social functions and some of the "less qualified" are consigned to more menial tasks. This is indicated in the fledgling bureaucracy of 1 Kings 4:1–6, in the naming of the tax officers in 4:7–19, and in the naming of the courtiers' wives who live close to power in 10:8. Clearly there were many inhabitants of Israel, Judah, and Jerusalem who were not on the horizon of these social delineations, the ones who take an initiative in 12:1–19.

Social stratification and differentiation of social roles are social realities that bring along with them the development of "surplus value." In Solomonic Jerusalem economic prosperity reached a level well beyond anything needed for survival. In a smaller agrarian economy there was little chance for the development of such surplus value, as "eating and drinking" more characteristically stayed closer to subsistence. To be sure, already in an agrarian economy the figure of Nabal represents an important example of surplus value (1 Sam 25); no doubt the cadre of people who gathered around David in 1 Samuel 22:2 were among those who were without such surplus value and who constituted David's "young men" in 25:5–13. With the concentration of power that permitted legitimated government to *tax* and to *draft* (cheap labor), an urban class close to royal power benefited from income that was not produced by real work but by the manipulation of symbols (priests, wise men). Thus emerged a contrast between a peasant community of villagers who lived at the subsistence level and an urban population that needed storage cities, great structures that both housed and symbolized wealth, and that provided affluence well beyond maintenance. That no doubt is the picture given in 1 Kings 4:22–23, with the support of taxes (1 Kgs 4:7–19), foreign tribute (21), and cheap labor (5:13).

We are, with some attentiveness, not able to read the Solomon narrative with its varying offers of innocence and/or irony without an awareness that this narrative act of royal imagination is deeply contested elsewhere in the disputatious community that is Israel. Thus Solomon provided peace and prosperity: "During Solomon's life-time Judah and Israel lived in safety, from Dan even to Beersheba, all of them under their vines and fig trees" (1 Kgs 4:25). That same phrasing, however, is employed by the peasant poet Micah to quite different ends, whereby he anticipates an end to the war machine that is a sine qua non for surplus wealth:

> But they shall all sit under their
> own vines and under their own fig trees,
> and no one shall make them afraid;
> for the mouth of the Lord of hosts has spoken. (Mic 4:4)

In the final form of the text, moreover, the Micah tradition that celebrates a peace-able "vine and fig tree" is the same tradition that castigates usurpatious land prac-tices:[15]

> Alas for those who devise wickedness
> and evil deeds on their beds!
> When the morning dawns, they perform it,
> because it is in their power.
> They covet fields, and seize them;
> houses, and take them away;
> they oppress householder and house,
> people and their inheritance.
> Therefore thus says the Lord:
> Now, I am devising against this family an evil
> from which you cannot remove your necks;
> and you shall not walk haughtily,
> for it will be an evil time.
> On that day they shall take up a taunt song against you,
> and wait with bitter lamentation,
> and say, "We are utterly ruined;
> the Lord alters the inheritance of my people;
> how he removes it from me!
> Among our captors he parcels out our fields." (Mic 2:1–4)

Eventually, it is the same tradition of poetic critique that anticipates the failure and demise of the royal-urban system of Jerusalem:

> Hear this, you rulers of the house of Jacob
> and chiefs of the house of Israel,
> who abhor justice and pervert all equity,
> who build Zion with blood
> and Jerusalem with wrong!
> Its rulers give judgment for a bribe,
> its priests teach for a price,
> its prophets give oracles for money;
> yet they lean upon the Lord and say,
> "Surely the Lord is with us!
> No harm shall come upon us."
> Therefore because of you
> Zion shall be plowed as a field;
> Jerusalem shall become a heap of ruins,
> and the mountain of the house a wooded height. (Mic 3:9–12)

It is instructive that this critical verdict on the royal-urban apparatus given by the village poet is quoted a century later in defense of Jeremiah, a starchy critic of the economic system put in place in and around Solomon:

And some of the elders of the land arose and said to all the assembled people, "Micah of Moresheth, who prophesied during the days of King Hezekiah of Judah, said to all the people of Judah: 'Thus says the Lord of hosts,

> Zion shall be plowed as a field;
> Jerusalem shall become a heap of ruins,
> and the mountain of the house a wooded height.'

Did King Hezekiah of Judah and all Judah actually put him to death? Did he not fear the Lord and entreat the favor of the Lord, and did not the Lord change his mind about the disaster that he had pronounced against them? But we are about to bring great disaster on ourselves!" (Jer 26:17–19)

In these latter references we are, to be sure, somewhat far afield from Solomon. I cite Micah and Jeremiah in an attempt to understand the economic achievement of Solomon. These prophetic citations are instructive because they remind us that the economic miracle of the globalization of Solomon did not happen in a vacuum. It happened on the backs of the villagers who had no access to the king's table. It happened, moreover, amid the shrill poetry of resistance that not even the memo-writing bureaucracy or the cadences of symmetrical liturgy could silence. At best, the economic miracle of Solomon is contested. At worst, it is exposed as a short-term deception with deep and durable costs for those who are to come after. And indeed, in 1 Kings 12 at the death of Solomon, we are able to see the beginnings of the cost that must then be paid.

CHAPTER 8

THE DEUTERONOMIC PROVISO:
THE VOICE OF IRONIC CRITICISM

The articulation of Solomon as temple builder, wise king, and economic
genius is an act of sustained, constructive imagination. This act of interpretive imagination most likely was undertaken by participants in the successful urban society of Jerusalem for whom Solomon is the epitome. Such a practitioner
of Solomonic imagination might have presented Solomon in such an imaginative
way as an ideological act to enhance the claims of the Davidic monarchy and the
legitimacy of the Jerusalem temple, or as an act of theological affirmation attesting
that YHWH effectively kept promises made to David and to Solomon, or as an act of
self-serving economics from one who benefited from the uncommon prosperity of
imagined Solomon, who perhaps sat at the table of the king. For that matter, it is
entirely plausible that these three motivations readily converged, as there is nothing
mutually exclusive about affirmations of Jerusalem, celebrations of YHWH, and self-
promotion. In any case, the outcome of such constructive imagination is a king like
whom there is no other:

> I give you also what you have not asked, both riches and honor all your life;
> no other king shall compare with you. . . . All Israel heard of the judgment that
> the king had rendered; and they stood in awe of the king, because they per-
> ceived that the wisdom of God was in him, to execute justice. (1 Kgs 3:13, 28)

> Solomon's wisdom surpassed the wisdom of all the people of the east, and all
> the wisdom of Egypt. . . . People came from all the nations to hear the wisdom
> of Solomon; they came from all the kings of the earth who had heard of this
> wisdom. (1 Kgs 4:30, 34)

> Twelve lions were standing, one on each end of a step on the six steps. Noth-
> ing like it was ever made in any kingdom. . . . Thus King Solomon excelled all
> the kings of the earth in riches and in wisdom. The whole earth sought the
> presence of Solomon to hear his wisdom, which God had put into his mind.
> (1 Kgs 10:20, 23–24)

In this reading Solomon is unrivaled and uncontested as the best in every regard. But
of course this royal-temple-urban act of constructive imagination, as sustained and

effective as it was (and continues to be), did not emerge uncontested in an interpretive vacuum. All around this remarkable royal-urban emergent in the imagination of Israel, and perhaps more deeply rooted, was another long-term act of constructive imagination that contested the royal-urban trajectory of imagination. This alternative is represented by the tag word "covenantal," even though the interpretive trajectory is itself complex and variegated.

CONFORMING KINGSHIP TO THE REQUIREMENTS OF COVENANT

The covenant tradition is rooted, according to the text, at Mount Sinai and receives its primal presentation in the so-called Sinai pericope of Exodus 19–24.[1] There is no scholarly consensus about the provenance or dating of this tradition, except that it is taken in ancient Israel to be very old and ultimately authoritative.[2] This covenant tradition articulates that in the mountain encounter between YHWH, the God of the exodus who dwells inscrutably on the mountain, and Israel, this people formed from a ragtag company of the "forced labor" of the Egyptian empire, YHWH and Israel are bound to each other in mutually exclusive oaths of loyalty. While the binding of covenant is mutual, there is no thought that the parties to covenant are equal or that this new relationship is symmetrical.[3] It is clear, characteristically, that YHWH, the God of emancipation and the God of storm, is the sovereign presiding officer of the covenant relationship to whom Israel is bound in oaths of obedience (Exod 24:3, 7).

Thus the centerpiece of the Sinai pericope is the Decalogue of Exodus 20:1–17, whereby YHWH's own voice at the mountain articulates the ten fundamental requirements of the relationship, centering on 20:3, the requirement of singular and exclusive loyalty to YHWH, the God of the exodus. That catalog of ten elemental requirements that constitute the condition of the covenantal relationship received an ongoing series of interpretations over time, a series of interpretations that came to constitute the corpus of "Torah" in the Old Testament. In the Sinai pericope itself, the first wave of interpretation of the ten elemental stipulations for covenant is given in the so-called Book of Covenant (Exod 21:1–23:19).[4] It is clear in this first exposition of the Decalogue that the sovereign will of the covenant God pertains to every sphere of Israel's life, public and personal, cultic and economic. Where the will of that covenant to God is faithfully enacted, Israel may understand and embody the reality of "the Kingdom of God," that is, the realm that is ordered according to the will of the covenanting God:

> Over and against the common world-view of the nations of its time which centred upon the well-being of the state, and was thus, as suggested above, a sort of "state-ideology," over against Israel's own apparent belief that its well-being was permanently secured by Yahweh, is a world-view in which the fulfilment

of God's righteousness is the goal, the very *raison d'être,* of the nation. Hence Yahweh's will confronts Israel and in its name a faithless Israel can be and is rejected, the goal of its promised reconstitution being again the service of Yahweh and the uncompromising demands of his will.

Here then we have evidence that Israel adopted significant aspects and features of the characteristic thought-world of its environment, with strong indications that the innate polytheism of that thought-world made deep inroads into Israelite life, but at the same time evidence also that in the most decisive and far-reaching manner Israelite religion as it finally found expression in the Old Testament rejected such a world-view and arrived at a radically different understanding of God and his relation to man and the world. Such is the gulf which separates them that we must think of it as the rejection of one world-view, initially significantly influential upon Israel, and the working out of a radically different one.[5]

Of particular interest is the initial declaration of this relationship in Exodus 19:3–6, perhaps the most elemental articulation of covenant theology.[6] The text begins in verses 3–4 with a reminder of the recent deliverance from Egypt, a parallel to Exodus 20:2. Then in verses 5–6, Moses enunciates the promise that a faithful, obedient Israel who "keeps my covenant" will be YHWH's special people among all the peoples of the world, "a priestly kingdom and a holy nation." Of particular importance for our study is the "if" utterance by Moses in verse 5. It is reinforced by the double absolute infinitive, a grammatical device for special rhetorical emphasis: "if you *really* obey my voice and if you *really* keep my covenant." The whole of the relationship is conditional upon obedience to the announced will of YHWH that consists of the Ten Commandments and most particularly focuses on the first commandment, to have "no other gods." It is fair to say that the rest of the extensive and complex Torah tradition of the Old Testament is an exposition of this most elemental and uncompromising "if."

The rootage of the Sinai tradition, and the Sinai pericope in particular, is in critical judgment quite obscure.[7] We are in a better circumstance when we come to a second wave of covenantal thinking in Israel that presents itself as a recovery of the Sinai tradition. In the eighth or seventh century B.C.E., there arose in Israel a sustained interpretive tradition that looked back to Sinai but at the same time focused on the contemporary reality of Israel as YHWH's special people, which sought to maintain its theological distinctiveness amid the demands, dangers, and vagaries of political reality. The centerpiece of this recovery of Sinai is in the book of Deuteronomy, which is concerned with the contemporaneity of covenant in the actual life of Israel. This tradition is concerned not with an ancient, remembered covenant but with one that has contemporary force and relevance, a force and relevance made possible through daring reinterpretation of what is taken for old tradition: "Not with our ancestors did the Lord make this covenant, but with us, who are all of us here alive today" (Deut 5:3).

The narrative of 2 Kings 22 reports the rediscovery of an old book of Torah teaching that evokes alarm on the part of King Josiah, who, in response to the rediscovered book, institutes a great theopolitical reform of the realm:

> Shaphan the secretary informed the king, "The priest Hilkiah has given me a book." Shaphan then read it aloud to the king. When the king heard the words of the book of the law, he tore his clothes. Then the king commanded the priest Hilkiah, Ahikam son of Shaphan, Achbor son of Micaiah, Shaphan the secretary, and the king's servant Asaiah, saying, "Go, inquire of the Lord for me, for the people, and for all Judah, concerning the words of this book that has been found; for great is the wrath of the Lord that is kindled against us, because our ancestors did not obey the words of this book, to do according to all that is written concerning us." (2 Kgs 22:10–13)

This rediscovered scroll is commonly understood to be some form of the book of Deuteronomy, out of which came the great "Deuteronomic revolution" in Israel. This royally authorized revolution was an attempt to revision contemporary Israel in terms of old covenantal teaching that passionately champions the "if" of Exodus 19:5 whereby the existence and well-being of Israel are taken to be conditional upon Torah obedience.

The corpus of commandments in Deuteronomy 12–25 is in a general way derivative from the Ten Commandments (see Deut 5:6–21). Some scholars, moreover, suggest that the sequence of commandments in Deuteronomy 12–25 is organized according to the Ten Commandments.[8] However that may be, it is clear that the Deuteronomic corpus of commandments is a remarkable innovation in Israel, introducing themes and topics that are nowhere explicit in the old Sinai traditions.[9]

Specifically in Deuteronomy 16:18–18:22, this Torah tradition introduces a series of offices that are together to govern Israel in the land of promise: judge, king, priest, and prophet. Dean McBride has proposed that the Deuteronomic corpus offers a "constitution" for Israel ordered according to the Sinai covenant; Norbert Lohfink has in particular noticed the provision for the separation of powers that precludes an excessive concentration and absolutizing of political authority.[10] In this sequence of judge, king, priest, and prophet, our attention, as we take up the study of Solomon, is drawn to the remarkable teaching on kingship in 17:14–20. This text is of profound importance for our general consideration of Solomon because it is the primary articulation in Deuteronomic rhetoric of the relationship of kingship to Torah.[11]

Because the "Deuteronomic revolution" is dated to the eighth or seventh century, and because this particular teaching coheres well with what is said of King Josiah at the end of the seventh century in 2 Kings 22, it is almost certain that Deuteronomy 17:14–20 is a late Deuteronomic reflection, certainly after Solomon and surely with Solomon in purview.

The intent of the teaching on kingship in Deuteronomy 17:14–20 is to curb the power of kingship and to conform kingship to the requirements of covenant as the Deuteronomists construe it. The effect of the teaching is to empty kingship of much of its ideological, mythological, or liturgical claim; consequently the king in this rendition is reduced simply to being one more member of the covenant community, who, like every other member of the covenant community, is subject to Torah requirements. Thus the teaching of Deuteronomy 17:14–20 provides at the outset that the king in the newly acquired land of promise must be "one from your own community," that is, one subject to and committed to Torah requirements (Deut 17:15). The threefold restraint upon the king concerns horses (signifying armaments and so military autonomy), wives (signifying self-securing political alliances), and silver and gold, (signifying attempts at self-securing resources): "Even so, he must not acquire many horses for himself, or return the people to Egypt in order to acquire more horses, since the Lord has said to you, 'You must never return that way again.' And he must not acquire many wives for himself, or else his heart will turn away; also silver and gold he must not acquire in great quantity for himself" (17:16–17).

This is a remarkable set of restraints upon kingship, for together they address the most characteristic means whereby any kingship may maintain and augment itself:

> The fact that the king was forbidden to have "many wives" in verse 17 is connected with the foreign policy relationships and marriages entered into by Solomon (1 Kg 3:1, 11.1ff.). The "turning away of the heart" can best be understood, if it is interpreted as dealing with the religious dangers connected with affairs of the heart. We need not comment upon the acquiring of gold and silver, the piling up of treasures at the expense of the people.
>
> We might regard all of Deuteronomy, especially the tax system, as a commentary upon this. The three-fold prohibition against "acquiring" (or "making much") is aimed at limiting these activities and it includes appropriate controls. Nevertheless, in this way there is notification that even these areas of the king's activity are under the control of law. The professional army, foreign policy relationships, administration of the state treasury were all part of his duties. On the other hand, he was denied control of cultic activity, the militia, which was certainly quite important at this time, the administration of justice, and taxation, a previously important source of revenue.[12]

This kingship, as conjured in Deuteronomic teaching, is to have none of the marks of autonomy that characterize kingship in general and Solomon in particular. It is clear that Solomon specialized exactly in the things here prohibited.

The positive counterpoint in this articulation of kingship is that the king need not pursue self-sufficiency through arms and wealth, but is free to study Torah, here no doubt specifically the Torah of Deuteronomy: "When he has taken the throne of his kingdom, he shall have a copy of this law written for him in the presence of the levitical priests. It shall remain with him and he shall read in it all the days of his life, so that he may learn to fear the Lord his God, diligently observing all the words of this law and these statutes, neither exalting himself above other members of the community nor turning aside from the commandment, either to the right or to the left" (Deut 17:18–20a). Crüsemann rightly observes that this teaching renders the king powerless by conventional standards: "Completely depriving the king of power, something so astonishing in the ancient Near East, raises the inescapable question, 'Who had the power and authority to do that?' The kingship law authorized the people to set up kings, and the authority speaking in this law must be over both king and people. We will see what this is all about in the provisions for the legal system and in prophetic material."[13]

The effect of this requirement is that the existence and well-being of monarchy is completely geared to Torah. The teaching culminates in a "so that" formula: "so that he and his descendants may reign long over his kingdom in Israel" (Deut 17:20b). This statement effectively reiterates the "if" of Moses in Exodus 19:5. *Monarchy, as authorized by Moses in Deuteronomic Torah, depends completely upon Torah obedience.* All the conventional accoutrements of monarchy—arms, treaties, economic resources—are of little value in this notion of royal power. It is clear that this remarkable and radical provision flies in the face of all conventional thinking about political power. It certainly tells, moreover, against the Solomon conjured by the royal-urban interpretation that celebrated temple building, royal wisdom, and royal economics.[14]

SOLOMON THROUGH THE PRISM OF TORAH OBEDIENCE

On the basis of this deeply rooted covenantal tradition with its uncompromising horizon of Torah obedience, the same circles that produced the Torah corpus of Deuteronomy subsequently produced a history of Israel that culminated in 1 and 2 Kings.[15] This text is constituted as a rewrite, a revisionist version of Israel's history according to the Torah commands that center around the Mosaic "if" of covenantal understanding. Our purpose in what follows is to consider how differently Solomon is articulated when presented through the contrasting interpretive prism of Torah obedience.

There is no doubt that much of the material in 1 Kings 3–11 is taken from extant sources, perhaps from the sources cited in 1 Kings 11:41. Here we are interested only in the texts that exhibit the distinctive interpretive agenda of the Deuteronomic covenantal horizon. First, we may particularly identify three statements of conditionality ("if") that decisively shape the final form of the text.

The divine grant of wisdom, riches, and honor (1 Kgs 3:12–13) in response to the king's request (3:9) is surely a free one without strings attached. The addition of 1 Kings 3:14, however, decisively changes that unconditional gift: "*If* you will walk in my ways, keeping my statutes and my commandments, as your father David walked, then I will lengthen your life." Now the "if" looms large, and effectively limits the prospects of Solomon's future to adherence to "my statutes and my commandments." (The appeal to the obedience of David is of course a rather curious one, given David's own departure from Torah.) Here that problematic is disregarded, though the problematic is frontally acknowledged in 1 Kings 15:5: "David did what was right in the sight of the Lord, and did not turn aside from anything that he commanded him all the days of his life, except in the matter of Uriah the Hittite." Clearly it is adherence to Torah and not the model of David that concerns this interpretive tradition.

A second instance of "if" is found in the extended account of preparation for building and furnishing the temple, where 1 Kings 6:12–13 constitutes a curious intrusion. These verses are, however, less of an intrusion if we notice that the "if" is characteristic of the covenantal traditions: "Concerning this house that you are building, *if* you will walk in my statutes, obey my ordinances, and keep all my commandments by walking in them, then I will establish my promise with you, which I made to your father David. I will dwell among the children of Israel, and will not forsake my people Israel" (1 Kgs 6:12–13). So understood, the verses are not an intrusion but are in fact the pivot point of interpretation. They have the effect of turning attention away from the temple so much celebrated in this narrative. They show that the temple, in itself, can guarantee nothing for king or for people. The only ground of YHWH's fidelity toward Jerusalem is adherence to Torah. The connection of 1 Kings 6:13 to 6:12 is not clear; in context, however, it is likely that YHWH's "dwelling in" (*skn*) and "not abandoning" (*ʿzv*) Israel is dependent upon the obedience of verse 12. It is remarkable that in verse 13 attention is turned away from the temple and the city and has in purview the people Israel, a people clearly antecedent to and not defined by the Jerusalem constitution.

The most important example of Deuteronomic conditionality is in the longer, symmetrical text of 1 Kings 9:4–9. The positive "if . . . then" connects Torah obedience and dynastic survival and, as in 6:12, easily takes a "good David" as a given. This positive "if . . . then" formulation is congruent with 3:14 and 6:12–13. The second "if . . . then" of verses 6–9, unlike the three previous cases, presents a negative scenario of disobedience and, consequently, judgment. This part of the formulation thus breaks new ground. It does so only after the temple has been built, dedicated, and duly celebrated. It does so by presenting a second dream that is the counterpoint to the first positive dream of 3:5–14. Thus the Deuteronomic shaping of the narrative, as Martin Noth has seen, slots most of the negative material concerning Solomon after the achievement of the temple.[16] In this "if . . . then" formulation the uncompromising conditionality concerns worship of other gods, a violation of the first command of Sinai (Exod 20:3; Deut 5:7).

The judgment to come based on disobedience is a savage one; clearly the interpreter has in purview both the curse tradition of Deuteronomy 28 and the events surrounding the destruction of Jerusalem and the deportation of some urban residents at the hand of the Babylonians (see 2 Kgs 24–25). The threat grounded in disobedience is that YHWH will "cut off" Israel from the land, that YHWH will "cast out" the temple, that Israel will become a visible humiliation and embarrassment in the eyes of the world (1 Kgs 9:7). The formulation is parallel to the covenant threat of Deuteronomy 28:37: "You shall become an object of horror, a proverb, and a byword among all the peoples where the Lord will lead you." First Kings 9:8–9 makes clear that such a disaster and demise is not caused by any failure on the part of YHWH; it is caused, rather, frontally and unmistakably by Israel. Israel will have "abandoned" ('zv) YHWH, the same word used in 6:13 wherein YHWH promises not to "forsake" ('zv) Israel. The breakdown that is to come is all on the side of disobedient Israel, or more specifically on the side of Solomon, who embodies and practices an ideology of self-securing that is inimical to the God of the first commandment. This negative "if . . . then," to be sure, is still in prospect in 1 Kings 9.

But that anticipation of judgment and deportation needs to be seen in larger perspective. This covenantal interpreter knows where the royal narrative is headed and knows the disastrous outcome that the violation of Torah by Solomon will have made inescapable. Solomon, the man who, with horses, wives, silver, and gold, violated Torah, will in due course bring upon himself, his realm, his city, and his temple a judgment about which Israel has been on notice since the days of Sinai. It is to be appreciated, moreover, that in this presentation Solomon's violation is not a mere act of commandment breaking. Rather the entire ideological system with imagined Solomon as its center constitutes a theory of power that is unreceptive to the conditional "if" of covenant. This is not a man versus a scroll, but in fact two theories of power and two systems of governance that are mutually exclusive. The Solomonic enterprise cannot tolerate the "if" of Sinai that requires kings (and communities) to forego conventional sources of self-securing.

It is clear that this tradition of interpretation counters the self-aggrandizement of the Jerusalem establishment. It is rooted in Sinai and articulated through a political idiom available in seventh-century Assyria. It asserts that the invisible Lord of the covenant will be the real ruler of the realm and that the Davidic officer in Jerusalem, even given the Davidic oracle and the continually reinforcing liturgy of the Jerusalem temple, should be a responsive member of the Torah community. This theological vision radically redefines the political landscape and insists that covenantal measures of political success, "riches and honor," are profoundly irrelevant in contemporary assessments of governance and in anticipations of the future. The uncompromising quality of the "if . . . then" structure of covenantal reasoning sweepingly diminishes the imagined achievements of Solomon that we have thus far considered.

The deep tension between these two acts of systemic imagination is—perhaps intentionally—indicated by the way in which the twofold Deuteronomic "if . . . then" of 1 Kings 9:4–9 (framed by 1 Kgs 9:1–3) is juxtaposed to the recital of royal achievements in 9:10–28. This latter inventory of success includes the several elements of royal accomplishment already noted: great buildings through forced labor and acquisition of armaments and gold. The odd and noteworthy fact is that the two competing versions of royal reality in verses 4–9 and verses 10–28 are juxtaposed without any hint, grammatical or rhetorical, about how they are to be linked together. I suppose that in the frame of reference of the urban elites around Solomon, the achievements of verses 10–28 are so spectacular as to render the warnings of verses 4–9 irrelevant. Conversely, from a Deuteronomic perspective, the warning of verses 4–9 has such gravity that it is not impinged upon at all by what follows in verses 10–28. While interpretation can run in either direction, it is clear that in the final form of the text—at the hand of the Deuteronomists—the Torah warning constitutes the decisive reality of the Jerusalem establishment.

The series of "if" statements in 1 Kings 3:14, 6:12, and 9:4–9 comes to fruition in the capstone of Deuteronomic commentary upon Solomon in 11:1–13. (In 9:7, the "then" that threatens Israel because of its disobedience is expulsion from the land.) These verses are cast in a conventional mode of a prophetic speech of judgment, organized as *indictment* and *sentence*.[17] The indictment of Solomon in 11:1–8 echoes the warning given in 9:6: "If you turn aside from following me, you or your children, and do not keep my commandments and my statutes that I have set before you, but go and serve other gods and worship them . . ." (9:6).

The most elementary indictment of Solomon is that he "loved many foreign women." This is a systemic judgment that Solomon compromised the pure vision of Israel's Torah and accommodated his power to alien theological loyalties and, consequently, to alien political policies and economic postures (1 Kgs 11:1). No doubt this indictment in 1 Kings 11:1 is a clear counterpoint to 3:3, wherein Solomon loved YHWH. As Noth has seen, however, even in that verse the claim for YHWH is compromised by the final clause introduced by "only" concerning "high places."[18]

Already in 3:3, Solomon is indicted for heterodox worship of which the Deuterono-mist disapproved.

The ground for the Deuteronomic indictment of 1 Kings 11:1, with its categoriza-tion of "foreign wives," is immediately given in verse 2, which is linked to Deuteron-omy 7:3–4: "Do not intermarry with them, giving your daughters to their sons or taking their daughters for your sons, for that would turn away your children from following me, to serve other gods. Then the anger of the Lord would be kindled against you, and he would destroy you quickly" (Deut 7:3–4).[19] The risk of "foreign wives" is a theological one; they bring their religious commitments with them, and those religious commitments in turn bring along social-economic-political postures and the policies that are alien to Israel's covenantalism.[20] Thus Solomon violates Torah and compromises loyalty to YHWH, putting the community at risk.

The remainder of the indictment of Solomon in 1 Kings 11:3–8 details his viola-tions. The facts of the case include an inventory of foreign alliances, at best a hyper-bolic statement made in order to indicate the vast network of international connections that were characteristically sealed with marriages among the families of kings and chieftains. The indictment is careful to place this distortion of Solomon's loyalty "when Solomon was old," thus keeping the temple builder free of the charge. The intention is to assert that the temple was built by the king who had not yet compro-mised his covenantal identity. That same verse 4 makes clear that the violation of Torah concerns the first commandment, the exclusive claim of loyalty that every Israelite must practice. For reasons of state, Solomon compromised that exclusive claim. And indeed, stepping outside Deuteronomic passion, one might reason that the development and maintenance of a network of international relations requires the easing of an exclusionary theological claim. Such an international network is pre-cluded if an uncompromising loyalty stands at the center.[21] The Deuteronomist of course has no patience with such political realism and so proceeds with the condem-nation.

The outcome of such royal compromise, in the horizon of the Deuteronomic indictment, particularly concerns Astarte, perhaps goddess of Solomon's Sidonian ally Hiram, Milcom of the Ammonites, Chemosh, the Moabite god, and Molech of the Ammonites. These names of gods are not to be taken with any precision, and we cannot determine anything precise from the names. They are standard names of a formulaic kind utilized for polemical purposes and are to be understood as represen-tatives of a greater host, as Solomon "did the same for all his foreign wives" (1 Kgs 11:8). The key point is the violation of the exclusive claim of YHWH as given in the first commandment, a violation so profound for covenantal theology that the negat-ing term "abomination" is used three times in this text (11:5, 7). For reasons of state,

Solomon has created an orgy of religious activity that surely spins off in political and economic policy; or in any case, so goes the Deuteronomic polemic.

The indictment itself is reiterated in 1 Kings 11:9–10: the king's "heart had turned away, from the Lord" (1 Kgs 11:9). This phrasing reiterates that of verse 3: "his wives turned away his heart." The king followed after other gods, the core point of the indictment of verses 2–8. The outcome of the theological failure of Solomon leads to the conclusive "therefore" of verse 11: "*Therefore* the Lord said to Solomon, 'Since this has been your mind and you have not kept my covenant and my statutes that I have commanded you, I will surely tear the kingdom from you and give it to your servant'" (11:11). The dynasty will lose land; YHWH will "tear away" territory from the Davidic house. This is of course the decisive judgment that can be made against any regime. The threat is immediately qualified in verses 12–13 introduced by the conjunction "yet" (*'ak*). The threat of verse 11 is unspecified, but the qualification of verses 12–13 makes clear that it is the loss of the northern territories in 922 B.C.E., at the death of Solomon, that is in purview.

Two matters are to be noted about 1 Kings 11:11–13. First, we should not miss the remarkable claim so characteristic of the Deuteronomists that *violation of Torah* leads to *land loss*. In the end, that Deuteronomic perception will concern the debacle of 587 B.C.E. and the deportation. Here, however, the land loss is the more modest one of the northern territories. The land loss, moreover, is declared with the verb "tear" (*qr'*) with YHWH as the active agent of the verb. This verb is a most important one in the development of Deuteronomic theology concerning the relation of land and Torah; in 2 Kings 22:11 Josiah—the Torah-keeping king—"tears" his robes in penitence. And conversely, Jehoiakim—the Torah-defying king—"tears" the scroll that threatens his rule (Jer 36:23).[22] The word usage in these three instances indicates that Deuteronomic thought on political continuity has in purview a dynamic that is at the edge of violence, a violence apparently congruent with the uncompromising quality of the rule of YHWH.

Second, as Gerhard von Rad has noted, the qualifying words of 1 Kings 11:12–13 show the skillful way in which the uncompromising Torah theology of Deuteronomy is compromised in order to accommodate YHWH's promise to David.[23] That accommodation may be a theological one, so great was the claim for David. At the same time, however, the theological settlement may be in the interest of credibility for these interpreters. The tradition has it that the house of David did indeed retain the territory of Judah and Jerusalem, while it lost the northern areas. In these verses, not much is made of the Davidic proviso; in the end, moreover, the Davidic proviso counted for nothing, because Babylon took everything (2 Kgs 24–25). Thus one can see in these verses the Deuteronomic interpreter making the adjustments that are required in order to present a coherent statement on monarchy that is congruent with the facts on the ground. The qualification "for the sake of David" is at best an interim arrangement; in the end, in this read, Torah strictness is decisive, and the monarchy is totally exposed to the "therefore" here uttered against Solomon (see 2 Kgs 23:26–27, 33–34; 25:6–7, 27–30).

The speech of judgment in 1 Kings 11:1–11 is the decisive word of the Deuteronomists on Solomon. In this rendering, the claim of Torah is completely vindicated. The cost of Torah disobedience is massive, and none of the props that Solomon established—temple, wisdom, wealth—amounted to anything. The claim, so characteristic of the Bible even if it must be imposed on the king, is that there is a resilient God-given purpose pervading the historical process that in the end cannot be accommodated or nullified.[24] In due course this God-given purpose will prevail. So goes the argument as we reach the end of the narrative of Solomon.

After the speech of judgment in 1 Kings 11:1–11, the text offers three additional texts that amount to implementations of the decisive judgment on Solomon already pronounced. The narrative of 11:14–40 includes a report on three adversaries (*stn*) who vexed and harassed Solomon. The text says "YHWH raised up" these adversaries. This formulation suggests that these historical threats constituted an implementation of the prophetic threat of verse 11. It indicates, moreover, a conviction that the historical process is the arena of YHWH's judging activity in the public domain. The first adversary is an Edomite who responds to David's earlier harshness vis-à-vis Joab (1 Kgs 11:14–23). The narrative is of interest because Pharaoh, father-in-law to Solomon, tried to restrain the Edomite, and no specific mention is made of action against Solomon. The second adversary is a Syrian who becomes king in Damascus (11:23–25). No particular initiative against Solomon is mentioned. We may imagine, nonetheless, that Syria was a perennial vexation to Israel. The third adversary, Jeroboam, is a homegrown product who receives the most narrative attention (11:26–40). This third case, however, is connected to a prophetic initiative whereby YHWH initiates a new rule that would displace much of the Davidic governance (11:29–39). The speech of the prophet Ahijah reiterates the decisive verb "tear" (11:31), reports the inventory of alternative gods to whom Solomon is attracted (11:33), restates the Davidic proviso (11:34–36), and, most remarkably, repeats the "if" of conditionality (11:38). In Deuteronomic purview, YHWH is still seeking a candidate for kingship who will honor the "if" of Torah. It is remarkable that the promissory honor to Jeroboam in verse 38 echoes the cadences of the divine oracle to David in 2 Samuel 7:11–16. As with Hadad in verses 17–22, Jeroboam also sought sanctuary with Pharaoh, Solomon's own father-in-law (11:40).

As we shall see, this third adversary has a historical and narrative future in Israel, unlike the first two who are only of passing interest. The list of three, with particular accent on Jeroboam, indicates that the prophetic "therefore" of 1 Kings 11:11 was not entirely Deuteronomic rhetoric. It pertained to real history. It is to be noted, in the report concerning Jeroboam, that the Deuteronomic historian manages the interface between *divine intentionality* and *historical reality* through prophetic utterance. The prophetic utterance of Ahijah, moreover, is the voice of the old tradition of Shiloh, an old-time competitor to the rising claims of preeminence for Jerusalem.[25] Thus not even the prophetic utterance is a disembodied divine voice. Rather, the divine voice—so costly to Solomon—is carried through the horizon and no doubt through the interests of a center of tradition that in principle was resistant to the Davidic establishment. The utterance of Ahijah is yet one more element in the rich way in which the imaginatively constructed Solomon is an arena for contention among interpretive traditions. Ahijah, of the old cultic center of Shiloh, is made a mouthpiece for the Deuteronomist in its dismissal of a failed Solomon and in its hope for an alternative social arrangement that may practice the "if" of Torah.

The brief notation of 1 Kings 11:41–43 is a characteristic narrative closure to a reign in Jerusalem given by the Deuteronomist. The formulaic character of the verses places the accent on continuity: "The king is dead; long live the king." Two other matters are to be observed in this death notice. First, the historian cites a primary source, "The Acts of Solomon." Such a citation frees the Deuteronomist from the necessity of being a historian who relates all of the data, freed then for interpretation of a very particular, even polemical kind. Second, the verdict "all that he did as well as his wisdom" is noticeably laconic. It leaves so much unsaid. In light of the seething hostility narrated in verses 14–40 and in light of the weighty speech of judgment in verses 1–13, the terseness of this notice is remarkable. Does the notice simply disregard negative elements in the narrative account of Solomon, after the manner of a death notice that eschews dirty linen in the life reported? Or does the notice in its very terseness wink at the reader, expecting that we belated readers will know better? The point is not clear; I will explore it in what comes below.

The narrative of 1 Kings 12:1–19 provides an account of the rule of Rehoboam immediately after the notice of his succession to Solomon in 11:43. This narrative functions as an implementation of the "therefore" of 11:11 and more particularly the prophetic initiative of Ahijah in 11:29–39. It has long been clear to scholars that the Israelite territory to the north did not subscribe to the absolutist pretensions of legitimacy claimed by the Jerusalem dynasty.[26] For that reason Rehoboam, upon succession to the throne, was required to renegotiate the allegiance of the North to the Jerusalem throne. The negotiation concerns "yokes" light and heavy, that is, tax burdens. The final offer of Rehoboam to his would-be northern subjects, following the advice of his young men, who are apparently alienated from the old covenantal traditions, is brusque and uncompromising: He "spoke to them according to the advice of the young men, 'My father made your yoke heavy, but I will add to your yoke; my father disciplined you with whips, but I will discipline you with scorpions'" (1 Kgs 12:14). The policy decision of the new king has the appearance of the embrace of bad advice. The narrator, however, knows better. It is the hidden rule of YHWH that causes "a turn of affairs" (*sbbh*) that bad advice should be followed. That is, YHWH has led Rehoboam to a foolish tax policy. The reason for such divine guidance, moreover, is to enact the revelatory oracle of Ahijah from chapter 11. Revolution is in the air! It is given prophetic impetus. We may believe, however, that it is the usurpatious economic policies of Solomon concerning tax and forced labor—rooted in the departure from YHWH, the God of the exodus and of covenant—that provides the energy for northern resistance. The notation of 1 Kings 12:15, once again, nicely interfaces *raw social reality* and *hidden divine intentionality*. The North rejects the rule of the Davidic dynasty that it had long experienced as greedy and acquisitive.[27]

The other notation of importance is the presence of Adoniram one more time in the narrative (1 Kgs 12:18). It is Adoniram, member of the royal cabinet (4:6) who had supervised the policy of forced labor (5:14), who now appears one more time, as a royal emissary to the North. What an act of obtuseness! Adoniram is clearly the epitome of the worst oppressive impulses of the regime, a lightning rod to attract whatever hostility and resistance are still latent in the North. Adoniram is murdered by the crowd of resisters, surely an act commensurate with the violence of Moses against the Egyptian foreman, also an agent of forced labor (12:18; see Exod 2:11–12). In both cases, the royal official killed is in the interest of symbolic resistance against an entire regime and its practices of exploitation. The juxtaposition of Ahijah—a revolutionary voice of the old northern sanctuary—and Adoniram—agent of the worst of the regime—nicely dramatizes the symbolic conflict in this confrontation as well as the clash of competing systems of social power.

The outcome of this narrative, located close to raw economic reality, is the loss of the North that is "torn" from David, just as the threat of 1 Kings 11:11 and the word of Ahijah (1 Kgs 11:31) had anticipated. The king of "riches and honor" ends with his governance in shambles. Even such a king who lived in opulence and who controlled every social lever could not succeed, for he violated the twin, allied forces of the will of YHWH and the reality of social pain that becomes bold energy. The demise of the monarchy in the narrative of 1 Kings 11–12 is remarkable; its telling, however, is not uncharacteristic of the interface of social reality and divine intentionality in Israel. In the end, Solomon disregarded both, imagining that his great achievements could make him safe. Solomon ends as an unsafe man, a jeopardized king. In the horizon of the Deuteronomist, there is only one source of safety and well-being: adherence to the Torah-giving God. On that count, the reality of Solomon is a dismal failure.

SOLOMON, EXPOSED AS A FAILURE

We may now consider this textual verdict in a more thematic way concerning the three great achievements of Solomon. We have seen that Solomon built a temple that was designed to assure the permanent residency of YHWH in Jerusalem:

> Then Solomon said,
> "The Lord has said that he
> would dwell in thick darkness.
> I have built you an exalted house,
> a place for you to dwell in forever." (1 Kgs 8:12–13)

The liturgical affirmation of "forever" (plural in the Hebrew) along with the verb "dwell" (*ysv*) indicates the intentionality of the temple and the liturgical claims made for it.[28]

As the Deuteronomist knows very well and says, however, the temple was a failure in its capacity to guarantee divine presence. As we have seen, in the great 1 Kings 8 itself, verse 9 attests to the "emptiness" of the ark, and verse 27 acknowledges that such a house cannot "contain" the Holy One of Israel. Beyond these theological-liturgical dissents to the high claims made for the temple, of course, the Deuteronomist has in purview that at the end of the sixth century the temple was sacked by the Babylonians. Nebuchadnezzar seized all of the precious contents of the temple that had been so carefully prepared and described in the temple narrative of 1 Kings 6–7. Everything was carried away with the deportees (2 Kgs 25:13–17; Jer 52:17–23).[29]

The dramatic awareness that the God resident in the temple did not or could not protect the temple is the basis for the Deuteronomic articulation of 1 Kings 8:28–53. There it is affirmed that YHWH is *not* present in the temple but in fact is "in heaven your dwelling place" (1 Kgs 8:30). The temple is a place of divine regard and attentiveness; but in fact it is per se a place of absence, a recognition that directly contradicts the claims of Solomon. Most particularly, the culmination of the temple prayer in 8:46–53 speaks explicitly of "the land to which they had been taken captive" (8:47). The temple may function in many salutary ways, but not among those ways is assured divine presence. The claims of Solomon ring hollow in Israel; its central tradition must deal with the reality of divine absence.[30]

We have observed the international reputation of Solomon for wisdom. That international reputation was based in part on his capacity to collect and codify available learning (1 Kgs 4:29–34). Much more, it was based on a pragmatic sense of statecraft whereby a centralized economy was made to work with remarkable effectiveness. The final form of the text continues the claim for Solomonic wisdom in the terse concluding verdict of 1 Kings 11:41. To be sure, the shaping of the tradition by the Deuteronomist nowhere explicitly calls that royal wisdom into question. I suggest, however, that in the hands of the Deuteronomist the celebrated wisdom of Solomon in the end is shown to be a *foolishness unto death*. Insofar as wisdom is the capacity to live with "the grain of creation" as ordered by the Creator, statecraft and economic management require a mix of freedom, responsibility, and restraint that does not violate the given ordering of social relationships.

By the end of this primary narrative on Solomon, it is apparent, in Deuteronomic horizon, that Solomon has indeed violated the given order of creation in two distinct ways, two ways that are offered in 1 Kings 11–12 as a basis for the demise of the regime. First, as the prohibition of Deuteronomy 7:2–4 was against marriage with "foreign women," so wisdom teaching is alert to the danger, threat, and seduction of "the strange woman."[31] Solomon's foolish embrace of foreign wives, so instrumental to his political-commercial policies, constituted a set of choices that led to the death of the regime.

Second, there can hardly be any doubt that forced labor, whereby the urban elites lived well off the produce of cheap labor, is against the grain of viable social relationships. It requires no revelation from Sinai to know that covenantal solidarity among "brothers" in the community cannot be sustained by social stratification designed for exploitation. In the end, that labor policy, intimately linked to an avaricious tax policy, eventuates in the revolutionary activity of 1 Kings 12:1–19 that culminates in the death of Adoniram, symbol of governmental foolishness practiced by this allegedly wise king.

Clearly, the celebrated riches and honor of Solomon are premised on exactly these two dimensions of foolishness: international trade relations sealed by marriages to foreign waves, and cheap-labor policies. The propaganda of the king (or of the urban elites who constructed the king) caused such policies to appear wise, that is, effective. The larger, more critical view, however, shows both to be defining contributions to failure. Wisdom invites and warns:

> And now, my children, listen to me:
> happy are those who keep my ways.
> Hear instruction and be wise,
> and do not neglect it.
> Happy is the one who listens to me,
> watching daily at my gates,
> waiting beside my doors.
> For whoever finds me finds life
> and obtains favor from the Lord;
> but those who miss me injure themselves;
> all who hate me love death. (Prov 8:32–36)

In the judgment of the Deuteronomist, Solomon "misses" wisdom and turns out to love death.[32]

We have seen that Solomon is celebrated as an economic genius for whom the wealth of the global economy pours into his royal treasury and into the lives of his courtiers and wives in Jerusalem (1 Kgs 10:8). In Deuteronomic perspective, however, the wealth of Solomon in Jerusalem is a sham that cannot be sustained. There are important hints that the final form of the text intends to recast Solomon as Pharaoh, albeit a homegrown pharaoh. Solomon is said by the Deuteronomist to put in motion the processes by which the wealth of Jerusalem was taken away. Solomon has amassed wealth by acquisitive policies and practices. But very soon his son Rehoboam is victim of the same acquisitiveness from Egypt: "In the fifth year of King Rehoboam, King Shishak of Egypt came up against Jerusalem; he took away the treasures of the house of the Lord and the treasures of the king's house; he took everything. He also took away all the shields of gold that Solomon had made; so King Rehoboam made shields of bronze instead, and committed them to the hands of the officers of the guard, who kept the door of the king's house" (14:25–28).

The sum of the Egyptian action on the part of Shishak is terse: "He took everything." The narrative lingers over the details of the process by which the precious treasure of Rehoboam was carried away, bit by bit, from temple to the guardroom. The confiscatory action of Shishak against the helpless son of Solomon is only the first of a sequence of such confiscations, eventually including those of Assyria:

> Ahaz sent messengers to King Tiglathpileser of Assyria, saying, "I am your servant and your son. Come up, and rescue me from the hand of the king of Aram and from the hand of the king of Israel, who are attacking me." . . . Then King Ahaz cut off the frames of the stands, and removed the laver from them; he removed the sea from the bronze oxen that were under it, and put it on a pediment of stone. The covered portal for use on the Sabbath that had been built inside the palace, and the outer entrance for the king he removed from the house of the Lord. He did this because of the king of Assyria. (2 Kgs 16:7, 17–18)

And, of course, the loss culminates in the seizure of Jerusalem's wealth by the Babylonians:

> The bronze pillars that were in the house of the Lord, as well as the stands and the bronze sea that were in the house of the Lord, the Chaldeans broke in pieces, and carried the bronze to Babylon. They took away the pots, the shovels, the snuffers, the dishes for incense, and all the bronze vessels used in the temple service, as well as the firepans and the basins. What was made of gold

the captain of the guard took away for the gold, and what was made of silver, for the silver. As for the two pillars, the one sea, and the stands, which Solomon had made for the house of the Lord, the bronze of all these vessels was beyond weighing.

The height of the one pillar was eighteen cubits, and on it was a bronze capital; the height of the capital was three cubits; latticework and pomegranates, all of bronze, were on the capital all around. The second pillar had the same, with the latticework. (2 Kgs 25:13–17)

They took everything. Nothing could be preserved or salvaged in Jerusalem because the gathering of wealth in Jerusalem in the first place was an act of greed and foolishness, without reference to the sustenance of viable social relationships.

On all three counts of his celebrated reputation, Solomon ends exposed as failure: A *temple* for presence becomes a *house of absence* for the deported; the gift of *wisdom* is transformed into *distorted foolishness*; and the accumulation of *wealth* culminates in *disastrous loss*.

The Deuteronomic verdict, we may think, is congruent with the facts on the ground. The real issue, however, is between a theological vision (ideology) that intends to subvert the celebrated claims of Solomon, and the ideology upon which those claims are premised.

SOLOMON'S ROLE IN MOVING ISRAEL FROM GIFT TO LOSS

The royal-temple-urban ideology fostered by the Jerusalem elites is an act of celebrative imagination that could view Solomon as an absolute fixed point of ideology not impinged upon by historical vagaries. Thus the Solomon of temple-wisdom-wealth dominates the horizon of the Jerusalem ideology, unscathed by the seething "underneathness" that will not be stilled. One can observe this absolutizing of ideology, mythology, and liturgy in the Songs of Zion (most notably Ps 46) and in the Royal Psalms, as, for example, Psalm 110:

> The Lord sends out from Zion
> your mighty scepter.
> Rule in the midst of your foes.
> The Lord has sworn and will
> not change his mind,
> "You are a priest forever
> according to the order of Melchizedek."
> The Lord is at your right hand;
> he will shatter kings on the
> day of his wrath. (Ps 110:2, 4–5)

The Deuteronomic interpreters, however, have a different interpretive horizon. They view Solomon not as a fixed ideology point immune from historical vagaries, but as an episode in the larger narrative of Israel that begins in YHWH's *gift of land* and culminates in the *loss of land* at the behest of YHWH. This interpretive tradition is preoccupied with the question of the role and status of Solomon in the larger narrative. Given such a question, this imaginative trajectory cannot accept a Solomon who is above the fray. Instead, he is seen as a decisive contributor as Israel moves from *gift* to *loss*.

To that end, Solomon is placed at the beginning of 1–2 Kings. To be sure, the two books of Kings are part of the larger narrative that includes Joshua, Judges, Samuel, and Kings, but 1 and 2 Kings themselves constitute a literary corpus that tells the tale of monarchy. By placing the failed Solomon of *temple absence, foolish wisdom,* and *lost wealth* at the beginning of the narrative, the story shows how Solomon is a key contributor not only to the failure that immediately surfaces for his son Rehoboam, but to the ultimate failure, the termination of the dynasty in 2 Kings 24–25. Thus the Deuteronomist, unlike the Jerusalem ideology, takes a very long view of the impact of Solomon and shows how the monarchy has gone wrong from the outset, gone wrong by the abusive distortion of the gracious gifts of YHWH to the regime, gifts of wisdom, riches, and honor.

In this telling there can be no doubt that Josiah is the good king who faithfully keeps Torah (2 Kgs 22–23): "Before him there was no king like him, who turned to the Lord with all his heart, with all his soul, and with all his might, according to all the law of Moses; nor did any like him arise after him" (23:25). Josiah is the model for effective kingship and, as Chaney has shown, the counterpoint of the Torah-teaching Joshua in Joshua 1:6–9, 16–18.[33] Thus the narrative of the Deuteronomist is bracketed by *Joshua* at the beginning and *Josiah* at the end. Midway between them is placed Solomon, who refuses Torah obedience and imagines an autonomy about his wealth and power, an autonomy he may have learned from his father-in-law Pharaoh, or from his father, David, as in 2 Samuel 11:1–27. Thus in a Deuteronomic reading Solomon is the quintessential practitioner of autonomy who violates Torah and so contributes to the failure of the whole. Writing in the seventh and sixth centuries, the Deuteronomist can credit failure of the whole to Manasseh: "Still the Lord did not turn from the fierceness of his great wrath, by which his anger was kindled against Judah, because of all the provocations with which Manasseh had provoked him. The Lord said, 'I will remove Judah also out of my sight, as I have removed Israel; and I will reject this city that I have chosen, Jerusalem, and the house of which I said, My name shall be there'" (2 Kgs 23:26–27; see 21:1–18).

Manasseh is judged to be evil, disobedient, heterodox, every bad verdict imaginable. Manasseh, however, only brings to fruition the way of rule that the Deuteronomist identifies already in Solomon. Thus Solomon at the beginning of the royal narrative functions as a type of bad king who will, in the end, be replicated by Manasseh and countered by Josiah. Already in 1 Kings 11:11, YHWH had sworn to "tear the kingdom from you."

Thus the reader of the whole is drawn away from the absolutist claims of the Jerusalem liturgy to the larger narrative that is written with the clarity of Deuteronomic ideology and with attentiveness to the facts on the ground. In that reading, Solomon at the beginning and Josiah at the end form the contrasting possibilities concerning *covenantal faith* and *public power.* The contrast between these models, surely products of determined imagination, is well voiced by Jeremiah, a child of the Deuteronomic tradition: "Thus says the Lord: Do not let the wise boast in their wisdom, do not let the mighty boast in their might, do not let the wealthy boast in their wealth; but let those who boast boast in this, that they understand and know me, that I am the Lord; I act with steadfast love, justice, and righteousness in the earth, for in these things I delight, says the Lord" (Jer 9:23–24 [Heb 22–23]).[34]

In the end, Solomon is one whose narrative features wisdom, might, and wealth; conversely, Josiah is a model for and embodiment of steadfast love, justice, and righteousness (see Jer 22:15–16 for such a positive reading of Josiah, "your father").[35] This motto in Jeremiah 9:23–24 is a clear either/or. The either/or given in prophetic cadence is a very old one in Deuteronomy:

> See, I have set before you today life and prosperity, death and adversity. If you obey the commandments of the Lord your God that I am commanding you today, by loving the Lord your God, walking in his ways, and observing his commandments, decrees, and ordinances, then you shall live and become numerous, and the Lord your God will bless you in the land that you are entering to possess. But if your heart turns away and you do not hear, but are led astray to bow down to other gods and serve them, I declare to you today that you shall perish; you shall not live long in the land that you are crossing the Jordan to enter and possess. I call heaven and earth to witness against you today that I have set before you life and death, blessings and curses. Choose life so that you and your descendants may live, loving the Lord your God, obeying him, and holding fast to him; for that means life to you and length of days, so that you may live in the land that the Lord swore to give to your ancestors, to Abraham, to Isaac, and to Jacob. (Deut 30:15–20)

The imagined Solomon of Jerusalem is much celebrated. In this subversive, ironic reread of Solomon, however, the king characteristically chose death, not in viciously evil ways but by imagining himself to be autonomous, unrestrained by Torah or by the "grain of creation" willed by the Creator. In Deuteronomic perspective, such autonomy can endure awhile and even be celebrated . . . but not finally! Finally comes the "tearing."

CHAPTER 9

CHRONICLES: SOLOMON GLORIOUS, ONE-DIMENSIONAL, MINUS IRONY

We have seen that the Deuteronomic history (Joshua, Judges, Samuel, and Kings) is an extended act of narrative imagination that reconstrues the memory of Israel in the seventh and sixth centuries B.C.E. It does so with particular reference to the dislocation and deportation of 597 and 587, and ponders how it is that the good land, city, and temple given by YHWH could be so brusquely forfeited. Specifically, we have seen how Solomon, in the narrative of 1 Kings 3–11, is reconstrued as a foil for the good king Josiah and as an embodiment of the royal pretensions that eventually led to land loss and deportation. This entire presentation, preoccupied with the Babylonian crisis, is an immensely imaginative articulation guided and shaped by theological convictions that were particularly pertinent to that time of crisis.

A REIMAGINED TEMPLE

When we turn to 1 and 2 Chronicles (the Chronicler), we find an artistic construction that is largely informed by the presentation of the Deuteronomists, thus an act of interpretive imagination derived from and informed by the prior act of imagination in the Deuteronomic literature.[1] The relationship of the Chronicler to the Deuteronomist is a characteristic example of the way in which the Old Testament is constituted of layers of interpretation that are themselves extrapolated from many prior layers of creative construction. It is a consensus judgment that the work of the Chronicler is from the Persian period (540–333 B.C.E.), though within that scope there is no agreement about a more precise dating, some dating it earlier, before the reformist work of Ezra and Nehemiah in mid-fifth century, some dating it after that time. Either way, there can be little doubt that the Chronicler seeks to reconstrue previous articulations of Israel's memory in a way that is informative and persuasive for that Persian period of Judaism. Only now is scholarship turning its primary attention to Jewish history, faith, and culture in the Persian period, and there is much that we do not yet know.[2] The primary point of historical circumstance concerns the bold and courageous efforts of elitist Jews deported by the Babylonians. A new initiative was taken with the support and credentialing of Persian authorities in order to reconstitute the Jerusalem community around a rebuilt temple, the latter reflected particularly in the prophetic utterances of Haggai and Zechariah. It is clear that Persian generosity toward restored Jerusalem made possible the reforming of the city and the restoration of the temple. It is equally clear that there were important limitations to Persian generosity, so that Judaism was restored largely through a cultic community that in all matters political and economic was dependent upon and compliant with the will of the Persian Empire. Within that general framework, there is dispute as to the extent of historically reliable reports in the Chronicles, though that issue is scarcely pertinent to our consideration of Solomon. The materials regarding Solomon in the Chronicler largely follow the Deuteronomist and make only a few suggestions of historical reliability beyond what may be adjudicated in the version of the Deuteronomist in 1 Kings 3–11.

From that broad enterprise of the reconstitution of Judaism as a cultic community, it does not surprise us that the interpretive imagination that constitutes this literature is content to reimagine Jerusalem not as a state but as a community of worship in the context of the restored temple. The kings in Jerusalem, moreover, are presented primarily as patrons and leaders of the temple cult. In the environment of the Persian period, the maintenance of a distinctive Jewish identity would seem to be a primary rhetorical-interpretive concern. This agenda, in the horizon of the Chronicler, is taken to be the maintenance of Jewish identity through participation in the temple cult. This means, in turn, that the temple cult in Jerusalem is imagined in this literature not in terms of its actual modesty but in terms of the remembered and imagined first temple that is the gift of Solomon. Thus the Solomon imagined here is a glorious figure without blemish or flaw.[3]

Before turning directly to the materials on Solomon in 2 Chronicles 1–9, we may briefly consider the shape of the entire literature of the Chronicler that is divided into four parts. First, in 1 Chronicles 1–9, the entire history of the world from Adam (1:1) to David is tersely summarized. Second, David is presented in 1 Chronicles 10–29 as founder of the cult and initiator of the temple. Third, Solomon is featured in 2 Chronicles 1–9 as the temple builder, and the remainder of the Davidic dynasty is quickly sketched out in 2 Chronicles 10–35. It is clear in the concluding verses of 36:22–23 that the story line is carried through the fall of Jerusalem and the exile, with an anticipation of return to the land from exile at the behest of YHWH and at the permit of Cyrus the Persian: "In the first year of King Cyrus of Persia, in fulfillment of the word of the Lord spoken by Jeremiah, the Lord stirred up the spirit of King Cyrus of Persia so that he sent a herald throughout all his kingdom and also declared in a written edict: 'Thus says King Cyrus of Persia: The Lord, the God of heaven, has given me all the kingdoms of the earth, and he has charged me to build him a house at Jerusalem, which is in Judah. Whoever is among you of all his people, may the Lord his God be with him! Let him go up'" (2 Chron 36:22–23).

The literature is designed so that contemporary Jewish readers in the Persian period are to understand themselves as the ones to enact the next phase of the story of the people of God, the next phase being the return movement around Ezra and Nehemiah. Solomon is presented in 2 Chronicles 1–9 as a memory of a past glory in Jerusalem, designed as an impetus for contemporary Jews in terms of what is promised, what is hoped for, and what is possible in return and restoration. For remembered Solomon and for contemporary Judaism, everything turns upon the temple cult. The passion for this memory and hope is very deep and is able, in this imagination, to override what must have been a dismal and shabby life in Jerusalem, a shabbiness no doubt reflected in Haggai.

THE UNITY OF THE DAVID AND SOLOMON NARRATIVES

While the Deuteronomist had given attention to Solomon's legacy from David with particular reference to the divine oracle in 2 Samuel 7, it is clear that in the horizon of the Chronicler, Solomon is not only David's heir but in fact the two are bound together so intimately as to be presented as a unity. Thus before we take up the Solomon narrative in 2 Chronicles 1–9, it is important to consider those aspects of the David narrative that tie the son to the father much more intimately than had been imagined by the Deuteronomist.

In the Davidic narrative we may give particular attention to 1 Chronicles 22, 28, and 29.[4] As we shall see in our consideration of the presentation of Solomon by the Chronicler, the presentation of David is now without any of the negations presented in the narratives of the books of Samuel, most especially the references to Uriah and Bathsheba. What interests us, however, is the way in which Solomon is already profoundly present in the David material, in contrast to the Samuel narrative, where Solomon's appearance is limited to the allusion in the oracle of 2 Samuel 7:12–15, the birth announcement of 2 Samuel 12:24–25, and the narrative of 1 Kings 1 and 2, where Solomon is largely a passive recipient of the throne. Here, by contrast, Solomon figures prominently in the David narrative, whereby Solomon is granted enormous legitimacy, and consequently the temple is more thoroughly rooted within the aegis of David (see 1 Chron 17:11–14).

In 1 Chronicles 22, David makes preparation for the temple and charges Solomon with the building task. David also recognizes that Solomon is "young and inexperienced" and will greatly benefit from David's anticipatory oversight and planning: "For David said, 'My son Solomon is young and inexperienced, and the house that is to be built for the Lord must be exceedingly magnificent, famous and glorified throughout all lands; I will therefore make preparation for it.' So David provided materials in great quantity before his death. Then he called for his son Solomon and charged him to build a house for the Lord, the God of Israel. David said to Solomon,

'My son, I had planned to build a house to the name of the Lord my God'" (1 Chron 22:5–7).

The particular charge given to Solomon that makes Solomon eventually the one who completes David's own faithful intention is in three parts.

First, in 1 Chronicles 22:9–10, David recalls YHWH's oracle identifying the son as "a man of peace" (ish ménuḥah) who will utilize "peace from all his enemies" in order to erect this house for YHWH's name.[5]

Second, David wills that Solomon should have "discretion and understanding" (skl wbinah) in order to obey covenant (vv. 12–13). The "if" of verse 13 is familiar to us from the Deuteronomist and is reiterated here, thus aligning the Chronicler with the conditionality of the Deuteronomist in terms of Torah obedience. Clearly in the fifth century, as in the seventh or sixth century, this act of prosperity pivots on Torah loyalty.

Third, David assures Solomon that there are sufficient funds and material for the task (vv. 14–18).

David's mandate to Solomon to have courage, in 1 Chronicles 22:13, is a commissioning formula. Lohfink, followed by Braun, notices that the speech of David utilizes a genre for installation into office that is closely paralleled to the text of the commissioning of Joshua in Joshua 1, also a mandate to Torah obedience.[6]

In 1 Chronicles 22:17–19 the mandate is extended beyond Solomon to rally the subjects to support Solomon "with mind and heart." The whole is designed to tie the next generation to the authorizing declaration of father David. Concerning Solomon, this text accomplishes two matters. First, it assures that the building of the temple is the single focus of his rule, a role well suited to Jerusalem in the Persian period since no ambitious Jewish power could do more under the watchful eye of the Persian Empire than to be preoccupied with the temple. Second, the text secures for Solomon the legitimacy of the whole community so that he does not, as in 1 Kings 1 and 2, need to secure the throne by palace intrigue and a series of assassinations. The throne is rightfully his and he has secured it through proper dynastic conventions. The throne is properly his "office."

In 1 Chronicles 28, Solomon's legitimacy and responsibility for the temple are reiterated. As to the first, the matter of Solomon's legitimacy, in verses 2–8 David addresses the assemblage of his "brothers" and his people. The address clarifies, as in 22:8, why David cannot build the temple.

The commendation given to Solomon accents two points. First, the verb "bḥr" (choose) is used for YHWH's designation of Solomon as king, the only time this word is used this way with reference to Solomon in all of scripture (1 Chron 28:5–6, 10; 29:1).[7] Thus not only is Solomon the only king so chosen by YHWH, but the rhetoric is utilized only in the Chronicler, a usage that clearly means to elevate and celebrate this awesome temple builder. Second, the free act of choice is immediately conditioned by the "if" of Torah in 1 Chronicles 28:7–8, so that the characterization of the king is a rhetorical maneuver to voice a more general Torah instruction to the whole community. The inference is that not only the imagined king but also the reading community are inescapably drawn to Torah.

First Chronicles 28 also addresses Solomon's responsibility for the temple. David again directs a charge to Solomon (1 Chron 28:9–10), consisting of three accent points: the Deuteronomic "if" of Torah and a commendation to love and serve YHWH wholly; an affirmation of Solomon's peculiar election (*bḥr*); and an imperative to act boldly in temple building. These two verses thus constitute a heavily laden rhetorical summary of the full authorization and legitimization of Solomon.

Then follows a narrative interlude in 1 Chronicles 28:11–19 that characterizes the written plan (*bnîth*) that YHWH has given to David that David now entrusts to Solomon. The plan is given in close detail so that Solomon, "young and inexperienced," need only enact what he has been given. The use of the word "*bnîth*" is of particular interest because it is a recurring term in the Priestly instruction given to Moses concerning the building of the tabernacle.

There are three detailed plans for sanctuaries in biblical sources outside Chronicles: the tabernacle in Exod. 25ff.; Solomon's temple in 1 Kings 6–7; and Ezekiel's future temple in Ezek. 40ff. Both the tabernacle and Ezekiel's visionary temple are explicitly described as following a divine plan. Thus in Exod. 25.9: "According to all that I show you concerning the pattern (*tabnît*) of the tabernacle and of all its furniture, so you shall make it" (also 25.40; 26.30; 27.8, etc.), and in different terms in Ezekiel's vision: "Son of man, look with your eyes, and hear with your ears, and set your mind upon all that I shall show you, for you were brought here in order that I might show it to you" (Ezek. 40.14). On the other hand, in sharp contrast to the version in Chronicles, the account in I Kings 6–7 gives no hint that Solomon's Temple was built according to any divine model or inspiration.[8]

It is plausible that the Chronicler here, given a statement of Deuteronomic conditionality, also incorporates Priestly teaching, so that both traditions of "holy place" are held together.

Finally, the chapter concludes with the third piece of the father's charge to the son, an address in which he again urges zeal, fidelity, and courage for this most singular task. Thus even though David is crucial for the project of the temple, it is clear that the temple to be built is not his plan but a plan given to him—in writing—by YHWH.

The Chronicler's account of the reign of David comes to a close in 1 Chronicles 29, where Solomon is mentioned in three connections. First, in verses 1–5, David addresses Solomon, again reinforcing the charge concerning the temple; the father assures the son that he, the father, has done all the hard work of planning and providing for supplies. In a quick phrase in verse 1, moreover, the Chronicler attests to a particular temple theology: "for the temple will not be for mortals but for the Lord God" (1 Chron 29:1b). Second, David's prayer in verses 10–19 moves from a ringing doxology (29:10–13) to a statement of needy deference in which Israel is said to have "no hope" (29:14–15) to a petition for son Solomon that he may be obedient and that he may build the temple (29:19). David cannot quit before he has reminded God— and the reader—that he has "made provision" for the building of the temple (29:19).

Third, Solomon is made king, in fact, "prince" (ngîd). This is the culminating act of David's reign; he secures the succession to his dynasty for his well-beloved son. The odd phrase "a second time" likely refers back to 1 Chronicles 23:1, where Solomon is made king by David, only this time there is proper ritual activity. The parallel mention of Zadok as priest likely reinforces the sacerdotal nuance of the entire text, for the Chronicler envisions a community at worship, not a state. The conclusion of verses 24–25 employs extravagant language for this young and inexperienced heir who is highly exalted and bearer of royal majesty: "The Lord highly exalted Solomon in the sight of all Israel, and bestowed upon him such royal majesty as had not been on any king before him in Israel" (1 Chron 29:25). Japhet suggests that the general pledge of allegiance to the new king in verse 24 is to counteract the narrative report of 1 Kings 1–2 that the throne was in dispute at the death of David, for here there was no dispute at all: "This remark's raison d'être is its polemic reference to I Kings 1–2. There, the struggle between the camps of Adonijah and Solomon culminate in the latter gaining the upper hand, but Solomon's enthronement was surely not the unanimous act of 'all the leaders.' . . . The Chronicler, on the other hand, stresses not only the consent of the entire people, but even more their active support in the accession of Solomon, by carefully including here members of both camps: 'the mighty men' and 'all the sons of king David.'"[9]

The throne is not in dispute. It belongs to son Solomon just as father David intended, and all are agreed. In what follows, Solomon is a great temple builder. In fact, so reports the narrative, there is little for him to do. The "plan" is in place and the materials are provided; all that is required is a faithful Torah keeper, exactly the kind of Jew required in Persian Judaism, exactly the kind of Jew produced by the imagination of Ezra, the great Torah scribe.

THE TEMPLE AS CULMINATION AND FULFILLMENT OF TRADITION

The best way into the Chronicler's account of Solomon in 2 Chronicles 1–9 is to see it as a report that closely follows the Deuteronomic construal of 1 Kings 3–11; there are, however, important adjustments that reflect the particular interests of the

Persian-period narrator. In sum, Japhet rightly judges: "Chronicles adds a number of motifs intended to enhance Solomon's image. . . . With some goal in mind, the Chronicler also deletes all the sore points from Solomon's reign."[10] The additions to and subtractions from the Kings narrative that are designed to make Solomon more impressive along the way have an additional effect, namely, all the acute irony begetting ambiguity in the Kings narrative has now been dissolved. There remains little playfulness to make room for interpretation of a genuinely historical figure. All that is narratively interesting from the Kings narrative has been dissipated in the service of a very different agenda.

Of the entire Solomon narrative in Chronicles (2 Chron 1–9), the extended central section of 2 Chronicles 2:1–7:11 concerns the temple, that section being framed by an introduction (1:1–17) and general conclusion containing a variety of different materials (7:12–9:31). It is clear in such an arrangement that the narrative is designed to cohere with the Davidic material we have already considered, in order to attest that Solomon's primal task as king is temple building. Rudolf Mosis observes that "everything else that the Chronicler knows to report concerning Solomon is subordinated to this primary content of his reign."[11] The extended material on the temple may be understood in three sequenced units: preparation (2:1–5:1), dedication (5:2–7:7), and sacrificial worship (7:8–10; 8:12–16).[12] The entire report on the temple is completed with the formula of completion in 7:11, a formula matched in 5:1 with the conclusion on the section concerning preparation. Because the single focus is upon Solomon as temple builder, we may give detailed attention to this report. (It is clear the Chronicler has little interest in Solomon as wise king and gives only passing attention to Solomon's economic prowess. Thus in the interest of the temple, the Chronicler has minimized the importance of two of the three primary themes we noted in 1 Kings 3–11.)

In the report, the preparation for the building of the temple in 2 Chronicles 2:1–5:1 is seen as implementation of the plan and provisions David had already put in place. The preparation begins with conscription of a labor force (2 Chron 2:2 [Heb 2:1]), a note reiterated in 2:17–18. In this presentation, Solomon now replicates the work of his father (see 1 Chron 22:2) and, like his father, recruits only "aliens" (*gerim*) who will do the work of stonecutting. Here the eventually odious practice of forced labor is exclusively in the service of temple construction. The capacity of this centralized government to recruit in such a way is reinforced by the equally odious practice of a census, a means of identifying the labor force (see 2 Sam 24:1; 1 Chron 21:1). In this narrative, no hint of criticism is noted for either the labor policy or the census. In other contexts we might expect a harsh critique of such royal practices, but none is forthcoming here.

This narrative report sandwiches two letters that serve to recount the indispensable report of Huram of Tyre. Solomon's initial letter presents to Huram a rationale for the temple and a brief temple theology (2 Chron 2:3–10). This theology, following the Deuteronomist, accepts that the house is to be for "the name" (2:1, 4), for it cannot "contain" the presence. The particular emphasis here, however, is that the house is for offerings and sacrifices and festivals. Thus in this purview, Solomon makes possible the identity-giving, identity-sustaining liturgic actions of Jews amid Persian power. The setting of cedar and cypress wrought through skilled labor is to make such offerings possible (2:7–10). In exchange for the contributions of the workmen from Tyre, Solomon will send to Tyre other materials secured in trade.

The response of Huram shows him to be a willing accomplice and subordinate to Solomon (2 Chron 2:11–16). It is evident that the report on crafts necessary to the temple is informed by Exodus 35:31–35, indicating that this narrator can draw from the Priestly account of the construction of the wilderness cult. More than simply the deference of Huram to Solomon, Huram, like the Queen of Sheba later in 2 Chronicles 9:8, is a good Yahwistic theologian who is capable of praise of YHWH and who confirms Solomon as king. Solomon, as a practitioner of "discretion and understanding," knows precisely what is needed for temple building (see parallel on the lips of David in 1 Chron 22:12).

The actual construction and completion of the temple is reported in close detail, and is in general congruent with the narrative account of 1 Kings 5–7. The temple yet again is in three chambers, the vestibule (2 Chron 3:4), the nave (3:5–7), and the most holy place (3:8–9). Particular attention is given to the carved cherubim and the holy of holies, perhaps in order to attest, as in Ezekiel, to the palpable presence and mobility of the God who is linked to the temple (see Ezek 43–44). As with the earlier report in the Kings narrative, the furnishings are lavish with ample gold, in order to enhance the place of presence (2 Chron 3:9–10; 4:7, 19–22). In 2 Chronicles 4:11, it is reported that Hiram, a very close associate in the project, finished his work for Solomon. In 5:1, moreover, Solomon is said to have finished the work of preparation, in fact completing what David had set in motion. We note only one other matter. The place of the temple is Mount Moriah, thus an allusion to the authority of Abraham (see Gen 22); beyond that, however, the site is "the threshing floor of Ornan," thus an appeal to the purchase of David (2 Chron 3:1; 2 Sam 24:18–25; 1 Chron 21:18–22):

Then the angel of the Lord commanded Gad to tell David that he should go up and erect an altar to the Lord on the threshing floor of Ornan the Jebusite. (1 Chron 21:18)

Then David said, "Here shall be the house of the Lord God and here the altar of burnt offering for Israel." (1 Chron 22:1)

It is clear that the son proceeds in full compliance with the mandate of the father. Of special interest in the narrative that legitimates the site is reference to the tabernacle of Moses: "For the tabernacle of the Lord, which Moses had made in the wilderness, and the altar of burnt offering were at that time in the high place at Gibeon" (1 Chron 21:29). In this skillful statement, the tradition at the same time appeals back to Mosaic authority and makes links to the shrine at Gibeon from where Solomon begins his rule (2 Chron 1:3). Thus the narrative incorporates a variety of sanctuary traditions and establishes the way in which the temple of Solomon is to be the culmination and fulfillment of all of those traditions. All the traditions serve to legitimate and enhance this new sanctuary.

DEDICATION OF THE TEMPLE

The report of temple dedication in 2 Chronicles 5:2–7:11 closely follows the narrative of 1 Kings 8, including the festival procession with the ark, thus linking the temple to the remembered traditions of the Covenant of Sinai (2 Chron 5:2–9), the dissenting note about presence in the ark (5:10), the high theology of "dwelling" (6:1), the prayers of doxology (6:4–11, 14–17), the caveat against presence (6:18, here reiterated from 2:6), and a series of prayers that may be addressed via this place to the God who dwells in heaven (6:19–40).

While the essential report is parallel to its antecedent source, we may note important, distinctive accents. The Levitical singers figure prominently in the liturgy of the new temple (2 Chron 5:11–13; 7:6). These two mentions are located as an envelope to the entire report. That placement suggests great intentionality and indicates the signature interest of the Levites in the horizon of the Chronicler, an ordering given elaborate attention in the preparation of David (see 1 Chron 23:1–25:31). The Levites in this reading are particularly connected to hymnic refrain: "It was the duty of the trumpeters and singers to make themselves heard in unison in praise and thanksgiving to the Lord, and when the song was raised, with trumpets and cymbals and other musical instruments, in praise to the Lord, 'For he is good, for his steadfast love endures forever,' the house, the house of the Lord, was filled with a cloud" (2 Chron 5:13; see 7:3).

It may well be that this hymnic phrasing was a conventional and distinctive mark of Second Temple choirs. The phrasing of course delineates a primary claim for YHWH's fidelity, a connection crucial to the courage and resolve of Jews in emerging Judaism.

The report twice narrates the coming of "the glory of the Lord" to inhabit the newly dedicated house:

The house . . . was filled with a cloud, so that the priests could not stand to minister because of the cloud; for the glory of the Lord filled the house of God. (2 Chron 5:13–14)

When Solomon had ended his prayer, fire came down from heaven and consumed the burnt offering and the sacrifices; and the glory of the Lord filled the temple. The priests could not enter the house of the Lord, because the glory of the Lord filled the Lord's house. When all the people of Israel saw the fire come down and the glory of the Lord on the temple, they bowed down on the pavement with their faces to the ground, and worshiped and gave thanks to the Lord, saying, "For he is good, for his steadfast love endures forever." (2 Chron 7:1–3)

While the report echoes 1 Kings 8:10–11, the accent on presence is much greater here, and surely intends close parallel to the tabernacle in Exodus 40:34–35 (see also the descent of fire in Lev 9:23–25).

The particular accent on teaching in 2 Chronicles 6:27 and foreigners in 6:32–33 is reiterated from the earlier account; they may have special force in the Persian period when Judaism, under scribal impetus, became a didactic enterprise and when the presence of foreigners in the community was equally contested, on which see Isaiah 56:3–8. The dynastic promise contained in Solomon's prayer reiterates the same prayer from 1 Kings 8, but with a decisive difference. In 2 Chronicles 6:16, the dynastic promise has been made conditional by the intrusive "if" into the earlier unconditional promise. This interpretive maneuver is of course congruent with the rigorous covenantalism of the Chronicler and the tight theory of retribution with which the heritage is relayed in this version. (See the same introduction of the "if" in Psalm 132 when compared with Psalm 89.)

THE TEMPLE'S OPENING FESTIVAL

With the completion and consecration of the temple with the climactic statement of the Lord's "steadfast love" (2 Chron 7:6–7), the work of dedication is finished. Finally, in 2 Chronicles 7:8–10, Solomon sponsors for "all Israel" a seven-day festival of exuberance. The performance of such liturgic acts had been the initial purpose of the proposed temple first communicated to Huram: "I am now about to build a house for the name of the Lord my God and dedicate it to him for offering fragrant incense before him, and for the regular offering of the rows of bread, and for burnt offerings morning and evening, on the sabbaths and the new moons and the appointed festivals of the Lord our God, as ordained forever for Israel" (2:4).

The language of these verses is permeated with the technical terminology of Priestly, liturgical practice, here making Solomon into a Priestly figure. The purpose of the temple is to give offerings to YHWH on every imaginable occasion, in order to enhance YHWH and surely to sustain the liturgic-Yahwistic identity of the worshiping community. Indeed, Solomon's father had already articulated a theology of gratitude as the ground for offerings:

> And now, our God, we give thanks to you and praise your glorious name. "But who am I, and what is my people, that we should be able to make this freewill offering? For all things come from you, and of your own have we given you. For we are aliens and transients before you, as were all our ancestors; our days on the earth are like a shadow, and there is no hope. O Lord our God, all this abundance that we have provided for building you a house for your holy name comes from your hand and is all your own. I know, my God, that you search the heart, and take pleasure in uprightness; in the uprightness of my heart I have freely offered all these things, and now I have seen your people, who are present here, offering freely and joyously to you. O Lord, the God of Abraham, Isaac, and Israel, our ancestors, keep forever such purposes and thoughts in the hearts of your people, and direct their hearts toward you." (1 Chron 29:13–18)

In the Chronicles, David and perhaps Solomon regard Israelites (in the Persian period) as "aliens and transients" (*gerim . . . wetosavim*) who are without hope in the world. The sheer existence of Judaism as it was reconstituted in Jerusalem in the Persian period is understood as a gift from YHWH. Surely the community around the Chronicler is intensely committed to the proposition that sustained liturgic engagement with this God from whom all things come is the indispensable condition of survival and well-being for this small vulnerable community in a world of threats and endlessly ambiguous imperial power. What the father verbalizes the son seeks to implement by the completion of the house of God.

Thus it is not surprising that the first act upon completion of the temple is a festival that remembers and replicates the same festival (*hg*) that ancient mothers and fathers had daringly proposed in the ancient days of slavery:

> Afterward Moses and Aaron went to Pharaoh and said, "Thus says the Lord, the God of Israel, 'Let my people go, so that they may celebrate a festival to me in the wilderness.'" (Exod 5:1)

Israel had understood in its inchoate beginning that such a festival is a dramatic act of identity, a daring act of subversion, a resolved act of freedom, all grounded in the affirmation of the God who can override every imperial power. Of course Pharaoh, in that ancient narrative, understood as well as Israel the dangerous significance of festival, and so resisted. Only in a belated act of vulnerability did Pharaoh bargain with Moses to allow a limited festival:

> Then Pharaoh summoned Moses and Aaron, and said, "Go, sacrifice to your God within the land." (Exod 8:25)

And Pharaoh, in response to the insistence of Moses, seeks an element of benefit for himself:

> But Moses said, "It would not be right to do so; for the sacrifices that we offer to the Lord our God are offensive to the Egyptians. If we offer in the sight of the Egyptians sacrifices that are offensive to them, will they not stone us? We must go a three days' journey into the wilderness and sacrifice to the Lord our God as he commands us." So Pharaoh said, "I will let you go to sacrifice to the Lord your God in the wilderness, provided you do not go very far away. Pray for me." (Exod 8:26–28)

The ante is upped in Exodus 10:3:

> So Moses and Aaron went to Pharaoh, and said to him, "Thus says the Lord, the God of the Hebrews, 'How long will you refuse to humble yourself before me? Let my people go, so that they may worship me.'" (Exod 10:3)

Pharaoh's grudging allowance, however, is not yet enough:

> Then Pharaoh summoned Moses, and said, "Go, worship the Lord. Only your flocks and your herds shall remain behind. Even your children may go with you." But Moses said, "You must also let us have sacrifices and burnt offerings to sacrifice to the Lord our God. Our livestock also must go with us; not a hoof shall be left behind, for we must choose some of them for the worship of the Lord our God, and we will not know what to use to worship the Lord until we arrive there." (Exod 10:24–26)

The narrative of course ends with Pharaoh's complete capitulation to Moses and to YHWH. Israel, in its seizure of freedom that is grudgingly granted, will worship YHWH:

> Then he summoned Moses and Aaron in the night, and said, "Rise up, go away from my people, both you and the Israelites! Go, worship the Lord, as you said." (Exod 12:31)

And only in passing does Moses leave a blessing for the one who has resisted YHWH (Exod 12:32):

Now of course there is no necessary linkage between the Exodus narrative and the festival of Solomon in our text. If, however, contemporary scholarship is correct in taking the final form of the Pentateuch as a Persian achievement, this festival in the Exodus narrative then is a subversive means of communal identity in the face of imperial reality whenever "we are slaves to this day" (see Neh 9:36). Thus the parallel between *Solomon's act* and the *Exodus narrative* is a credible one. In 2 Chronicles 7:8–10 Solomon does what he anticipated in his opening communication to Huram in 2:4. If this is an act that substantiates a specific, particular identity, then there is ample reason that the people went away to their homes, joyful and in good spirits because of the goodness that the Lord had shown to David and to Solomon and to his people Israel (2 Chron 7:10).

Solomon's commitment to a sustained practice of offerings is evidenced in the derivative text of 2 Chronicles 8:12–15. That text is presumably based on 1 Kings 9:25, but now it is greatly expanded in length, in detail, and in the many practices of sacrifice and offering that are listed: "Then Solomon offered up burnt offerings to the Lord on the altar of the Lord that he had built in front of the vestibule, as the duty of each day required, offering according to the commandment of Moses for the sabbaths, the new moons, and the three annual festivals—the festival of unleavened bread, the festival of weeks, and the festival of booths" (2 Chron 8:12–13).

Along with new moons and sabbaths and "the duty of each day," the major festivals are named, whereas they were only summarized in the introductory text. It is clear that the makers of this tradition are quite intentional about liturgic detail. The practice of festivals, moreover, is marked in two other ways. First, everything is performed as David had provided. Second, the leadership concerns the Levites. On both counts Solomon is in full compliance with his charge and in agreement with the interests of the text makers: "According to the ordinance of his father David, he appointed the divisions of the priests for their service, and the Levites for their offices of praise and ministry alongside the priests as the duty of each day required, and the gatekeepers in their divisions for the several gates; for so David the man of God had commanded. They did not turn away from what the king had commanded the priests and Levites regarding anything at all, or regarding the treasuries" (2 Chron 8:14–15).

This second report on offerings and sacrifices, after 2 Chronicles 7:8–10, evidences a perfectly conformed liturgy presided over by a profoundly pious, obedient king. The cult guaranteed by Solomon is everything for this community amid the empire. It is no wonder that at the end of these liturgical acts the text offers yet one more formula of conclusion: "Thus all the work of Solomon was accomplished from the day the foundation of the house of the Lord was laid until the house of the Lord was finished completely" (2 Chron 8:16).

SUCCESSFUL COMPLETION OF THE TEMPLE

The concluding formula of 2 Chronicles 7:11 is a notably strong one: "Thus Solomon finished the house of the Lord and the king's house; all that Solomon had planned to do in the house of the Lord and in his own house he successfully accomplished." It reports that the work has been "successfully accomplished" and oddly credits Solomon for all that was done, omitting the plan of David, on which see 1 Chronicles 28:11–19. Now it may be that this formula of completion, already anticipated in 2 Chronicles 4:11 and 5:1, is nothing more than a literary convention, a way of closing a narrative report.

We may, however, be instructed by the shrewd analysis Joseph Blenkinsopp has made of the literary, rhetorical structure of the Pentateuch. He has paid particular attention to the formulaic expressions that shape the literature. Specifically, he is attentive to the fact that

> the most solemn of these conclusion formulas occur at three points of the P history:
>
> (1) Creation of the world (Gen 2:1–2): "Thus the heavens and the earth were finished and all their hosts . . . God finished his work which he had done."
> (2) Construction of the wilderness sanctuary (Exod 39:32; 40:33): "Thus all the work of the tabernacle of the tent of meeting was finished . . . so Moses finished the work."
> (3) Setting up of the sanctuary in Canaan and allotment of territory (Josh 19:51): "So they finished dividing the land."

In a certain sense, therefore, the construction of the sanctuary is the completion of the work begun in creation, a conclusion toward which P leads us by the parallel wording of the two narratives:

Creation of the world	Construction of the sanctuary
And God saw everything that he had made, and behold, it was very good (Gen 1:31).	And Moses saw all the work, and behold, they had done it (Exod 39:43).
Thus the heavens and the earth were finished (Gen 2:1).	Thus all the work of the tabernacle of the tent of meeting was finished (Exod 39:32).
God finished his work which he had done (Gen 2:2).	So Moses finished the work (Exod 40:33).
So God blessed the seventh day (Gen 2:3).	So Moses blessed them (Exod 39:43).

The parallelism is completed by the injunction to observe sabbath which concludes the instructions for the setting up of the cult and is repeated immediately before the account of their implementation (Exod 31:12–17; 35:1–3).

It is difficult to avoid the conclusion that this basic structure of the P narrative is related in some way to the project of rebuilding the temple and restor-
ing the cult in the land of Israel.[13]

To be sure, Blenkinsopp's analysis concerns only the Pentateuch, with an accent
upon the Priestly material on the construction of the tabernacle in Exodus 25–31.
But since his analysis looks beyond the Pentateuch into Deuteronomic materials and
since the Chronicler pushes to the extreme some Deuteronomic matters, we may
suggest an extrapolation from Blenkinsopp to consider the formula of completion
in 2 Chronicles 7:11 (with reference also to 4:11, 5:1). It is clear in 7:11 that the
Chronicler has reached the point of heavy significance. If Solomon is primarily,
almost exclusively, noted as a temple builder, then the completion of the temple merits notation, not only completed but completed "successfully," according to all that
the dutiful son imagined from his commanding father. In the narrative of the Chronicler, the imagined—reimagined—temple of Solomon with its choirs and luxurious
furnishings and fire of presence surely provides a fixed point of identity for Jews who
had little to go on except the practices, disciplines, and teachings that cluster in the
temple apparatus. In this "finishing," Judaism was made safe for Jews into the next
generation, safe from Persian dissolution, safe from detractions from non-Jerusalem
Jews, and safe from mixed marriages and all manner of compromise. Blenkinsopp's
triad of creation, tabernacle, and land surely operate as well in the horizon of the
Chronicler.[14] The tabernacle as a place of glory is echoed in the imagined temple. The
land around Jerusalem is now a place of safety and security and blessing, even if
guaranteed by the Persians, and surely the temple with its "sea" (2 Chron 4:15) and
dynastic pillars (3:17) bespeaks the solidity and firmness of creation. We may conclude that the Chronicler trades upon and makes use of the Priestly theology of "finish" that was already in some form available. That this resolution of all the vagaries
of history in temple absoluteness is here and there subverted by the conditional "if"
(6:16) and by reservation about presence (2:6; 5:10; 6:18) does not detract from that
powerful absolutist claim. It is the wonder of Solomon that in this act of interpretive
imagination he is able to host, sponsor, and legitimate this richness of assurance
without compromising the starchy candor of covenant and without adjudicating
all of the complexities of the traditions utilized in this retelling. At 7:11, it is done.
It is accomplished. The formula is a triumphant affirmation, not unlike the "finished"
formula Christians cherish on the lips of the dying Jesus (John 19:30).

FRAMING OF THE SOLOMON NARRATIVE IN CHRONICLES

With this consideration of the temple text, we may now return to comment upon the framing of the narrative of Solomon in 2 Chronicles 1:1–17 and 7:12–9:31. The introduction to the Solomon narrative in 2 Chronicles 1:1–17 contains familiar material, first the initial dream narrative that legitimates his rule (2 Chron 1:2–15), and second, a report on Solomon's commercial activity (1:14–17). That familiar material, however, is now shaped in a particular way. The opening formula of 1:1 ties Solomon securely to David as "son of David" and so refers back to the legitimating statements of 1 Chronicles 22, 28, and 29. The formula nicely juxtaposes Solomon's own initiative, for he is the subject of the verb "establish" (hzq), and the gift of YHWH who is the subject of "make great" (gdl) plus the adverbial modifier. Braun suggests that the verb "establish" (hzq) is a reference to the assassinations necessary to the throne in 1 Kings 2 that have now been overlooked in the Chronicler's account.[15] The completed formula of the first verse refers back to David's legitimacy and particularly to 1 Chronicles 28:20, David's affirmation that "the Lord my God is with you." Indeed, the remainder of the Solomon narrative to follow is a substantiation and demonstration of the opening declaration of Solomon's greatness and of his accompaniment by YHWH.

The dream narrative is a public event at Gibeon. In this articulation the narrative gathers together a variety of cultic memories and places them all at Gibeon, the great cult antecedent to Jerusalem that is the place of legitimization. Thus at this great shrine was Moses's "tent of meeting," the ark that David had confiscated, and the bronze altar that relates to the Priestly tradition of tabernacle. Clearly Solomon (and his temple) is the heir of all of these traditions of presence. The legitimization offered here is not only of the king but also of the temple that he will "decide to build" (2 Chron 2:1 [Heb 1:18]).

The dialogic exchange of 2 Chronicles 1:7–12 reports Solomon receiving from YHWH what is needed for the coming narrative. In a prayer framed by deferential doxology, the kind surely offered by a person of great piety, Solomon asks for "wisdom and knowledge." The divine response notices all that Solomon might have asked and did not, including "the life of those who hate you." The new king is granted "wisdom and knowledge," but also "riches, possessions, and honor in comparable measure." The divine response is of course the same as in the narrative of 1 Kings 3, except that here it is escalated. The list of divine gifts in verse 12 plays upon the list of things "not asked" in verse 11. The sum of both, in hyperbolic form, centers on riches and honor. While the request and grant is for wisdom, it is readily noticed in what follows that the Chronicler has no interest in the king's judicial practice or in his capacity for wise rule. At the most, royal wisdom concerns temple construction, but even that shades over into wealth.

The focus upon wealth moves the narrative easily to 2 Chronicles 1:14–17, a celebration of royal wealth gained through commercial activity. This paragraph is basically a reiteration of the report in 1 Kings 10:26–29. The narrative of the Chronicler has no particular interest in Solomon's commercial activity, his wealth being primarily of interest for the lavish decor of the temple. The two introductory topics of dream legitimization and wealth together position Solomon for his proper work of temple building. He is fully legitimated and equipped financially for the work.

The transitional verse that leads to temple construction is a bit curious (2 Chron 2:1 [Heb 1:18]), for it concerns the royal decision to build the temple (and royal palace) as if it were an entirely new idea, when in fact the preceding Davidic report readied Solomon for this moment. In any case, the legitimated, resolved, pious Solomon is now up to the task. It is worth noting that in his unqualified orthodoxy, there is no distracting mention of Pharaoh's daughter (as in 1 Kgs 3:1), nor any mention of high places (as in 1 Kgs 3:2), for Gibeon is a centralized sanctuary without any competition or distraction.

THE CONCLUDING FRAMEWORK OF THE SOLOMON NARRATIVE

The conclusion of the framework of Solomon's narrative of temple building in 2 Chronicles 7:12–9:31 is made up almost entirely of familiar materials, though here the text is more complex. The concluding framework begins in 7:12–22 with the second dream narrative. The two dream reports help to shape the entire narrative, as they do the narrative in 1 Kings 3–11. The warning and conditional "if" of Torah here pertain to the people as to the king, as they did not in the Deuteronomic narrative (2 Chron 7:14). Thus the text is much more didactically aimed at the community in the Persian period. The symmetrical "if . . . then" formulation in positive and negative modes is reiterated, again with an accent upon the negative warning (7:17–22). The intent of the whole, of course, is a rigorous insistence upon Torah obedience with particular emphasis upon the first commandment and the great risk of "other gods." Along with rigorous demand, Hugh Williamson has seen that this passage (referring to vv. 17–22) is acutely responsive to the "paradigmatic 'exilic' situation," assuring the reader that "no circumstances are too formidable to prevent God's immediate, direct, and, if necessary, miraculous move to fulfill his promise."[16]

The report of 2 Chronicles 8 includes statements about Solomon's building projects, including storage towns made possible by forced labor from captured peoples (2 Chron 8:1–10) and commercial activity (8:17–18) that has made his wealth secure. One has the impression that the narrator is not especially interested in these matters but reports them from already known material.

In this account of royal success, two matters merit attention. First, as already mentioned, the liturgical activity of Solomon in 2 Chronicles 8:12–15 displays Solomon's punctilious piety and exhibits the newly completed temple in its proper festival function as a place of offerings and sacrifices. Second, the daughter of Pharaoh is treated to an exclusionary formula. We have seen in the Kings narrative that her fingerprints are all over the Solomonic narrative. In the Chronicles version, Pharaoh's daughter and other foreign women are purged from the narrative even as the daughter is purged according to this report: "Solomon brought Pharaoh's daughter from the city of David to the house that he had built for her, for he said, 'My wife shall not live in the house of King David of Israel, for the places to which the ark of the Lord has come are holy'" (2 Chron 8:11). The temple where the ark is placed is holy; this foreign princess is incompatible with Israelite holiness and must be kept apart from temple precincts, "outside the camp." This formula of expulsion is terse and without comment. It takes little imagination, however, to relate this notation to the reforming zeal of Ezra and Nehemiah in the mid–fifth century. Specifically Ezra and Nehemiah regarded "foreign wives" as a decisive threat to the faithfulness and therefore the well-being of Judaism, and so required a purging of such women from the community (Ezra 9:1–4; Neh 13:1–3, 23–29). It may well be that the polemic of 1 Kings 11:1–8 also reflects this agenda of reformed Judaism, but the connection is more direct in Chronicles.[17] Ezra and Nehemiah are concerned to foster and protect the holiness of the Jewish community, specifically the "holy seed" of Jewishness. In Chronicles, Solomon is portrayed as readily compliant with that requirement, so that Pharaoh's daughter receives only minimal attention, and the entire readiness of Solomon to be open to culture beyond his own is severely circumscribed.

Chapter 9 of 2 Chronicles contains the narrative of the visit of the Queen of Sheba (2 Chron 9:1–12) and an inventory of Solomon's immense wealth. There is little that is new in this version. The visit of the queen is an opportunity to celebrate Solomon's wisdom that otherwise is not much in play in this narrative. The wisdom celebrated here consists in "practical skills of speech, wit, craftsmanship and statesmanship."[18] The inventory of wealth, with particular attention to much gold and ivory, evidences an extraordinary situation: "The like of it was never made in any kingdom" (9:19); and "Thus King Solomon excelled all the kings of the earth in riches and in wisdom" (9:22).

The detailed inventory is confirmation that the divine promise of 2 Chronicles 1:12 has indeed been fulfilled: "Wisdom and knowledge are granted to you. I will also give you riches, possessions, and honor, such as none of the kings had who were before you, and none after you shall have the like" (2 Chron 1:12). Thus 1:12 and 9:19, 22 provide an envelope for the entire narrative. All of the gains of immense energy and ingenuity are bracketed by divine favor, fidelity, and generosity. Solomon's wealth bespeaks divine blessing. The theological intentionality of this report is suggested by Donald D. Schley Jr., who notices that in 2 Chronicles 9:28 the Chronicler has added the phrase "from all the earth," suggesting celebrative hyperbole rather than reportage.[19]

The text moves on to a conventional concluding formula in 2 Chronicles 9:29–31 with appropriate footnotes. The concluding mention of Solomon's wisdom in 1 Kings 11:41 is omitted, again indicating a lack of interest in that royal capacity. More important, of course, is the lack of all of the materials in 1 Kings 11 concerning indictment (2 Kings 11:1–8), sentence of pending land loss (11:9–13), and threats instigated by YHWH of "raising up" adversaries (11:14, 23), and by prophetic instigation (11:29–40). None of that is on the horizon of this narrative, because now the narrative serves to articulate the "superlative blessing" of Rehoboam, son of Solomon:

> The themes of the new material in II Chron. 11 are: building projects (vv. 5–12), aspects of religious life (vv. 13–17), wives and sons (vv. 18–23)—which in the Chronicler's concept of history are signs of God's blessing. These are precisely the topics around which the excised story of Jeroboam in I Kings revolves: Jeroboam's constructions (I Kings 12.25), religious reforms and reactions to them (12.26–13.14), and Jeroboam's wife and son (14.1–18). Moreover, in each case there is an antithesis; the transgressions of Jeroboam are noted by the Chronicler only for the benefit incurred by Judah with the influx of emigrant faithful Israelites; in contrast to the death of Jeroboam's son and the dire prophecy of the extinction of his line, Chronicles enlarges the superlative blessing of Rehoboam. This element of literary counterpoint is in itself a theological statement, probably making a more profound impression than explicit comment.
>
> . . . In addition, there is a peculiar philosophy of history which determines the structure of Rehoboam's history. As the correlation between circumstances and religious conduct is taken to be absolute, the course of history must bear this out. The theologically motivated reconstruction has two points of departure: I Kings 12.24, "So they hearkened to the word of the Lord," and I Kings 14.25, "Shishak king of Egypt came up against Jerusalem." The beginning of Rehoboam's reign is marked by obedience to God's word, while its continuation is marked by an enemy invasion. Since it is the Chronicler's understanding both that Rehoboam's obedience should be properly rewarded and that Shishak's campaign is God's punishment for transgression, the intermediate period, from the first to the fifth year of Rehoboam, in Chronicles becomes an interim of transition, from three years of following "in the ways of David and Solomon" (11.17) to the fourth year in which Rehoboam "forsook the law of

God" (12.1). Then, in full accord with the Chronicler's theology, all the land-
marks of success and well-being are placed in these first three years.[20]

In what follows for the Chronicler among the kings after Israel, heirs to David and
Solomon, critiqued in polemic expressed, but not for David and not for David's son.

SOLOMON, THE IMMACULATE BUILDER OF THE PERFECT HOLY PLACE

The product of this narrative imagination is a Solomon who stands above the
vagaries of history, who is untempted and unseduced by royal power, and who is
therefore the immaculate builder of the perfect holy place where dwells the name (2
Chron 2:1 [Heb 1:18]), where prayers are heard (6:20–21), and where offerings and
sacrifices are given and festivals are celebrated (1:4–6, 7:8–10, 8:12–15). By the
elimination of all the seductions and compromises elsewhere assigned to Solomon,
the narrative has constructed a perfect place of presence and, we may hazard, a time-
less sanctuary that is immune to historical threat. As Solomon is removed from the
vagaries of time in this narrative, so his time stands immune to such risks.

We may imagine that such an offer of a place for unmitigated Jewishness in the
presence of the God of Israel was a response to a profound need for the holy community of Judaism in Jerusalem amid destruction and threats, local and imperial.
Thus the imagined temple, surely well beyond the reality of the Second Temple, gave
imaginative space for Judaism because it counted on promise and engaged in the
disciplines of altar and scroll in order to preserve and practice a distinctive covenantal identity. The actual practice of the Jerusalem cult may have relied on Persian
funding; in the imagination of this tradition, however, the necessary resources for
institutional maintenance are gifts of God wrought through faithful, pious worldly
achievement. Thus the worldly achievement of Solomon in 2 Chronicles 1:14–17,
8:17–18, and 9:13–27 is all in the service of the temple, which is a cipher for resolved
faithfulness to the God of covenant.

Given the context of that required maintenance of a distinct community without
great resources, we are able to appreciate the imaginative vision of the Chronicler.
We can, moreover, appreciate the way Solomon can give himself over to that imaginative vision or, more properly, the way in which Solomon can be taken over for that
vision. The context seems to have required precisely such a one-dimensional king
who really had no interest beyond temple. It was, in addition, important for the
enhancement of the temple that Solomon should in every way be glorious, invested
with "riches, possessions, and honor." What we have then is a king responsive to circumstance, glorious and one-dimensional. The reader will notice, however, that in
the imaginative production of this king, much of what is interesting in the narrative
of 1 Kings 3–11 has been lost. There is no critical counterpoint within the text and

therefore no playful irony upon which the interpreter can capitalize. It may well be that such irony is a luxury this particular community could ill afford. In this narrative, then, Solomon pales from his previous imaginative appearance as a point of interest. But then, the Chronicler was manifestly not interested in entertaining us belated readers or providing grist for playful ambiguity. The need in that community was far too urgent for playfulness. As a consequence the move from Kings to Chronicles entails a loss of irony in the material. That loss is itself an occasion for our own ironic interpretation.

CHAPTER 10

SOLOMON AS DURABLE
TEACHER: PROVERBS

The two narratives we have considered, 1 Kings 3–11 and 2 Chronicles 1–9, constitute what we have of Solomon as a historical personality. In both cases, however, we have seen that these narrative accounts offered as reportage are in fact vigorous and bold acts of interpretive imagination that plausibly are rooted in some historical memory to which we have no compelling access. These sustained acts of narrative imagination are designed to offer theological perspective of a quite insistent kind, respectively concerning the destruction of Jerusalem (1 Kgs 3–11) and the sustenance of the Jerusalem community in the Persian period (2 Chron 1–9). While historical rootage was likely important to the shapers of these traditions, it is clear in any case that they exercised immense interpretive freedom with whatever they had of rooted memory for the sake of contemporary interpretation. Both narratives make claim to historicity, but the claim itself is subject to careful interpretive query.

In the discussion of the book of Proverbs here undertaken—plus subsequent consideration of the Song of Songs and Ecclesiastes—the text itself makes only passing claim that connects the literature to Solomon, so that we are in a different world of interpretation. The book of Proverbs cites Solomon three times and seems to treat the matter with casual interest at best (Prov 1:1; 10:1; 25:1). Critical scholarship in general gives no credence to the apparent claim of Solomonic authorship of the book of Proverbs, even though in popular interpretation the connection is as readily entertained as the Davidic authorship of the book of Psalms.[1] There is no doubt that the book of Proverbs is a collection of already existing collections of proverbs, as indicated by the several introductory formulae (1:1; 10:1; 25:1; 30:1; 31:1). There is also no doubt that the secondary connection to Solomon is based on his general reputation for wisdom (see 1 Kgs 3:12, 16–28; 10:1–5, 23–24) and more specifically on the report of 1 Kings 4:29–34 (Heb 5:9–14) that Solomon authored a myriad of proverbs and catalogued available knowledge in an encyclopedic way. That connection to Solomon is not supportable, and in fact the wisdom in these several collections arose in a variety of contexts and circumstances.[2]

THE INTERFACE OF SOLOMON AND PROVERBS

In what follows, we will consider the interface of Solomon and Proverbs in terms of the critical discussion that has recently taken a provocative and compelling turn.

Gerhard von Rad, among the most prominent Wisdom interpreters of the last generation, offered a quite distinctive interpretive claim for Solomonic literature and culture on the basis of some strands of the Pentateuch plus the narratives clustered around David.[3] Von Rad proposed that in the tenth century B.C.E., in the new cultural environment generated by Solomon, there was a new spirit that reflected human emancipation from older understandings of the world and the usual role assigned to human beings in the world of the gods. He observed that in the new literature of the tenth century, human persons were now portrayed as actors in their own history and their own destiny, and not simply as obedient beings dependent upon the workings of the gods. This new literary offer he likened to an Enlightenment, using the term to appeal to the eighteenth-century notion of "man come of age": "In consequence, the figures in the stories now move in a completely demythologised and secular world. Unquestionably, we have here to do with the traces of an Enlightenment on a broad basis, an emancipation of the spirit and a stepping out from antiquated ideas."[4]

In the development of this hypothesis, von Rad imagined something of a decisive cultural transformation in the tenth century. While von Rad's argument is based on narrative art, it clearly has important implications for the sapiential tradition that is solidified in the book of Proverbs. The proverbs, like the narratives to which von Rad appeals, present human persons with a freedom and capacity to exercise choice that determines futures. Neither the narratives nor the proverbs, of course, lose sight of the elemental governance of the providence of the Creator God. That providential governance, however, leaves enormous room for human choice, human freedom, and human responsibility. Von Rad does not go so far as to connect Proverbs directly to the Solomonic moment, but the way is open to imagine the encyclopedic wisdom of Solomon in 1 Kings 4:29–34 as an important human initiative to gather the world around human capacity.[5]

And if sapiential teaching offers a close connection between deed and consequence, as it obviously does, then the successful outcome of Solomon's reign in terms of wealth, in sapiential interpretation, attests to his good conduct.[6] Crenshaw shrewdly observes: "As the wealthiest king in Israel's memory, Solomon must naturally have invited thoughts associating him with extraordinary wisdom."[7] The connection of this Solomonic revolution to Proverbs is not explicit in either von Rad or Crenshaw; the connection, however, is a thinkable one given the hypothesis of "Enlightenment." Von Rad's proposal was for a time an influential one in scholarship, making plausible Solomon's major contribution to Israelite wisdom. This connection was further enhanced when it was recognized that Israel's Wisdom tradition was intimately linked to that of Egypt, and Solomon is of course said to be deeply connected to Egyptian power and Egyptian culture.[8]

A more popular treatment of Solomon that coheres with von Rad's hypothesis is that of E. W. Heaton's *Solomon's New Men: The Emergence of Ancient Israel as a National State*.[9] Heaton analyzes the traditions of Solomon assuming that these traditions bear a great deal of historical reliability, and he expresses no skepticism concerning the claims made therein. The title of Heaton's book, *Solomon's New Men*, refers to the emerging scribal class in the tenth century reflective of a new "cultural milieu" that produced a "New Democracy" and a new literature from the "educated men."[10] The critique that has been subsequently made of von Rad's hypothesis pertains as well to the analysis offered by Heaton.

In the long-term development of scholarship concerning Wisdom, von Rad's hypothesis was not sustained. While the connection of monarchy and Wisdom seems credible, and Crenshaw, for example, does not directly deny a possible tenth-century locus, von Rad's hypothesis has been defeated by more general historical studies. The decisive argument against a Solomonic date for Wisdom material that is presented with the Book of Proverbs is that of R. B. Y. Scott, who in 1955, just at the time von Rad's proposed his Enlightenment theory, reached the conclusion that "it is quite out of the question that the king was in fact the composer of the whole book of Proverbs, of Ecclesiastes, and Wisdom, of psalms canonical and extra-canonical."[11] In considering the key texts in 1 Kings 3:16–28, 4:29–34, and 10:1–13, Scott concludes that the texts are products of folklore and, on the basis of legitimate parallels, the texts are likely to be postexilic and could not be early. Thus the evidence for Solomon as a Wisdom teacher is quite late and without historical basis. In this, Scott has generally been followed by other scholars.

Scott then goes on to consider the references to Solomon in the superscriptions of the book of Proverbs and focuses upon Proverbs 25:1, "These are other proverbs of Solomon that the officials of King Hezekiah of Judah copied." He concludes that during the time of Hezekiah there was considerable literary activity that makes the collection of proverbs at that time, under royal aegis, plausible. Whatever may lie behind Hezekiah, with reference to Solomon, is beyond recovery, but Scott is representative of scholarship that denies Solomon any important role in Wisdom collection, precisely because there are no textual attestations that are credible.

It is important to notice that since publication of Scott's essay, scholarship is recently in a mood to date things much later, so that many scholars now would no more credit to the time of Hezekiah such a collection than Scott would credit them to the time of Solomon. Thus we may give a consensus interpretive point that Solomon has no historical connection to the book of Proverbs. The Wisdom materials have, moreover, been subjected to close scrutiny by R. N. Whybray in *The Intellectual Tradition in the Old Testament*.[12] Whybray quotes Scott and advances Scott's conclusion that the Wisdom traditions of the Old Testament have no discernible base in Solomon's tenth century. More specifically, against Heaton's sort of argument, Whybray judges that "there is no evidence in the Old Testament for existence of a class of writers known as 'the wise men' nor indeed *any* class of men so designated."[13] Whybray would deny any sustained continuing tradition of Wisdom teaching and sees the evidence only for ad hoc emergents: "There was over a long period 'an educated class' . . . and among them there arose from time to time men of literary ability and occasionally genius who provided the literature, which satisfied their demand."[14] On such a basis, of course, it is untenable to imagine any continuity between a tenth-century Solomon and the book of Proverbs.

That, however, leaves evidence in Proverbs 1:1, 10:1, and 25:1 that remains to be interpreted "canonically." Brevard Childs, as a part of his canonical proposal, has commented upon the canonical issues that are at stake once it is agreed that there is no historical connection between Solomon and the book of Proverbs. Whereas Crenshaw inclines to think that Wisdom, in popular imagination, gravitated to Solomon, Childs's characteristic propensity is to judge that the canonical marker, Solomon, is imposed upon the sapiential collection in a way that causes the liturgy to become something that it was not. By drawing the collection (or collection of collections) toward Solomon, two important moves were made.

First, the superscription guards against forcing the proverbs into a context foreign to wisdom, such as the Decalogue. The superscription serves canonically to preserve the uniqueness of the sapiential witness against attempts to merge it with more dominant biblical themes.[15] It is evident that the temptation to move the book of Proverbs toward more dominant themes was an important one in mid–twentieth century in the so-called biblical theology movement. That is, the Solomon connection helps to assure that the wisdom literature will be treated on its own terms, a guarantee given by the ascription to the great wise king.

Second, the superscription that assigns the proverbs to Solomon serves an important canonical function in establishing the relative age of wisdom in Israel.[16]

Critically, however, reference to Egyptian parallels and the awareness of the international culture of wisdom do not assure a sense of antiquity. Childs of course does not refer to modern critical judgment but rather to the need in the ancient world wherein antiquity was a crucial aspect of authority. Thus Childs's assessment of the canonical superscriptions is that the Solomonic claim for Proverbs does not at all touch the internal processes of the collection but only situates the literature intentionally.

We may take the sequence of von Rad (bold theological inventiveness), Scott (denial on close historical grounds), and Childs (canonical twist when historical claims are no longer credible) as a characteristic sequence of modern scholarship.

The outcome of the argument culminating in a canonical judgment is altogether congruent with how we have understood Solomon in the two traditions of historical reportage. That is, the Solomon given us in the canon has no historical claim to which we have access but is to be understood as a product and outcome of Israel's daring theological imagination. In the book of Proverbs, then, Solomon is shown to be the great practitioner of reasoned learning that is grounded in experience and observation, a reasoned learning that is rooted in a theological conviction that takes the world in its quotidian reality seriously. Solomon thus becomes a means whereby the *reality of faith* and the *reality of life* are deeply joined by sustained observation, imagination, and artistic articulation.

> But behind our assertion that experiences of Yahweh were, for Israel, experiences of the world, and *vice versa,* there lurks the question: Were there actually two areas of experience which Israel in the last resort did differentiate, or was there only one? That we can now no longer separate a realm of religious experience from a realm of secular experience is clear. On the other hand, Yahweh and the world were certainly not identical. Yahweh encountered man in the world. But why did there still exist parallel series of statements about "experiences of Yahweh" and "experiences of the world" as we saw above in Prov. 16.7–12 (an example typical of the book of Proverbs as a whole)? We can only answer as follows. Obviously Israel, in her "enlightened" understanding of the world, has stumbled upon a dialectic of experience which could no longer be simply resolved and released. Indeed, if Yahweh and the world had been identical, then everything could have been expressed in simple terms. But Yahweh encountered man in the world always and only in the individual act of experience, and this certainly did not presuppose any identity of God and world. Again, the expressions "experience of Yahweh" and "experience of the world" perhaps did not entirely coincide, otherwise the statements in the sentences could simply have been interchanged. But that was certainly never attempted.[17]

It is to be noted that von Rad here still says "enlightened," though that particular usage does not tell importantly against his shrewd conclusion.

THE STRANGE WOMEN IN THE SOLOMON NARRATIVE

The denial of a historical link between Solomon and Proverbs is a settled matter in critical scholarship. The attempt to connect the two canonically is offered by Childs, but it does not take us very far. Given the lack of generativity from these approaches, we may turn to the very different perspective of Claudia V. Camp.[18] Camp's general subject of study is "the strange woman," a study that begins with the "strange woman" in the book of Proverbs. She then extends the topic to other parts of the Bible. In the book of Proverbs, the "strange woman" is juxtaposed with "wisdom" or "Dame Wisdom" as a binary gender construct that reflects a generally binary approach to the instruction of the book of Proverbs. It is clear that this characteristic binary antithesis extends to right and wrong, righteous and wicked, wise and foolish, holy and profane, and eventually to life and death.

In the postexilic period it became a central concern of Judaism, in the wake of the disaster of the sixth century, to delineate boundaries in order to protect the community by safeguarding its holiness.[19] That protection of boundaries was a primary agenda of Ezra in the fifth century, epitomized by the expulsion of "foreign women" (Ezra 9:1–4; Neh 13:1–2, 23–27). Thus in a study of postexilic interpretive practice, Camp draws a close connection between the "strangeness" of women in Proverbs and in Ezra and Nehemiah, a strangeness that will jeopardize the "holy seed" of the community of Jerusalem. The defense of "holy seed" is of course an ideological construct in her reading that represents the interests and the power of an elite body of men; we must for that reason be alert to the polemic and its motivation in all of this trajectory. The presentation of the strange woman in Proverbs includes the following characterization of the woman, who is each time contrasted with the life-giving figure, wisdom:

> You will be saved from the loose woman,
> from the adulteress with her smooth words,
> who forsakes the partner of her youth
> and forgets her sacred covenant;
> for her way leads down to death,
> and her paths to the shades;
> those who go to her never come back,
> nor do they regain the paths of life. (Prov 2:16–19)

> My child, be attentive to my wisdom;
> incline your ear to my understanding,
> so that you may hold on to prudence,
> and your lips may guard knowledge.
> For the lips of a loose woman drip honey,
> and her speech is smoother than oil;
> but in the end she is bitter as wormwood,
> sharp as a two-edged sword.
> Her feet go down to death;

her steps follow the path to Sheol.
She does not keep straight to the path of life;
her ways wander, and she does not know it. (Prov 5:1–6)

My child, keep your father's commandment,
and do not forsake your mother's teaching.
Bind them upon your heart always;
tie them around your neck.
When you walk, they will lead you;
when you lie down, they will watch over you;
and when you awake, they will talk with you.
For the commandment is a lamp and the teaching a light,
and the reproofs of discipline are the way of life,
to preserve you from the wife of another,
from the smooth tongue of the adulteress.
Do not desire her beauty in your heart,
and do not let her capture you with her eyelashes;
for a prostitute's fee is only a loaf of bread,
but the wife of another stalks a man's very life. (Prov 6:20–26)

Say to wisdom, "You are my sister,"
and call insight your intimate friend,
that they may keep you from the loose woman,
from the adulteress with her smooth words.
For at the window of my house
I looked out through my lattice,
and I saw among the simple ones,
I observed among the youths,
a young man without sense,
passing along in the street near her corner,
taking the road to her house in the twilight, in the evening,
at the time of night and darkness.
Then a woman comes toward him,
decked out like a prostitute, wily of heart.
She is loud and wayward;
her feet do not stay at home;
now in the street, now in the squares,
and at every corner she lies in wait.
She seizes him and kisses him,

and with impudent face she says to him:
"I had to offer sacrifices,
and today I have paid my vows;
so now I have come out to meet you,
to seek you eagerly, and I have found you!
I have decked my couch with coverings,
colored spreads of Egyptian linen;
I have perfumed my bed with myrrh, aloes, and cinnamon.
Come, let us take our fill of love until morning;
let us delight ourselves with love.
For my husband is not at home;
he has gone on a long journey.
He took a bag of money with him;
he will not come home until full moon."
With much seductive speech she persuades him;
with her smooth talk she compels him.
Right away he follows her,
and goes like an ox to the slaughter,
or bounds like a stag toward the trap
until an arrow pierces its entrails.
He is like a bird rushing into a snare,
not knowing that it will cost him his life.
And now, my children, listen to me,
and be attentive to the words of my mouth.
Do not let your hearts turn aside to her ways;
do not stray into her paths,
for many are those she has laid low,
and numerous are her victims.
Her house is the way to Sheol,
going down to the chambers of death. (Prov 7:4–27)

The foolish woman is loud;
she is ignorant and knows nothing.
She sits at the door of her house,
on a seat at the high places of the town,
calling to those who pass by,
who are going straight on their way,
"You who are simple, turn in here!"
And to those without sense she says,

"Stolen water is sweet,
and bread eaten in secret is pleasant."
But they do not know that the dead are there,
that her guests are in the depths of Sheol. (Prov 9:13–18)

In every case, the strange woman is seductive, attractive, and dangerous. She is dangerous because she will bring big trouble and death; consequently, wisdom instruction urges resistance to her and, instead, embrace of wisdom—the good woman who will bring life, prosperity, and well-being. It is the gain of Camp, in conversation with Marc Brettler and David Jobling, to have shown that wisdom instruction concerning the two women is a heavily freighted ideological polemic aimed at the defense of a particular mode of power and social organization.[20]

With this background Camp turns to the narrative of Solomon and notices that the narrative is much occupied by "strange women," notably the daughter of Pharaoh mentioned four times, the two strange women in 1 Kings 3:16–28, and finally the Queen of Sheba.[21] It is clear, following Deuteronomy 17:16, that the narrative intends to critique Solomon's "many foreign wives" whom he "loves," and who in 1 Kings 11:1–8 are the cause of his downfall. It is also the case, however, that the material is careful to protect Solomon as best it can from excessive contamination by the strange women. Thus in 3:16–28, Solomon chooses the good-mother strange woman and rejects the strange, really strange woman. In 10:1–13, Solomon bests the Queen of Sheba:

By the end of the Queen of Sheba episode, however, conventional expectations have been fulfilled. On one level, Woman Wisdom [the Queen] has lost her spirit to, been absorbed into, the Royal Man. On the narrative surface, the woman departs (10.13) and the man remains, but the effect is the same. This analysis leaves us not far, then, from Jobling's observations about the depiction of sexuality in mythic narratives (1991b: 59), where the male is the "real human" or, in this case, the "truly wise." On the other hand, the spirit taken by this man was not only that of Wisdom, but also of a Strange Woman. In this way, as well as in the sublimated sexuality of their wise discourse, Solomon's fall is anticipated in his relationship with the Queen of Sheba, at the same time that his ideal kingship is celebrated.[22]

WOMAN WISDOM / WOMAN FOOLISHNESS

For our purposes, the gain of Camp's shrewd reading of the narrative is twofold. The primary narrative of 1 Kings 3–11 in its final form, along with the Proverbs presentation of Woman Wisdom and the Strange Woman, propels the narrative into the orbit of Ezra and Nehemiah and their passionate concern to establish boundaries in order to protect the holy people and the "holy seed." Read in this way, the narrative of Solomon serves to affirm the regime of holiness and purity and the high risk presented by foreign women. The narrative of 1 Kings 3–11 is shown to be permeated with sexuality that serves as a cipher for ideology. Thus Camp refers, in her introductory chapter prior to a discussion of 1 Kings 3–11, to Bathsheba and Abishag. In the narrative itself, reference is readily made to the two strange women in chapter 3, to the four mentions of the daughter of Pharaoh, to the many foreign women of chapter 11, and most importantly, to the Queen of Sheba. The ideology of self-sufficiency and the critique of that ideology are gathered in the narrative around the women in the text.

Because of the prominence of women in the text, David Jobling, a conversation partner of Camp, has made the case that the narrative of Solomon contains a heavy critique of the distorted sexuality of his regime but at the same time is silent on the economic issues related to extravagant wealth, heavy taxation, and forced labor.[23] And indeed, the critique of Solomon's economics seems to be largely held in abeyance until 1 Kings 12, falling beyond the reign of Solomon. In this primary accent on sexuality as the point of critique in the narrative, Camp and Jobling are agreed.

We may, however, note since those publications the important work of Christine Yoder, who offers an alternative reading of Proverbs and "the two women," namely, "a socioeconomic reading of Proverbs 1–9 and 31:10–31."[24] Yoder's analysis begins with a study of women in the socioeconomic context of the Persian Empire. On the basis of extant documentation, she concludes:

> In marriage, often negotiated as "business" arrangements between families, a Persian-period woman was a bride of specified financial "worth" from whose dowry and additional inheritances, bequests, or gifts men might derive monetary gain.
>
> "Women's work" in the Achaemenid economy was varied. Among their responsibilities as managers of the household, women manufactured textiles, traded in the marketplaces, and might own and supervise slaves. Women also made and received deliveries, managed properties, and were parties to the purchase and sale of slaves and land. As workers in the royal economy, non-royal women engaged in a wide range of skilled and unskilled professions in numbers equivalent to or greater than men; women also worked at varying ranks and degrees of specialization. Moreover, women with sufficient amounts of capital might get into the credit business, making loans of cash and other goods at favorable interest rates.

Finally, royal women and women of high rank were often property holders and estate owners.[25]

That is, women were major economic players in both the domestic and the public economy. On the basis of this evidence, Yoder proposes that the "Woman of Substance" in Proverbs 31:10–31 is one who is effective and successful in the public economy. As a result, "To marry the Woman of Substance is to live a life of luxury."[26] Thus the "wise thing" (smart thing) for a prudent, well-connected man is to secure a wife who by competence and shrewdness will secure a comfortable or elite living for her husband and her family:

> Who, then, is this Woman of Substance? The embodiment of a goddess? This socioeconomic reading suggests not. Rather, the Woman of Substance in Prov 31:10–31 is a *composite figure of real—albeit exceptional—women in the Persian period*. She is a bride priced high for her wealth and socioeconomic potential. She brings home "loot" (her dowry and earnings) that makes her husband a wealthy man. She manufactures and trades in textiles with Phoenician merchants. She moves about, buying and selling, in the marketplaces and around the storehouses. She wears fine garments and clothes her family in the same. She manages workers. She buys real estate, develops it for profit, and still has money left over to give or loan to the poor. In short, her socioeconomic activities mirror those of affluent and royal women in the Persian period. She may be hard to find and even harder to attain, but she is not a figment of the imagination. As is expected in the wisdom tradition, it was the world—*indeed, the women*—known to the Persian-period writer that provided the pedagogical device for this wisdom poem. Images from the socioeconomic lives of women are here transformed into instruction for the socioeconomic survival of young men in the postexilic community.[27]

After a study of Proverbs 31:10–31 and "the Woman of Substance," Yoder turns to a study of Woman Wisdom in Proverbs 1–9. She concludes: "Interpreters tending to the parallels between Woman Wisdom (1–9) and the Woman of Substance (31:10–31) highlight the 'wisdom' dimensions of the Woman of Substance. This socioeconomic reading has reversed that approach, with new results. Significant portions of the father's instruction to his son in Proverbs 1–9 have been shown to personify Wisdom as a Woman of Substance."[28]

By exploring the connection between Woman Wisdom in Proverbs 1–9 and the Woman of Substance in chapter 31, Yoder is able to show that Woman Wisdom is one who continually performs well to the benefit of her husband:

She is a bride and a commodity to be sought after before all other possessions (4:4–7). She is a profitable businesswoman: her merchant profits (Hebrew, 3:14), revenues, and earnings (Hebrew, 8:19) are considerable. She is worth more than precious jewels (3:15; 8:11). She looks after her husband, offering him security, material advantage, storerooms filled to the brim (8:21), and an honorable place in the community. Finally, her household is a mansion filled with the trappings of privilege—servants and fine foods (9:1–3). Wisdom is a Woman of Substance and, as such, is a composite image of (exceptional) real women in the Persian period. In her, the lives of women become instruction for life.[29]

Thus Yoder's analysis alerts us to the fact that Proverbs, in its preoccupation with Woman Wisdom and Woman Foolishness, need not be read according to Freudian assumptions, in terms of repressed sexuality as Camp and Jobling propose. It is possible to turn in an economic (Marxist?) direction to see that wisdom is about a prosperous economy, a point certainly made in the Solomon narrative of 1 Kings 3–11.

In light of Yoder's hypothesis we may return to the Solomon narrative to suggest that perhaps the critique expressed through narrative attention to women does not pertain to sexuality but to the economy. It is possible that the several women noted are a cipher for a distorted economy in which neighborly covenantal relations are completely ignored in a stratified economy of surplus and wealth.[30] Thus we may ask again about the relationship of 1 Kings 11:1–8 and the tax revolt of 12:1–19 and see that Solomon is critiqued for a system of autonomous power that is expressed in a variety of ways. I do not believe that the question of the critique of Solomon is an either/or, between Yoder on the one hand and Camp and Jobling on the other, a critique of sexuality or of economics. Rather it is a both/and in which *exploitative sexuality* and *exploitative economics* (signified together in Deuteronomy 17:16–17 by "gold and silver and wives") function together in ways that distort "a more excellent way." In the hands of the Deuteronomist, the better way is in obedience to Torah. In the sapiential traditions, the better way is wisdom, acting congruently "with the grain of creation" as willed by the Creator. Both the Deuteronomist in 1 Kings 3–11 and the wisdom teachers in Proverbs know about the better way. Our narrative offers Solomon as an example of commoditization of both sexuality and economics in a futile effort at self-sufficiency.

CORE TEACHINGS OF THE BOOK OF PROVERBS

Thus the interface between the Solomonic narrative and Proverbs is immensely instructive. In my judgment, it is not necessary to draw a historical-critical judgment about dating the Solomonic narrative in order to be instructed by the arguments of

Camp, Jobling, and Yoder. It is enough to see that there is a sustained trajectory of critical reflection—whenever it is dated—that concerned the distinctiveness of Israel, the orderliness of creation, and the careless or cynical disregard of both that distinctiveness and that orderliness. In the Deuteronomic critique of Solomon, Solomon is rendered in the final form of the text as a covenant breaker who chooses death. Insofar as the Solomon narrative is drawn close to wisdom reflection, Solomon is shown to order his power against the grain of creation as ordered by the Creator.[31] The complex narrative of Solomon shows the king to have been a juggler, endlessly moving back and forth between the close demands of the covenant tradition and the opportunities for well-being that are offered on an international scale. This tension is intrinsic to the character of Israel and pervasive in Israel's text. The Solomon tradition is shaped by the Deuteronomist to give instruction about this tension. In a very different idiom the tradition of the proverbs attests that there are givens in lived reality that have been rightly discerned and cannot be violated with impunity.

Aside from forcing too much into a theory of repressed desire, we can nonetheless see that the wisdom tradition of Proverbs offers an immense illumination of royal power. In the most cited text, wisdom speaks and seems to look beyond ideology and repression to state the baseline of the entire sapiential worldview:

> The fear of the Lord is hatred of evil.
> Pride and arrogance and the way of evil and perverted speech I hate.
> I have good advice and sound wisdom;
> I have insight, I have strength. (Prov 8:13–14)

The "fear of the Lord" is championed as alternative to pride and arrogance. The fear of the Lord is equivalent to "hatred of evil." And then this primal utterance becomes more specific:

> By me kings reign,
> and rulers decree what is just;
> by me rulers rule,
> and nobles, all who govern rightly.
> I love those who love me,
> and those who seek me diligently find me.
> and nobles, all who govern rightly,
> I love those who love me,
> and those who seek me diligently find me.
> Riches and honor are with me,
> enduring wealth and prosperity.

My fruit is better than gold, even fine gold,
and my yield than choice silver.
I walk in the way of righteousness,
along the paths of justice,
endowing with wealth those who love me,
and filling their treasuries. (Prov 8:15–21)

Wisdom will indeed offer riches and honor, enduring wealth, and prosperity to kings. The condition here is not unlike the "if" we have seen in the Solomonic narrative; it concerns righteousness and justice. Perhaps the Queen of Sheba knew about this connection with more wisdom than the king who bested her: "Blessed be the Lord your God, who has delighted in you and set you on the throne of Israel! Because the Lord loved Israel forever, he has made you king to execute justice and righteousness" (1 Kings 10:9). Solomon, we are told, knew about this connection. Apparently he, or the urban elite who continued to imagine him, suffered from amnesia, a forgetfulness caused by commoditization. The Deuteronomist of course already knew that wealth produces amnesia, which seduces into autonomy:

> Take care that you do not forget the Lord your God, by failing to keep his commandments, his ordinances, and his statutes, which I am commanding you today. When you have eaten your fill and have built fine houses and live in them, and when your herds and flocks have multiplied, and your silver and gold is multiplied, and all that you have is multiplied, then do not exalt yourself, forgetting the Lord your God, who brought you out of the land of Egypt, out of the house of slavery, who led you through the great and terrible wilderness, an arid wasteland with poisonous snakes and scorpions. He made water flow for you from flint rock, and fed you in the wilderness with manna that your ancestors did not know, to humble you and to test you, and in the end to do you good. Do not say to yourself, "My power and the might of my own hand have gotten me this wealth." But remember the Lord your God, for it is he who gives you power to get wealth, so that he may confirm his covenant that he swore to your ancestors, as he is doing today. (Deut 8:11–18)

Wisdom is deeply rooted; when it is displaced by sheer technical capacity, everything important is put at risk. No wonder the tradition could imagine Proverbs in relationship to Solomon. The wise king had learned the core teaching of the book of Proverbs . . . the hard way!

CHAPTER 11

SOLOMON IN CANONICAL EXTRAPOLATION: ECCLESIASTES AND SONG OF SONGS

I n the third canon of the Hebrew Bible, "The Writings," one element of the canonical literature is constituted by the Megilloth, five small scrolls that in Jewish tradition are linked to the celebration of five festivals: Song of Songs (Passover); Ruth (Weeks); Lamentations (Ninth of Av); Ecclesiastes (Booths); and Esther (Purim).[1] Of these five small scrolls, two of them, Ecclesiastes and Song of Songs, have tradition connections to Solomon. For that reason we take up these two pieces of literature in turn. It is a common critical judgment that neither Ecclesiastes nor the Song of Songs has any historical connection to Solomon, for both of them are quite late in the Old Testament literature. Indeed, it is clear that even a canonical connection to Solomon is limited to little more than superscriptions that belatedly assign authorship of the material to Solomon. Since neither historical nor substantive canonical connections are forthcoming, the most we are able to do, in a study of Solomon, is to see what heuristic value there may be in imagining these literatures in relationship to Solomon.

ECCLESIASTES: THE WISDOM OF RESIGNATION

The book of Ecclesiastes is a collection of wisdom sayings that is conventionally dated to the late Persian or early Hellenistic period.[2] In the development of the Wisdom literature of the Old Testament, the book of Ecclesiastes seems to come belatedly, after the buoyant affirmation of the book of Proverbs and the defiant disputation of the book of Job, as a statement of resignation when Israel has lost its sense that "God acts in history" and when Israel (and even its sages) has become skeptical about the moral connection and coherence between acts and consequences. It is difficult to identify the precise context that evoked such a crisis of faith and intellect, where the thought was entertained that the world is not governed in a morally reliable way.[3] Scholarly hypotheses suggest that the voice heard in this text is of one who had been economically secure and socially established but then experienced immense loss and displacement. While the mood of skepticism is powerful, Roland Murphy has nicely made the point that the quarrel voiced in this text is not one that rejects the wisdom traditions of critical reflection; rather, it is one that extends the dispute in a way characteristic of wisdom teachers. This sage, according to Murphy, carries the dispute to its logical conclusion.[4]

The genre of material (beyond the observation that the teaching consists of characteristic wisdom sayings and sentences) and the ordering of the material are problematic. We can, however, identify governing and recurring themes that pervade the literature. We may take note in turn of the ways in which von Rad, Crenshaw, and Murphy delineate those themes.

Von Rad

Von Rad identifies three recurrent accents: the "vanity" of life, the role of the "mysterious decree of God" in governing the world, and the inability of humans to comprehend God's decrees.[5]

"Life is vanity."[6] Every human enterprise and every achievement, even the ones that "succeed," are in the end futile and meaningless. "I, the Teacher, when king over Israel in Jerusalem, applied my mind to seek and to search out by wisdom all that is done under heaven; it is an unhappy business that God has given to human beings to be busy with. I saw all the deeds that are done under the sun; and see, all is vanity and a chasing after wind" (Eccl 1:12–14).

As explicated by von Rad, the teacher reflects on a number of human options in the pursuit of meaning:

Pleasure is a false pursuit (Eccl 2:1).
Making "great works" through toil is essentially an empty performance (Eccl 2:4–8):
"Then I considered all that my hands had done and the toil I had spent in doing it, and again all was vanity and a chasing after the wind, and there was nothing to be gained under the sun" (2:11).
Wealth, possession, and honor are a futility: "There is an evil that I have seen under the sun, and it lies heavy upon humankind: those to whom God gives wealth, possessions, and honor, so that they lack nothing of all that they desire, yet God does not enable them to enjoy these things, but a stranger enjoys them. This is vanity; it is a grievous ill" (Eccl 6:1–2).
Righteousness comes to nothing:

All this I laid to heart, examining it all, how the righteous and the wise and their deeds are in the hand of God; whether it is love or hate one does not know. Everything that confronts them is vanity, since the same fate comes to all, to the righteous and the wicked, to the good and the evil, to the clean and the unclean, to those who sacrifice and those who do not sacrifice. As are the good, so are the sinners; those who swear are like those who shun an oath.

This is an evil in all that happens under the sun, that the same fate comes to everyone. Moreover, the hearts of all are full of evil; madness is in their hearts while they live, and after that they go to the dead. (Eccl 9:1–3)

Wisdom is "chasing after the wind": "I said to myself, 'I have acquired great wisdom, surpassing all who were over Jerusalem before me; and my mind has had great experience of wisdom and knowledge.' And I applied my mind to know wisdom and to know madness and folly. I perceived that this also is but a chasing after wind. For in much wisdom is much vexation, and those who increase knowledge increase sorrow" (Eccl 1:16–18).

The teacher's verdict is of course in conflict with the confidence of the older teaching of the book of Proverbs that believed these sorts of efforts—work, wisdom, righteousness—would produce life.

The world is governed by the mysterious decree of God. There is a proper time for every intention (Eccl 3:1–8, 17). There is a time and a way for everything (8:6). God determines everything, and there is nothing human agents can do to impact God's intention or to avert the divine will. The world is determined, and therefore human choices are rendered irrelevant.

The decrees of God that are sure are beyond human comprehension: "Yet they cannot find out what God has done from the beginning to the end" (Eccl 3:11).

The outcome of this set of convictions, identified by von Rad, is resignation, but the speaker does not end as a nihilistic agnostic.[7] Rather, the speaker offers advice on proximately preferred conduct in a world where human options are limited. First, the speaker urges a submission to God in obedience that need not be passionate but must be attentive enough to conform to the givenness of God's hidden will and purpose. Thus the advice offered in the addendum of Ecclesiastes 12:13–14 is a bland submissiveness that ceases to continue the struggle of Job:

Though sinners do evil a hundred times and prolong their lives, yet I know that it will be well with those who fear God, because they stand in fear before him, but it will not be well with the wicked, neither will they prolong their days like a shadow, because they do not stand in fear before God. (Eccl 8:12–13)

The end of the matter; all has been heard. Fear God, and keep his commandments; for that is the whole duty of everyone. For God will bring every deed into judgment, including every secret thing, whether good or evil. (Eccl 12:13–14)[8]

Second, the teacher does not simply counsel quiet submission. Alongside an admonition to obey, the speaker urges an immediate, concrete enjoyment of what is given in one's life, without endless torment about ultimate meanings:

> There is nothing better for mortals than to eat and drink, and find enjoyment in their toil. This also, I saw, is from the hand of God; for apart from him who can eat or who can have enjoyment? (Eccl 2:24–25)

> I know that there is nothing better for them than to be happy and enjoy themselves as long as they live; moreover, it is God's gift that all should eat and drink and take pleasure in all their toil. (Eccl 3:12–13)

> This is what I have seen to be good: it is fitting to eat and drink and find enjoyment in all the toil with which one toils under the sun the few days of the life God gives us; for this is our lot. Likewise all to whom God gives wealth and possessions and whom he enables to enjoy them, and to accept their lot and find enjoyment in their toil—this is the gift of God. (Eccl 5:18–19)

> In the day of prosperity be joyful, and in the day of adversity consider; God has made the one as well as the other, so that mortals may not find out anything that will come after them. (Eccl 7:14)

> Go, eat your bread with enjoyment, and drink your wine with a merry heart; for God has long ago approved what you do. Let your garments always be white; do not let oil be lacking on your head. Enjoy life with the wife whom you love, all the days of your vain life that are given you under the sun, because that is your portion in life and in your toil at which you toil under the sun. (Eccl 9:7–9)

It is possible that these statements envision a kind of ready hedonism and self-indulgence, but the tone of the whole seems much too sober for such an offer. More likely, the teacher urges a kind of modesty that is not excessively ambitious but that is gratefully receptive of the small gifts given in the daily processes of life. This teaching would seem to cohere with the modesty of Psalm 131:

> O Lord, my heart is not lifted up,
> my eyes are not raised too high;
> I do not occupy myself with things
> too great and too marvelous for me.
> But I have calmed and quieted my soul,

like a weaned child with its mother;
my soul is like the weaned
child that is with me. (Ps 131:1–2)

Third, the teacher is not morally indifferent but is able to make important distinctions, even given the inscrutability of the whole. The "better sayings" of Ecclesiastes 7:1–13 show an enduring conviction that moral discrimination is still possible and important. And with particular reference to wisdom, the teacher advises:

So I said, "Wisdom is better than might; yet the poor man's wisdom is despised, and his words are not heeded."

The quiet words of the wise are more to be heeded
than the shouting of a ruler among fools.
Wisdom is better than weapons of war,
but one bungler destroys much good. (Eccl 9:16–18)

James Crenshaw

The work of James Crenshaw articulates the same issues as von Rad, in a somewhat different way.[9]

First, wisdom could not achieve its goal. The capacity of human wisdom to discern the "way of life" soon confronts the hiddenness of the mystery of God. Thus the teacher knows about the "remoteness and profundity" of wisdom while recognizing that "of course, limited bits of insight were accessible, enabling their possessors to walk in light rather than darkness. Nevertheless, no one could really discover wisdom's hiding place, however much he or she claimed to have done so. Consequently, the future remained hidden and mysterious, even for the wise, who could not discern the right moment for any given action."[10]

Second, God is remote and the world crooked. The teacher finds the world to be fundamentally alien and unfriendly, and finds no comfort or succor in God, thus the teacher has no access to the traditional God of Israel and the gifts of fidelity, mercy, and compassion. The God for whom testimony is given here is cold and inaccessible, severely in charge but inattentive to human need or want.

Third, death does not take virtue or vice into consideration, so that the moral urgency of the older sages is dismissed as busywork. Thus the human person is fated to an indifferent death:

So I turned to consider wisdom and madness and folly; for what can the one do who comes after the king? Only what has already been done. Then I saw that wisdom excels folly as light excels darkness.

The wise have eyes in their head,
but fools walk in darkness.

Yet I perceived that the same fate befalls all of them. Then I said to myself, "What happens to the fool will happen to me also; why then have I been so very wise?" And I said to myself that this also is vanity. (Eccl 2:12–15)

Moreover I saw under the sun that in the place of justice, wickedness was there, and in the place of righteousness, wickedness was there as well. I said in my heart, God will judge the righteous and the wicked, for he has appointed a time for every matter, and for every work. I said in my heart with regard to human beings that God is testing them to show that they are but animals. For the fate of humans and the fate of animals is the same, as one dies, so dies the other. They all have the same breath, and humans have no advantage over the animals; for all is vanity. All go to one place; all are from the dust, and all turn to dust again. Who knows whether the human spirit of animals goes downward to the earth? (Eccl 3:16–21)

Again I saw that under the sun the race is not to the swift, nor the battle to the strong, nor bread to the wise, nor riches to the intelligent, nor favor to the skillful; but time and chance happen to them all. For no one can anticipate the time of disaster. Like fish taken in a cruel net, and like birds caught in a snare, so mortals are snared at a time of calamity, when it suddenly falls upon them. (Eccl 9:11–12)

Light is sweet, and it is pleasant for the eyes to see the sun. Even those who live many years should rejoice in them all; yet let them remember that the days of darkness will be many. All that comes is vanity. Rejoice, young man, while you are young, and let your heart cheer you in the days of your youth. Follow the inclination of your heart and the desire of your eyes, but know that for all these things God will bring you into judgment. Banish anxiety from your mind, and put away pain from your body; for youth and the dawn of life are vanity.

Remember your creator in the days of your youth, before the days of trouble come, and the years draw near when you will say, "I have no pleasure in them"; before the sun and the light and the moon and the stars are darkened and the clouds return with the rain; in the day when the guards of the house tremble, and the strong men are bent, and the women who grind cease working because they are few, and those who look through the windows see dimly;

when the doors on the street are shut, and the sound of the grinding is low, and one rises up at the sound of a bird, and all the daughters of song are brought low; when one is afraid of heights, and terrors are in the road; the almond tree blossoms, the grasshopper drags itself along and desire fails; because all must go to their eternal home, and the mourners will go about the streets; before the silver cord is snapped, and the golden bowl is broken, and the pitcher is broken at the fountain, and the wheel broken at the cistern, and the dust returns to the earth as it was, and the breath returns to God who gave it. (Eccl 11:7–12:7)

Fourth, the wisest course of action is to enjoy life during youth before the cares of advancing years make that impossible. In Ecclesiastes 12:1–7, the teacher knows that soon enough the vigor and chance of human life fail and fade into frailty and infirmity. That awareness, however, does not evoke anger or even sadness, rather, it leads to an urging that one must make the most of what one has been given, without hoping for more and without deferring enjoyment until later.

Roland Murphy

Roland Murphy, in slightly different phrasing, finds two thematics plus an addendum: Life is vanity; fear God and keep the commandments; and enjoy life.[11] It is not possible, according to Murphy, to summarize this teaching or to reduce it to a coherent pattern of instruction. The flavor of the whole, nonetheless, is that the real wisdom is to submit on the big issues of life and death and meaning and purpose, and to take initiative in the modest zone of human life wherein human agency can make a difference. If we hold this teaching to the well-known "serenity prayer," this teacher wants to "know the difference": "Give me courage to change what can be changed, patience to accept what cannot be changed, and wisdom to know the difference." Much cannot be changed because it is hidden in God's inscrutable will. Some things can be changed, and that concerns the gifts and blessings of the day. This wise teacher delineates the differences and urges his students to live and accept severe limitation and make the most of the rest. Such an instruction is very different from the affirmative urgency of the book of Proverbs. This teacher, however, still engages in the same task of discernment. In the limited scope of human possibility, there are things that are "better"; and they are enacted by calm resolve to conform to what is known of God's will, namely, the commandments.

SOLOMONIC WISDOM IN PROVERBS AND ECCLESIASTES

Once it was established, on the basis of 1 Kings 4:29–34, that Solomon could be utilized as an ongoing source of wisdom for subsequent generations (as was evidently the case in emerging Judaism), it was apparently not problematic to assign belated literature to that remembered, imagined, wise king. Once that possibility was seized upon in the ongoing work of traditioning, it was easy enough to imagine, as we have seen, that the collection of sentences and sayings that became the book of Proverbs could be assigned to Solomon. And once the buoyant, affirmative wisdom of Proverbs was linked to the great king, it was, apparently, inevitable that the later wisdom of resignation in the book of Ecclesiastes would also be assigned to him. That was possible even though, as we have seen, that collection of sayings is quite late and has no credible claim to a Solomonic connection.

In fact, Solomon is not named in the book of Ecclesiastes, even though he is linked to it in traditional interpretation. Rather, the name of the alleged author is "the Preacher" (*Qoheleth*), rendered in NRSV as "Teacher" (Eccl 1:1–2; 7:27; 12:8–10). The Hebrew term so rendered means the one who convenes the community in meeting, hence, traditionally the preacher. The term by itself would only signify an anonymous wisdom teacher; the term, however, is promptly modified and illuminated in Ecclesiastes 1:1 by the additional characterization of the author as "son of David, king in Jerusalem." And since David had only one son who reigned in Jerusalem, the reference is unmistakably to Solomon who is now accepted in the traditioning process as the source of wisdom for life.[12] That, however, is a subordinate counterpoint to the main claim established in the tradition.

The traditional, fictive claim of Solomonic authorship is served by the utilization of a genre of "royal testimony" in Ecclesiastes 1:12–2:26.[13] This text purports to be conclusions drawn by the king after a long reflection as a way of counsel to the realm: "I, the Teacher, when king over Israel in Jerusalem, applied my mind to seek and to search out by wisdom all that is done under heaven; it is an unhappy business that God has given to human beings to be busy with. I saw all the deeds that are done under the sun; and see, all is vanity and a chasing after wind" (Eccl 1:12–14).

The opening words of this unit of text articulate the primary theme of vanity, a judgment reiterated at the close of the unit: "This also is vanity and a chasing after wind" (Eccl 2:26b). The unit contained in the envelope of Ecclesiastes 1:12–14 and 2:26 is the world-weary testimony of one who had opportunity for every success in any venture and finds it all ultimately futile and meaningless. Thus the "wisdom" of this weary king, according to this royal fiction, is to see life for what it is; what it is, moreover, is emptiness and illusion. The statement is astonishing enough in itself, certainly made more so if taken as counsel from this king who in the remembered tradition had the Midas touch. For good reason, Crenshaw terms this text "Solomon's confession."[14]

If we now pursue the fiction of Solomon, certain conclusions illuminate the text.

The voice that speaks here is the voice of an old man who has lived long enough to have seen everything more than once: "Better is a poor but wise youth than an old but foolish king, who will no longer take advice. One can indeed come out of prison to reign, even though born poor in the kingdom. I saw all the living who, moving about under the sun, follow that youth who replaced the king; there was no end to all those people whom he led. Yet those who come later will not rejoice in him. Surely this also is vanity and a chasing after the wind" (Eccl 4:13–16).[15]

More importantly, the voice in Ecclesiastes 11:7–12:7 is a reflection on the glory and goodness of youth, and on the fact that old age renders one helpless and dependent. This voice can remember better days of vigor and effectiveness but now must acknowledge the loss.

It is of course not necessary to link this awareness to Solomon. It is nonetheless worth noticing that in the Deuteronomic arrangement of 1 Kings 3–11, the harsh judgments against the king are gathered together as a comment on his old age, presumably when he was frail and vulnerable and easily exploited: "For when Solomon was old, his wives turned away his heart after other gods; and his heart was not true to the Lord his God, as was the heart of his father David" (1 Kgs 11:4). The text does not exonerate Solomon, but it does make him the heedless object of the active verb "turn away," of which his foreign wives are the accused subject. Thus the mood of resignation is, in this rendering, not unrelated to the condition of helpless old age when one is acted upon. Of course Solomon is not the only one who became old and vulnerable, but since we are studying successes that are vanity, Solomon is an apt candidate for such articulation.

The list of futilities reviewed in this literature, particularly in the royal testimony of Ecclesiastes 1:12–2:26—concerning pleasure, wisdom, wealth, toil—cohere with Solomon's greatest successes (and, as we have seen, acts judged later to be failures). The list, moreover, is not widely remote from the Deuteronomic prohibition of Deuteronomy 17:16–17. In that text, the inventory is a list of prohibitions. In the more nuanced rendering of wisdom instruction, these goals are not prohibited but are found to be futile. Thus in royal fiction, the voice of the speaker is the old king who is belatedly able to see that the achievements on which he has spent his life add up to nothing. The text thus constitutes a belated critique of concerns of self-aggrandizement for which Solomon is the primary example in Israel. The text is a refutation of ambitious, aggressive displays of self-achieving power. In this way, Solomon by inference is made a didactic example in Judaism for how *not* to live in the world.

The critique of the Solomonic enterprise, point by point, is fairly obvious. We should not, however, miss the counterpoint in the text. As noted above, this text precisely challenges the moral connection between act and consequence, and concludes that human choices are irrelevant and unimportant because in fact fate is given indiscriminately according to God's hidden will:

Moreover I saw under the sun that in the place of justice, wickedness was there, and in the place of righteousness, wickedness was there as well. I said in my heart, God will judge the righteous and the wicked, for he has appointed a time for every matter, and for every work. I said in my heart with regard to human beings that God is testing them to show that they are but animals. For the fate of humans and the fate of animals is the same; as one dies, so dies the other. They all have the same breath, and humans have no advantage over the animals; for all is vanity. All go to one place; all are from the dust, and all turn to dust again. (Eccl 3:16–20)

All this I laid to heart, examining it all, how the righteous and the wise and their deeds are in the hand of God; whether it is love or hate one does not know. Everything that confronts them is vanity, since the same fate comes to all, to the righteous and the wicked, to the good and the evil, to the clean and the unclean, to those who sacrifice and those who do not sacrifice. As are the good, so are the sinners; those who swear are like those who shun an oath. This is an evil in all that happens under the sun, that the same fate comes to everyone. Moreover, the hearts of all are full of evil; madness is in their hearts while they live, and after that they go to the dead. (Eccl 9:1–3)

It is clear enough that this judgment deeply challenges the old assumptions of wisdom teaching concerning deeds and consequences.[16] With reference to Solomon, however, we should also notice that a trusting commitment to the connection between deeds and consequences is a hallmark of the Deuteronomic tradition as much as of the sapiential tradition. Indeed, as we have seen, this assumption is at the heart of the Deuteronomic critique of Solomon. That tradition is insistent that keeping Torah will preserve the dynasty and keep the land. The good consequences come from good deeds, as in Deuteronomy 30:15–20 (see also Ps 1).

This teaching in Ecclesiastes not only rejects the common sense connection made by the tradition of Proverbs; it also rejects the more aggressive, ideological claim of the Deuteronomist. In this judgment, Torah obedience does not lead to security and longevity, because fate is indifferent to obedience and disobedience.

Thus if Ecclesiastes is related to Solomon, one can see that this teaching tells against both the positively imagined Solomon of wealth, wisdom, and temple and against the Torah judgment made on Solomon by the Deuteronomist. This teaching insists that neither promotion of self—as in the imagination of the urban elites—nor the critique of that picture—as in the Deuteronomist—is reflective of reality. This text, then, more or less dissolves the disputatious issues that occupy 1 Kings 3–11 and at the most settles for a posture of accommodation that does not try too hard and does not expect too much, not too wicked and not too righteous (Eccl 7:16–17). Such counsel may make particular sense in the third century B.C.E. when the Jewish community had to live life on terms set by others. This critical teaching warns against heroic faith and against excessive accommodation. Neither option advocated in the Solomonic narrative—"occupation with great things, too great and too marvelous" (Ps 131:1) or particular compliance to Torah—is recommended. The urging here is modesty that permits the joys of daily life but does not look beyond them in any passionate way. The settlement offered arises out of exhaustion and trying too hard:

> Go, eat your bread with enjoyment, and drink your wine with a merry heart; for God has long ago approved what you do. Let your garments always be white; do not let oil be lacking on your head. Enjoy life with the wife whom you love, all the days of your vain life that are given you under the sun, because that is your portion in life and in your toil at which you toil under the sun. (Eccl 9:7)

> The end of the matter; all has been heard. Fear God, and keep his commandments; for that is the whole duty of everyone. (Eccl 12:13)

We may now reflect on the juxtaposition of Proverbs and Ecclesiastes as they are both drawn to Solomon. We have seen that the life of Solomon (in 1 Kgs 3–11 and in a less clear way in 2 Chron 1–9) is arranged to put a positive spin on Solomon's life as temple builder and a negative spin on his post-temple life, each pivoting on a dream (1 Kgs 3:5–14, 9:1–9; 2 Chron 1:7–13, 7:12–22). It may be of some value to observe that the good Solomon of the first dream who builds the temple is the Solomon who voices the buoyant trust of the book of Proverbs. Conversely, the failed Solomon of the second dream is the one who offers resigned teaching about modest joy and passionless devotion to Torah. The interface of good Solomon and failed Solomon and the interface of Solomonic wisdom in Proverbs and Ecclesiastes, each and both together, offer a double read of life in the world under the rule of God. That double read, accessed through the aging process, is perhaps the truth of Israel's wisdom. Either account, read by itself in buoyancy or in resignation, is inadequate. Thus the twinning of the two in relationship to the wise king perhaps exhibits the wisdom of the traditioning process itself, a wisdom that is not at all deterred by our critical severing of wisdom teaching from Solomon.

THE SONG OF ALL SONGS

The Song of Songs is the second of the Megilloth in the third canon of the Hebrew Bible that is canonically linked to Solomon.[17] The title of the book, first of all, indicates that this is the superlative song of which there is none better, "The Song of Songs," that is, the song of all songs. But then the phrase in Song of Songs 1:1 is immediately extended by the addition "which is from Solomon." The preposition introducing the last phrase of course links the literature to Solomon, but it does not perforce indicate authorship, for the same formula with the same preposition is used in many psalms that are thereby related to David without implying authorship (for example, Pss 3, 4, 5, 6, 7).

The "song" of this book is a love song in which the two lovers, a man and a woman, articulate their unrestrained, unencumbered desire for each other in elegant and suggestive rhetoric without any sense of shame, embarrassment, guilt, or restraint. The song is the fullest articulation of erotic desire and attachment that is offered anywhere in scripture and may be taken as an affirmation of the goodness of creation, of course specifically the goodness of human sexuality. (This affirmation is contemporarily of immense importance, given the sorry history of the church, now so dramatically exposed, concerning the fear and eventual pathology of human sexuality, a fear and a pathology that are rooted in the deepest traditions of church theology and practice.)[18]

The history of the interpretation of the poetry has been quite double-minded. On the one hand, most critical interpretation has proceeded on the premise that the song concerns an erotic articulation of human romanticism preoccupied with unrestrained desire. Conversely, most church interpretation has taken a mystical approach to the poetry and has understood the poetry to be an expression of a relation of desire between God and God's people Israel and, derivatively, that between Christ and Christ's church.[19] It is not to be thought that this second mode of interpretation is propelled by embarrassment about the erotic tone of the literature, for in fact such interpretation has fully appreciated the richest erotic tone of the poetry in order to make a theological claim for God's (Christ's) passion for God's people. Thus in both agendas, the uncurbed reality of desire has been uppermost in interpretation, whether concerning human or divine desire.

It is perhaps not necessary to choose between these two readings, but enough to recognize the claim of raw, intense, intimate relatedness that is more elemental than either cognitive or moral (deontological) categories of a conventional kind. Read either way or read both ways, the poems celebrate the rich interactive process of mutual giving and receiving that constitutes the truth of human life and the truth of God's life in the world.[20] Such an affirmation functions as a powerful and surely healthy counterpoint to the characteristic accent of Protestant theology that was vigorously articulated by Anders Nygren, who champions the self-giving of agape and denies any healthy dimension to eros.[21] It is clear in this poetry that the reader is led to a dimension of testimony about the intimacy and interactive quality of human or divine relationships that is remote from conventional church theology and, we may perhaps say, also remote from conventional accents in ancient Israel dominated either by cautious conservatism of the wisdom teachers or the rigors of Sinai mediated through the Deuteronomists, or more immediately, the restraining strictures of Ezra and Nehemiah.

Phyllis Trible, in an interpretive tour de force, has suggested that the Song of Songs be read as a response to and revision of the narrative of Genesis 2–3, wherein the idyllic sexual possibility of the garden of delight has been skewed and forfeited.[22] Thus Trible juxtaposes "a love story gone awry"[23] and "Love's Lyrics Redeemed."[24] Unlike Gerleman, Trible has no interest in placing the Song of Songs in the tenth century where the narrative of Genesis 2–3 has been situated in recent critical thought. She is indifferent to such a critical historical question, and takes the two pieces of literature as they stand in scripture.

Trible notices the way in which the Song of Songs reiterates the accent and plot from Genesis 2–3:

> Expanding upon the lyrics of eroticism in Genesis 2, three human voices compose this new song. They belong to a woman, a man, and a group of women, the daughters of Jerusalem. Independent of logical progression or plot development, these voices flow freely and spontaneously to yield a series of metaphors in which many meanings intertwine simultaneously. At times, the standard, the figurative, and the euphemistic converge so compellingly that one cannot discern where vehicle ends and tenor begins. Often the language is elusive, holding its treasures in secret for the lovers themselves. Occasionally the identity of the speaker is uncertain, creating a problem for observers but not for participants who know that in Eros all voices mingle. Hence, the poetry of the Song resists calculations and invites imagination. The visual must be heard; the auditory, seen. Love itself blends sight, sound, sense, and non-sense. In these ways, the voices of the Song of Songs extol and enhance the creation of sexuality in Genesis 2.

> Of the three speakers, the woman is the most prominent. She opens and closes the entire Song, her voice dominant throughout. By this structural emphasis her equality and mutuality with the man is illuminated. The arrangement recalls the stress placed upon the woman at the conclusion of Genesis 2: although equal with the man in creation, she was, nonetheless, elevated in emphasis by the design of the story. In the Song of Songs, accent upon the female is further increased by the presence of the daughters of Jerusalem. As a

foil and complement to the lovers, this group aids the flow of the action. Women, then, are the principal creators of the poetry of eroticism.[25]

Trible's detailed analysis is a most important offer on the poem. For our purposes, it is enough to notice that the skewed sexuality, as narrated in Genesis 2–3, can be corrected and redeemed by a poetic scenario that has nothing of either the rigorous prohibition of Eden, the defiant disobedience of Eden, or the forfeiture of delight in a narrative that ends in shame and dislocation. Juxtaposed to the Genesis narrative, the Song of Songs thus may be read as a second chance in the imagination of Israel, a chance to begin again in a kind of easy innocence that is unafraid and unembarrassed. Of course, one could read the Song of Songs in terms of secular drinking songs by those who are simply untroubled by an indifference to restraint. But because the song is appropriated late in the Hebrew Bible, long after Genesis and long after the Deuteronomists, such an uncaring is implausible.

Thus Trible's work, beyond its close offer of analysis, has the heuristic value of emancipated eros on offer after the failure of the characteristic pattern of prohibition-disobedience-expulsion. Such an "after" will be important for what follows in this discussion. Trible's study greatly supports such an "after" reading; her close juxtaposition of the song to Genesis 2–3 is not indispensable for an "after" reading, for the song simply comes after so much that is shabby and forfeited in Israel. The wonder is that after all of that, Israel could still muster canonical courage and imagination to embrace a second innocence.[26]

SOLOMON'S CONNECTION TO THE SONG OF SONGS

The connection of Solomon to the Song of Songs is traditional and eventually canonical, but certainly not historical. The initial mention of Solomon in Song of Songs 1:1 associates Solomon with the book but, as noted above, does not convey authorship. Indeed, it may suggest Solomon as one of the characters, or it may suggest that the book belongs in royal orbit, thus useful for royal celebration, pageantry, and lovemaking as, for example, with a wedding.[27]

The poetry five times mentions Solomon with reference to royal accoutrement: the curtains of Solomon (Sg 1:5), alluding to the skins that give a black color to tents, a metaphor for "black and beautiful"; the "litter of Solomon" surrounded by "sixty mighty men of the mighty men of Israel" (3:7); a palanquin made by King Solomon himself (3:9; see also verses 6 and 10), composed of silver, gold, and purple, bespeaking splendor and opulence; and a reference to Solomon passing by (3:11), a connection with his wedding and consequently his gladness of heart. The reference seems to be a way to articulate deep joy. The mentions of Solomon in Song of Songs 3:7, 9, and 11 altogether suggest a royal wedding procession. Murphy judges verses

6–11 to be an abrupt intrusion in the text and comments: "The man who is the hero of the love song is likened to Solomon, and the description of his wedding procession is meant as a tribute to him."[28] We are told in a fifth reference to Solomon that "Solomon had a vineyard" (8:11–12). The verses refer to the production of income (silver), but perhaps "vineyard" is also used with a sexual connotation (see Isa 5:1).

The reference to Solomon's vineyard begins with an allusion to the productive wealth of his territory. Very quickly, however, it is clear that the vineyard is a metaphor for a woman or, more properly, for many women. Thus the text alludes to Solomon's harem (1 Kgs 11:3), and then the speaker moves on to speak about "my vineyard, my very own" and compares his own wondrous vineyard to the "vineyard of Solomon."[29] Thus Solomon is referred to in order that the boastful, eager voice of desire can imagine that his own treasured woman whom he loves surpasses even the sexual achievements of Solomon. Murphy comments: "The symbolism of vineyard representing the woman is essential to an understanding of these lines."[30]

The references are rhetorical maneuvers designed to evoke an imagined environment of wealth, joy, beauty, and well-being, with Solomon here regarded as a full embodiment of such satiations. The primacy of the great king is a poetic convention for hyperbole but permits the poet to give full voice to desire. The comparison of Solomon's wives to the speaker's lover in Song of Songs 8:11–12 fully evokes for the speaker-lover a direct address to Solomon (Sg 8:12). Critically this particular address makes clear that the author cannot be Solomon but someone else who addresses Solomon. Beyond that critical observation, however, the rich point is that with "the eyes of eros," this lusted-after woman surpasses even the wives of Solomon. Thus Solomon is a point of reference that permits the poetry to supersede even the desire of Solomon in the fuller desire of the present poetry and the subject of the poetry. Childs observes that the tone in 8:11–12 democratizes the poetry, celebrating such love for "every man . . . even the poorest."[31] It is to be observed that Childs keeps the reference on the male lover, which may indeed, as Clines suggests, indicate a patriarchal inclination either in the poetry or in the interpretive tradition that results in Childs's own comment.[32]

Solomon figures internally in the poetry itself in order to justify poetic hyperbole. The reference in Song of Songs 1:1 is somewhat different, for it more immediately serves the final form of the text.[33] The function of Solomon in 1:1, according to Childs, is to link the poetry to wisdom, in order to assure that the poetry is not taken as either a secular song or as an allegory. Such a one-dimensional equation of Solomon with wisdom in this context seems difficult to maintain, for there is little evidence for a wisdom component in the poetry, as Childs himself seems to recognize. I suggest that in this context it is credible to take "canonical Solomon" in 1:1 not as a wisdom figure but as quintessential lover, an interpretation that pays attention to Solomon's twofold love of the Lord (1 Kgs 3:3) and many foreign women (1 Kgs 11:1). If Song of Songs 8:11–12 alludes to Solomon's harem, as Murphy suggests, then perhaps in a context of exuberant love the harem is appreciated as a full articulation of love, here so celebrated, without the deep reservation of Deuteronomic critique.

Thus the interface of Solomon and Song of Songs leads us to consider Solomon as lover. There is no doubt that Solomon's love of God is commended in 1 Kings 3–11, whereas Solomon's love of women is profoundly censored. In Song of Songs, however, such human love remains uncensored, indeed celebrated; consequently, we may ask if the Solomonic connection does not entail or at least permit a reclamation of Solomon's human love as a positive, celebrated good, without placing it in competition with the love of YHWH, which the Song of Songs clearly does not do. Thus the poem may permit us to reconsider Solomon's two loves in a way that is remote from the ironic critique of 1 Kings 3–11, for Solomon's many women are here taken to be a wondrous good.

Such an inverted verdict would of course be a most daring maneuver. Camp has made clear that the sexual overtones of 1 Kings 3–11 are immense.[34] In particular, the narrative of 10:1–13 concerning the visit of the Queen of Sheba would seem to suggest desire on the part of the queen, a desire that is resisted by the king who does not respond in such terms (see 1 Kgs 10:5, 13). In the midst of the report on the economic summit, the sexual dimension of the interaction is not to be missed.

But what if the connection of Solomon to Song of Songs, by way of a heuristic gain, invites a reread of this material? Janie Hunter proposes, following Loader, that the Song of Songs is a literature of protest against patriarchy on behalf of the legitimacy of woman's experience.[35] The Song of Songs expresses, says Hunter, "the refutation of the 'normal' in Israelite consciousness and wisdom teaching . . . Israelite (and indeed our concepts of what should be deemed 'holy' need radical adjustment. The book does not present negative protest but a positive celebration that protests by implication."[36] We may provisionally follow Hunter to note that the connection between Solomon and the Song of Songs suggests two protests. First, a protest is implicit against Deuteronomic strictures concerning sexual activity, permitting Solomon to be read as "the good king," sexuality and all. Second, there is a protest against Solomonic sexuality in the Succession Narrative whereby women are commodities and objects that function to support commercial and political interests. That is, Solomon's women are, so it appears, means toward an end, not persons to be loved as "ends." The Song of Solomon may be a revision that refuses condemnation of sexuality but that equally refuses sexual commoditization, insisting against both that love is a legitimate passion for its own sake. The book is permeated with a single affirmation: "Love for the sake of love is its message."[37]

By appeal to Trible, we may suggest that the Song of Songs is not only a redescription of the failure of the narrative of Genesis 2–3 but a redescription as well of the failure of the Solomon narrative in 1 Kings 3–11. In this rewrite, there is no need to imagine that Solomon's two loves are in competition or mutually exclusive. There is no need that Solomon's love of women should be enmeshed in commoditization or that it should lead to idolatry, for all those entanglements of commoditization and idolatry are absent in the horizon of the Song of Songs. If we read backward then from the Song of Songs to Solomon, we may reread Solomon in a "second innocence" after his failure and self-destruction. To read "after" does not deny his failure or dislocation, as Israel in Deuteronomic fashion has no chance to deny the royal failure that produced deportation. But Israel does not linger there. It imagines (and undertakes!) the reconstruction of life that is in touch with deep and genuine humanness.

We may understand this "after-read" of the Song of Songs via Solomon by considering the interface of passion and interest as they have been elucidated by Albert O. Hirschman.[38] Hirschman has considered the interface of passion and interests as they were treated in the Renaissance and into the modern period with reference to, among others, Machiavelli, Hobbs, Vico, Hume, James Madison, and Adam Smith. By "passion," Hirschman means the most elemental desires and yearnings of "man as he really is" in a state of nature, marked, for example, by greed and lust.[39] Hobbs identifies as passion "oppressive pursuit of riches, glory, and dominion."[40] It was, in the eighteenth century, taken to be self-evident that such passions of a most intimate and individual kind, if unchecked, constituted a threat to public order and to the public good. Thus it became imperative to repress and harness those passions for the sake of the public good,[41] the preferred strategy being the principle of "'countervailing passion' that would check a dangerous passion."[42] Thus Vauvenargues avers: "Passions are opposed to passions and one can serve as a counterweight to another."[43] And d'Holbach agrees: "The passions are the true counterweights of the passions; we must not at all attempt to destroy them but rather try to direct them. Let us offset those that are harmful by those that are useful to society."[44]

In the end, however, the argument moved from countervailing passion to a focus on "interest," by which is meant a concern for commercial and economic activity. Thus in the work of Adam Smith, economic activity becomes not only a restraint on passion but is in itself a venture that enhances the body politic.[45] In the appreciation of economic activity as a good, it was noted that a world governed by "interest" is marked by predictability and constancy,[46] so that money making and commerce come to be viewed as "innocent" in a way that conveys "sweetness, softness, calm, and guiltiness and is the antonym of violence."[47] Moneymaking is a "Calm Passion" that serves the common good.[48]

Of this remarkable argument that eventually culminated in the work of Adam Smith, Hirschman comments: "The opposition between interests and passions could also mean or convey a different thought, much more startling in view of traditional values: namely, that *one set of passions, hitherto known variously as greed, avarice, or love of lucre, could be usefully employed to oppose or bridle such other passions as ambition, lust for power, or sexual lust.*"[49]

This verdict by Hirschman suggests that his categories may illuminate the significance of Solomon's link to Song of Solomon. It is, I am fully aware, an enormous leap backward from the analysis of modern economic development to the imagined world of Solomon with its drastically different political economy. Fully aware of the anachronistic character of this interpretive move, I nonetheless suggest that the interplay of dangerous passions and calming interest may illuminate the connection of Solomon to the Song of Songs.

In the narrative of 1 Kings 3–11 (less so with 2 Chron 1–9), Solomon is largely an economic man, motivated by and celebrated for his economic prowess in his commercial success. Indeed, it is plausible that his wisdom turns out to be a capacity for commercial management (as in 1 Kgs 10:23–25), that his military achievement is in the service of his commerce (10:15–19), and that even the temple is appreciated especially for its lavish furnishings that match the king's extravagant table. It is entirely credible, moreover, that Solomon's "many foreign wives" are a function of political economy, in the service of a network of commercial interests. Solomon is characteristically portrayed as a king with an *interest*; it takes no imagination, moreover, to think that the urban elites who imagined him in this way valued and admired him as the best of their kind, hugely successful in the "calming interest" of wealth that produced order, predictability, and constancy.

Indeed, the Solomon portrayed in these royal narratives is such a man of "interest" that it is difficult to entertain the thought of his passion. And in the narrative concerning the visit of the Queen of Sheba, the narrative has a subtext of the queen's "every desire" that may well have a sexual connotation (1 Kgs 10:13). Unlike her, however, there is no hint of the "desire" of the king, so restrained or distracted or otherwise preoccupied is he. In the narrative, it is possible to conclude, according to Hirschman's categories, that interest has driven out the passion in the persona of the king.[50]

As we have seen, the narrative of 1 Kings 3–11 shows that Solomon failed; his great commitment to "interest" did not and could not deliver the life promised and hoped for. And if the connection between the Song of Songs and Genesis 2–3 can be entertained as Trible has forcefully suggested, then we may notice in Genesis 2–3 that the human couple is a model of unmasked passion (Gen 2:25) . . . until the serpent introduces "interest" into the narrative and into the horizon of the human characters (3:1). As soon as the human couple begins to think about knowledge and access, the zone of passion given by the Creator is promptly put beyond their access. Not only has interest driven out passion, but it has eventually driven the couple out of the garden of delight (3:23–24).

Now if the imagined Solomon of 1 Kings 3–11 is given over to interest at the cost of passion, and if the story of Genesis 2–3 narrates the deathly triumph of interest over passion according to Hirschman's categories, then we may consider the Song of Songs as a rendition of Solomon after the embrace of interest and the failure of interest. In this poetry, Solomon—or one who exalts himself even in comparison with Solomon—is a man of pure passion matched to a woman of pure passion. The Song of Songs is, as regularly recognized, an articulation of mutual, unrestrained passion and desire in which "the other" is the aim and end of the interaction and of the poetry. The interaction is not aimed at anything else, does not intend to "produce" anything or become anything other than what it is. By contrast, Psalm 45, a royal psalm, in celebrating a wedding aims at sons:

> In the place of ancestors you,
> O king, shall have sons;
> you will make them princes in
> all the earth.
> I will cause your name to be
> celebrated in all generations;
> therefore the peoples will
> praise you forever and ever. (Ps 45:16–17)

While that is a notion that is certainly credible for Solomon, it is not on the horizon of the Song of Songs.

Thus I suggest that after the failure of interest as reported in 1 Kings 3–11 and after critique by the Deuteronomist, the Song of Songs belatedly redescribes Solomon after the failure of interest as a man of passion who takes his passion with playful seriousness and who gives full and free articulation to desire, no longer restrained by calculating interest. Thus in an elongated interpretive process to which we had no access, the failed Solomon of interest is redeemed as a full creature who exults in his creatureliness. His partner in this poem is no cipher for commerce, no sign of commercial networks, no measure of wealth. She is who she is in her passion, and he is who he is in his passion. It is like a return to the singularity of passion from a "fall" into interest: "And the man and his wife were both naked, and were not ashamed" (Gen 2:25). The desire is no doubt celebration of the self in its elemental disposition, but it is desire that reaches beyond self to "thou," something economic Solomon had never done:

How beautiful you are, my love,
how very beautiful!
Your eyes are doves behind your veil.
Your hair is like a flock of goats,
moving down the slopes of Gilead.
Your teeth are like a flock of shorn ewes
that have come up from the washing,
all of which bear twins,
and not one among them is bereaved.
Your lips are like a crimson thread,
and your mouth is lovely.
Your cheeks are like halves of a pomegranate
behind your veil.
Your neck is like the tower of David,
built in courses;
on it hang a thousand bucklers,
all of them shields of warriors.
Your two breasts are like two fawns,
twins of a gazelle,
that feed among the lilies.
Until the day breathes and the shadows flee,
I will hasten to the mountain of myrrh
and the hill of frankincense.
You are altogether beautiful, my love;
there is no flaw in you.
Come with me from Lebanon, my bride;
come with me from Lebanon.
Depart from the peak of Amana,
from the peak of Senir and Hermon,
from the dens of lions,
from the mountains of leopards. (Sg 4:1–8)

The Solomon connection in this poetry is secondary. It nonetheless invites an interpretation that is stunningly contemporary in a world that has commoditized sexuality as much as economics.

CHAPTER 12

SOLOMON AMONG
"THE PRAISES OF ISRAEL"

T
he book of Psalms, which reached its final form in the period of emerging
Judaism—likely in the same period as the formation of the books of Ecclesiastes and Song of Songs—belongs to the father, David. Thus the foremost
superscription in the Psalms is "1david," for David (see, e.g., Pss 3, 4, 5, 6, 7). The
particular superscriptions concerning the life of David, moreover, relate the psalms
to particular critical moments in the remembered life of David (see, e.g., Pss 3, 34,
51, 52, 54, 60, 63, 106).[1] As a consequence, father David dominates the Psalter, and
son Solomon has only ad hoc entry, and that of a most marginal kind.

SOLOMON'S APPEARANCE IN THE PSALTER

The name of Solomon occurs only twice in the Psalter, in Psalms 72 and 127, both
times only in the superscription. The superscriptions concerning Solomon, in both
cases using the preposition *lamedh* (rendered in NRSV as "of Solomon," that is,
"pertaining to Solomon"), does not imply authorship. The careful study of superscriptions by Brevard Childs begins with the recognition that the superscriptions
do not reflect any "independent historical tradition," so that in these two psalms we
have no reference that in any direct historical way connects to Solomon.[2] Rather, as
with Proverbs, Ecclesiastes, and the Song of Songs, here also the connection is secondary and at most provides some heuristic clues about reading the psalms according to traditional intent. Thus, Childs concludes, "The Psalter titles do not appear to
reflect independent historical traditions but are the result of an exegetical activity
which derived its material within the text itself."[3] While Childs's study focuses on the
fuller, more numerous references to David, surely the same conclusion pertains to
the two references to Solomon. The outcome of such a judgment is that we may look
within the psalms themselves to see what may have occurred in the traditioning
process that evoked the superscription reference to Solomon and that in turn invited
canonical readers to entertain the psalms in the horizon of the imagined Solomon of
the canon.

THE KING IN PSALM 72

Psalm 72, the first of the two mentions of Solomon, counts among the royal psalms
and so in any case has "the king" as its subject, even though the superscription

becomes more specific concerning which king (see Pss 2, 18, 20, 21, 51, 72, 89, 101, 110, 114).[4] The royal psalms taken altogether, as in the work of Aubrey Johnson, present a full liturgical picture of the people of God organized around the Davidic king who is the proximate source of life for the entire realm.[5] This royal ideology, closely attached to the Zion theology embodied in the temple, is deeply at variance with the old covenantal memories of Sinai, though the tradition works hard to integrate the two.[6]

In Psalm 72, we may identify two specific markings of Solomon in addition to the superscription. First, the poetic parallelism in verse 1 of "the king" and "a king's son" need not be a reference to Solomon. But since the dynastic promise to David in 2 Samuel 7 explicitly mentions David's son, this is most plausibly Solomon. Second, the reference to "tribute" (*mnhh*) and "kings of Sheba" may explicitly connect to Solomon; see 1 Kings 4:21 (Heb 5:1) on "tribute" and of course 1 Kings 10:1–13 on the Queen of Sheba. Both of these matters could possibly be generic, but the connection to Solomon seems obvious.

Beyond these particulars, the psalm exhibits characteristic royal and surely Solomonic markings. David Jobling has observed how the Psalter is shot through with an economic dimension, surely reflecting an "Asiatic mode of production" whereby the central government extracted surplus value from the peasant productivity in village economics.[7] Thus Psalm 72 is alert to economic issues in which the king is involved, notably with reference to the poor (Ps 72:1–4, 12–14) and the oppressor (72:4; see 72:14).

The king is recognized, in a celebrative mood of high-court hyperbole, as a source of all things good: he is the giver of peace (*shalom*) (Ps 72:7); he is entrusted with dominion (clear to the Euphrates River), generative of income from international tributes, and honored before all kings (72:8–11); he is the recipient of many blessings, embodied in agricultural activity (72:15–17). On all counts of power, wealth, and honor, the king is the exalted figure in the community and in the known world around Israel. Clearly the convergence of power, wealth, and honor is appropriate to Solomon as to no other king that was ever celebrated in ancient Israel.

Psalm 72:18–19, taken by Kraus and Jobling to be a later addendum, turns attention away from the king to YHWH, the God of Israel, "who alone does wonders."[8] The effect of these two verses is to transfer the affirmation of the preceding away from the king, who is, in fact, the recipient of the noted achievements above and not the agent. Thus royal prosperity and prominence are all a gift of God, a theme noted in 1 Kings 3–11 but in the surge of exuberance mostly forgotten. As noted above, the concluding formula of 1 Kings 2:12, 46 is a bit ambiguous concerning Solomon's achievement as gift or as accomplishment.

These prominent themes are what one might expect in royal affirmation. As Jobling has made clear, however, there is an additional motif that may claim our attention. In verses 1–4 and 12–14, Psalm 72 identifies the king—the wise, just king (see 1 Kgs 3)—as committed to justice and righteousness. In 72:1–2, the term "justice and righteousness" is stated twice, in chiastic fashion. That royal commitment to justice, moreover, has as its special object "your poor" (Ps 72:2), "the poor of the people," and "the needy" (72:4). Jobling has noted that in verse 2 "your poor" is parallel to "your people" and that the verse therefore raises a generic concern for justice in the community or, alternatively, a commitment to the poor.[9] While the difference in the phrasing is to be noted, there is no doubt that the consistent accent is upon a particular group within the community. The king is designated to be protector and adjudicator precisely for the politically and economically disenfranchised who are vulnerable to assault from the powerful and the wealthy.[10]

The same motif is sounded in Psalm 72:12–14 concerning "the needy," "the poor and those who have no helper," "the weak and the needy," and "the needy," who are in the context of "oppression and violence." Jobling, moreover, judges that the introductory "*ki*" (For) in verse 12 is situated to affirm that the advocacy for the vulnerable in verses 1–4 is the *cause* of dominion, longevity, and prosperity in verses 5–11. Thus Jobling rightly observes a wondrous tension in the psalm between the claim that YHWH, the God of Israel, alone does wondrous things (on behalf of the monarch) and the claim that royal well-being is the consequence of a concern for the vulnerable. The tension reflects very old tensions in Israelite tradition between conditional and unconditional promises. While the two can be harmonized, it seems plausible that the primary accent in this psalm is upon the condition of compassionate justice as a prerequisite for monarchal well-being.

If that is so, then the psalm amounts to an important critique, if not an exposé, of the Solomon who occupies the superscription. As we have seen, Solomon is said to begin his reign with a listening heart, a wise and discerning heart (1 Kgs 3:9, 11), and his first royal act is to execute justice (3:16–18). But that is all. There is never after this initial episode any mention of justice, and nowhere in the mouth of Solomon is there any mention of the poor and the needy, that is, nowhere is there any recognition of social differentiation so that the poor and needy might be singled out for royal attention, even compassionate conservatism.[11] Indeed the only mention of justice and righteousness in the primary narrative of 1 Kings 3–11 is in 10:9, where it is on the lips of the Queen of Sheba: Blessed be the Lord your God, who has delighted in you and set you on the throne of Israel! Because the Lord loved Israel forever, he has made you king to execute justice and righteousness. It is likely that the phrasing is standard royal hyperbole; in any case, the phrasing is quickly passed over and disregarded by Solomon. The narrative promptly moves on in verse 10 to gold, spices, and precious stones. The absence of the social category of the poor and needy in the text, the absence of any mention of justice and righteousness except for the queen's utterance, and the general tone of self-aggrandizement all converge to suggest that the Solomonic enterprise practiced by the urban elites was completely lacking in the conditions stated in Psalm 72 for royal well-being. It may be that Psalm 72 is standard liturgical usage, and Jobling notes that even in verses 1–4 and 12–14, no hint is given of a way through which the king might redress the poverty and vulnerability. I am not as sure as Jobling that such technical matters might be expected in liturgical utterance, as grand public piety does not usually touch specific policy implementation. It is possible, alternatively, that the psalm is not only an ideal of what the just king must do, but also a public critique of the unjust king who fails to merit the condition and therefore cannot sustain peace and prosperity. This of course is how the tale unfolds in 1 Kings 11–12; by 12:1–19, the king with every kind of wealth and honor is a failure, not only by conventional standards but by the very standards of peace and prosperity.

In order to get leverage on this remarkable critique of the king, we may reference two additional texts, Jeremiah 22:15–16 and Ezekiel 34:1–24.

As to the Jeremiah text, we have already suggested that Solomon is offered by the Deuteronomist as the model bad king and as a foil for Josiah, the model good king, in the extended royal history. The poetry of Jeremiah, in a general critique of the later kings of the Davidic dynasty in his contemporary period, singles out Josiah for affirmation:

> Did not your father eat and drink
> and do justice and righteousness?
> Then it was well with him.
> He judged the cause of the poor and needy;
> then it was well.
> Is not this to know me? says the Lord. (Jer 22:15b-16)

Unlike his sons and grandson who are critiqued in Jeremiah 22, Josiah, the good king, is good—and therefore prosperous—precisely because he actively intervened for ("judged") "the cause of the poor and the needy." In this affirmative verdict concerning the king, the cause of the poor and the needy is juxtaposed precisely to the large terms "justice and righteousness." Thus it may be concluded that Josiah, a contrast to Solomon, exactly fulfilled the conditions of Psalm 72, and in particular the "because" of verse 12.

Ezekiel 34:1–24, the second text, offers a prophetic critique of kingship, affirming that Israel is in deep trouble precisely because the kings (shepherds) have been self-serving and have not attended to the flock (realm) (Ezek 34:1–6). The sheep are "scattered," that is, in exile, because of the failure of kingship (34:6). No direct connection is made to Solomon, and no doubt this later text is immediately preoccupied with later generations of kings. Nonetheless it is the case that Solomon stands as the model figure for self-serving governance to the neglect of the kingdom. Thus Ezekiel 34 converges well with Psalm 72. The psalm affirms the positive possibility of governance and insists upon that possibility; by contrast Ezekiel 34 details the cost of failure to embrace the possibility of justice and righteousness toward the vulnerable. After YHWH's resolve to take "direct rule" of the realm, that is, without a king (34:11–16), the text anticipates a new, proper David to come: "I will set up over them one shepherd, my servant David, and he shall feed them: he shall feed them and be their shepherd" (34:23). While that text may eventually carry messianic overtones, the image of this expected king coheres with the positive characterization of Josiah, whereas the failed model of kingship, so well embodied in imagined Solomon, is nullified. Thus Psalm 72 offers a theory of governance that permeates the Old Testament. The Solomon of the superscription, moreover, represents a model for what could have been a royal possibility but in the event was not. It may be for that reason that in verses 18–19 the psalm turns away from the king toward the "real" king, who does indeed practice justice and righteousness toward the poor and needy: "And I, the Lord, will be their God, and my servant David shall be prince among them; I, the Lord, have spoken" (Ezek 34:24).[12] Psalm 72 is placed last in book 2 of the Psalter, and perhaps it is there with the superscription to bespeak a "shutdown" of the royal possibility. In the king of the superscription, the great hope for justice through royal power has not come to fruition. Israel can still hope, but it cannot appeal to this Solomon who reneged on the conditions of verse 12 of the psalm.

It may be instructive that Psalm 72 with its Solomonic superscription is the conclusion of book 2 of the Psalter, signaled by the doxology in verse 20. Books 1 and 2 focus on the Davidic king, but then in book 3, culminating in the loss described in Psalm 89:38–51, the accent moves away from the human king to the divine king in book 4, suggesting that liturgically human kingship, culminating with Solomon, has run its course. If we entertain the newer canonical study of the psalms, as in the work of Gerald Wilson, we may note that Psalm 73, at the beginning of book 3, stands next to Psalm 72, though it posits a new beginning.[13] Psalm 73 of course has no relationship to Solomon; if, however, we can extend the heuristic suggestion of the superscription of Psalm 72 toward Psalm 73, we may provisionally entertain Solomon as the speaker in Psalm 73. In this psalm, the speaker—for the moment of this interpretation, Solomon—characterizes conventional Torah faith in verse 1 in an echo of Psalm 1.[14] The speaker then tells how he was lured to imitate the cynical wealthy who were able to control their own lives and who mocked God's rule (Ps 73:2–14). The speaker is almost lured but at the last moment turns to "the sanctuary of God" and has his life refocused upon the goodness of God, who is the only genuine desire of his life:

> Whom have I in heaven but you?
> And there is nothing on earth
> that I desire other than you. (Ps 73:25)

We have seen how Solomonic desire has been channeled away from "passion" and toward "interest," economic interest, so that his desire—even if he did not ask it from God—was for riches, honor, and power. And all of his considerable energy and acumen were devoted to that pursuit. In Psalm 73, however, we are face-to-face with Solomon *after* the rejection of the condition of Psalm 72, *after* the lure of his self-serving desire, *after* the failure of his regime that did not serve in justice and righteousness, *after* the disregard of the poor and the weak. The speaker of Psalm 73:19–28 is a chastened Solomon who begins again in new possibility. As we have seen in the belated wisdom of Proverbs, the belated awareness of Ecclesiastes, and the belated restoration of passion in the Song of Songs, here belatedly is a king who returns to Torah reality and communion with God after the lure of eyes that "swell out with fatness" and hearts that "overflow with follies" (Ps 73:7). Life was all about eating and drinking and being happy (1 Kgs 4:20).

Now of course this reading is all an extrapolation from the superscription of Psalm 72, well beyond any critical judgment about Psalm 73. But because Solomon so entranced the imagination of Israel, a venture from Psalm 72 toward Psalm 73 is, in my judgment, tentatively permitted and heuristically suggestive.

PSALM 127

The other psalm with a Solomonic superscription is Psalm 127, among the Psalms of Ascent (Pss 120–34), rendered by Hans-Joachim Kraus (452) as "A Pilgrim Song." This psalm has less to connect it directly to Solomon than did Psalm 72, but, as we shall see, the primary themes of "house" and "sons" readily lend themselves to a royal, even Solomonic, reading.

Psalm 127 divides into two parts. In the first part, verses 1–2, the psalm reflects on "vain labor" and contrasts such labor at the end of verse 2 with sleep given to the beloved. The contrast is between the effort of an autonomous human agent who labors endlessly and ineffectively to secure his own world and a worker who rests from work and is not devoured by anxiety. The contrast, perhaps with reference to the maintenance of a family and with reference to governance of a city, is between one who takes himself to be ultimate and without any fallback reserve, and one who recognizes himself to be penultimate in his efforts and achievements and who relies, after doing all that can be done, on the ultimacy of God, who governs the day of work and the night of rest (see Ps 104:19–23). The sense of verses 1–2 is that life conducted apart from YHWH is bound to be a profound failure and futility; there is, however, an alternative to anxiety, and that is entrustment of self and life to YHWH.

When these verses are drawn toward Solomon, as the superscription may suggest, the "house" may be taken as either "temple" or "dynasty," for in 2 Samuel 7:1–16, a founding dynastic oracle, the term "house" is utilized in both ways.[15] The term "city," moreover, would certainly be Jerusalem, "city of David."[16] Both house and city are presided over by the king, in this instant, Solomon. Both house and city sought to be places free of anxiety, where good sleep is possible if it is YHWH who builds and guards. If, however, the house is built and the city is guarded without reference to YHWH, all is futility.

If we focus on the threefold "in vain" (*sw'*), and if we take this term in the same semantic field as "vanity" (*hbl*) in the book of Ecclesiastes, then we can see that this psalm, not unlike Ecclesiastes, utters a critique of the Solomonic enterprise. While the house (temple) of Solomon is in a formal way deeply connected to YHWH, it is possible to see its construction as an act of royal self-aggrandizement, for it cannot in any case "contain" YHWH. While the city of Jerusalem is founded as a gift of YHWH to David, it is possible to see that it became an autonomous royal city that the king sought to secure by standard military devices (see 1 Kgs 10:15–19). If this psalm is drawn toward Ecclesiastes, which in turn is linked to Solomon, then we may hear echoes of the futility of anxious toil, a toil of self-serving:

> What has been is what will be,
> and what has been done is
> what will be done;
> there is nothing new under the sun.
> Is there a thing of which it is said,
> "See, this is new"?
> It has already been,
> in the ages before us.
> The people of long ago are not remembered,
> nor will there be any remembrance
> of people yet to come
> by those who come after them. (Eccl 1:9–11)

I hated all my toil in which I had toiled under the sun, seeing that I must leave it to those who come after me—and who knows whether they will be wise or foolish? Yet they will be master of all for which I toiled and used my wisdom under the sun. This also is vanity. So I turned and gave my heart up to despair concerning all the toil of my labors under the sun, because sometimes one who has toiled with wisdom and knowledge and skill must leave all to be enjoyed by another who did not toil for it. This also is vanity and a great evil. What do mortals get from all the toil and strain with which they toil under the sun? For all their days are full of pain, and their work is a vexation; even at night their minds do not rest. This also is vanity. (Eccl 2:18–23)

All human toil is for the mouth, yet the appetite is not satisfied. (Eccl 6:7)

One can imagine that the Jerusalem enterprise under Solomon was one of endless, feverish acquisitive activity—of arms, of gold, of wives, of everything that enhanced kingship. And now, so the psalmist concludes—all is in vain! There is an alternative: "for he gives sleep to his beloved" (Ps 127:2b). The alternative is to leave the future finally to God:

Therefore I tell you, do not worry about your life, what you will eat or what you will drink, or about your body, what you will wear. Is not life more than food, and the body more than clothing? Look at the birds of the air; they neither sow nor reap nor gather into barns, and yet your heavenly Father feeds them. Are you not of more value than they? And can any of you by worrying add a single hour to your span of life? And why do you worry about clothing? Consider the lilies of the field, how they grow; they neither toil nor spin, yet I tell you, even Solomon in all his glory was not clothed like one of these. (Matt 6:25–29)

This alternative, available even to the self-serving king, is an alternative to which the king may come only "after," as in Psalm 73; we may, moreover, find a royal connection in the positive affirmation of Psalm 127:2b, for the term "beloved" (*ydid*) is exactly the term used by Nathan in naming the son of David, a name deeply linked to the name of father David: "[The Lord] sent a message by the prophet Nathan; so he named him Jedidiah, because of the Lord" (2 Sam 12:25). The son is called *Jedidiah,* and in the Psalm it is to *ydid* that good sleep is given, sleep free of toil and beyond anxiety. The king may know that the alternative is possible.

The second part of Psalm 127, verses 3–5, concerns sons who are a gift and blessing of God. If the term "house" in verse 1 refers to the family, then in a patriarchal society sons are the guarantee of survival and continuity of the family. When the psalm is drawn toward Solomon, however, sons become an urgent topic for the guarantee of the dynasty into the next generation. Indeed the Davidic dynasty rests on YHWH's promise to give sons:

When your days are fulfilled and you lie down with your ancestors, I will raise up your offspring after you, who shall come forth from your body, and I will establish his kingdom. (2 Sam 7:12)

> The Lord swore to David a sure oath
> from which he will not turn back:
> "One of the sons of your body
> I will set on your throne." (Ps 132:11)

Then the Lord will establish his word that he spoke concerning me: "If your heirs take heed to their way, to walk before me in faithfulness with all their heart and with all their soul, there shall not fail you a successor on the throne of Israel." (1 Kgs 2:4)

Thus the generic requirement of sons in a patriarchal society may be understood specifically in dynastic terms (see Ps 45:16–17). The man (king) who has sons will be endlessly secure and honored, partly because he is manifestly blessed and partly because his sons will take his part.

In the long story of the Davidic dynasty, however, the end did come. Concerning the boy-king Jehoiachin, the last on the throne, Jeremiah can write:

Thus says the Lord:

> Record this man as childless,
> a man who shall not succeed in his days;
> for none of his offspring shall succeed
> in sitting on the throne of David,
> and ruling again in Judah. (Jer 22:30)

The future for every dynasty, including this one, is tenuous. There can be gifts of sons; but there is anxiety that there may not be. While Psalm 127 is altogether positive in verses 3–5, we may read these verses in the context of the "unless" of verse 1: Unless the family stays close to the God of blessing . . . there will be no sons. Thus the second part of the psalm, like the first part, states a profound either/or about all of life and, according to this exposition, about royal life. Solomon (and Israel) learned the hard way. Solomon tried to raise a house without the Lord building it. Solomon tried to rule a city without the Lord guarding it. Solomon tried to produce a dynasty of sons without the Lord's blessing it . . . or so the critique goes. But the critique comes along with an affirmation; an alternative is always again potentially embraced.

YHWH'S OFFER OF AN ALTERNATIVE TO FUTILITY AND ANXIETY

Too much should not be made of the Solomonic connection in these two psalms. Our discussion may only explore the heuristic value of the superscription in each case. These psalms—given a Solomonic reference—seek to redescribe the Solomon achievement in the arena of Yahwistic governance. Psalm 72 makes the success of monarchy dependent upon care for the poor and weak, who are the special object of YHWH's concern. Psalm 127 makes the well-being of the house, city, and dynasty dependent upon reliance on YHWH. It is clear in the liturgic world of Solomon that lip service was certainly paid to these claims. The extent to which the lip service matched reality is an open question. While the open question is variously answered, the news carried by these two psalms is that an alternative to futility and anxiety is on offer from YHWH. The alternative offered to Solomon and all his ilk concerns the rule of YHWH, the God who attends to the poor and weak, the God who is the only sure defense of house and city, the God who is the only giver of the next generation. Solomon and all his kind could be "happy" (Ps 127:5) but only on terms other than the usual royal terms of self-grounded life. It is clear that Solomon and his ilk always again keep relearning this hard truth.

CHAPTER 13

SOLOMON IN FOUR
BELATED REFRACTIONS

I n this chapter we will consider in turn four derivative, quite late, and quite different extrapolations from the memory and tradition of Solomon. These four extrapolations have no historical connection to or claim upon Solomon; they are, however, impressive exhibits of the way in which the memory of Solomon has continued to feed and energize the interpretive imagination of ongoing communities of faithful interpretation.

THE WISDOM OF SOLOMON

The Wisdom of Solomon is a collection of instructions and exhortations that address the problematic interface between Judaism and its Hellenistic environment.[1] The text is commonly dated to the first century B.C.E. after a long period of rapprochement between Jewish practice and Hellenistic culture, when thinking Jews were disillusioned and disappointed by that interface of faith and culture that had seemed so promising. The text, authored in Greek, is commonly thought to be situated in Alexandria, where there flourished a vibrant Jewish community that had long and deep connections with Greek thought and culture. (It may be recalled that in the second century of the Common Era, the Christian theologians Clement and Origen worked vigorously to rearticulate Christian faith in terms of the categories of the Hellenistic philosophic culture of Alexandria.)

The connection of the book to Solomon is, of course, a late, imagined connection that can only be inferred, because the name of Solomon does not occur in the book. While the title "Wisdom of Solomon" is offered in Greek for the book, "Solomon" is dropped from the title in Latin, which refers to it only as the book of Wisdom.[2] There is no doubt that the title and the argument of the book appeal to the tradition of Solomon as a wise man and wise king. The attachment of the book to Solomon, in the text itself and beyond the title, is by inference only. It is clear, nonetheless, that the text intends quite deliberately to learn from the tradition of Solomon as it is taken up by a Jewish author concerned for Jewish distinctiveness in the midst of a powerful Hellenistic (Egyptian) culture.

The middle portion of the book, Wisdom 6:22–10:21, most directly refers to Solomon and celebrates the wonder of Solomon's wisdom. In an appeal to the initial piety of Solomon in 1 Kings 3:5–14, it is affirmed that in great piety and humility Solomon received wisdom as a gift from God. The speaker, assuredly Solomon, who bears testimony to his own fate and experience, attests that he prayed for understanding: "No king begins life in any other way; for all come into life by a single path, and by a single path go out again. Therefore I prayed, and prudence was given to me; I called for help, and there came to me a spirit of wisdom. I valued her above scepter and throne, and reckoned riches as nothing beside her; I counted no precious stone her equal, because all the gold in the world compared with her is but a little sand, and silver worth no more than clay. I loved her more than health and beauty; I preferred her to the light of day; for her radiance is unsleeping" (Ws 7:6–10).

Solomon here attests that wisdom is more valuable and more to be treasured than "scepters and thrones and riches" (Ws 7:8), more than "priceless gems" (7:9), more than "health and comeliness" (7:10). As a result of this wondrous gift of God, Solomon received unerring knowledge of all things: "He himself gave me true understanding of things as they are: a knowledge of the structure of the world and the operation of the elements; the beginning and end of epochs and their middle course; the alternating solstices and changing seasons; the cycles of the years and the constellations; the nature of living creatures and behaviour of wild beasts; the violent force of winds and the thoughts of men; the varieties of plants and the virtues of roots. I learnt it all, hidden or manifest, for I was taught by her whose skill made all things, wisdom" (7:17–22).

It is of special notice, of course, that in Wisdom 7:22, wisdom (as in Prov 8:22–31) is the teacher of all and is a feminine agent of instruction. In Wisdom 7:26–8:1, Solomon offers an ode in celebration of wisdom and moves in a speculative or philosophic direction not unlike that of Proverbs 8:22–31, articulating the unparalleled closeness between wisdom and God. While the king yearns for wisdom, it is clear that the king cannot of his own initiative acquire wisdom, for it is singularly in the gift of God: "But I saw that there was no way to gain possession of her except by gift of God—and it was a mark of understanding to know from whom that gift must come" (Ws 8:21). As a result of this awareness, the initiative-taking king assumes a posture of humble prayer and offers petition to the sovereign God who in mercy may give the wisdom that the king must have to rule wisely. The king reports his earnest prayer of petition: "God of our fathers, merciful Lord, who has made all things by thy word, and in thy wisdom hast fashioned man, to be the master of thy whole creation, and to be steward of the world in holiness and righteousness, and to administer justice with an upright heart, give me wisdom, who sits beside thy throne, and do not refuse me a place among thy servants. I am thy slave, thy slave-girl's son, a weak ephemeral man, too feeble to understand justice and law; for let a man be ever

so perfect in the eyes of his fellow-men, if the wisdom that comes from thee is wanting, he will be of no account" (9:1–6).

The prayer is congruent with the simple petition of 1 Kings 3:9, but now is filled
out as a full articulation of piety. This extensive prayer in praise of wisdom, extend-
ing through Wisdom 11:1, links the power and gift of wisdom decisively to the sovereign God who is "God of the fathers," that is, God of the Jewish tradition. Thus the
preoccupation with wisdom, a notion that could be understood in broad cultural
terms, is firmly submitted to the God known in Jewish faith. Consequently, the petition for wisdom is indeed a petition addressed to the God of Jewish faith. This elab-
oration of the simple exchange of 1 Kings 3:4–14 links worldly wisdom to theological
rootage in the Jewish tradition of faith. The king who asks for and receives wisdom
is indeed a Jewish king.

This centerpiece of the book is the primary link of the text to Solomon, here a
model of piety and prayer, grateful recipient of God's sovereign gift. From that central section of the book, we may see how the first section of the book, Wisdom
1:1–6:21, focuses upon quintessential Jewish themes but develops them in a way
pertinent to a Hellenistic milieu. In these chapters the text makes a characteristic
Jewish argument that the world is morally coherent, sinners are punished, and they
bring death upon themselves as the sure outcome of their actions: "For the spirit of
the Lord fills the whole earth, and that which holds all things together is well aware
of what men say. Hence no man can utter injustice and not be found out, nor will
justice overlook him when she passes sentence. The devices of a godless man will be
brought to account, and a report of his words will come before the Lord as proof of
his iniquity" (Ws 1:7–9).[3]

The equation is a simple one that is reflected in all parts of Old Testament tradition, in the teaching of Deuteronomy (Deut 30:15–20), in the Psalms (Ps 1), and
in wisdom (Prov 8:32–36): "The creative forces of the world make for life; there
is no deadly poison in them. Death is not king on earth, for justice is immortal"
(Ws 1:15–16). The text at length then exposits this simple, sapiential statement of
theodicy. The careless, self-indulgent way of sinners is characterized at some length.
Indeed, that self-indulgence sounds much like the kind of life that is at last proposed
in Ecclesiastes: "Come then, let us enjoy the good things while we can, and make full
use of the creation, with all the eagerness of youth. Let us have costly wines and per-
fumes to our heart's content, and let no flower of spring escape us. Let us crown ourselves with rosebuds before they can wither. Let none of us miss his share of the good
things that are ours; who cares what traces our revelry leaves behind? This is the life
for us; it is our birthright" (Ws 2:6–9; see Eccl 9:7).

The speaker knows of course that the righteous go to their death unrewarded for
their piety and their Torah obedience. Such an unarguable fact, however, does not

diminish confidence in the theodicy offered here, for the righteous are safe in death and safe beyond death: "But the souls of the just are in God's hand, and torment shall not touch them. In the eyes of foolish men they seemed to be dead; their departure was reckoned as defeat, and their going from us as disaster" (Ws 3:1–4). Thus the argument goes well beyond what was characteristic of the Old Testament itself and takes full advantage of the religious development of subsequent Judaism in terms of immortality and the ongoing life of the righteous who are kept safe by God.

The theme of the righteous and the sinners, respectively destined for peaceful well-being or deep torment, is developed with rhetorical flourish:

> The hope of a godless man is like down flying on the wind, like spindrift swept before a storm and smoke which the wind whirls away, or like the memory of a guest who stayed for one day and passed on. (Ws 5:14)

> But the just live forever; their reward is in the Lord's keeping, and the Most High has them in his care. Therefore royal splendour shall be theirs, and a fair diadem from the Lord himself; he will protect them with his right hand and shield them with his arm. (Ws 5:15–16)

While this trajectory can be developed richly and at length, it is not to be missed that the argument turns on the characteristic conviction that the guarantees of moral coherence that connect deed and consequence are offered by the sovereign God, who is sure and reliable and cannot be deceived or circumvented. The world of reward and punishment is very sure. This is the quintessence of wisdom, and it is, of course, the foundational conviction of Jewish faith that is rooted in the ancient articulation of blessings and curses. The world will hold according to the rule of God to which this writer (and his community) is firmly committed. The address of this argument is ostensibly to "kings and judges" (Ws 6:1), but that king-to-king rhetoric is an appeal that the wise one makes to every member of the community who by cultural seduction may be led away from the simple certitudes of faith.

As the opening argument of Wisdom 1:1–6:21 makes an appeal for the most elemental Jewish conviction of theodicy—and thereby offers reason to continue in faith—by contrasting the righteous and sinners, so the final section of the book (Ws 11:21–19:22) makes a sustained contrast between Israel and Egypt. While the argument appeals to the old exodus tradition, it is clear that the contrast in fact concerns faithful Jews in first-century Alexandria (in Egypt, of course) and those who submit to Alexandrian, Hellenistic culture. Thus the old narrative of exodus becomes an interpretive vehicle for a contemporary polemic engagement. The text does not define terms but abruptly begins to speak of "they" who turn out to be the Israelites who were wondrously protected and provided for by God: "They made their way across an unpeopled desert and pitched camp in untrodden wastes; they resisted every enemy, and beat off hostile assaults. When they were thirsty they called upon thee, and water to slake their thirst was given them out of the hard stone of a rocky cliff. . . . All the infants should be killed, while to these thou gavest abundant water unexpectedly" (Ws 11:2–4, 7).

Conversely, the adversaries who opposed them and opposed the God who led them are subject to terrible punishments:

> In return for the insensate imagination of those wicked men, which deluded them into worshipping reptiles devoid of reason, and mere vermin, thou didst send upon them a swarm of creatures devoid of reason to chastise them, and to teach them that the instruments of a man's sin are the instruments of his punishment. For thy almighty hand, which created the world out of formless matter, was not without other resource: it could have let loose upon them a host of bears or ravening lions or unknown ferocious monsters newly created, either breathing out blasts of fire, or roaring and belching smoke, or flashing terrible sparks like lightning from their eyes, with power not only to extermi- nate them by the wounds they inflicted, by their mere appearance to kill them with fright. (Ws 11:15–19)

The text looks beyond Egypt in following Israel's traditional story line and considers "the old inhabitants of the holy land" (Ws 12:3), the Canaanites. But the argument is the same concerning the Canaanites as the Egyptians. Thus the arguments of the first part of the book are now reiterated with specific reference to current cultural temptations and seductions.

While the judgment against the outsider is severe, the text is at pains to testify to the mercy of God that is extended to sinners who repent, and to the patience of God toward wayward peoples. The intention of the argument is to maintain God's fair- ness, justice, and compassion toward all peoples:

> But thou art merciful to all men because thou canst do all things; thou dost overlook the sins of men to bring them to repentance; for all existing things are dear to thee and thou hatest nothing that thou hast created—why else wouldst thou have made it? How could it have endured unless called into being by thee? Thou sparest all things because they are thine, our lord and master who lovest all that lives; for thy imperishable breath is in them all.
>
> For this reason thou dost correct offenders little by little, admonishing them and reminding them of their sins, in order that they may leave their evil ways and put their trust, O Lord, in thee. (Ws 11:23–12:2)

Thus the argument does not concern Israel's special status; rather, the argument is an affirmation of God's wondrous providential care for all people, with the sorry recognition that some—Egyptians, Canaanites—eventually place themselves beyond that gracious providence. Whereas the argument about theodicy in Wisdom 1–6 concerned individual persons, here the argument concerns whole peoples with the eventual affirmation of Israel's blessedness as God's righteous people.

In Wisdom 13:1 the text shifts from providential mercy to a critique of idolatry in chapters 13–15. This indictment of the worshippers of idols is rooted in such texts as Jeremiah 10:1–16, Psalm 115, and Isaiah 44:9–20, which already in early accounts had mocked the nations that placed their trust in what is not more than a human product: "The really degraded ones are those whose hopes are set on dead things, who give the name of gods to the work of human hands, to gold and silver fashioned by art into images of living creates, or to a useless stone carved by a craftsman long ago" (Ws 13:10). The practice of idolatry—of worshiping what is not God—is not simply a religious activity but has practical consequences: "All is in chaos—bloody murder, theft and fraud, corruption, treachery, riot, perjury, honest men driven to distraction; ingratitude, moral corruption, sexual perversion, breakdown of marriage, adultery, debauchery. For the worship of idols, whose names it is wrong even to mention, is the beginning, cause, and end of every evil" (14:26–27).

The text knows very well who the idolaters are—Egyptians and Canaanites. But the text also knows that trust in this true God is a possible alternative that will lead to immortality: "But thou, our God, art kind and true and patient, a merciful rule of all that is. For even if we sin, we are thine; we acknowledge thy power. But we will not sin, because we know that we are accounted thine. To know thee is the whole of righteousness, and to acknowledge thy power is the root of immortality" (Ws 15:1–3).

The sharp either/or that permeates the entire text culminates in an affirmation of Israel as YHWH's chosen people:

The whole creation, with all its elements, was refashioned in subservience to thy commands, so that thy servants might be preserved unscathed. Men gazed at the cloud that overshadowed the camp, at dry land emerging where before was only water, at an open road leading out of the Red Sea, and a grassy plain in place of stormy waves, across which the whole nation passed, under the shelter of thy hand, after all the marvels they had seen. They were like horses at pasture, like skipping lambs, as they praised thee, O Lord, by whom they were rescued. For they still remembered their life in a foreign land: how instead of cattle the earth bred lice, and instead of fish the river spewed up swarms of frogs; and how, after that, they had seen a new sort of bird when, driven by greed, they had begged for delicacies to eat, and for their relief quails came up from the sea. (Ws 19:6–12)

Thus the argument returns to the dominant story line of Israel's faith and is constituted by a normative recital of miracles. Conversely, sinners—in this context Egyptians—are heartily condemned. The either/or dominates every section of the book: Wisdom 1–6, either righteousness to immortality or sin to death and torment; 6–12, either wisdom or foolishness; 11–19, either righteous Israelites who live by mercy or idolatrous Egyptians. The development of the argument is rich and imaginative; in its main points, however, it stays with the core of Israel's faith. The literary achievement of the book is to place the defining either/or on the lips of the wise king in a way that gives royal sanction and support to Israel's deepest conviction. In the mouth of this king, the either/or of Torah constitutes wisdom that even the nations might recognize and embrace.

Read critically, the Wisdom of Solomon is a sapiential articulation of dominant themes from first-century Judaism in a context (Alexandria) where Judaism attended to its distinctive faith and identity amid a seductive culture that threatened and challenged that distinctiveness. This sapiential articulation contains no big surprises; it exposits themes and connections that are at the very core of Israel's faith.

The heuristic value of the connection of the book of Wisdom of Solomon to King Solomon, albeit a late interpretive maneuver, makes rather commonplace theological themes into a project of considerable interest. The reason the Solomon connection evokes interest is that, as we have seen in our analysis of 1 Kings 3–11, the king there seems at deep variance with the accents of this later text. In the narrative of 1 Kings 3–11, the initial dream narrative of 3:4–14 did indeed portray Solomon as pious, submissive, modest, and receptive. After that initial presentation, however, the Solomon of that narrative seems to have departed in dramatic ways from his initial piety and submissiveness: instead of profound trust in God, Solomon proceeds as an autonomous entrepreneur; instead of wisdom that leads to justice, wisdom is transposed into commercial chutzpah; instead of devotion to God's holy people, interaction at an international level leads away from focus upon distinctiveness of this people in its faith; instead of devotion to Torah as the clue to the future, Solomon practices a public life that is indifferent to Torah requirements. The Solomon narrative of 1 Kings 3–11 in its large sweep is about a movement of the king away from Israel's core convictions in pursuit of the new world of control.

Such a textual reality concerning Solomon, however, leaves the imaginative traditioning process undaunted. That process is unembarrassed about placing in the mouth of Solomon the very convictions that the narrative life of Solomon contradicts. It is clear that the traditioning process engages in a daring act of making a connection to the king only by disregarding what is remembered of Solomon. If, however, we provisionally accept the connection and remain inside the daring of the text itself, we are bound to say that Solomon by this time has learned a great deal and has returned to his initial trusting innocence. In 1 Kings 11:4 we are told that when "Solomon was old," his heart turned away. By the time with which the Wisdom of Solomon concerns itself, Solomon is older still, and he has abandoned the pursuit of autonomy (see Nebuchadnezzar in a similar maneuver in Daniel 4). It is as though Solomon had his "reason returned" to him (see Dan 4:34), as though he has "come to himself" (see Luke 15:17) and is now able to move beyond his waywardness so condemned by the Deuteronomists, able to affirm the core faith of his people. Whereas his earlier broad internationalism led him away from Torah, he now knows better and is able to see and to say the decisive either/or of Torah faith against which he had lived his life.

Thus at the center of this book, Solomon is able to affirm the gift of wisdom with no cynical transposition of wisdom into the technical competence of commercial life: "Therefore I prayed, and prudence was given to me; I called for help, and there came to me a spirit of wisdom" (Ws 7:7). Wisdom is indeed to be preferred to all riches and honor the king can imagine. At the beginning of this book, moreover, Solomon is able to affirm the rigorous symmetry of deeds and consequences, that righteousness leads to life and wickedness to death. This symmetrical conviction is of course rooted in the Deuteronomist, who critiqued Solomon. Clearly the Solomon of the royal narrative did not act on the basis of such a theory of accountability but acted instead as though his actions were disconnected from the gifts God might give. Surely there is high irony that this king has become a mouthpiece for the simple moral passion of the Deuteronomist, who had found it so necessary to critique him. At the end of this book, Solomon can celebrate the mercy of God and see it as a contrast to the idolatry of the Egyptians. It is for that reason that the ancient exodus contrast between Israel and Egypt serves so well for Jews in Alexandria. What gives us pause, however, is that it is this very king who condemns the Egyptians (16:15–16). In the royal narrative, Solomon is much connected to Egypt, married to Pharaoh's daughter, has perhaps imitated Egyptian wisdom, and perhaps has appropriated Egyptian patterns of bureaucracy. But now the attraction of Egypt is exhausted. Earlier Solomon had not understood that his many foreign wives—no doubt including Pharaoh's daughter—could lead him into idolatry and turn his heart away from God. But now, in this book, he knows. He knows all about the dangerous power of idolatry and about the "good light" given to the "holy ones" (18:1).

Now there is no attraction in Egypt, for Solomon is content to be a trusting Israelite, relying on the faithful God of mercy. Inside the drama of the text attached to Solomon, Solomon has learned a great deal, has moved on from his autonomy to a second naiveté. Read critically, Judaism in the first century has recovered enough nerve to claim its own faith, to resist in critical, even polemical ways the attraction of Hellenism that would eventually erode the faith. Wisdom now given to Judaism in the figure of the king is intensely Jewish, intentionally Yahwistic, and intensely Torah-centered. Wisdom is the delight of this king and the delight of the people that now remember and trade upon him: "She is an inexhaustible treasure for mankind, and those who profit by it become God's friends, commended to him by the gifts they derive from her instruction" (Ws 7:14).

SOLOMON, THE QUEEN OF SHEBA, AND THE QUR'AN

The tradition of Solomon, most especially the narrative tradition of Solomon's meeting with the Queen of Sheba (1 Kgs 10:1–13), remained a lively, generative tradition throughout the Mediterranean world. We have seen that this narrative, not unlike the narrative of 1 Kings 3:16–28, is marked by a tone of folklore tradition and that it is saturated with sexual subtlety.[4] Edward Ullendorff particularly notes that the statement in 10:2—the queen "came to Solomon"—is freighted language, for the Hebrew verb *bo'* (to come, to enter) is also used as a technical term for coitus.[5] In verse 13, moreover, it is reported that "Solomon gave to the Queen of Sheba all her desire." The usage of the term readily suggests a sexual dimension to the interaction. These two ingredients, folkloristic imagination plus a sexual subtext, have caused the narrative to be of continuing power and continuing interest in ongoing interpretive communities.

Here I will consider only two of the many such narrative developments, those of the Qur'an and Ethiopic traditions with particular reference to the document *Kibra Nagast*. In taking up these materials, I (probably like most readers) am a novice and so am largely dependent on secondary sources.[6]

When we enter the world of these ongoing interpretive traditions that are marked by passion, intensity, and great imagination, the reader will find, as I have found, that we enter a world completely unfamiliar to Western parlance. At the same time, we are aware that the imaginative interpretation, albeit extravagant in its reach, is not unlike the imaginative interpretation that we have seen underway already in the biblical text itself. It is of course incumbent upon us now, in Western communities of biblical faith, to enter as best we can this world reflective of another culture, both to discover how differentiated and variegated is the interpretive process, and to be instructed in interpretative traditions other than our own. In the Qur'an, the episode of Solomon and the Queen of Sheba is related in one brief passage (27:15–44).[7] In this rendering, deeply rooted in the biblical text but obviously transposed into a vigorous Islamic statement, Solomon is confronted with a message concerning the Queen of Sheba:

> I have brought you a sure message
> from Sheba.
> I have found a woman ruling over them
> who had been given something of everything
> and who had a great throne. (Qur'an 27:22–23)

Thus the Queen of Sheba begins in the narrative as a genuine peer of Solomon and perhaps as a rival. But the narrative turns in the next comment of the report to mount a critique of the queen:

> I found her and her people
> worshipping the sun instead of God.
> The devil had made these works seem fair to them,
> and had barred the way to them,
> so that they are not proceeding aright
> that they are not worshipping God
> brings out the hidden things
> in the heavens upon the earth
> and knows what you conceal and what you publish. (Qur'an 27:24–25)

Solomon's response to this message is to issue a command to the queen he has not met that she should come to see him: "Do not act proudly against me, / but come to me in humble submission [to God]." It is clear that the summons from Solomon to the queen is an ultimatum. And while the phrase "to God" may be understood as implied, submission to Solomon seems also clearly implied.

After some indecision the queen comes to Jerusalem, where Solomon tests her two times. First, he disguises her throne, which he has brought to Jerusalem. She recognizes her throne, evidencing her intelligence. Second, Solomon sits on a throne that is set on glass, which looks to the queen like water. She is deceived and lifts her robes for the sake of the water and uncovers ankles. Thus the test conducted by Solomon is a strategy for humiliating her. In a peculiarly disjunctive maneuver, the narrative moves to its culmination with the conversion of the queen to Islam. The narrator comments:

> What she worshipped apart from God
> has barred the way to her;
> She was of an unbelieving people. (Qur'an 27:43)
> In the end, the queen herself declares:
> I have wronged myself;
> to God, the God of the worlds
> with Solomon I submit. (Qur'an 27:44)

Thus the queen has submitted to God (Allah) and has, like Solomon, become a Muslim.

At the same time, however, the queen's speech makes clear that she has *not* submitted to Solomon. Lassner comments that the dominant theme is "the argument against unbelief";[8] Solomon is the true believer and creates an environment in which even the sun-worshiping queen from the South is brought to true faith. The text is a clear example of the way in which ancient Jewish tradition is taken up and taken over to serve the interests of Islam that all be brought to faith in Allah. While the transposition of Solomon into a zealous Muslim may seem strange to a Western Christian reader, this maneuver in the text is of course quite parallel to the interpretive maneuvers long practiced in a precritical way in Christian appropriation of texts from the Hebrew Bible.

ETHIOPIC TRADITIONS CONCERNING
SOLOMON AND THE QUEEN OF SHEBA

The second narrative account that we will consider is that of the Ethiopic tradition concerning Solomon and the Queen of Sheba. The principal text is *Kibra Nagast,* upon which Ullendorff has commented in helpful detail.[9] Whereas Solomon summoned Sheba to Jerusalem in the Qur'anic account, in the Ethiopic version Sheba takes the initiative because she has heard reports from her trading caravans of the opulence and wisdom of Solomon in Jerusalem. Thus she goes to Jerusalem and has the rumors confirmed that Solomon is her most impressive peer; she marvels at his wisdom and justice. In this Ethiopic version, she also abandons sun worship, but here worships the Creator, the God of Israel. Thus the story is supple enough that it can serve different religious traditions, even in their competing exclusivist claims. Whereas the narrative in the Qur'an is permeated with Islamic passion, the Ethiopic version knows of no such singular theological commitment. While the new worship is of the God of Israel, in this account the agenda is not theological passion but political legitimacy.

The Queen of Sheba is ready to depart Solomon and Jerusalem. Except that the king in Jerusalem is taken with her, and resolves to beget a son by her. He must, however, engage in deception in order to make this possible. The queen agrees that she will go to his tent for the night only when he promises not to take her by force. In turn, Solomon makes her promise to bring nothing to the tent with her; he establishes the condition that if she brings something to the tent with her, then he may take her. In the night, however, she is thirsty and drinks from a bowl, thus violating her pledge to come to the tent empty-handed. Because she has reneged on her promise, the king is now free from his promise as well. Ullendorff concludes laconically: "Solomon seized her hand and accused her of having broken her oath. He then worked his will with her."[10]

Out of this night in the tent was born a son, Menelik. He became the king and founder of the dynasty in Ethiopia, but not before he had spent time in Jerusalem. He was feted by his father Solomon, anointed king by the priest Zadok, and inculcated into Jewish faith. When he returned home with the ark of the covenant that Solomon entrusted to him, he became head of a dynasty linked to the house of David: "From this time onwards, the people abandoned their idols and accepted the God of the Hebrews, and Menelik sat upon the throne of David, king of Israel."[11] It is clear that the object of this tradition was to prove that Ethiopia was the successor and heir of Israel as the chosen people of God.[12] As a consequence, "In Ethiopic historical, religious, and legal documents there clearly emerges the national dogma of dynastic continuity stretching from David to Haile Selassie."[13]

It is remarkable that the vision is so pliable in interpretive imagination that the same narrative encounter can, in different retellings, witness to the sovereignty of Allah and alternatively provide legitimization for a throne rooted in Jewishness. As Ullendorff has made clear, Ethiopia from early time on was a remarkably synchronistic culture in which Jewish, Christian, and Islamic traditions could readily interface, all subject to the rich and vibrant interpretation that can generate new readings and, out of new readings, new social relationships. Thus the narrative of the meeting of king and queen is incorporated into a theory of kingship that legitimates power by rootage in this ancient tradition.

Alongside this clearly political, ideological agenda, we may notice that gender politics are at work as they undeniably are in the central narrative of 1 Kings 10:1–13. The Ethiopic tradition continued to pay attention to the subtext of sexuality and to give it important attention.[14] Ullendorff observes that in this version there is something of role reversal. Now it is the queen and not Solomon who is the wise one. Whereas Solomon met the queen's desire in the narrative in the book of Kings, here the account is upon the purity of the queen: "No longer is Solomon exposed to the wiles of the seductress, Lilith, the earthly demon, but he himself assumes the role of seducer and, by a ruse, takes the virgin queen who . . . gives birth to a son Menelik."[15] Lassner has reported on a Yemenite folktale concerning the same visit. Here the narrative takes a very different turn. It is now "a tale of competing intellects, carnal knowledge, a case of ritual purity and risky sex. . . . The need to gratify his [Solomon's] sexual desire ultimately led to Nebuchadnezzar's conquest."[16] In this account it is the aggressive desire of Solomon that leads to a sexual transaction that causes the birth of Nebuchadnezzar, now not as with Menelik, the noble king of Ethiopia, but rather the destructive king of Babylon. Along the way, moreover, Solomon is indicted for intercourse with an impure woman in violation of Jewish law.[17] In this account, Solomon is indicted in quite specific ways that are congruent with the generic indictment of 1 Kings 11:1–3. Here, as in the analysis of Camp,

Solomon is judged by standards of postexilic Judaism concerning ritual purity, especially in relationship to foreign, impure women.[18]

The sexual dimension of the narrative permitted enormously imaginative reading; we may note the two directions in which this agenda is developed. On the one hand, as we have just seen, in the Ethiopic tradition Sheba is revered and Solomon is the seducer. In the other direction, Lassner has chronicled the way in which Islamic tradition demonizes the queen as a threat and a corrupter of faith. Thus in a reading of Solomon by Tha'lobi, the Queen of Sheba is a threat to be contravened: "We turn then to the Queen of Sheba, a proud and presumptuous woman whose very presence threatens to jar Solomon's balanced and harmonious world. She too chooses to deny men their due; she too will need to be put in her place."[19]

This narrative of *Tha'lobi* builds from the text of the Qur'an cited above. In this version, however, the queen puts herself forward in a way that is dangerous and unacceptable in a patriarchal society, thus challenging not only male order but also the divine order that men are to maintain.[20] In the episode whereby Solomon tests the queen concerning her throne, in which she responds that the throne Solomon presents looks like her throne, the queen "sought to demonstrate that women are the equivalent of men and that she, therefore, was entitled to the great domain that she had obtained and now rules with female cunning."[21] This in the end cannot be the last word. Lassner's account of Islamic tradition leads in general to the judgment that "this haughty woman who had never been touched by a 'blade' and who had trained great men as if they were wild stallions to be broken, will be rejected by the greatest stallion of them all. By all accounts, Solomon was the greatest of all lovers. He had the sexual potency of forty men and clearly needed all of it, because as in Jewish tradition, he had no less than one thousand concubines and wives."[22]

It is clear that the narrative of 1 Kings 10:1–13 has had immense generative power in a variety of traditions wherein narrative art operates with great freedom and imagination. Lassner's account shows how the patriarchal tradition of Islam told against the queen, while in Ethiopia, the contrary is the case. At the same time, it is important to recognize that when the narrative is taken with irony, it is not difficult to find a feminist agenda at work as well.[23] Of the rich potential of the narrative, Watt concludes: "The elaborations and interpretations of the story of Belais [the traditional name of the queen] and her meeting with Solomon are an interesting example of the function of what may be called 'imaginative forms' in man's intellectual life. Because the story was mentioned in the *Qur'an* it had *droit de cite* in Islam. It had already been developed somewhat in Jewish literature. And now in an Islamic context and with various specifically Islamic features it gathered to itself many themes from popular imaginative thinking."[24]

This rich imaginative development of the narrative is what we have already seen in the canonical literature, albeit somewhat more restrained and in the service of other ideological-religious passions. Ullendorff seconds the judgment of Watt: "The main components of the story must have had a very long period of gestation in Ethiopia and elsewhere and have possessed all the elements of a gigantic conflation of legendary cycles."[25] Ullendorff's final paragraph, clearly light and humorous, nonetheless reflects the continuing force of gender ideology in the long reading of the narrative. Concerning the meeting: "'Behold, the half was not told to me,' she said in taking leave of Solomon. Had his answer been recorded, he might well have said, 'Nor to me, madam, about you.' But probably he said nothing. As the wisest of men and the husband of seven hundred wives he must surely have known where the last word belongs."[26]

FREEMASONRY AND THE SOLOMONIC TRADITION

The fourth tradition extrapolated from the Solomonic tradition is that of Freemasonry, which originated early in the eighteenth century and quickly became a powerful cultural and political force in Europe and the New World.[27] The emergence of Freemasonry was in the congenial context of the Enlightenment; it drew upon the notions of freedom, beauty, and imagination that were rooted in the earlier Renaissance and resulted in the quite orderly world of imagination. It seems likely that we may identify the specific origin of the Masons to be in a first meeting of the "Grand Lodge of England" in London on June 24, 1717, after which James Anderson, from 1717 to 1723, compiled the founding documents of Freemasonry, *The Statutes of Freemasonry* and the *Old Charges*. It is clear that this movement that began on English soil capitalized on an intellectual climate of trust in rational and free thought that opposed any notion of particular "revealed religion." The movement, moreover, was part of a general response, chronicled by Stephen Toulmin and Klaus Scholder, to the war weariness of Europe after the Thirty Years War, when the great divide in Christendom produced neither security nor certitude.[28] When such apparently failed religious traditions collapsed into barbarism, the time was right for a new quasi-religious alternative that championed toleration and refused to commit to the particularity of any identifiable creed beyond a commitment to sensible social life that encouraged peace and well-being.

While we are able to mark quite specifically the origins of the Masonic movement, it obviously did not arise de novo, even though the antecedents are not easy to identify. Josef S. Roucek has made the interesting suggestion that a major contributor to the founding lore of the Masonic movement is John Amos Comenius (b. 1592), a well-known Moravian educational theorist who championed children and developed important pedagogical theories and methods. Roucek suggests that Comenius, out of the Moravian religious community of Unitas Fratrum, the Unity of Bohemian Brothers, sought to mobilize "the architects of the new edifice [of tolerance] on the ruins of the old world. . . . The aim of Comenius was to create a new social possibility amid the ruins of weary Europe, and he consistently used the imagery and metaphor of *building a temple* for his wisdom concerning a new society of 'justice, love, peace, and progress.' . . . Thus the language is variously of 'a temple of wisdom,' or 'a Temple of Seven Chambers.'"[29]

Roucek observes, moreover, that behind Comenius's vision is the ordered and disciplined religious community of Brethren who were divided into four classes: beginners, those growing in grace, the perfect, and the fallen. As we will see, Masonic imagery has a powerful propensity to order and classify into degrees and various classes. Now, whether this role assigned to Comenius is correct I cannot judge; but Roucek suggests that these ideas served James Anderson well in his initial formulation of the order.[30] In any case, the hopes and visions here assigned to Comenius were very much in the air by the beginning of the eighteenth century; they contribute to our understanding of the environment that permitted and encouraged Freemasonry as an alternative to the exhausted claims of Christendom. The imagery of mason or builder that is crucial to the movement of course did not arise as a metaphor but derived from concrete imagery. Once the metaphor of building a temple is popularized as a term referring to the reconstitution of a defeated society, then it is inescapable that one should push back to real temple builders, namely, those who constructed the great medieval cathedrals.

W. Kirk MacNulty, in his study of Freemasonry, pays particular attention to the pattern of myth and symbol in Masonry, for the lodge is essentially a ritual meeting that enters into and endlessly reconstitutes and relegitimates an imagined world taken as "temple."[31] MacNulty's perspective is much informed by a Jungian approach to symbol, and understands the emergence of Masonry as an attempt to formulate and live according to generic universal myths (sustained by ritual) in a social context that tried excessively to rely upon the paradigm of "scientific materialism" that was readily seen to be inadequate and incomplete.[32]

If we look to the world of the mythic, we may particularly point to two references. First, it is commonly recognized that Masonic lore, especially in the various documents produced by James Anderson, strongly appeals to rabbinic and kabbalistic interpretations that move in gnostic directions, that is, in the development of secret knowledge to which only the initiated can possibly have access. Along with such interpretive practice, however, MacNulty also notes that the great medieval cathedrals are architectural "monuments" to the "mystery" of the gospel, designed through patterns of entrances and barriers and through the management of light and darkness. They serve at the same time to give access to the mystery (in the medieval church, the mystery as sacrament) and to preserve the sense of the inscrutable even in the very process of granting access.[33] In the medieval church, of course, the access to the mystery of the gospel—offered in the sacraments—was governed by the priest-hood that managed the cathedrals and administered the sacraments. And of course the dreaded capacity of excommunication is the dramatic indication that access and exclusion were matters of enormous importance. Thus the political administration of the mystery assures the quite worldly realism about the process; it is, however, a realism that is characteristically infused with mystical attractiveness, dread, and awe. Of course, the Masonic movement not only appropriated patterns of interpretation and architecture but then appropriated them in a particular way so that the mysti-cal dimension of the rites was juxtaposed to an ethical vision that was clear and rea-sonably ordered. But then the Enlightenment, as heir to medieval "mystery" and to emancipation, managed, characteristically, to hold together the mystical and the rational-ethical in a way that sought to preclude the sectarianism that had so wea-ried Europe in the seventeenth century.

Thus the Masons would build these "great temples" in a mystical tradition of care-fully governed access. MacNulty observes the characteristic structure in four parts: the nave, the choir, the sanctuary, and the altar.[34] He proposes, moreover, that this ritual formulation is at the same time a "model for man and universe."[35] That is, the fourfold structure is a model for human personality in its four dimensions; it is at the same time a model for the universe in its several aspects so that a new world and a new human being are evoked and vouched for in the temple construction and in the ritual that gives access to the mysterious gift of newness.

With rootage in a certain intellectual climate that a mystical tradition articulated in both interpretation and architecture, the Masonic order offered in the eighteenth century a quasi-secular religion that overcame every embarrassing "scandal of partic-ularity." At the same time that we notice the newness of Enlightenment modality, we notice with equal clarity that the Masonic world of myth and ritual is deeply based in an appeal to the triumph of Solomon in the Old Testament. And that, of course, is why the subject is pertinent to our Solomonic exploration. Alex Horne makes clear that in the earliest codifications of James Anderson in the *Old Charges,* it is asserted that "at the making of Solomon's temple that King David began . . . Solomon had four score thousand Masons at his work, and . . . Solomon confirmed the charges that David his father had given to the Masons and Solomon himself taught them these manners little differing from the manners that are now used."[36]

That same appeal to Solomon is articulated in other early Masonic literature in-cluding *A Mason's Examination* (1723) and *The Mystery of Freemasonry* (1730). Horne notes that the claims of the literature are "still believed at the present time."[37] The Masonic appeal to the temple of Solomon includes several elements:

The *multichamber* construction that creates a puzzle of access and barriers that pro-tects secret knowledge. While it is characteristic that the Masonic temple has four parts and Solomon's temple reflects the typical three-chamber pattern of the ancient Near East, the distinction is no barrier to Masonic appeal.

The *appeal to Hiram* (cited as Huram Abiff in Masonic lore after 2 Chron 4:16) as the master architect and Mason.[38] Horne observes in the medieval mystery plays there was present a "Huronic Dream" that was celebrated by Catholics.[39]

The *many craftsmen* of Solomon and Hiram, divided into "Three Grades," apprentices, fellows, and masters, thus anticipating the degrees that became important in Masonic order and discipline.[40]

The *Pillars of Boaz and Jachim* as permanent features in the Masonic temple, even though their meaning is enigmatic.[41]

Thus the Masonic formulation was able to draw on long-standing mythic-liturgical notions that gave deep rootage to its venturesomeness in the eighteenth century whereby a new social order, symmetrical, hierarchical, and reliably ordered, is an important antidote to the chaos of the seventeenth century. Horne opines that the Masonic appeal to Solomon's temple drew upon lively recent tradition and was able to capitalize on the "moralizing apparatus offered" in this tradition.[42] Thus the temple of Solomon becomes a legitimator for a new, quite modern, quasi-religious perspective; participants in the new ritual construction of a world of peace and justice could re-perform the ancient temple of Solomon. As we have seen with our forays in this chapter exploring the great imaginative leaps of interpretation, it is a long way to leap in interpretation of ancient text to new usage in the seventeenth century. The connectors between old texts and new usage in this case are variously medieval imagination given in architecture and liturgy and the new world of reason that could accommodate mystical thought and interpretation alongside. The connections are immensely playful and imaginative even if, in new usage, they are taken seriously, literally, and historically.

Having said that, however, we may circle back to the temple of Solomon in order to suggest that in a subtle, indirect, and intuitive way, the Masonic appeal to Solomon's temple has more to its credit than a historical study might suggest. In early consideration of Solomon's temple in the text of 1 Kings 5–8, we have seen that the temple, in its architecture and liturgy, moved away from the particularities of Israel's historical memory to the broader, generic myths and rituals of common ancient Near Eastern faith. Specifically, the temple seems to have been a venue for the enthronement of the divine king who as Creator God sustained all of creation; in that imagined world, the particularities of Israel's historical recital did not figure prominently and indeed could not figure prominently if the temple was to serve a broad constituency that included non-Israelites in the polyglot regime of King Solomon. Given that general perspective, we may take notice of the work of two scholars in particular.

Jon D. Levenson has written at length about "Zion," the "mountain of the temple."[43] Levenson has seen that the temple in Jerusalem participated in, embodied, and bore witness to the God of Israel as the key character in the great creation myths whereby cosmic order is enacted and assigned. Given the liturgic claim of the temple, "it is clear that the temple precincts are perceived as radically and qualitatively different from the rest of the world. . . . The sanctuary, then, is a place in which reality is perceived as a whole, as fresh and untarnished, where the costs exacted by the harshness of normal life are not paid. . . . Words like 'ideal,' 'perfection,' and 'unblemished,' suggest that the temple was, in fact a paradise."[44] In a second study, *Creation and the Persistence of Evil,* Levenson has shown how the temple is a microcosm of creation.[45]

Philip Peter Jenson has studied "the Priestly conception of the world" with reference to its mythic structure and claim. He identifies three "zones" in the temple whereby there are varying degrees of holiness: the court, the holy place, and the holy of holies.[46] These gradations of holiness mean that there are both barriers and accesses, that some people are more qualified and given access to holiness and others are given partial access but denied full access. The rules of holiness, as in the book of Leviticus, are ways to govern access in a liturgical world that is well-ordered and managed in hierarchical ways.

A reflection on these texts suggests that a Masonic appropriation of Solomon's temple and his Priestly architecture and its codes of access nicely serves the several classes of Masons and readily serves the degrees whereby Masons are variously ranked and qualified for ritual participation.[47]

It may be that the initial appeal of the Masons to the temple of Solomon was not based on an awareness of such matters. It is clear, moreover, that the Masonic appropriation of Solomon's temple was, in a characteristically eighteenth-century way, concerned with the strange interface of rationalism and mysticism. In that enlightened world with its particular commitment to "merit," the degrees of the Masonic qualification are coherently ordered. But then, the same was true of the ordering of the priests in the ancient world. Thus the temple serves the Masons by offering a generic religious system without sectarian affront, a clear order of access with mystery at the center. In the ancient world, that temple merited harsh Deuteronomic critique and in the end was a failed temple. It is possible that such a critique of the Masonic appropriation could be offered, but that is beyond the scope of our study.

SOLOMON WRIT LARGE IN ONGOING INTERPRETATION

I have selected four representative examples of Solomonic tradition that are belatedly developed in very different contexts to accomplish very different purposes: the Wisdom of Solomon, a quasi-canonical book that employs Solomon in order to reassert the distinctiveness of Jewishness in the face of Hellenistic culture; an excerpt from the Qur'an that appropriates Solomon for Islamic purposes; Ethiopic traditions that utilize Solomon to legitimate the very ancient dynasty of Ethiopia and assert that that dynasty is the legitimate heir to the Davidic dynasty; and the Masonic traditions that evidence the way quite modernist interpretation can appropriate Solomon as a legitimization of an Enlightenment usage that sustains an interface of ethical romanticism and mystical wisdom. In these several probes I have commented on literature that is outside my own field of expertise and have, perforce, relied on the judgment of other interpreters in the secondary literature. Certain conclusions suggest themselves to me from this study.

First, we have already seen that the biblical traditions themselves are immense acts of interpretive imagination, whether the imagination of urban elites who would take Solomon as model king, or the imagination of Jewish zealots in the Persian period, or the imagination of poets and sages in late Judaism who explored the tricky, complex interface between Jewish traditions and Gentile context. In any case, what emerges clearly in the present discussion is that these ancient textual acts of imagination continue to be open to and generative of subsequent acts of interpretive imagination whereby ancient memories could be readily aligned with contemporary agendas. It is this tricky way in which the biblical memory of Solomon negotiates self-conscious covenantal faith while still accommodating lived reality that makes the tradition enormously supple and open to belated use. While these belated acts of imagination go far beyond whatever may have been historical and biblical memory, it seems reasonable to conclude that the enterprise of interpretive imagination in later tradition is different in degree from what goes on in the Bible, but not different in kind.[48]

The second conclusion that very much surprised me is that for all the venturesomeness of these interpretive acts of imagination, in each case it is my judgement that the later interpretation in legitimate ways did appeal to some aspect of the biblical tradition, even if the biblical tradition took great liberties in extrapolation. Thus, the Wisdom of Solomon, with its appeal to the God of Israel as Lord of Wisdom, is faithful, I suggest, to the Deuteronomic redescription of Solomon. That is, the Wisdom of Solomon, as did the Deuteronomist, calls Israel back to a rigorous Torah-based covenantalism. The summons to Torah-based conventalism in turn produces strictures against idolatry and voices deep hope for Torah keepers in this age and in the age to come. The brief Solomonic excerpt in the Qur'an can articulate Solomon as the one who bests the Queen of Sheba and who satisfies her "desire" and yet does not capitulate to her. To be sure, the Solomonic "victory" in the biblical tradition is more an act of machismo power than it is pure faith, but the victory in both cases in parallel belongs to Solomon. Conversely, in the Ethiopic traditions, it is the Queen of Sheba who bests Solomon. We may imagine that the capacity of foreign wives to "turn away his heart" is operative here, for in this tradition the queen does prevail, as do the foreign wives in the Deuteronomic tradition (1 Kgs 11:1–9). The Masonic tradition rightly sensed that Solomon's temple and generic ideology that moved against close particularism were useful in fashioning an ideology of tolerance. Given that objective, it turns out that the temple of Solomon is as generic and as lacking in the "scandal of particularity" as eighteenth-century Enlightenment thought needed it to be.

On all these counts, the supple memory of Solomon lends itself to ongoing usage in a variety of contexts where there is a great deal·at stake. If we consider the spectrum of belated usages reviewed here, we are able to see that the contested dimensions of the scriptural tradition continue to surface in a variety of ways, as these primal traditions are variously taken up: Deuteronomic rigor in the Wisdom of Solomon; Solomon's defeat of the Queen of Sheba in the Qur'an; the power of the foreign wife over Solomon in the Ethiopic tradition; and the generic quality of the temple articulated in the Masonic formulation. When viewed altogether, these belated usages go in different, even competing directions. All, however, can appeal to these ancient traditions, and each makes powerful, albeit complex claim in contemporary context. It is no wonder that Solomon is indeed David's "greater son"; he continues to be writ large in ongoing interpretation among all "the peoples of the book."

CHAPTER 14

POSTSCRIPT: SOLOMON IN NEW TESTAMENT PERSPECTIVE

Solomon's father, David, is profoundly important and prominent in the New Testament. The early church sought ways to understand and interpret Jesus through the memory of David. Jesus of course was situated in Old Testament memory and imagery and yet could not be contained in such images and memories. David's son Solomon, by contrast, is mentioned only marginally in the New Testament. Here I will comment on three uses that exhaust the interpretive grist of New Testament usage but that together constitute an important body of testimony concerning the way in which the early church understood and utilized the tradition of Solomon.[1]

JESUS' LINEAGE

The first New Testament usage is in Matthew 1:6–7: "and Jesse the father of King David. And David was the father of Solomon by the wife of Uriah" (Matt 1:6). This verse occurs in the royal genealogy of Matthew that connects Jesus, through his father Joseph, back to Abraham through the royal Davidic line (1:1–17). This genealogy is of special interest because of the mention of four "mothers" in Israel who in other contexts might be unmentionable embarrassments. The other three mothers beyond Bathsheba are Tamar (1:3), Rahab (1:5), and Ruth (1:5).

Of course in the verse that concerns us, the mother of Solomon, Bathsheba, is not mentioned by name but only alluded to as "the wife of Uriah" (Matt 1:7). The point of such phrasing of course is the insistence of the tradition of Matthew that Bathsheba, mother of Solomon, never became legitimately David's wife; she remains after the sordid narrative of 1 Samuel 11–12 forever the wife of Uriah. It is plausible that the tradition of Matthew alludes back to the birth narrative of 2 Samuel 12:24–25, in which Bathsheba figures prominently, and declines to treat the birth process and succession from David to Solomon as illegitimate. The tradition of Matthew makes nothing of this allusion to David's sordid affair with the wife of Uriah the Hittite and is in any case focused on the conclusion of the genealogy, the birth of Jesus in Matthew 1:16. Nonetheless this passing reference to the wife of Uriah, which receives no special comment, raises questions of illegitimacy that haunt the entire genealogy.

In this quick verdict, moreover, the tradition of Matthew is fully consonant with the Deuteronomic verdict of 1 Kings 15:4–5: "Nevertheless for David's sake the Lord his God gave him a lamp in Jerusalem, setting up his son after him, and establishing Jerusalem; because David did what was right in the sight of the Lord, and did not turn aside from anything that he commanded him all the days of his life, except in the matter of Uriah the Hittite."

The Deuteronomic tradition per se does not want to make too much of the origin of Solomon, but it cannot pass over it in silence. There as well, the tradition (not unlike that of Matthew) cannot bring itself to sound the name of the illicit mother but must line it out by reference to Uriah, the wronged legitimate husband. The notation in Matthew 1:6, after the fashion of the notation in 1 Kings 15:4–5, is only in passing. The wonder of course is that it is there at all, thus aligning the gospel tradition, it would seem, with the Deuteronomic critique of the great king.

A METAPHOR FOR THE FUTILITY OF AN AUTONOMOUS LIFE

The Deuteronomic critique of Solomon is advanced in the parallel texts of Matthew 6:29 and Luke 11:31. The instruction of Jesus here is an address to his disciples concerning trust in the generous gifts of "your father" as an alternative to the anxiety that is produced by futile self-serving effort. The address begins with reference to anxiety, and recognizes that anxiety is a product of endless labor to acquire all of the priorities of life, food, drink, and clothing: "Therefore I tell you, do not worry about your life, what you will eat or what you will drink, or about your body, what you will wear. Is not life more than food, and the body more than clothing?" (Matt 6:25). The ones who trust the father (birds and flowers) are free of anxiety; indeed, they are not only free of anxiety but they are more gloriously clothed in beautiful, rich apparel than even Solomon, who was of course opulent in dress as in everything else. The core teaching of this instruction and its elemental contrasts are not difficult to grasp. We may nonetheless marvel at the rhetorical maneuver of the contrast. If we wanted to find a contrast to the loveliness of birds, the trustfulness of flowers, the security of all creatures beyond the human, one could hardly have imagined a more breathtaking counterpoint than Solomon, the cipher in Israel's memory for extravagant wealth. The contrast is total.

It is clear that more is accomplished here than a clear contrast. In fact, the rhetoric serves to deconstruct Solomon, to suggest that his unparalleled wealth is in fact a pretentious empty show that does nothing to relieve anxiety: "Yet I tell you, even Solomon in all his glory was not clothed like one of these" (Matt 6:29). Solomon is singled out as a cipher for failed wealth and for futile, empty self-securing. There is no doubt that Solomon in 1 Kings 3–11 is an endlessly driven acquisitor—of horses, chariots, silver, gold, wives (see Deut 17:16–17). If we sneak a look at Ecclesiastes, moreover, we can see how the entire process of acquisitiveness that defines Solomon is a profound futility, a vanity that yields nothing.[2] Thus Solomon's glory is an emptiness that should not be replicated. The alternative to Solomonic acquisitiveness, which inescapably ends in anxiety, is God and "God's righteousness," the righteousness commended to royalty in Psalm 72 but surely not on the horizon of remembered Solomon. Thus Solomon is taken as the quintessential metaphor for the futility of autonomous life that cannot, in the end, find peace or well-being for itself, for such peace and well-being are a gift of the Creator God; the gifts of peace and well-being are already underway in the processes of life lived congruently and obediently as God's creatures.

The point of contrast is shaped in the tradition of Matthew by the fact that the instruction is prefaced with the simple contrast of Matthew 6:24: "No one can serve two masters; for a slave will either hate the one and love the other, or be devoted to the one and despise the other. You cannot serve God and wealth." The last term in that instruction is variously translated "wealth," "capital," or "mammon," but the point is clear. Jesus calls for a radical act of trust that invites the disciples to a deep either/or.[3] Any attempt to choose both God and wealth eventually cannot be sustained, for by default one will inevitably be chosen. If we connect verse 24 to verse 29, it is clear that remembered Solomon wanted to sustain the both/and but eventually could not. In the end, when he was old (1 Kgs 11:4), Solomon opted for acquisitiveness, and in practice he abandoned the God of the Torah and ended in harsh judgment. The memory of Solomon makes clear that in practical matters it was Solomon's wealth, and his wisdom in the service of his wealth, that came to characterize his life. Thus not unlike the Deuteronomist who contrasts bad king Solomon with good king Josiah, the tradition of Matthew portrays Solomon as a model of failed life, defined by acquisitiveness that would not rely on the gracious gifts of the Creator.

The same instruction in the Lucan version is more complex and therefore more interesting. Luke of course has no counterpart to the dictum of Matthew 6:24; instead, the instruction in Luke is preceded by a parable that also concerns greed, covetousness, and acquisitiveness (Luke 12:13–21). The rich man had more than enough and wanted yet more. And when the tradition thinks of "a rich man," it might before very long think of Solomon as the quintessentially rich man. Of course that is not required in the Lucan parable, unless we permit mention of Solomon in verse 27 to inform our hearing of the parable. We may notice the following elements of the narrative that may be provisionally illuminated by reference to Solomon: The rich man needs more storage space for his surplus produce and surplus wealth (12:18). Solomon was perpetually preoccupied with accumulation that required more "storage cities" (1 Kgs 9:9), a habit we have noted that is not unlike the need of Pharaoh (Exod 1:11):

The phrasing of verse 15 is significant. "Covetousness" (*pleonexia, lit.*, "the desire for more"), also translated as avarice or greed, is one of the vices most scorned by Hellenistic moralists. They call it "the metropolis of all evil deeds" (Diodorus Siculus) or "the greatest source of evil" (Dio Chrysostom). It is found in the early Christian "vice lists" (Rom. 1:29; *1Clement* 35:5). In Col. 3:5 it is equated with "idolatry," which Rom. 1:24–25 describes as serving "the creature rather than the Creator." It is a vice that turns its victim away from both God and neighbor. While the first half of the introductory verse is a warning, the second is a maxim: human life does not consist in an "abundance" (*en tô perisseuein*). The Greek term literally means "in what is more than enough," with pejorative overtones, since moderation and having nothing in excess (*mçden agan*) was prized in the Hellenistic world. It is not the mere possession of material goods which will spell the downfall of the rich man but his constant desire for more which leads to surplus possession, which today we might call "conspicuous consumption."[4]

The self-admiration of the rich man is summarized in the triad of "eat, drink, be merry," a formula that seems a direct reminiscence of the affirmation of Solomon in 1 Kings 4:20: "Judah and Israel were as numerous as the sand by the sea; they ate and drank and were happy." That triad, moreover, seems closely related to the verdict of Ecclesiastes 9:7 that settles for enjoyment without excessive ambition: "Go, eat your bread with enjoyment, and drink your wine with a merry heart; for God has long ago approved what you do."

Finally, the verdict of the rich man is "fool" (Luke 12:20). The rich man had called himself "soul" (*psyche*), likely bespeaking an autonomous self that has no reference beyond himself. Such autonomy of necessity is committed to endless acquisitiveness that is, so we are taught here, a commitment to self-destruction. The verdict of "fool" is of course an undoing of the claim of wisdom that was in the service of wealth. That is, Solomon's much celebrated wisdom turned out to be the foolishness of death. If the Solomon connection is to be entertained here, then the narrative is a verdict that the wisdom of Solomon, so much admired by the world, is in the end foolishness. Such wisdom that did not begin in "the fear of the Lord" but is instead only driven by a fear of scarcity inevitably ends in anxiety.

The conclusion of the parabolic instruction in Luke 12:21 permits a defining contrast between *treasures for themselves* and *rich toward God*. Solomon is an obvious case study in this contrast. By 1 Kings 11 his acquisitiveness had caused him to abandon his initial "love of YHWH" in 1 Kings 3:3. His life and reign had turned away from that love to seek "treasures for themselves." By 1 Kings 12:1–19 those self-serving treasures are placed in acute jeopardy.

The parable, if not intentionally reminiscent of Solomon, is at least congruent with the imagined Solomon of the Old Testament. The man who asks the question that evoked the parable is concerned about the "family inheritance," that is, about the acquisition of land (Luke 12:13). It is of course recognized that Solomon is devoted in every possible way to acquiring more territory (see 1 Kgs 4:21 [Heb 5:1]). In both cases, the remembered king and the man with the question in the parable, the issue is recognized as a case of self-destructive greed in pursuit of "the abundance of possessions" (Luke 12:15).

But the man who asks the question, the man in the parable who is a "fool," and the inferred ancient king all together constitute a foil for the instruction that Jesus will provide his disciples in Luke 12:22–34. The point of that instruction is that the disciples are summoned to an alternative existence of trust that does not seek to secure self but trusts that their Father knows what they need (Luke 12:30). The Lucan version of the teaching, moreover, adds an addendum for the "little flock" that engages in the alternative (12:32–33). The radical behavior enjoined in this instruction is about "treasure" that accompanies "heart" (12:34). We are of course aware that in 1 Kings 11:3–4 Solomon had redirected his heart toward other treasures, and so forfeited "the kingdom" that it had been his "father's good pleasure" to give (Luke 12:32). Read in this way, it is no wonder that Solomon merits mention as a negative exemplar in the instruction of Jesus: "Even Solomon in all his glory was not clothed like one of these" (12:27b). Solomon is the very best of his genre, the wisest and the richest. He is, however, no recommended model, for such a life as his can in the end only be devoured by anxiety. The alternative is "do not be anxious"; one cannot have it both ways.

ONE WHO IS GREATER THAN SOLOMON

The third citation of Solomon is in an instruction of Jesus that is again common to both Matthew and Luke (Matt 12:38–42; Luke 11:29–32).[5] The two versions of the instruction in Matthew and Luke vary slightly. In the Lucan version, the reference to Jonah is interrupted by a reference to Solomon, so that Jonah is cited both before (Luke 11:29–30) and after (11:32) the citation of Solomon (11:31). Both versions, however, move to the same point, namely, that the disbelieving crowd wants a "sign" but fails to recognize that in Jesus the ultimate sign of the new rule of God is fully manifest and present among them.

The teaching makes two appeals to the Old Testament, in each case in order to contrast the ancient sign in Israel with the new sign present in Jesus. The first such contrast concerns the significance of Jonah. In Matthew, Jonah is cited because of the wonder of rising on the third day from "the belly of the sea monster." The people of Nineveh repented at the preaching of Jonah. The three-day venture of Jonah is a type for the three-day resurrection of Jesus to come, but those of the contemporary generation, unlike the people of Jonah's time, miss the sign and do not repent, and they are therefore condemned, even by the Ninevites. The Ninevites are seen to contrast their own repentance with the obduracy of the new generation.

The second citation, the one of interest to us, concerns Solomon as a type for Jesus. The teaching refers to the visit of the Queen of Sheba, "the queen of the South," because she recognized the wisdom of Solomon, which, along with his wealth, took her breath away (1 Kgs 10:5) and satisfied her every desire (10:13). By contrast, the present generation in its recalcitrance fails to come to terms with the greater wisdom now embodied in Jesus.

It is evident in both cases that the resurrection tale of Jonah and the visit of the queen to Solomon are cited in order to assert that a "greater" is now present in the person of Jesus. The resurrection of Jesus is *greater* than the resurrection of Jonah. The wisdom of Jesus is *greater* than the wisdom of Solomon. Those who listen to Jesus and are scandalized by him are condemned—by the Ninevites, by the queen of the South, by Jesus, and by the voice of the Q tradition. They are condemned because they fail to recognize and to come to terms with this one who is "greater."

As with the teaching of Matthew 6:25–33 and Luke 12:22–34, Solomon is cited in this teaching of Matthew 12:38–42 and Luke 11:29–32 as the supreme case from the old tradition. In the instruction of Matthew 6 and Luke 12, Solomon is the supreme case of "glory" (wealth and honor). In the instruction of Matthew 12 and Luke 11, Solomon is a supreme case of wisdom, readily recognized as such by the queen of the South. These texts assert that even in wisdom, Solomon is surpassed by Jesus. Indeed, Jesus surpasses all that was previously known and recognized in Israel, or beyond Israel, even among the Gentiles. Thus Solomon is employed by this teaching in order to exalt and celebrate Jesus, who is quintessentially superior in every regard, including wisdom. Joseph Fitzmeyer observes: "Luke enhances the warning with a wisdom motif. In not heeding Jesus' preaching, the men of his generation have failed to recognize the heaven-sent wisdom which he has come to preach. . . . This episode suggests an identification of preaching and wisdom with that 'Word of God.'"[6]

The claim made for Jesus, in Israelite context, is breathtaking, because the old memory of Solomon is vigilant in its assertion of the preeminence of Solomon in wisdom:

I now do according to your word. Indeed I give you a wise and discerning mind; no one like you has been before you and no one like you shall arise after you. I give you also what you have not asked, both riches and honor all your life; no other king shall compare with you. (1 Kgs 3:12–13)

All Israel heard of the judgment that the king had rendered; and they stood in awe of the king, because they perceived that the wisdom of God was in him, to execute justice. (1 Kgs 3:28)

So that Solomon's wisdom surpassed the wisdom of all the people of the east, and all the wisdom of Egypt. He was wiser than anyone else, wiser than Ethan the Ezrahite, and Heman, Calcol, and Darda, children of Mahol; his fame spread throughout all the surrounding nations. . . . People came from all the nations to hear the wisdom of Solomon; they came from all the kings of the earth who had heard of his wisdom. (1 Kgs 4:30–31, 34)

When the queen of Sheba had observed all the wisdom of Solomon, the house that he had built, the food of his table, the seating of his officials, and the attendance of his servants, their clothing, his valets, and his burnt offerings that he offered at the house of the Lord, there was no more spirit in her. So she said to the king, "The report was true that I heard in my own land of your accomplishments and of your wisdom, but I did not believe the reports until I came and my own eyes had seen it. Not even half had been told me; your wisdom and prosperity far surpass the report that I had heard." (1 Kgs 10:4–7)

Thus King Solomon excelled all the kings of the earth in riches and in wisdom. The whole earth sought the presence of Solomon to hear his wisdom, which God had put into his mind. (1 Kgs 10:23–24)

But now—"greater"! The utilization of Solomon in this instruction is different from that of Matthew 6 and Luke 12. In that teaching, the matter was a simple contrast between the anxiety of Solomon and trust in the Father. In this teaching, Solomon and Jesus are in the same category, but Solomon is surpassed by the one who possesses greater wisdom.

It is important to recognize that this teaching is in Q, a primal gospel tradition that focuses upon teaching, that offers true teaching to which the world has no access, teaching that moves in the direction of secret teaching, gnosis. Thus the "greater" wisdom of Jesus is not more knowledge, not, as with the knowledge of Solomon, about governance or about the economy. Rather, the greater wisdom of Jesus concerns the very mystery of life that is given, not to the wise and intelligent, but to "infants," that is, the disciples:

At the same hour Jesus rejoiced in the Holy Spirit and said, "I thank you, Father, Lord of heaven and earth, because you have hidden these things from the wise and the intelligent and have revealed them to infants; yes, Father, for such was your gracious will. All things have been handed over to me by my Father; and no one knows who the Son is except the Father, or who the Father is except the Son and anyone to whom the Son chooses to reveal him." Then turning to the disciples, Jesus said to them privately, "Blessed are the eyes that see what you see! For I tell you that many prophets and kings desired to see what you see, but did not see it, and to hear what you hear, but did not hear it. (Luke 10:21–24; see Matt 11:25–27)

Thus Jesus is celebrated in this tradition not for the kind of earthly management in which Solomon excelled, but in the secret of true life to which the disciples—but none of Solomon's ilk—have access.

This instruction about Jesus as "greater" is situated in Matthew in a context of teaching where Jesus is said to have power over evil (Matt 12:22–32, 43–45) and in which Jesus' "true family" consists of those who do "the will of my Father" (12:46–50). W. F. Albright and C. S. Mann see this teaching in a context that condemns contemporary Judaism for its failure to receive Jesus.[7] But they also notice that "lines of separation are being drawn ever within Israel."

In Luke the same teaching is preceded by a call to radical obedience (Luke 11:28) and followed by instruction about light (11:33–36) and a warning against those who focus on trivial or destructive matters to the neglect of "the key of knowledge" (11:52). The whole of the text, in both presentations, invites the listening disciples to a radically alternative existence, certainly radically alternative to the life, the riches, and the wisdom in which Solomon excelled.

THE MEMORY OF SOLOMON AS A TESTIMONIAL TO THE TRUTH OF JESUS

These three citations of Solomon (Matt 1:6–7, Matt 6:29, and Luke 12:27), and Matthew 12:42 and Luke 11:32 constitute a major interpretive play upon the imagination and memory of Solomon.

The genealogical note of Matthew 1:6–7 insists that Solomon can be kept in the ambiguity of his life, in the context of David's sordidness, a judgment congruent with the Deuteronomist. Raymond E. Brown comments: "It is the combination of the scandalous or irregular union and of divine intervention through the woman that best explains Matthew's choice of genealogy."[8] Brown further suggests that in the citation of a woman not free of scandal, Matthew may foreshadow the role of Mary, herself not free of scandal in the narrative. The contrast of Solomon's greedy autonomy and trust in the father (Matt 6:29; Luke 12:27) is a radical summons away from acquisitiveness to trust in the father's generosity, and the teaching on "greater" dissolves the authority of the worldly wisdom of Solomon and points the disciples to an alternative life-giving wisdom. In all these citations, the memory of Solomon is utilized in order to testify to the truth of Jesus: that the purposes of God can utilize human sordidness as a route to Messianic possibility; that an alternative to greedy, anxious acquisitiveness is possible, grounded in God's generous abundance; that the wisdom that gives life is not the capacity to manage and accumulate but is given in vulnerability where God's newness is operative. On all counts, not even Solomon, not the best of the old order, can give what the harbinger of the new age brings. Not even Solomon!

NOTES

INTRODUCTION

1. See Frank S. Frick, *The Formation of the State in Ancient Israel* (SWBA 4; Sheffield: Almond Press, 1985); and David Noel Freedman and David Frank Graf, eds., *Palestine in Transition: The Emergence of Ancient Israel* (SWBA 2; Sheffield: Almond Press, 1983).

2. On such "thickness," see Clifford Geertz, *The Interpretation of Cultures: Selected Essays* (New York: Basic Books, 1973), 3–30.

3. Wayne Booth, "The Empire of Irony," *Georgia Review* 37 (1983): 12.

4. Gail R. O'Day, *Revelation in the Fourth Gospel* (Philadelphia: Fortress Press, 1986), 31.

CHAPTER 1

1. See Edward W. Said, *Culture and Imperialism* (New York: Vintage Books, 1994); and Howard Zinn, *People's History of the United States* (New York: New Press, 1997).

2. See L. G. Running, "William Foxwell Albright," in *Dictionary of Biblical Interpretation A-J* (ed. John H. Hayes; Nashville, Tenn.: Abingdon Press, 1999), 22–23; and John A. Miles, "Understanding Albright: A Revolutionary Etude," *HTR* 69 (1976): 151–75.

3. The programmatic book of Albright is *From the Stone Age to Christianity: Monotheism and the Historical Process* (Baltimore: Johns Hopkins University Press, 1957). See the critical assessment of his work by Burke O. Long, *Planting and Reaping Albright: Politics, Ideology, and Interpreting the Bible* (University Park: Pennsylvania State University Press, 1997).

4. John Bright, *A History of Israel* (4th ed.; Louisville, Ky.: Westminster John Knox Press, 2000).

5. See William P. Brown, introduction to Bright, *History of Israel*, 1–22.

6. Bright, *History of Israel*, 211–28.

7. Brown, introduction, 21, 22.

8. Bright, *History of Israel*, 227.

9. Ibid., 215.

10. James B. Pritchard, "The Age of Solomon," in *Solomon and Sheba* (ed. James B. Pritchard; London: Phaidon, 1974), 17–39.

11. Ibid., 32–33.

12. Ibid., 35, 36.

13. Ibid., 30–31.

14. See John Bright, *Early Israel in Recent History Writing: A Study in Method* (London: SCM Press, 1956).

15. Martin Noth, *The History of Israel* (rev.; New York: Harper and Row, 1960), 204.

16. Ibid., 219.

17. Ibid., 219–20.

18. Noth cites von Rad in ibid., 223.

19. Ibid., 223–24.

20. G. Ernest Wright, *Biblical Archaeology* (Philadelphia: Westminster Press, 1957).

21. Ibid., 132.

22. On the connection between temple and creation, see Jon D. Levenson, *Creation and the Persistence of Evil: The Jewish Drama of Divine Omnipotence* (San Francisco: Harper and Row, 1988), 53–127; and Levenson, *Sinai and Zion: An Entry into the Jewish Bible* (New York: Winston Press, 1985), 89–184.

23. See G. Ernest Wright, *The Old Testament against Its Environment* (SBT 2; London: SCM Press, 1950).

24. Wright, *Biblical Archaeology,* 142–45.

25. Ibid., 143.

26. The core of biblical theology, for Wright, consists of a confession of "God's mighty acts" enacted in the historical process. See Wright, *God Who Acts: Biblical Theology as Recital* (SBT 8; London: SCM Press, 1952).

27. J. Alberto Soggin, "The Davidic-Solomonic Kingdom," in *Israelite and Judean History* (ed. John H. Hayes and J. Maxwell Miller; Philadelphia: Westminster Press, 1977), 332–80.

28. Ibid., 332.

29. Ibid., 340–43.

30. Ibid., 373–80.

31. Ibid., 365–70.

32. Ibid., 370.

33. On that common pattern of ideology, see Ivan Engnell, *Studies in Divine Kingship in the Ancient Near East* (Oxford: Blackwell, 1967).

34. See Henri Frankfort, *Kingship and the Gods: A Study of Ancient Near Eastern Religion as the Integration of Society and Nature* (Chicago: University of Chicago Press, 1948).

35. J. Maxwell Miller and John H. Hayes, *A History of Ancient Israel and Judah* (Philadelphia: Westminster Press, 1986).

36. Ibid., 189.

37. Ibid. See also J. Maxwell Miller, "Separating the Solomon of History from the Solomon of Legend," in *The Age of Solomon: Scholarship at the Turn of the Millennium* (ed. Lowell K. Handy; Leiden: Brill, 1997), 1–24.

38. Miller and Hayes, *History of Ancient Israel and Judah,* 190.

39. Ibid., 193.

40. Ibid., 196.

41. R. A. Carlson, *David: The Chosen King: A Traditio-Historical Approach to the Second Book of Samuel* (Stockholm: Almqvist and Wiksell, 1964).

42. Langdon Gilkey, "Cosmology, Ontology, and the Travail of Biblical Language," *JR* 41 (1961): 194–205.

43. See the works of Wright cited in notes 23 and 26.

44. Gerhard von Rad, *Old Testament Theology* (New York: Harper and Row, 1962), 1:302.

45. Walther Eichrodt, *Theology of the Old Testament,* 2 vols. (trans. J. A. Baker; Philadelphia: Westminster Press, 1961), 1:512–13.

46. The problem faced by careful readers of the text, I suggest, is not the historicity of Old Testament traditions; it is, rather, the flat, one-dimensional notions of history from the nineteenth century that continue to inform criticism. See Yosef Hayim Yerushalm, *Zakhor: Jewish History and Jewish Memory* (Seattle: University of Washington Press, 1982).

47. Thomas L. Thompson, *The Historicity of the Patriarchal Narratives: The Quest for the Historical Abraham* (BZAW 133; Berlin: DeGruyter, 1974). Thompson's later works continue to develop the project set forth in Thompson, *Historicity: Early History of the Israelite People: From the Written and Archaeological Sources* (Leiden: Brill, 1994); Thompson, *The Mythic Past: Biblical Archeology and the Myth of Israel* (New York: Basic Books, 1999); and Thompson, *The Origin of Tradition in Ancient Israel: The Literary Formation of Genesis and Exodus 1–23* (Sheffield: Sheffield Academic Press, 1987).

48. John Van Seters, *Abraham in History and Tradition* (New Haven: Yale University Press, 1975).

49. John Van Seters, *In Search of History: Historiography and the Ancient World and the Origins of Biblical History* (Winona Lake, Ind.: Eisenbrauns, 1997); Van Seters, *The Life of Moses: The Yahwist as Historian in Exodus-Numbers* (Louisville, Ky.: Westminster John Knox Press, 1994); Van Seters, *The Pentateuch: A Social-Scientific Commentary* (Sheffield: Sheffield Academic Press, 1999); and Van Seters, *Prologue to History: The Yahwist as Historian in Genesis* (Louisville, Ky.: Westminster John Knox Press, 1992).

50. Philip R. Davies, *In Search of "Ancient Israel"* (JSOTSup 148; Sheffield: Sheffield Academic Press, 1992).

51. Niels Peter Lemche, *The Israelites in History and Tradition* (Louisville, Ky.: Westminster John Knox Press, 1998).

52. Ibid., 148–56.

53. Ibid., 161.

54. A. R. Millard and D. J. Wiseman, eds., *Essays on the Patriarchal Narratives* (Leicester: InterVarsity Press, 1980).

55. Baruch Halpern, *The First Historians: The Hebrew Bible and History* (San Francisco: Harper and Row, 1988). Notice should be taken of Iain Proven, V. Philips Long, and Tremper Longman III, *A Biblical History of Israel* (Louisville, Ky.: Westminster John Knox Press, 2003).

56. On ideology, see Paul Ricoeur, *Lectures on Ideology and Utopia* (New York: Columbia University Press, 1986).

57. See James Barr, *History and Ideology in the Old Testament: Biblical Studies at the End of the Millennium* (Oxford: Oxford University Press, 2000), for an unsympathetic view of the current practice of "ideology critique" in Old Testament studies.

58. This is the import of the critique that Long has made of Albright's work, cited in note 3 above.

59. For such a critique of the ideological dimension of historical criticism, see Musa W. Dube, "Villagizing, Globalizing, and Biblical Studies," in *Reading the Bible in the Global Village: Cape Town*, by Justin S. Ukpong et al. (Atlanta, Ga.: Society of Biblical Literature, 2002), 41–63. The other essays in the volume merit attention on the same issue.

60. See Erhard S. Gerstenberger, *Theologies in the Old Testament* (Minneapolis, Minn.: Fortress Press, 2002), chap. 8. Notice that Donald Akenson, *Surpassing Wonder* (New York: Harcourt, Brace, 1998), designates the exilic author as "the Great Inventor," suggesting that a sweeping theological vision was generated and imposed upon Israel during the crises of the exile. This vision became decisive for all subsequent generations of Jews and Christians.

61. See Lester L. Grabbe, ed., *Leading Captivity Captive: "The Exile" as History and Ideology* (JSOTSup 278; Sheffield: Sheffield Academic Press, 1988); and James M. Scott, ed., *Exile: Old Testament, Jewish, and Christian Conceptions* (Leiden: Brill, 1997), especially the essay by Daniel Smith-Christopher.

62. See Hans M. Barstad, *The Myth of the Empty Land: A Study in the History and Archeology of Judah During the "Exilic" Period* (Oslo: Scandinavian University Press, 1996).

63. This accent has been effectively championed by Brevard S. Childs, *Introduction to the Old Testament as Scripture* (Philadelphia: Fortress Press, 1979); and Childs, *Biblical Theology of the Old and New Testaments: Theological Reflection on the Christian Bible* (Minneapolis, Minn.: Fortress Press, 1993).

64. Keith Whitelam, *The Invention of Ancient Israel: The Silencing of Palestinian History* (London: Routledge, 1996).

65. See the acute analysis of Michael Prior, *Zionism and the State of Israel: A Moral Inquiry* (London: Routledge, 1999).

66. See Walter Brueggemann, *Theology of the Old Testament: Testimony, Dispute, Advocacy* (Minneapolis, Minn.: Fortress Press, 1997), 726–29.

67. Israel Finkelstein and Neil Asher Silberman, *The Bible Unearthed: Archaeology's New Vision of Ancient Israel and the Origin of Its Sacred Texts* (New York: Free Press, 2001).

68. Ibid., 128.

69. Ibid., 133.

70. Ibid., 134.

71. Ibid., 141.

72. Ibid., 142.

73. Ibid., 144.

74. Ibid., 167, 168.

75. William G. Dever, *What Did the Biblical Writers Know, and When Did They Know It?* (Grand Rapids, Mich.: Eerdmans, 2001). See also Dever, "Monumental Architecture in Ancient Israel in the Period of the United Monarchy," in *Studies in the Period of David and Solomon and Other Essays* (ed. Tomoo Ishida; Winona Lake, Ind.: Eisenbrauns, 1982), 269–306.

76. Dever, *What Did the Biblical Writers Know,* 100, 101.

77. Ibid., 101.

78. Ibid., 106–8.

79. Ibid., 125.

80. Ibid., 133.

81. Ibid., 135–37.

82. Ibid., 144–57.

83. Ibid., 145, 157.

84. Ibid., 126–31.

85. Ibid., 127.

86. See chap. 13.

87. Finkelstein and Silberman, *The Bible Unearthed,* 168.

88. See Dever, *What Did the Biblical Writers Know?,* 100; and Morton Smith, *Palestinian Parties and Politics That Shaped the Old Testament* (New York: Columbia University Press, 1971).

CHAPTER 2

1. David Noel Freedman, *The Unity of the Hebrew Bible* (Ann Arbor: University of Michigan Press, 1993), 5–6.

2. David Harman Akenson, *Surpassing Wonder: The Invention of the Bible and the Talmuds* (New York: Harcourt Brace, 1998).

3. Ibid., 23.

4. Ibid., 24–25.

5. Ibid., 21–22.

6. Ibid., 22.

7. See Peter R. Ackroyd, "The Temple Vessels: A Continuity Theme," in *Studies in the Religious Tradition of the Old Testament* (London: SCM Press, 1987), 46–60.

8. See Isaiah 55:12–13 on a new beginning, with the "thorns and thistles" of Genesis 3:14–19 now eliminated.

9. The classic hypothesis of such an editorial process is the documentary hypothesis, on which see Ernest Nicholson, *The Pentateuch in the Twentieth Century: The Legacy of Julius Wellhausen* (Oxford: Clarendon Press, 1998); and Richard Elliot Friedman, *The Bible with Sources Revealed: A New View into the Five Books of Moses* (San Francisco: Harper San Francisco, 2003).

10. See the classic formulation of this hypothesis by Martin Noth, *The Deuteronomistic History* (JSOTSup 15; Sheffield: JSOT Press, 1981).

11. There is now a great deal of scholarly ferment that seeks to refine or modify the dominant hypothesis of Noth. See, for example, Anthony F. Campbell and Mark A. O'Brien, *Unfolding the Deuteronomistic History: Origins, Upgrades, Present Text* (Minneapolis, Minn.: Fortress Press, 2000).

12. Gerhard von Rad, *The Problem of the Hexateuch and Other Essays* (New York: McGraw-Hill, 1966), 27.

13. Ibid., 28–29.

14. George Mendenhall, *Law and Covenant in Israel and the Ancient Near East* (Pittsburgh, Pa.: Biblical Colloquium, 1955).

15. See the critical review of the issues by Ernest W. Nicholson, *God and His People: Covenant and Theology in the Old Testament* (Oxford: Clarendon Press, 1986), 56–82.

16. Georg Braulik, *The Theology of Deuteronomy: Collected Essays of Georg Braulik* (trans. Ulrika Lindblad; N. Richland Hills, Tex.: BIBAL Press, 1994). See also Stephen Kaufman, "The Structure of the Deuteronomic Law," *Maarav* 1 (1979): 105–58.

17. See Delbert R. Hillers, *Treaty-Curses and the Old Testament Prophets* (BibOr 16; Rome: Pontifical Biblical Institute, 1964).

18. See Morton Smith, *Palestinian Parties and Politics That Shaped the Old Testament* (New York: Columbia University Press, 1971).

19. See note 10, above.

20. In addition to the work of Campbell and O'Brien cited in note 11, see Gary N. Knoppers and J. Gordon McConville, *Reconsidering Israel and Judah: Recent Studies on the Deuteronomistic History* (Sources for Biblical and Theological Study 8; Winona Lake, Ind.: Eisenbrauns, 2000); Raymond F. Person, Jr., *The Deuteronomic School: History, Social Setting, and Literature* (Studies in Biblical Literature 2; Atlanta, Ga.: SBL, 2002); and Johannes C. de Moor and Harry E. van Rooy, *Past, Present, Future: The Deuteronomistic History and the Prophets* (Leiden: Brill, 2000).

21. See Gerhard von Rad, *Old Testament Theology* (vol. 1; New York: Harper and Row, 1962); and Hans Walter Wolff, "The Kerygma of the Deuteronomic Historical Work," in *The Vitality of Old Testament Traditions*, by Walter Brueggemann and Hans Walter Wolff (2d ed.; Atlanta, Ga.: John Knox Press, 1982), 83–100.

22. See Walter Brueggemann, "Social Criticism and Social Vision in the Deuteronomic Formula of the Judges," in *Die Botschaft und die Boten: Festschrift fuer Hans Walter Wolff* (ed. Joerg Jeremias and Lothar Perlitt; Neukirchen-Vluyn: Neukirchener Verlag, 1981), 101–14.

23. Noth, *The Deuteronomistic History*, 42–53.

24. See Dennis J. McCarthy, "The Inauguration of Monarchy in Israel: A Form-Critical Study of I Samuel 8–12," *Int* 27 (1973): 401–12.

25. Leonhard Rost, *The Succession to the Throne of David* (Sheffield: Almond Press, 1982).

26. See Gerhard von Rad, *Studies in Deuteronomy* (SBT 9; Chicago: Henry Regnery, 1953), 75.

27. See Marvin L. Chaney, "Joshua," in *The Books of the Bible: The Old Testament /
Hebrew Bible* (ed. Bernhard W. Anderson; New York: Charles Scribner's Sons, 1989),
1:103–12.

28. See Dennis J. McCarthy, "II Samuel 7 and the Structure of the Deuteronomic History," *JBL* 84 (1965): 131–38.

29. Von Rad, *Studies in Deuteronomy*, 84.

30. Ibid., 85.

31. Ibid., 86.

32. Ibid., 89.

33. Von Rad, *Old Testament Theology*, 1:339.

CHAPTER 3

1. R. A. Carlson, *David, the Chosen King: A Traditio-historical Approach to the Second
Book of Samuel* (trans. Eric J. Sharpe and Stanley Rudman; Stockholm: Almqvist and Wiksell, 1964). See Tomoo Ishida, "Solomon's Succession to the Throne of David—A Political Analysis," in *Studies in the Period of David and Solomon and Other Essays* (ed. Tomoo
Ishida; Winona Lake, Ind.: Eisenbrauns, 1982), 175–87; and David S. Williams, "Once
Again: The Structure of the Narrative of Solomon's Reign," *JSOT* 86 (1999): 49–66.

2. David M. Gunn, *The Story of King David: Genre and Interpretation* (JSOTSup 6;
Sheffield: JSOT Press, 1978), 63–70.

3. Carlson, *David, the Chosen King*, 131–259.

4. Leonhard Rost, *The Succession to the Throne of David* (Sheffield: Almond Press,
1982), 65–114. See Walter Brueggemann, "2 Samuel 21–24—An Appendix of Deconstruction?" *CBQ* 50 (1988): 383–97.

5. Gerhard von Rad, "The Beginnings of Historical Writing in Ancient Israel," in *The
Problem of the Hexateuch and Other Essays* (New York: McGraw-Hill, 1966), 198–204.

6. Ibid., 199.

7. See W. L. Moran, "The Ancient Near Eastern Background of the Love of God in
Dt," *CBQ* 29 (1963): 77–87.

8. This dual sense of the person of the king pervades the memory of Israel. The narratives make clear that the king is "truly human"; at the same time the liturgical dimensions of the royal drama draw the king beyond the human toward the holiness of God.
See Aubrey R. Johnson, *Sacral Kingship in Ancient Israel* (Cardiff: University of Wales
Press, 1967).

9. See Claudia V. Camp, *Wise, Strange, and Holy: The Strange Woman and the Making
of the Bible* (JSOTSup 320; Gender, Culture, Theory 9; Sheffield: Sheffield Academic
Press, 2000).

10. David Jobling, *1 Samuel* (Berit Olam; Collegeville, Minn.: Liturgical Press, 1998),
129–94. See especially 168, 173.

11. This rendering conventionally follows the Greek text at the point where the Hebrew
text lacks the introductory clauses.

12. Reinhold Niebuhr, *The Nature and Destiny of Man: A Christian Interpretation* (New York: Charles Scribner's Sons, 1951), 262, 267, illumines the danger of unchecked and disproportionate power, the kind evidenced in our texts:

All historic forms of justice and injustice are determined to a much larger degree than pure rationalists or idealists realize by the given equilibrium or disproportion within each type of power and by the balance of various types of power in a given community. It may be taken as axiomatic that great disproportions of power lead to injustice, whatever may be the efforts to mitigate it. . . . It is nevertheless important to recognize that government is also morally ambiguous. It contains an element which contradicts the law of brotherhood. The power of the rulers is subject to two abuses. It may actually be the dominion which one portion of the community exercises over the whole of the community. Most governments until a very recent period were in fact just that; they were the consequence of conquest by a foreign oligarchy. But even if government does not express the imperial impulse of one class or group within the community, it would, if its pretensions are not checked, generate imperial impulses of its own towards the community. It would be tempted to destroy the vitality and freedom of component elements in the community in the name of "order." It would identify its particular form of order with the principle of order itself, and thus place all rebels against its authority under the moral disadvantage of revolting against order *per se*. This is the sin of idolatry and pretension, in which all government is potentially involved. This evil can be fully understood only if it is recognized that all governments and rulers derive a part of their power, not only from the physical instruments of coercion at their disposal, but also from the reality and the pretension of "majesty." The uncoerced submission which they achieve, and without which they could not rule (since coerced submission applies only to marginal cases and presupposes the uncoerced acceptance of the ruler's authority by the majority) is never purely "rational" consent. It always includes, explicitly or implicitly, religious reverence for "majesty." The majesty of the state is legitimate in so far as it embodies and expresses both the authority and power of the total community over all its members, and the principle of order and justice as such against the peril of anarchy. (262, 267)

In my commentary on the Books of Kings, *1 & 2 Kings* (Smyth and Helwys Bible Commentary; Macon, Ga.: Smyth and Helwys, 2000), I have found frequent opportunity to connect the narrative of the text to the acute critical categories of Niebuhr.

CHAPTER 4

1. See the discussion of Robert Alter, *The Art of Biblical Narrative* (New York: Basic Books, 1981).

2. On the cruciality of the term in other contexts, see Joseph Blenkinsopp, *The Pentateuch: An Introduction to the First Five Books of the Bible* (London: SCM Press, 1992), 217–18.

3. On that crisis, see Walter Brueggemann, "The Crisis and Promise of Presence in Israel," *HBT* 1 (1979): 47–86; and, more broadly, Samuel Terrien, *The Elusive Presence: Toward a New Biblical Theology* (San Francisco: Harper and Row, 1978).

4. On the role of the king in the administration of justice, see Keith Whitelam, *The Just King: Monarchal Judicial Authority in Ancient Israel* (JSOTSup 12; Sheffield: JSOT Press, 1979).

5. The following observations are pertinent to the issue of Solomon as a practitioner of justice: (1) In the commands of Deuteronomy, tradition has anticipated a "supreme court" "in that place which the Lord will choose" (Deut 17:8–13). This provision for a superior court is thought by some to be the constitutional innovation of Jehoshaphat (2 Chron 19:8–11). This citation has the merit of linking judicial responsibility to the king and yet leaving the work of judgment in the hands of the Levitical priests, thus making a nice connection between the provision of Deuteronomy 17 and the responsibility of Solomon as king. (2) There is no doubt that this petition on the part of the king is to be connected to the narrative of 1 Kings 3:16–28, a narrative designed to confirm that Solomon has indeed received a "listening heart." (3) It may perhaps be the case that the "supreme court" here is not to be thought of as a high urban institution but rather as the function of the chief in a bucolic context. Among some African tribal communities, for example, the chief settles matters of dispute, rules on guilt, and assigns proportionate punishment and compensation. Such governance does indeed entail careful, attentive listening. It is to be noticed that in the petitionary response of Solomon to YHWH, the king asked nothing for himself, but only the capacity to be a good king.

6. See the analysis of Claus Westermann, *Basic Forms of Prophetic Speech* (Philadelphia: Westminster Press, 1967).

7. The extent to which Israel participated in the general cultural notion of divine kingship is much in dispute. See the contrasting judgments of Ivan Engnell, *Studies in Divine Kingship in the Ancient Near East* (Oxford: Blackwell, 1967); S. H. Hooke, ed. *Myth and Ritual: Essays on the Myth and Ritual of the Hebrews in Relation to the Culture Pattern of the Ancient East* (London: Oxford University Press 1933); and Henri Frankfort, *Kingship and the Gods: A Study of Ancient Near Eastern Religion as the Integration of Society and Nature* (Chicago: University of Chicago Press, 1948).

8. In addition to the works cited in note 7, see Aubrey R. Johnson, *Sacral Kingship in Ancient Israel* (Cardiff: University of Wales Press, 1967).

9. Johnson, ibid., is helpful on the role of the human king in the drama of order and chaos. See also Jon D. Levenson, *Creation and the Persistence of Evil: The Jewish Drama of Divine Omnipotence* (San Francisco: Harper and Row, 1988), for an appreciation of the cruciality of the temple in that drama.

10. See Martin Buber, *Kingship of God* (3d ed.; London: Humanities Press International, 1967), 119.

11. Frank M. Cross, *Canaanite Myth and Hebrew Epic: Essays in the History of the Religion of Israel* (Cambridge, Mass.: Harvard University Press, 1973), 135.

12. Buber, *Kingship of God,* 136.

13. See an English summary of Mowinckel's hypothesis in Sigmund Mowinckel, *He That Cometh* (Nashville, Tenn.: Abingdon Press, n.d.). See a critical assessment of the hypothesis by Ben C. Ollenburger, *Zion the City of the Great King: A Theological Symbol of the Jerusalem Cult* (JSOTSup 41; Sheffield: Sheffield Academic Press, 1987), 23–33.

14. J. J. M. Roberts, "Mowinckel's Enthronement Festival: A Review." Photocopy, Princeton Seminary, 16.

15. On "common theology," see Morton Smith, "The Common Theology of the Ancient Near East," *JBL* 71 (1952): 135–48; and Norman K. Gottwald, *The Tribes of Yahweh: A Sociology of the Religion of Liberated Israel, 1250–1050 B.C.* (Maryknoll, N.Y.: Orbis Books, 1979), 670–75.

16. Frankfort, *Kingship and the Gods.*

17. See Patrick D. Miller, *The Religion of Ancient Israel* (Library of Ancient Israel; Louisville, Ky.: Westminster John Knox Press, 2000), 51–79.

CHAPTER 5

1. J. J. M. Roberts, "Zion in the Theology of the Davidic-Solomonic Empire," in *Studies in the Period of David and Solomon and Other Essays* (ed. Tomoo Ishida; Winona Lake, Ind.; Eisenbrauns, 1982), 93–108.

2. See John M. Lundquist, "What Is a Temple? A Preliminary Typology," *The Quest for the Kingdom of God: Studies in Honor of George E. Mendenhall* (ed. H. B. Huffman et al.; Winona Lake, Ind.: Eisenbrauns, 1983), 205–19.

3. See Carol Meyers, "David as Temple Builder," in *Ancient Israelite Religion: Essays in Honor of Frank Moore Cross* (ed. Patrick D. Miller Jr. et al.; Philadelphia: Fortress Press, 1987), 357–76.

4. Ibid., 360.

5. Ibid., 359.

6. G. Ernest Wright, *Biblical Archaeology* (Philadelphia: Westminster Press, 1957), 136–45. See William G. Dever, "Archaeology and the Israelite Monarchy," in *The Blackwell Companion to the Bible* (ed. Leo G. Perdue; Oxford: Blackwell, 2001), 195–200.

7. William G. Dever, *What Did the Biblical Writers Know, and When Did They Know It?* (Grand Rapids, Mich.: Eerdmans, 2001), 155; see 144–57.

8. Israel Finkelstein and Neil Asher Silberman, *The Bible Unearthed: Archaeology's New Vision of Ancient Israel and the Origin of Its Sacred Texts* (New York: Free Press, 2001), chap. 1.

9. To place the site in context, see Dever, *What Did the Biblical Writers Know?,* 155.

10. Meyers, "David as Temple Builder," 365–66. See her citation of the extensive literature with reference to the works of C. Renfrew, C. S. Peebles and S. M. Kus, and T. Earle.

11. Walter Brueggemann, "The Tearing of the Curtain (Matt. 27:51)," in *Faithful Witness: A Festschrift Honoring Ronald Goetz* (ed. Michael J. Bell et al.; Elmhurst, Ill.: Elmhurst College, 2002), 77–83.

12. Meyers, "David as Temple Builder," 362.

13. See Walter Brueggemann, *1 and 2 Kings* (Smyth and Helwys Bible Commentary; Macon, Ga.: Smyth and Helwys, 2000), 105–20; also see the historical perspective of Jon D. Levenson, "From Temple to Synagogue: 1 Kings 8," in *Traditions in Transformation: Turning Points in Biblical Faith* (ed. Baruch Halpern and Jon D. Levenson; Winona Lake, Ind.: Eisenbrauns, 1981), 143–66.

14. Meyers, "David as Temple Builder," 362–63. See J. J. M. Roberts, "Zion," 93–108.

15. Samuel Terrien, *The Elusive Presence: Toward a New Biblical Theology* (San Francisco: Harper and Row, 1978), 194.

16. Ibid., 195–96.

17. See the classic discussion of this matter of praxis by Jose Miranda, *Marx and the Bible: A Critique of the Philosophy of Oppression* (trans. John Eagleson; Maryknoll, N.Y.: Orbis Books, 1974), 44–53.

18. See Walter Brueggemann, "The Travail of Pardon: Reflections on slh," in *A God So Near: Essays on Old Testament Theology in Honor of Patrick D. Miller* (ed. Brent A. Strawn and Nancy R. Bowen; Winona Lake, Ind.: Eisenbrauns, 2003), 283–97.

19. See Thomas Raitt, *A Theology of Exile: Judgment / Deliverance in Jeremiah and Ezekiel* (Philadelphia: Fortress Press, 1977).

20. Fredrik Lindström, *Suffering and Sin: Interpretations of Illness in the Individual Complaint Psalms* (ConBOT 37; Stockholm: Almqvist and Wiksell, 1994), has made a compelling case for the temple as pivotal for the life and faith of Israel.

21. See Hans Walter Wolff, "The Kerygma of the Deuteronomic Historical Work," in *The Vitality of Old Testament Traditions* (ed. Walter Brueggemann and Hans Walter Wolff; Atlanta, Ga.: John Knox Press, 1982), 83–100.

22. Frank Moore Cross, *From Epic to Canon: History and Literature in Ancient Israel* (Baltimore: Johns Hopkins University Press, 1998), 91–92, 95.

23. Ben C. Ollenburger, *Zion the City of the Great King: A Theological Symbol of the Jerusalem Cult* (JSOTSup 41; Sheffield: Sheffield Academic Press, 1987).

24. Ibid., 66; and see John H. Hayes, "The Tradition of Zion's Inviolability," *JBL* 82 (1963): 419–26.

25. See the summary statement of Lindström, *Suffering and Sin*, 435–51.

26. See Ollenburger, *Zion the City of the Great King*, 23–33; and J. J. M. Roberts, "Mowinckel's Enthronement Festival: A Review."

27. Lindström, *Suffering and Sin*, 402, 412–13.

CHAPTER 6

1. See Martha Nussbaum, *Poetic Justice: The Literary Imagination and Public Life* (Boston: Beacon Press, 1997).

2. See the major characterizations of wisdom in the Old Testament by James L. Crenshaw, *Urgent Advice and Probing Questions: Collected Writings on Old Testament Wisdom* (Macon, Ga.: Mercer University Press, 1995); Gerhard von Rad, *Wisdom in Israel* (Nashville, Tenn.: Abingdon Press, 1972); and Roland E. Murphy, *The Tree of Life: An Exploration of Biblical Wisdom Literature* (New York: Doubleday, 1990).

3. This is a central point for von Rad, *Wisdom in Israel,* especially against the notion of William McKane, *Proverbs: A New Approach* (OTL; Philadelphia: Westminster Press, 1970), who proposes a pretheological, secular wisdom in Israel.

4. Walther Zimmerli, "The Place and Limit of the Wisdom in the Framework of the Old Testament Theology," *SJT* 17 (1964): 148.

5. The point is well made in numerous publications of James Crenshaw. See, for example, Crenshaw, "Wisdom and Authority: Sapiential Rhetoric and Its Warrants," in *Urgent Advice,* 326–43.

6. See Carole R. Fontaine, "The Sage in Family and Tribe," in *The Sage in Israel and the Ancient Near East* (ed. John G. Gammie and Leo G. Perdue; Winona Lake, Ind.: Eisenbrauns, 1990), 155–64. Note especially her citation of Erhard Gerstenberger.

7. See F. W. Golka, *The Leopard's Spots: Biblical and African Wisdom in Proverbs* (Edinburgh: T. and T. Clark, 1993).

8. See the discussion of von Rad, *Wisdom in Israel,* 97–110; and Hartmut Gese, *Essays on Biblical Theology* (Minneapolis, Minn.: Augsburg Publishing House, 1981), 190–99.

9. Erhard Gerstenberger, *Wesen und Herkunft des sogenannten "apodiktischen Rechts" im Alten Testament* (WMANT 20; Neukirchen-Vluyn: Neukirchener Verlag, 1965), 49.

10. See E. W. Heaton, *Solomon's New Men* (London: Thames and Hudson, 1974).

11. See Walter Isaacson and Evan Thomas, *The Wise Men: Six Friends and the World They Made: Acheson, Bohlen, Harriman, Kennan, Lovett, McCloy* (New York: Simon and Schuster, 1988).

12. On the odd way in which political wisdom matched with pride turns readily to destructive foolishness, see Kai Bird, *The Color of Truth: McGeorge Bundy and William Bundy, Brothers in Arms. A Biography* (New York: Simon and Schuster, 1998).

13. Stephen Toulmin, *Cosmopolis: The Hidden Agenda of Modernity* (New York: Free Press, 1990), for example, offers a critical appreciation of the "modern" modes of knowledge that are necessary to the great modern states. Toulmin of course is acutely aware of the costs of such cultural modes of power as well.

14. See Heaton, *Solomon's New Men;* and George Mendenhall, "The Shady Side of Wisdom: The Date and Purpose of Genesis 3," in *A Light unto My Path: Old Testament Studies in Honor of Jacob M. Myers* (ed. Howard N. Bream et al.; Philadelphia: Temple University Press, 1974), 319–34.

15. See R. N. Whybray, *The Intellectual Tradition in the Old Testament* (BZAW 135; Berlin: De Gruyter, 1974).

16. In addition to the classic work of F. W. Golka cited in note 7, see M. Masenya, "Proverbs 31:10-31 in a South African Context: A Reading for the Liberation of African (Northern Sotho) Women," *Semeia* 78 (1997): 55-68.

17. See Jenny Strauss Clay, "The Real Leo Strauss," *New York Times,* 7 June 2003.

18. See Lennart Bostrom, *The God of the Sages: The Portrayal of God in the Book of Proverbs* (ConBOT 29; Stockholm: Almqvist and Wiksell International, 1990).

19. See R. N. Whybray, "Wisdom Literature in the Reigns of David and Solomon," in *Studies in the Period of David and Solomon and Other Essays* (ed. Tomoo Ishida; Winona Lake, Ind.: Eisenbrauns, 1982), 13-26.

20. See Keith Whitelam, *The Just King: Monarchal Judicial Authority in Ancient Israel* (JSOTSup 12; Sheffield: Sheffield Academic Press, 1979).

21. On this and related texts, see the discussion of Claudia Camp, *Wise, Strange, and Holy: The Strange Woman and the Making of the Bible* (JSOTSup 320; Gender, Culture, Theory 9; Sheffield: Sheffield Academic Press, 2000), 144-86.

22. On *rhm* as mother love, see the classic discussion of Phyllis Trible, *God and the Rhetoric of Sexuality* (OBT; Philadelphia: Fortress Press, 1978), 31-59.

23. On mother love broadly, see John Bowlby, *Attachment* (New York: Basic Books, 2000); and D. W. Winnicott, *The Maturational Processes and the Facilitating Environment: Studies in the Theory of Emotional Development* (New York: International Universities Press, 1965).

24. See Martha Nussbaum's work cited in note 1, above.

25. Anthony Amsterdam and Jerome Bruner, *Minding the Law* (Cambridge, Mass.: Harvard University Press, 2000).

26. On this formulation as verdict, see Gerhard von Rad, "Faith Reckoned as Righteousness," in *The Problem of the Hexateuch and Other Essays* (New York: McGraw-Hill, 1966), 125-30.

27. On the scope of wisdom beyond Israel, see von Rad, *Wisdom in Israel,* 117, 287, 310, and passim.

28. The reference to "wisdom of all the people of the east" is no doubt in the purview of the narrative of the magi in Matthew 2:1-12.

29. Scholars have in general now rejected that hypothesis. See the critical review and assessment of the issue by James L. Crenshaw, "Studies in Ancient Israelite Wisdom: Prolegomenon," in *Urgent Advice,* 90-140.

30. See the decisive argument of R. Y. B. Scott, "Solomon and the Beginnings of Wisdom in Israel" in *Studies in Ancient Israelite Wisdom: Selected with a Prolegomenon,* ed. James L. Crenshaw (New York: KTAV Publishing House, 1976), 84-101.

31. Von Rad, *Wisdom in Israel,* 117-18.

32. Gerhard von Rad, "Job xxxviii and Ancient Egyptian Wisdom," in von Rad, *Problem of the Hexateuch and Other Essays,* 281-91.

33. Annie Dillard, *Pilgrim at Tinker Creek* (1974; New York: McGraw-Hill, 2000); for a review of the work of John Muir, see Dennis C. Williams, *God's Wilds: John Muir's Vision of Nature* (College Station: Texas A & M University Press, 2002).

34. John Muir, in his mix of faith and science, understood the world as God's creation. For a more studied presentation of nature as creation, see Alister E. McGrath, *Nature* (vol. 1 of *A Scientific Theology;* Grand Rapids, Mich.: Eerdmans, 2001).

35. John Barton, "Natural Law and Poetic Justice in the Old Testament," *Understanding Old Testament Ethics: Approaches and Explorations* (Louisville, Ky.: Westminster John Knox Press, 2003), 32–44.

36. See Kenneth Suskin, *Autonomy in Jewish Philosophy* (Cambridge: Cambridge University Press, 2001).

CHAPTER 7

1. See the presentation of G. Ernest Wright, *Biblical Archaeology* (Philadelphia: Westminster Press, 1957), 132–36. The initial explorations were by Nelson Gleuck.

2. See Yataka Ikedea, "Solomon's Trade in Horses and Chariots in Its International Setting," in *Studies in the Period of David and Solomon and Other Essays* (ed. Tomoo Ishida; Winona Lake, Ind.: Eisenbrauns, 1982), 215–38.

3. See J. Alberto Soggin, "Compulsory Labor under David and Solomon," in Ishida, *Studies,* 259–67.

4. On the general theory of such an economy, see Peter L. Berger, *Pyramids of Sacrifice: Political Ethics and Social Change* (New York: Basic Books, 1974).

5. See T. N. D. Mettinger, *Solomonic State Officials: A Study of the Civil Government Officials of the Israelite Monarchy* (ConBOT 5; Lund: C. W. K. Gleerup, 1974).

6. On the archaeology of the fortifications and gates of Solomon, see William G. Dever, *What Did the Biblical Writers Know, and When Did They Know It?* (Grand Rapids, Mich.: Eerdmans, 2001), 124–38.

7. Francis Fukuyama, *The End of History and the Last Man* (New York: Free Press, 1992).

8. The notion of "realized eschatology" is especially connected to the work of C. H. Dodd, *The Parables of the Kingdom* (New York: Scribner's, 1961).

9. See the debunking and dismissal of such claimed evidence by Israel Finkelstein and Neil Asher Silberman, *The Bible Unearthed: Archaeology's New Vision of Ancient Israel and the Origin of Its Sacred Texts* (New York: Free Press, 2001), 135–45.

10. See Frank S. Frick, *The Formation of the State of Ancient Israel* (SWBA 4; Sheffield: Almond Press, 1985); and David Noel Freedman and David Frank Graf, eds., *Palestine in Transition: The Emergence of Ancient Israel* (SWBA 2; Sheffield: Almond Press, 1983).

11. See James W. Flanagan, *David's Social Drama: A Hologram of Israel's Early Iron Age* (Sheffield: Sheffield Academic Press, 1989).

12. It is this socioeconomic totalism that the prophets characteristically critique; see D. N. Premnath, *Eighth Century Prophets: A Social Analysis* (St. Louis, Mo.: Chalice Press, 2003).

13. On social stratification reflected in the organization of worship, see Philip P. Jenson, *Graded Holiness: A Key to the Priestly Conception of the World* (JSOTSup 106; Sheffield: Sheffield Academic Press, 1992); and Walter Houston, *Purity and Monotheism: Clean and Unclean Animals in Biblical Law* (Sheffield: Sheffield Academic Press, 1993).

14. See Walter Brueggemann, "The Tearing of the Curtain (Matt. 27:51)," in *Faithful Witness: A Festschrift Honoring Ronald Goetz* (ed. Michael Bell et al.; Elmhurst, Ill.: Elmhurst College, 2002), 77–83.

15. See Hans Walter Wolff, "Micah the Moreshite—The Prophet and His Background," in *Israelite Wisdom: Theological and Literary Essays in Honor of Samuel Terrien* (ed. John G. Gammie et al.; Missoula, Mont.: Scholars Press, 1978), 77–84; and Walter Brueggemann, "'Vine and Fig Tree': A Case Study in Imagination and Criticism," in *A Social Reading of the Old Testament: Prophetic Approaches to Israel's Communal Life,* (ed. Patrick D. Miller; Minneapolis, Minn.: Fortress Press, 1994), 91–110.

CHAPTER 8

1. On this text, see Ernest W. Nicholson, *God and His People: Covenant and Theology in the Old Testament* (Oxford: Clarendon Press, 1986), 121–78.

2. See Frank Crüsemann, *The Torah: Theology and Social History of Old Testament Law* (Minneapolis, Minn.: Fortress Press, 1996), 27–200.

3. See Martin Buber, *Kingship of God* (London: Humanities Press International, 1967).

4. Crüsemann, *The Torah,* 109–200.

5. Nicholson, *God and His People,* 201.

6. See James Muilenburg, "The Form and Structure of the Covenantal Formulations," *VT* 9 (1959): 347–65.

7. Moving quickly past the vexing critical questions, Terence E. Fretheim, *Exodus* (Interpretation; Louisville: John Knox Press, 1991), 201–7, offers compelling interpretive access to this critical text.

8. See Georg Braulik, *The Theology of Deuteronomy: Collected Essays of Georg Braulik* (N. Richland Hills, Tex.: BIBAL Press, 1994); and Stephen Kaufman, "The Structure of the Deuteronomic Law," *Maarav* 1 (1979): 105–58.

9. See Crüsemann, *The Torah,* 201–75.

10. Dean S. McBride, "Polity of the Covenant People: The Book of Deuteronomy," *Int* 41 (1987): 229–44; and Norbert Lohfink, "Distribution of the Functions of Power: The Laws Concerning Public Offices in Deuteronomy 16:18–18:22," in *Great Themes from the Old Testament* (Chicago: Franciscan Herald, 1981), 55–75.

11. See Gary N. Knoppers, "The Deuteronomist and the Deuteronomic Law of the King: A Reexamination of a Relationship," *ZAW* 108 (1996): 329–46.

12. See Crüsemann, *The Torah,* 237.

13. Ibid., 238.

14. The intimate connection between kingship and Torah is evidenced in the beginning of the Psalter by the juxtaposition of Psalm 1, a text on Torah obedience, and Psalm

2, a text on the cruciality of the king. See Patrick D. Miller, "The Beginning of the Psalter," in *Israelite Religion and Biblical Theology: Collected Essays* (JSOTSup 267; Sheffield: Sheffield Academic Press, 2000), 269–78.

15. The classic treatments are those of Martin Noth and Gerhard von Rad. There is a new ferment on the subject, a new literature represented by, for example, Anthony F. Campbell and Mark A. O'Brien, *Unfolding the Deuteronomistic History: Origins, Upgrades, Present Text* (Minneapolis, Minn.: Fortress Press, 2000).

16. Martin Noth, *The Deuteronomistic History* (JSOTSup 15; Sheffield: JSOT Press, 1981), 57–62.

17. See Claus Westermann, *Basic Forms of Prophetic Speech* (Philadelphia: Westminster Press, 1967).

18. Noth, *The Deuteronomistic History*, 58.

19. The tradition clearly intends that the indictment of Solomon in 1 Kings 11:1 should refer back to the prohibition in Deuteronomy 7. It is not clear, however, which text is in fact older; the commandment in Deuteronomy may be a construct after the Solomonic indictment. In any case, they are related, and that relationship brings Solomon to judgment, the clear intention of the tradition.

20. This is clearly the case in the tradition's harsh indictment of the Omri dynasty in 1 Kings 21, a clear example of the way in which faith claims are defining for socioeconomic practice.

21. This of course is the dilemma for Christian "evangelicals" in the United States, for whom any serious internationalism must perforce violate narrow ideological commitments that run in the direction of theocracy.

22. See the shrewd analysis of Ernest W. Nicholson, *Preaching to the Exiles: A Study of the Prose Tradition in the Book of Jeremiah* (Oxford: Blackwell, 1970), 38–46, concerning the juxtaposition of 2 Kings 22 and Jeremiah 36.

23. Gerhard von Rad, *Old Testament Theology* (San Francisco: Harper and Row, 1962), 1:334–47.

24. Klaus Koch, *The Assyrian Period* (vol. 1 of *The Prophets*; Philadelphia: Fortress Press, 1982), 5, 73, 88, 99, and *passim*, happily uses the term "metahistory" for the affirmation of YHWH's decisive governance of the public processes of history.

25. On the continuing force of the Shiloh tradition and its serious challenge to the Jerusalem establishment, see Martin A. Cohen, "The Role of the Shilonite Priesthood in the United Monarchy of Ancient Israel," *HUCA* 36 (1955): 59–98.

26. See Albrecht Alt, *Essays on Old Testament History and Religion* (Oxford: Blackwell, 1966), 241–59.

27. The statement in verse 15 is not unlike those of 2 Samuel 17:14 and 2 Samuel 24:1 in which the hidden yet decisive governance of YHWH is attested.

28. The liturgic claim that puts the Jerusalem temple beyond the ambiguity of history is a common accent of the "Songs of Zion." See Ben C. Ollenburger, *Zion the City of the*

Great King: A Theological Symbol of the Jerusalem Cult (JSOTSup 41; Sheffield: Sheffield Academic Press, 1987), 81–100 and passim.

29. See Peter R. Ackroyd, *Studies in the Religious Tradition of the Old Testament* (London: SCM Press, 1987), 46–60.

30. The absence of YHWH from the Jerusalem temple is, as Lindström has observed in *Suffering and Sin,* a common theme in the Psalms. It is also well articulated in Ezekiel 9–10 with its vision of the palpable departure of the glory of YHWH from the temple.

31. See Claudia Camp, *Wise, Strange, and Holy: The Strange Woman and the Making of the Bible* (JSOTSup 320; Gender, Culture, Theory 9; Sheffield: Sheffield Academic Press, 2000).

32. On the relation of the tradition of Deuteronomy and sapiential teaching, see Moshe Weinfeld, *Deuteronomy and the Deuteronomic School* (Oxford: Clarendon Press, 1972).

33. Marvin L. Chaney, "Joshua," in *The Books of the Bible I: The Old Testament / Hebrew Bible* (ed. Bernhard W. Anderson; New York: Scribner's Sons, 1989), 103–12. See also Marvin A. Sweeney, "The Critique of Solomon in the Josianic Edition of the Deuteronomic History," *JBL* 1214 (1995): 607–22.

34. See Walter Brueggemann, "The Epistemological Crisis of Israel's Two Histories (Jeremiah 9:22–23)," in *Old Testament Theology: Essays on Structure, Theme, and Text* (Minneapolis, Minn.: Fortress Press, 1992), 270–95.

35. The utilization of the word pair "justice and righteousness" in 1 Kings 10:9 is remarkable and surely carries ironic intention. On the use of such phrasing, see Jose Miranda, *Marx and the Bible: A Critique of the Philosophy of Oppression* (trans. John Eagleson; Maryknoll, N.Y.: Orbis Books, 1974), 214–29.

CHAPTER 9

1. See Gerhard von Rad, *Old Testament Theology* (New York: Harper and Row, 1962), 1:347–54.

2. See Jon K. Berquist, *Judaism in Persia's Shadow: A Social and Historical Approach* (Minneapolis, Minn.: Fortress Press, 1995).

3. See Roddy L. Braun, "Solomonic Apologetic in Chronicles," *BJL* 92 (1973): 503–16.

4. See Roddy L. Braun, "Solomon, the Chosen Temple Builder: The Significance of I Chronicles 22, 28, and 29 for the Theology of Chronicles," *JBL* 95 (1976): 581–90.

5. Ibid., 584.

6. Norbert Lohfink, "Die deuteronomistische Darstellung des Übergangs der Führung Israels von Moses and Joshue," *Scholastik* 37 (1962): 32–44; Braun, "Solomon, the Chosen Temple Builder," 586. See also Dennis J. MCarthy, "An Installation Genre?" *JBL* 90 (1971): 31–41. I am grateful to Patrick D. Miller for the reference to Lohfink.

7. Braun, "Solomon, the Chosen Temple Builder," 588–90; George E. Mendenhall, "Election," *IDB* E-J, 79.

8. Sara Japhet, *I and II Chronicles: A Commentary* (OTL; Louisville, Ky.: Westminster John Knox Press, 1993), 493.

9. Ibid., 514–15.

10. Sara Japhet, *The Ideology of the Book of Chronicles and Its Place in Biblical Thought* (BEATAJ 9; Berlin: Peter Lang, 1989), 478–79. Japhet's commentary, *I and II Chronicles,* 522–24, details the way in which the Chronicler on Solomon follows and does not follow the Deuteronomist.

11. Rudolf Mosis, *Untersuchungen zur Theologie des Chronistischen Geschichtswerk* (Freiburg: Herder, 1973), 162.

12. Roddy L. Braun, *Understanding the Basic Themes of 1, 2 Chronicles* (Dallas: Word Publications, 1991), 5–6, proposes a detailed chiastic structure for the whole of the narrative of Solomon.

13. Joseph Blenkinsopp, *The Pentateuch: An Introduction to the First Five Books of the Bible* (London: SCM Press, 1992), 217–18.

14. Ibid., 217–20.

15. Braun, *Understanding the Basic Themes of 1, 2 Chronicles,* 11.

16. H. G. M. Williamson, *1 and 2 Chronicles* (New Century; Grand Rapids, Mich.: Eerdmans, 1982).

17. On this connection, see Claudia Camp, *Wise, Strange, and Holy: The Strange Woman and the Making of the Bible* (JSOTSup 320; Gender, Culture, Theory 9; Sheffield: Sheffield Academic Press, 2000).

18. Japhet, *I and II Chronicles,* 635; see also von Rad, *Old Testament Theology,* 1:429–37.

19. Donald D. Schley Jr., "1 Kings 10:26–29: A Reconsideration," *JBL* 106 (1987): 599–601.

CHAPTER 10

1. See the summary of the history of critical study of the book of Proverbs by Brevard S. Childs, *Introduction to the Old Testament as Scripture* (Philadelphia: Fortress Press, 1979), 547–51; and James L. Crenshaw, *Urgent Advice and Probing Questions: Collected Writings on the Old Testament* (Macon, Ga.: Mercer University Press, 1995), 355–70.

2. Crenshaw, *Urgent Advice,* 355, refers to them as "an anthology."

3. Gerhard von Rad, *The Problem of the Hexateuch and Other Essays* (New York: McGraw-Hill, 1966), 69–74, 202–4; von Rad, *Old Testament Theology* (San Francisco: Harper and Row, 1962), 1:48–56.

4. Ibid., 53.

5. Gerhard von Rad, *Wisdom in Israel* (Nashville, Tenn.: Abingdon Press, 1972), 58.

6. On reasoning concerning wealth as a consequence of good conduct, see Klaus Koch, "Is There a Doctrine of Retribution in the Old Testament?," in *Theodicy in the Old Testament* (ed. James L. Crenshaw; Philadelphia: Fortress Press, 1983), 57–87.

7. Crenshaw, *Urgent Advice*, 357.

8. C. Kayatz, *Studien zu Proverbien 1–9* (WMANT; Neukirchen-Vluyn: Neukirchener Verlag, 1966), has suggested that the wisdom material of Proverbs 1–9 has close connections to Egyptian wisdom material; on the basis of this connection, she proposes an early date for the material, as early as the tenth century.

9. E. W. Heaton, *Solomon's New Men: The Emergence of Ancient Israel as a National State* (London: Thames and Hudson, 1974).

10. Ibid., chap. 7; see 47, 130.

11. See R. B. Y. Scott, "Solomon and the Beginnings of Wisdom in Israel," in *Wisdom in Israel and in the Ancient Near East* (ed. D. Winton Thomas; VTSup 3; Leiden: Brill, 1955), 262; see also Martin Noth, "Die Bewährung von Solomons 'Götterlicher Weisheit,'" in Thomas, *Wisdom*, 224–37. For another rendition of the "Enlightenment" by von Rad, see *Holy War in Ancient Israel* (Grand Rapids, Mich.: Eerdmans, 1991), 74–93.

12. R. N. Whybray, *The Intellectual Tradition in the Old Testament* (BZAW 135; Berlin: de Gruyter, 1974).

13. Ibid., 54.

14. Ibid., 69.

15. Childs, *Introduction*, 552.

16. Ibid.

17. Von Rad, *Wisdom in Israel*, 63.

18. Claudia V. Camp, *Wise, Strange, and Holy: The Strange Woman and the Making of the Bible* (JSOTSup 320; Gender, Culture, Theory 9; Sheffield: Sheffield Academic Press, 2000).

19. See Mary Douglas, *Purity and Danger: An Analysis of Concepts of Pollution and Taboo* (London: Routledge, 1966).

20. Marc Brettler, "The Structure of 1 Kings 1–1," *JSOT* 49 (1991): 87–97; and David Jobling, "'Forced Labor': Solomon's Golden Age and the Question of Literary Representation," *Semeia* 54 (1991): 57–76.

21. Notice that in the Chronicles, the daughter of Pharaoh is put at the edge of society due to her impurity (2 Chron 8:1).

22. Camp, *Wise, Strange, and Holy*, 178.

23. Jobling, "Forced Labor."

24. Christine Roy Yoder, *Wisdom as a Woman of Substance: A Socioeconomic Reading of Proverbs 21–9 and 31:10–31* (BZAW 304; Berlin: De Gruyter, 2001).

25. Ibid., 71.

26. Ibid., 83.

27. Ibid., 90–91.

28. Ibid., 101.

29. Ibid.

30. See, for example, the role of Jezebel and the characterization of women in Amos 4:1–3.

31. On the relation between wisdom and the Deuteronomic tradition, see Moshe Weinfeld, *Deuteronomy and the Deuteronomic School* (Oxford: Clarendon Press, 1972).

CHAPTER 11

1. See Donn F. Morgan, *Between Text and Community: The "Writings" in Canonical Interpretation* (Minneapolis, Minn.: Fortress Press, 1990), 118.

2. See James L. Crenshaw, *Urgent Advice and Probing Questions: Collected Writings on Old Testament Wisdom* (Macon, Ga.: Mercer University Press, 1995), 499–585.

3. See Frank Crüsemann, "The Unchangeable World: The 'Crisis of Wisdom' in Koheleth," in *God of the Lowly: Socio-historical Interpretations of the Bible* (ed. Willy Schottroff and Wolfgang Stegemann; Maryknoll, N.Y.: Orbis Books, 1984), 57–77.

4. See Roland E. Murphy, "Qoheleth's 'Quarrel' with the Fathers," *From Faith to Faith: Essays in Honor of Donald G. Miller on His Seventieth Birthday* (ed. Dikran Y. Hadidian; Pittsburgh, Pa.: Pickwick Press, 1979), 235–45.

5. Gerhard von Rad, *Wisdom in Israel* (Nashville, Tenn.: Abingdon Press, 1972), 227–29.

6. Ibid., 228.

7. See Gerhard von Rad, *Old Testament Theology* (San Francisco: Harper and Row, 1962), 1:456.

8. On the postscript to the book of Ecclesiastes, see Brevard S. Childs, *Introduction to the Old Testament as Scripture* (Philadelphia: Fortress Press, 1979), 584–86; and G. T. Sheppard, "The Epilogue to Qoheleth as Theological Commentary," *CBQ* 39 (1977): 182–89.

9. Crenshaw, *Urgent Advice*, 509–13.

10. Ibid., 509–10.

11. Roland E. Murphy, *The Tree of Life: An Exploration of Biblical Wisdom* (Garden City, N.J.: Doubleday, 1990), 52.

12. Childs, *Introduction*, 584, finds trace that "the fiction of Qoheleth as a pseudonym for Solomon is clearly abandoned within the book itself."

13. Von Rad, *Old Testament Theology*, 1:454; see Crenshaw, *Urgent Advice*, 500, 506.

14. Crenshaw, *Urgent Advice*, 506.

15. Here I follow the translation of NRSV; the Hebrew text is less than clear.

16. On the assumption of a connection between "deeds and consequences," see Klaus Koch, "Is There a Doctrine of Retribution in the Old Testament?" in *Theodicy in the Old Testament* (ed. James L. Crenshaw; Philadelphia: Fortress Press, 1983), 57–87.

17. The fullest critical discussion is by Roland E. Murphy, *The Song of Songs: A Commentary on the Book of Canticles or the Song of Songs* (Hermeneia; Minneapolis, Minn.: Fortress Press, 1990); see also Tremper Longman III, *Song of Songs* (NICOT; Grand Rapids, Mich.: Eerdmans, 2001).

18. It is a common critical consensus that this series of love poems has important affinities to the secular poems in Egyptian culture and that the poems are to be dated quite late in the biblical period, certainly after the exile. (The exception is Gillis Gerleman, *Ruth, Das Hohelied* [BKAT 18; Neukirchen-Vluyn: Neukirchen Verlag, 1965], 63–77, who proposes a tenth-century date. Gerleman appeals to the so-called Solomonic Enlightenment and so situates the book in the environs of Solomon. Gerleman's advocacy is singular in the face of a rough scholarly consensus.)

19. See Murphy, *Song of Songs,* 11–41, on the history of interpretation.

20. See the discussion of Andre LaCocque and Paul Ricoeur, "The Song of Songs," in *Thinking Biblically: Exegetical and Hermeneutical Studies* (Chicago: University of Chicago Press, 1998), 235–303.

21. Anders Nygren, *Agape and Eros* (trans. Philip S. Watson; New York: Harper and Row, 1969).

22. Phyllis Trible, *God and the Rhetoric of Sexuality* (OBT; Philadelphia: Fortress Press), 144–65.

23. Ibid., 72–143.

24. Ibid., 144–65.

25. Ibid., 144–45.

26. Such a second innocence is not unrelated to the "second naiveté" of Paul Ricoeur: see Mark I. Wallace, *Second Naiveté: Barth, Ricoeur, and the New Yale School* (Macon, Ga.: Mercer University Press, 1995).

27. See Psalm 45 on a royal wedding, a song that could also be readily linked to Solomon in its inventory of opulence.

28. Murphy, *Song of Songs,* 152.

29. Ibid., 199.

30. Ibid., 194; see Marvin Pope, *Song of Songs* (AB 7C; Garden City, N.J.: Doubleday, 1977), 326.

31. Childs, *Introduction,* 577–78.

32. See David J. A. Clines, "Why Is There a Song of Songs, and What Does It Do to You If You Read It?" in *Interested Parties: The Ideology of Writers and Readers of the Hebrew Bible* (JSOTSup 205, Gender, Culture, Theory 1; Sheffield: Sheffield Academic Press, 1995), 122–44.

33. See Childs, *Introduction,* 574–77.

34. Claudia V. Camp, *Wise, Strange and Holy: The Strange Woman and the Making of the Bible* (JSOTSup 320, Gender, Culture, Theory 9; Sheffield: Sheffield Academic Press, 2000), 144–86.

35. Janie Hunter, "The Song of Protest: Reassessing the Song of Songs," *JSOT* 90 (2000): 109–24.

36. Ibid., 111.

37. Trible, *God and the Rhetoric of Sexuality,* 162; see also Brevard S. Childs, *Biblical Theology in Crisis* (Philadelphia: Westminster Press, 1970), 191–95.

38. Albert O. Hirschman, *The Passions and the Interests: Political Arguments for Capital-ism Before Its Triumph* (Princeton, N.J.: Princeton University Press, 1977). Hirschman's categories have been taken up by Gerald M. Pomper, *Passions and Interests: Political Party Concepts of American Democracy* (Lawrence: University of Kansas Press, 1992), in a dis-cussion of more recent and contemporary political reality in the United States.

39. Hirschman, *Passions and Interests*, 12–14.

40. Ibid., 31. ·

41. Ibid., 14–20.

42. Ibid., 20–31.

43. Ibid., 27.

44. Ibid.

45. Ibid., 39–40.

46. Ibid., 48–56.

47. Ibid., 59.

48. Ibid., 63.

49. Ibid., 40–41.

50. Reference might be made here to the work of J. Robert Lifton on "psychic numb-ing," in this case, numbness to need.

CHAPTER 12

1. See Brevard S. Childs, *Introduction to the Old Testament as Scripture* (Philadelphia: Fortress Press, 1979), 143–48.

2. In connection with the canonical psalms linked in the tradition to Solomon, we may mention as well the Psalms of Solomon, eighteen psalms in the later, postcanonical literature of the Pseudepigrapha. These psalms reflect conventional psalmic types. They are likely dated in the first century B.C.E. and of course have nothing to do historically with Solomon. They reflect the piety of Judaism as the community sought to maintain itself amid the cultural environment of the empire. These psalms constitute an important resource for the religious practices and assumptions of Judaism in the period. For an older but reliable discussion of these psalms, see Otto Eissfeldt, *The Old Testament: An Introduction: The History of the Formation of the Old Testament* (trans. Peter R. Ackroyd; New York: Harper and Row, 1965), 610–13.

3. See Brevard S. Childs, "Psalm Titles and Midrashic Exegesis," *JSS* 16 (1971): 137–50. See Gerald T. Sheppard, "The Relation of Solomon's Wisdom to Biblical Prayer," *TJT* 8 (1992): 16–21.

4. Childs, *Introduction*, 143.

5. See Keith Crim, *The Royal Psalms* (Richmond, Va.: John Knox Press, 1962); Hans-Joachim Kraus, *Theology of the Psalms* (Minneapolis, Minn.: Augsburg Publishing House, 1986), 107–23; and James L. Mays, *The Lord Reigns: A Theological Handbook to the Psalms* (Louisville, Ky.: Westminster John Knox Press, 1994).

6. See Aubrey R. Johnson, *Sacral Kingship in Ancient Israel* (Cardiff: University of Wales Press, 1967).

7. See Jon D. Levenson, *Sinai and Zion: An Entry into the Jewish Bible* (New York: Winston Press, 1985).

8. David Jobling, "Deconstruction and the Political Analysis of Biblical Texts: A Jamesonian Reading of Psalm 72," *Semeia* 59 (1992): 95–127.

9. Hans Joachim Kraus, *Psalms 60–150: A Commentary* (Minneapolis, Minn.: Augsburg Publishing House, 1989), 80. Note that verse 20 is a doxological formulation that serves to conclude book 2 of the Psalter.

10. Jobling, "Deconstruction," 95–127.

11. On this role for the king, see Keith Whitelam, *The Just King: Monarchal Judicial Authority in Ancient Israel* (JSOTSup 12; Sheffield: JSOT Press, 1979).

12. On the emergence of such social differentiation in early Christian culture, see Peter Brown, *Poverty and Leadership in the Later Roman Empire* (Hanover, N.H.: University Press of New England, 2002).

13. See Christopher R. Seitz, *Word without End: The Old Testament as Abiding Theological Witness* (Grand Rapids, Mich.: Eerdmans, 1998), 150–67.

14. Gerald Henry Wilson, *The Editing of the Hebrew Psalter* (Chico, Calif.: Scholars Press, 1985).

15. The juxtaposition of Torah instruction and royal mandate is suggested in the interface of Psalms 72 and 73. The same juxtaposition of course is crucial for the beginning of the Psalter in Psalms 1 and 2. See Patrick D. Miller, "The Beginning of the Psalter," in *Israelite Religion and Biblical Theology: Collected Essays* (JSOTSup 267; Sheffield: Shefsfield Academic Press, 2000), 269–78; and Patrick D. Miller and Walter Brueggemann, "Psalm 73 as Canonical Marker," *JSOT* 72 (1996): 45–56.

16. Kraus, *Psalms 60–150,* 454, takes the term to refer to the temple.

CHAPTER 13

1. On critical judgments about the book, see Roland E. Murphy, *The Tree of Life: An Exploration of Biblical Wisdom Literature* (Garden City, N.J.: Doubleday, 1990), 83–96; and James L. Crenshaw, *Old Testament Wisdom: An Introduction* (Atlanta, Ga.: John Knox Press, 1981), 174–89.

2. Murphy, *Tree of Life,* 83.

3. On the tight connection of deeds and consequences affirmed here, see Klaus Koch, "Is There a Doctrine of Retribution in the Old Testament?," in *Theodicy in the Old Testament* (ed. James L. Crenshaw; Philadelphia: Fortress Press, 1983), 57–87.

4. See Claudia Camp, *Wise, Strange, and Holy: The Strange Woman and the Making of the Bible* (JSOTSup 320; Gender, Culture, Theory 9; Sheffield: Sheffield Academic Press, 2000), 144–90.

5. Edward Ullendorff, *Ethiopia and the Bible: The Schweich Lectures of the British Academy* (Oxford: Oxford University Press, 1968), 132–33.

6. I have found especially helpful Jacob Lassner, *Demonizing the Queen of Sheba: Boundaries of Gender and Culture in Postbiblical Judaism and Medieval Israel* (Chicago: University of Chicago Press, 1933); James B. Pritchard, ed., *Solomon and Sheba* (London: Phaidon, 1974), with particular appreciation of the essays by W. Montgomery Watt and Edward Ullendorff; Ullendorff, *Ethiopia and the Bible;* A. H. Jenkins, "Solomon and the Queen of Sheba: Fakhr al-Din al Razi's Treatment of the Qur'anic Telling of the Story," *AbrN* 24 (1968): 58–82; and Jacob Lassner, "Ritual Purity and Political Exile: Solomon, the Queen of Sheba, and the events of 586 B.C.E. in Yemenite Folktale," in *Solving Riddles and Untying Knots: Biblical, Ethiopic and Semitic Studies in Honor of Jonas C. Greenfeld* (ed. Ziony Zivit et al.; Winona Lake, Ind.: Eisenbrauns, 1995), 117–36.

7. *The Holy Qur'an: Arabic Text with English Translation and Commentary of Malik Ghulam Farid* (Rabuah: Oriental and Religious Publishing Corporation, 1969), 18–126; the text is also provided by W. Montgomery Watt, "The Queen of Sheba in the Islamic Tradition," in Pritchard, *Solomon and Sheba,* 92–94.

8. Lassner, *Demonizing the Queen of Sheba,* 45.

9. Ullendorff, *Ethiopia and the Bible,* chap. 3.

10. Edward Ullendorff, "The Queen of Sheba in Ethiopian Tradition," in Pritchard, *Solomon and Sheba,* 109.

11. Ibid., 110.

12. Ibid., 108.

13. Ibid., 105.

14. Ibid., 111–12.

15. Ibid., 111.

16. Lassner, "Ritual Purity," 119.

17. Ibid., 132–34.

18. See Camp, *Wise, Strange, and Holy,* 144–90; and Lassner, "Ritual Purity," 136.

19. Lassner, *Demonizing The Queen of Sheba,* 73.

20. Ibid., 79.

21. Ibid., 82–83.

22. Ibid., 85–86.

23. See Camp, *Wise, Strange, and Holy;* and Dory Preven, "Sheba and Solomon," *USQR* 43 (1989): 59–66.

24. Watt, "Queen of Sheba," 103.

25. Ullendorff, *Ethiopia and the Bible,* 141.

26. Ibid., 145, reporting a footnote to *The Times,* 28 June 1954.

27. The literature that has been most helpful to me concerning the Masons includes W. Kirk MacNulty, *Freemasonry: A Journey through Ritual and Symbol* (London: Thames and Hudson, 1991); Marie Mulrey Roberts and Hugh Ormsby-Lennon, eds., *Secret Texts: The Literature of Secret Societies* (New York: AMS Press, 1995); Alex Horne, *King Solomon's Temple in the Masonic Tradition* (London: Aquarin Press, 1972); and Helen Rosenau, *Vision*

of the Temple: The Image of the Temple of Jerusalem in Judaism and Christianity (London: Oresko Books, 1979).

28. Stephen Toulmin, *Cosmopolis: The Hidden Agenda of Modernity* (New York: Free Press, 1990); and Klaus Scholder, *The Birth of Modern Critical Theology: Origins and Problems of Biblical Criticism in the Seventeenth Century* (London: SCM Press, 1990).

29. Josef S. Roucek, "Jan Amos Komensky: The Spiritual Founder of Modern Masonic Movement," *ZRGG* 15 (1963): 374–76.

30. James Anderson is credited with authoring the founding documents of Masonry: *The Book of Constitutions* (1723), *A Mason's Examination* (1723), and *The Mystery of Free Masonry* (1730). See Horne, *King Solomon's Temple*, 27–30.

31. MacNulty, *Freemasonry*, characterizes the appeal to the temple in the lore of Masonry.

32. Ibid., 6.

33. See Ross King's recent report on the building of "Brunelleschi's Dome," an architectural wonder that sought to provide access to holy mystery: *Brunelleschi's Dome: How a Renaissance Genius Reinvented Architecture* (New York: Walker and Company, 2000).

34. MacNulty, *Freemasonry*, 9.

35. Ibid., 74.

36. Horne, *King Solomon's Temple*, 29.

37. Ibid., 30–37.

38. Ibid., 184, 262, 282.

39. Ibid., 329.

40. Ibid., 183–93.

41. Ibid., 224.

42. Ibid., 63.

43. Jon D. Levenson, *Sinai and Zion: An Entry into the Jewish Bible* (New York: Winston Press, 1985), 89–143.

44. Ibid., 127–28.

45. Ibid., 78–99.

46. Philip Peter Jenson, *Graded Holiness: A Key to the Priestly Conception of the World* (JSOTSup 106; Sheffield: Sheffield Academic Press, 1992).

47. Horne, *King Solomon's Temple*, 183–93.

48. On the dynamism of imagination in the tradition, see David Brown, *Discipleship and Imagination: Christian Tradition and Truth* (Oxford: Oxford University Press, 2000); and Brown, *Tradition and Imagination: Revelation and Change* (Oxford: Oxford University Press, 1999).

CHAPTER 14

1. Beyond these three references the other New Testament references to Solomon are incidental. They do not need to concern us as we consider the interpretive inclinations

of the early church. In John 10:23, Acts 3:11, and 5:12, Solomon is mentioned only to identify the "portico of Solomon," a particular location in the temple. It is of course instructive that Jesus, and after him the apostles, are operative in the temple. Nothing is made of it, but clearly the narratives are concerned not with the building but with those freighted carriers of God's power. The only other use, in John 7:47, concerns the "tent of testimony" and Solomon's temple as a place of presence. But not unlike the Deuteronomist, the report in Acts precisely denies the capacity of the temple to contain the presence. Thus we may for now disregard these texts and take up the three texts that hold promise of especially rich interpretive possibility.

2. See chap. 11.

3. See Heinz Joachim Held, "Matthew as Interpreter of the Miracle Stories," in *Tradition and Interpretation in Matthew* (by Guenther Bornkamm, Gerhard Barth, and Heinz Joachim Held; Philadelphia: Westminster Press, 1963), 178–21.

4. John R. Donahue, *The Gospel in Parable: Metaphor, Narrative, and Theology in the Synoptic Gospels* (Philadelphia: Fortress Press, 1988), 177.

5. The parallel text in Mark 8:11–12 lacks a reference to Solomon.

6. Joseph Fitzmeyer, *Luke* (AB 28; Garden City, N.Y., 1985), 2:933–34.

7. William F. Albright and C. S. Mann, *Matthew* (AB 26; Garden City, N.Y., 1971), 160.

8. Raymond E. Brown, *The Birth of the Messiah: A Commentary on the Infancy Narratives in Matthew and Luke* (London: Geoffrey Chapman, 1977), 74.

SUBJECT INDEX

SCRIPTURE INDEX

NEW TESTAMENT

DEUTEROCANONICAL BOOKS